MW00628339

LIGHTS OF CREATION & TRANSCENDENCE

David Birnbaum / Mesorah Matrix Series

www.MesorahMatrix.com

VOLUME 4

KADDISH

David Birnbaum / Mesorah Matrix Series
LIGHTS OF CREATION & TRANSCENDENCE

Editors

David
Birnbaum & Cohen
Martin S.

Associate Editor: **Saul J. Berman**

New Paradigm Matrix™

EXPLORING HIGHER DIMENSIONS

Published by NEW PARADIGM MATRIX

Library of Congress Cataloging-in-Publication Data

Birnbaum, David.

Kaddish / David Birnbaum and Martin S. Cohen.

ISBN 978-0-9961995-6-8

1. Kaddish.   2. Jewish Spiritual.   I. Title.

21st CENTURY PUBLISHING

New Paradigm Matrix
att: David Birnbaum
Tower 49
Twelve E. 49th St.,
11th Floor,
New York, NY 10017

www.NewParadigmMatrix.com

Direct contact to Editor-in-Chief

David.Birnbaum.NY@gmail.com

Frydman-Kohl
Berkowitz
Walfish
Marx
Oitzky
Claussen
Kunin
Blech
Yoskowitz
Thiede
Greenstein
Marmur
Glazer
Cohen
Jacobson-Maisels
Bronstein Triguboff
Bulka
Greenspan
Kaunfer
Ornstein Kepnes
Rosen Farkas
Reisner
Knobel
Lockshin

Kaddish

The Kaddish Prayer

David Birnbaum and Martin S. Cohen

Editors

NEW PARADIGM MATRIX

www.NewParadigmMatrix.com

David Birnbaum & Martin S. Cohen

Kaddish
The Kaddish Prayer

with essays by

Adena K. Berkowitz, Benjamin Blech, Herbert Bronstein, Reuven P. Bulka,
Geoffrey Claussen, Martin S. Cohen, Noah Zvi Farkas, Baruch Frydman-Kohl,
Aubrey L. Glazer, Mark B. Greenspan, David Greenstein,
James Jacobson-Maisels, Elie Kaunfer, Steven Kepnes, Peter S. Knobel,
David A. Kunin, Martin I. Lockshin, Michael Marmur, Dalia Marx, Avi S. Olitzky,
Kerry M. Olitzky, Dan Ornstein, Avram Israel Reisner, Jeremy Rosen,
Barbara Thiede, Orna Triguboff, Ruth Walfish, and Herbert A. Yoskowitz

Saul J. Berman
Associate Editor

New Paradigm Matrix Publishing
New York
2016

21st CENTURY PUBLISHING

From the Editor-in-Chief

May 10, 2016

It is a privilege to be serving as Editor-in-Chief of this unique 10-theme series. I am honored to be working with world-class editors Benjamin Blech, Martin S. Cohen, Saul J. Berman, and Shalom Carmy.

It is our hope and prayer that the series be a catalyst for intellectual and spiritual expansion – as well as a unifying force both for our people as well as for individuals of good will globally.

Sincerely,

David Birnbaum

Mesorah Matrix series

jewish thought & spirituality

10-theme

10-volume

200+ original essays

150+ global thought leaders

a decade-long unified endeavor

genre: *applied scholarship*

www.MesorahMatrix.com

21st CENTURY PUBLISHING

Mesorah Matrix series

Sanctification

Tikkun Olam

Birkat Kohanim

> *Kaddish*

Modeh Ani

Havdalah

Search for Meaning

U-vacharta Ba-chayim

Ehyeh asher Ehyeh

V'Shamru

A POTENTIALLY ICONIC LEGACY SERIES
FOR THE 21ST CENTURY

10-VOLUME SERIES......200+ ESSAYS......A GLOBAL EFFORT

150+ ESSAYISTS....SPANNING THE WORLD'S TOP JEWISH THOUGHT LEADERS

A DYNAMIC CONTEMPORARY GLOBE-SPANING ENDEAVOR AND COLLEC-
TION

ESSAYISTS COVER A VERY WIDE SPECTRUM OF JUDAISM:

THE COMPLETE SERIES TO DATE IS AVAILABLE ON-LINE GRATIS
IN FLIP-BOOK FORM......AND DOWNLOAD-ABLE GRATIS
+
AVAILABLE IN SOFTCOVER VIA AMAZON
+
AVAILABLE IN E-BOOK FORM VIA VARIOUS MODALITIES

A UNIQUE STUDY AND REFERENCE TOOL FOR CLERGY, ACADEMICS,
STUDENTS & LAY INTELLIGENSIA

A STELLAR CORE COURSE OF STUDY – WHETHER FOR ONE SEMESTER OR
MULTI-YEAR

AND... AS AN UNINTENDED CONSEQUENCE, THE SERIES HAS
BROKEN DOWN BARRIERS - AND SERVED AS A FORCE-MULTIPLIER –
IN UNIFYING THE JEWISH PEOPLE

IN DEPTH & BREADTH......SCOPE & SPECTRUM
A LANDMARK SERIES
UNIQUE ACROSS THE 3,500+ YEAR SPAN OF JEWISH HISTORY

a unique, timeless and potentially multi-semester

Contemporary Jewish Thought

Course Text

a *sui generis* series • all original essays • broad spectrum authorship

a potentially iconic Jewish resource

Am ha-Sefer

This New Paradigm Matrix work
is available via multiple modalities:

amazon: www.AmazonX1000.com

eBooks: www.eReader1000.com

online: www.MesorahMatrix.com

contact: NPM1000@yahoo.com

The ten volumes of the Mesorah Matrix series amount to a contemporary encyclopedia of the best of traditional and new creative thinking on the central issues of Jewish Spirituality for the 21st century. People grappling with the place of truth, personal virtues and social values in their lives, will find multiple essays which challenge them to grow intellectually and spiritually in their Jewish identity. The ideas are all deeply rooted in Jewish texts in ways that enlighten the early texts and brighten the path into the future of the Jewish People.

- Rabbi Saul Berman
  Yeshiva University
  Chanukah, 2018

About the Editors

Martin S. Cohen has been a Senior Editor of the inter-denominational Mesorah Matrix series since 2012.

From 2000-2014, he served as Chairman of the Editorial Board of the quarterly journal *Conservative Judaism*, which was published under the joint auspices of the Jewish Theological Seminary and the Rabbinical Assembly.

Rabbi Cohen also served as the senior editor of *The Observant Life*, a landmark compendium of Jewish law and custom published by the Rabbinical Assembly in 2012.

His weekly blog can be viewed at www.TheRuminativeRabbi.blogspot.com. He has served as rabbi of the Shelter Rock Jewish Center in Roslyn, New York, since 2002.

Rabbi Cohen was educated at the City University of New York and at the Jewish Theological Seminary, where he was ordained a rabbi and received his Ph.D. in Ancient Judaism. He is the recipient of fellowships at the Hebrew University in Jerusalem in 1983 and Harvard University in 1993.

Martin Cohen has taught at Hunter College, the Jewish Theological Seminary, the Institute for Jewish Studies of the University of Heidelberg, as well as at the University of British Columbia and the Vancouver School of Theology.

His published works include *The Boy on the Door on the Ox* (2008) and *Our Haven and Our Strength: A Translation and Commentary on the Book of Psalms* (2004), as well as four novels and four books of essays.

Rabbi Cohen is currently writing a translation and commentary on the Torah and the Five Megillot.

MARTIN S. COHEN MAJOR WORKS

As Senior Editor

Mesorah Matrix series 2012 - present

Conservative Judaism 2000 - 2014

The Observant Life 2012

As Author (Non-Fiction)

Travels on the Private Zodiac: Reflections on Jewish Life, Ritual and Spirituality (1995)

In Pursuit of Wholeness: The Search for Spiritual Integrity in a Delusional World (1996)

Travels on the Road Not Taken: Towards a Bible-Based Theology of Jewish Spirituality (1997)

Sefer Ha-ikarim Li-z'maneinu (2000)

Our Haven and Our Strength: The Book of Psalms (2004)

Siddur Tzur Yisrael (2005)

Zot Nechamati for the House of Mourning (2006)

Riding the River of Peace (2007)

The Boy on the Door on the Ox (2008)

As Author (Fiction)

The Truth About Marvin Kalish (1992)

Light from Dead Stars (1996)

The Sword of Goliath (1998)

Heads You Lose (2002)

About the Editors

David Birnbaum is a philosophical writer, historical chronicler and *conceptual theorist*. His first work *God and Evil* (KTAV, 1988) is considered by many to be a breakthrough *modern day classic* in the field of theodicy. See God-And-Evil.com.

Editor-in-Chief Birnbaum is known globally as "the architect of Potentialism Theory" – a unified philosophy/cosmology/metaphysics. The paradigm-challenging theory (see ParadigmChallenge.com) is delineated in Birnbaum's 3-volume *Summa Metaphysica* series (1988, 2005, 2014). See Philosophy1000.com.

A riposte to *Summa Theologica* of (St.) Thomas Aquinas, the Birnbaum treatise challenges both the mainstream Western philosophy of Aristotelianism and the well propped-up British/atheistic cosmology of Randomness. See Potentialism Theory.com.

The focus of 150+ reviews/articles, Summa Metaphysica has been an assigned Course Text at over 15 institutions of higher learning globally. See SummaCoverage.com.

Summa Metaphysica was the focus of an international academic conference on Science & Religion in April 16-19 2012 (see Conference1000.com). The work has been very widely covered globally. See RewindSumma.com.

David Birnbaum is the Editor-in-Chief of the *Mesorah Matrix* series on Jewish thought and spirituality. The *sui generis* series spans 10-volumes and 10 themes. The entire series is comprised of 200+ specially commissioned original pieces from 150-180 global Jewish thought leader essayists. See Mesorah1000.com.

In the history realm, David Birnbaum is the author/chronicler of the 2-volume *The Crucifixion – of the Jews*, and of the 7-volume *Jews, Church & Civilization*. His Crucifixion series, in particular, traces a direct trajectory from the Canonical Gospels in the First Century to Auschwitz in the Twentieth. See History1000.com.

David Birnbaum has served on the faculty of the New School for Social Research in Manhattan. He is a graduate of Yeshiva University High School (Manhattan), CCNY (City College of New York) and Harvard. His commentary blog is www.ManhattanObserver.com.

DAVID BIRNBAUM MAJOR WORKS

As Author

4-volume *Summa Metaphysica** (www.philosophy1000.com)

2-volume *The Crucifixion* (www.crucifixion1000.com)

7-volume *Jews, Church & Civilization* (www.civilization1000.com)

As Editor-in-Chief

10-volume *Mesorah Matrix* (www.mesorah1000.com)

As Conceptualizer

3-volume *Summa Spinoffs* (www.Spinoffs1000.com)

8-volume *Potentialism Theory* via Graphic-Narrative
(www.TheoryGraphics1000.com)

As Commentator

www.ManhattanObserver.com

YouTube channels

Summa Metaphysica

Mesorah Matrix

*

Summa I: Religious Man / God and Evil
Summa II: Spiritual Man / God and Good
Summa III: Secular Man / The Transcendent Dynamic
Summa IV: Quantum Man / Morphed Cosmic Order

>>

DAVID BIRNBAUM MAJOR WORKS

FOCUS ON 4-VOLUME -

Summa Metaphysica series

presenting new paradigm
Potentialism Theory
a universal, unified, seamless & fully-integrated
overarching philosophy

www.SummaMetaphysica.com

Summa I:
Religious Man: God and Evil: focus: *theodicy & eternal origins* [1988]**

Summa II:
Spiritual Man: God and Good: focus: *metaphysics & teleology* [2005]

Summa III:
Secular Man: The Transcendent Dynamic: focus: *cosmology & evolution* [2014]

Summa IV:
Quantum Man: Morphed Cosmic Order: focus: *quantum-potential* [2020]

see also secondary site PotentialismTheory.com

see also: RewindSumma.com 222+ panel Scroll-Down tour

YouTube Channel: Summa Metaphysica

see also Supplement: Articles on Summa
(only online - on www.SummaMetaphysica.com)

** see also: www.GodOfPotential.com
** see special YouTube channel: www.UnifyingScienceSpirituality.com

www.BirnbaumAcademic.com

www.David1000.com

www.Major1000.com

Mesorah Matrix
SENIOR EDITORIAL BOARD

Kaddish

Kaddish

TABLE OF CONTENTS

Preface   1

Mourner's Kaddish: A New Framing   9
ELIE KAUNFER
The Mourner's Kaddish is often framed in American synagogues by short readings that make short but overarching claims about the nature of this prayer. This essay examines some of these implicit and explicit claims and challenges them based on a close reading of the biblical and rabbinic intertexts of the prayer.

The Kaddish Is the Song of Songs   29
DAVID GREENSTEIN
Surprisingly, the Mourner's Kaddish has been described as a great love song. What love is being expressed? The answer emerges as much from how the prayer says what it says, as well as from what it leaves unsaid.

For a God Who Mourns   45
NOAH ZVI FARKAS
In this theological reading of the Mourner's Kaddish, we find a God who mourns the death of every living creature. In an act of courage, the mourner comforts God and becomes God's partner in bringing life back to the world.

Death Is But a Dream   67
MARTIN S. COHEN
It is a commonplace for modern Jews to speak about saying Kaddish "for" someone, but what is the real force of the preposition in that expression? When we say that we are saying Kaddish "for" someone, do we truly suppose that person somehow benefits posthumously from our efforts? If so, how exactly do we imagine the trajectory of that beneficence? If not, then in what sense is it "for" that person at all? This essay explores these questions in light of classical sources.

Do We Expect Too Much from Kaddish…Or Not Enough?   89
REUVEN P. BULKA
This essay suggests that the original purpose of Kaddish recitation for mourners was to inspire those who were disaffected from Judaism to come back to active communal involvement through the effort to sanctify God via the performance of good deeds, with the consolation benefits of Kaddish recitation being entirely tangential. It is not only possible, but most appropriate, to attempt to re-capture that original Kaddish "magic."

Kaddish and the Red Heifer   107
BENJAMIN BLECH
Death is a frightening challenge to faith; Kaddish as our traditional response to its harsh decree can best be understood with reference to the biblical law regarding the *parah adumah*, the red heifer, as well as the sin of the golden calf.

Is the Kaddish About You and Me…or God?   131
AVI S. OLITZKY
By understanding the true meaning of the Mourner's Kaddish, as well as by considering carefully who says it and why, we can strengthen our relationships to ourselves, to each other, and to God.

Mysteries of the Kaddish   143
ORNA TRIGUBOFF
The Kaddish prayer, when said with the appropriate intention, is understood by the Zohar and Lurianic Kabbalah to be a gateway leading to different states of consciousness. This essay explores how this takes place.

Say the Kaddish, Create the World (for the Very First Time)   161
BARBARA THIEDE
We do not heal through denial, nor can we praise without understanding God may be hidden, but Kaddish asks us to pray as adults responsible for the world.

Kaddish as a Vehicle for Rabbinic Political Revolution   173
KERRY M. OLITZKY
While the Kaddish today serves primarily to comfort the mourner and has become part of the folk-religion of the Jewish people, it was intentionally used as a powerful tool in the claim of rabbinic authority over the community. As a result, the Kaddish stands as a creative model of the way one generation's leaders may wrest authority from their predecessors, thus providing a model for future generations to follow.

The Mourner's Kaddish: An Enduring Inspiration and Challenge   183
PETER S. KNOBEL
Taking the Mourner's Kaddish as more than a simple doxology (that is, a prayer of praise), this essay attempts to demonstrate that its recitation connects one generation to the next and in that specific way provides comfort and reconciliation. But it is also true that, in a post-Shoah world, the Kaddish pays tribute to victims and protests the seeming silence of God. The Kaddish is thus both liturgy and an experience that transcends its place in the prayerbook.

Sound and Silence in Response to Grief   195
MARTIN S. COHEN AND DALIA MARX
Jewish tradition offers two distinct paths for the mourner: the path of silence and the path of public speech. Both are grounded in ancient tradition and both can assist mourners struggling to come to terms with their loss. This essay shows how this ancient dichotomy manifests itself in kibbutz culture in pre-state and contemporary Israel.

My Kaddish   221
HERBERT BRONSTEIN
The Kaddish prayer, a "marker" of particular Jewish identity for Jews and non-Jews alike, is generally known as a mourner's prayer. Yet, by considering its various textual versions and the various roles those versions play in Jewish religious observance, we can understand the Kaddish not only as an essential component of Jewish liturgy, but as a prayer possessed of universal meaning for all people facing the inevitable trials of everyday life. Rooted in antiquity, the Kaddish confronts modern philosophic materialism with a continuing affirmation of the reality of the spiritual dimension of reality.

Kaddish as Prayer and Confession   235
JEREMY ROSEN
The Kaddish is known as the Jewish memorial prayer. However, it has a long history as a marker within the framework of Jewish prayer. Furthermore, the Kaddish does not mention death at all, but rather exists to give the mourner a role in the daily services. Over the centuries, though, the Kaddish has acquired a quasi-mystical function in the efforts of the living to remember the dead, while simultaneously giving verbal expression to the grief of the individual by providing an opportunity for the mourner to acknowledge the Divine at work in the universe.

The Recitation of Kaddish: A Personal Odyssey   255
RUTH WALFISH
The essay summarizes some of the halakhic background regarding the recitation of the Mourner's Kaddish and the growing participation of women in that ritual. The author presents her experience in taking this practice upon herself after the death of her mother.

An Enigma Wrapped in A Mystery   267
ADENA K. BERKOWITZ
The daily recitation of Kaddish by those in mourning, traditionally a ritual seen as only open to men, has been embraced by more and more Orthodox Jewish women. This essay explores what Jewish law and rabbinic decisors have said about women saying Kaddish, and the experiences of the author throughout her year of mourning.

Reflections on Saying Kaddish   281
HERBERT A. YOSKOWITZ
This essay sets forth its author's sense that the Kaddish exemplifies the relevance of Jewish wisdom as a palpable source of intellectual and spiritual power for Jewish people, and that this is so regardless of whether it emanates from the pew or the *bimah*.

The Kaddish: How We Name the Blessed Holy One   297
STEVEN KEPNES
The Kaddish prayer is used to mark both transitions in Jewish liturgy and the
transition of the individual from life to death to eternal life. The Kaddish is
a sign of the eternality of the soul of the departed as well as the eternality of
the Jewish people.

The Kaddish, the Allegory of the Cave, and the Golden Calf:
Meditations on Education and the Encounter with God   307
GEOFFREY CLAUSSEN
Grounded in the idea that God is a moral ideal that invites our continual
reflection and growth, and drawing on the biblical narrative of the golden
calf and the Platonic allegory of the cave, this essay considers how the words
of the Kaddish may help Jews encounter God through the activity of study.

An Unlikely Prayer   337
MARTIN I. LOCKSHIN
The Kaddish prayer is anomalous in many ways and has relatively weak
roots in Jewish history and law. Its power derives from folk-religion and
from the deep psychological need that it helps fulfill.

"Let the Power of the Eternal Be Great":
Kaddish, Cosmos, and Covenant   349
BARUCH FRYDMAN-KOHL
Two biblical phrases, examined as examples of rabbinic augmentation
theology, were occasionally recited along with the Kaddish. In addition to
reviewing the halakhic debate about their liturgical suitability, this essay
explores their adaptation by Abraham Joshua Heschel and Hans Jonas
and their implications for contemporary efforts to develop a relational
understanding of God that bridges cosmology and covenant, scientific
theory, and theological belief.

L'eilla L'eilla (**Higher and Higher**): **The Kaddish as Allusion to** *Tikkun*   375
DAVID A. KUNIN
The mysterious text of the Kaddish appears to have no overt connection to the way it is traditionally used in synagogue. Yet, when considered closely, it may be interpreted as a call to community responsibility and *tikkun olam*.

Kaddish as Expansiveness   387
JAMES MOSHE JACOBSON-MAISELS
The essay explores the recitation of Kaddish as a performative spiritual practice of expansiveness which allows the practitioner to hold the fullness of loss, the fullness of life, and the fullness of everything that has arisen in their prayer experience in a container of awe and love.

Kaddish as *Neuzeit*: **Between the Nameless and the Named**   415
AUBREY L. GLAZER
This essay argues that normative Jewish liturgy with all its mystical undertones provides a way to live life in a less accelerated manner, thus allowing for more expansiveness through the indivisible layers of time embedded in a prayer like Kaddish. The ritual of reciting Kaddish, viewed through a Zoharic lens but also through some current exemplars in popular culture as well as the post-secular songbook of Leonard Cohen, sheds light on how much the divine name is in need of restoration.

Kaddish and God's "Great Name"   427
MARK B. GREENSPAN
One of the mysteries of the Kaddish is the absence of a specific name of God in this prayer. The Kaddish speaks of praising "the Great Name of God." While "name praise" dates back to the Bible, it took on special significance as the liturgy developed. Eventually, the contemplation of God's name became the link that connects heaven and earth. Speaking of God in this fashion emphasizes both God's immanence and transcendence, and creates a common language to which all people can easily relate.

Kaddish: The Practice of Praise   449
AVRAM ISRAEL REISNER
The author finds the origins of the Kaddish prayer in the texts of Heikhalot
mysticism. In this view, Kaddish signals the completion of earthly prayers
so that heavenly praise might begin, thus serving as an essential cog in the
cycle of praise that supports God's world.

The Kaddish as a Speech Act   475
MICHAEL MARMUR
This essay argues that in order to understand the centrality of the Kaddish
in Jewish liturgy and culture, aspects of its language—among them the
interplay of past, present. and future, as well as the interplay of Hebrew
and Aramaic—deserve attention.

Oseh Shalom: Giving Peace a Chance in Heaven and on Earth   493
DAN ORNSTEIN
The prayer that closes the Kaddish in almost all its versions, the Oseh
Shalom, is not a mere request to God for peace, but a demand that God
impose peace upon the Jewish people and all people.

YouTube   513

About the Contributors   515

Preface

Martin S. Cohen

When Allen Ginsberg famously began his idiosyncratic eulogy of his mother by asking the reader to imagine him "up all night, talking, talking, talking, reading the Kaddish aloud, listening to Ray Charles," he did not pause to explain what exactly this thing called Kaddish was or why he would have been reading it aloud in his mother's memory. Nor did he need to: there is no Jewish prayer better known to the non-Jewish world than Kaddish, and the concept of saying Kaddish "for" someone has entered the American lexicon of cultural phrases known to all and used freely without the need to translate or explain. Neither Imre Kertesz's *Kaddish for an Unborn Child* nor Leon Wieseltier's 1998 bestseller *Kaddish* provides a translation or explanation on the dustjacket, for example, the assumption being that anyone cultured enough to want to read either book—and surely not only Jewish readers—would know what the word means and what its use as the title implies about the book's content. Nor did Leonard Bernstein seem to feel the need for any explanation when he named his third symphony "Kaddish," and left it at that.

And yet, for all that everybody "knows" what Kaddish is, the truth is that it remains—even for those well-versed in Jewish prayer—mysterious in many ways. There are, for example, several different version of Kaddish, each assigned its particular place in the larger liturgical world of traditional Judaism, but the specific relationship of all these versions remains obscure: it is even unknown whether the shorter versions are abridgements of the longer ones, or if the longer ones are elaborations of the shorter texts. Another riddle has to do with the language of the Kaddish: why is it primarily composed in Aramaic, the street language of Roman Palestine, rather than Hebrew, the regular language for Jewish prayer? (And it is unclear as well why its author would have used a hodge-podge of Aramaic *and* Hebrew, when the prayer could easily have been written solely in one language or the other.) Nor do we know the precise relationship between the Kaddish and the text presented in the New Testament and later known to Christians as the "Lord's Prayer"—despite the obvious similarities in vocabulary, grammar, and meaning between the two prayers. The Kaddish, in each of its versions, has eschatological overtones—but what specifically the prayer means to suggest about the messianic future, and how that vision interfaces with other related rabbinic concepts (including the resurrection of the dead, the redemption of the world, the kingdom of God on earth, and the sanctification of God's name as the salvific trigger of redemption) is unclear...as is the place or prominence of Kaddish in Jewish worship during the first centuries of the Common Era. We do not even know with certainty the date of the Kaddish.

In its own category of obscurity is the use of Kaddish as the memorial prayer for the dead *par excellence*—a role so widely understood that the expression "to have Kaddish for someone" will be easily unpacked by even the casual Jewish listener to mean that the speaker has lost a parent, sibling, spouse, or child, that the anniversary of that relative's death is coming up, and that the speaker intends to attend synagogue services on that day in order to recite the Kaddish in memory of that deceased individual. But what it means precisely to say Kaddish "for" someone—that is another matter entirely, and a far more obscure one. Do the dead derive some posthumous benefit when someone says Kaddish "for" them? If not, in what sense is it "for" them at all? But if the departed themselves do not derive any benefit at all from the recitation of the prayer, then who does benefit from its recitation? And in what specific way?

These questions, and many, many others, are addressed by the authors who have contributed to this volume. They come from a wide range of backgrounds: some are congregational rabbis, while others are teachers and academics, and still others work in the Jewish world in different capacities. They are a diverse group, our authors: men and women, older and younger, staunchly traditionalist and more liberally oriented, Israeli and diaspora-based. Yet, for all that they are different, they are also united by the common belief that the written word, and particularly in the form of the short essay, is a medium in which readers may meaningfully explore Judaism and Jewishness itself. This is not a book solely for Jews of any particular spiritual orientation; nor, for that matter, is it a book solely for Jewish readers. Rather, my hope is that this anthology of essays may open a door for all who possess of the kind of curiosity regarding Jewish religion and culture that cannot be dealt with by platitudes, or even heartfelt op-ed pieces, but solely with thoughtful, text-based studies intended to inform, persuade, and convince. The authors in this volume invite readers along on an investigative journey that will lead, if successful, to a deeper appreciation of the larger Jewish enterprise through the informed contemplation of a single one of its myriad parts. I feel privileged to present the work of these authors to the reading public for its—for *your*—contemplation, and I hope our readers come to feel as I do that this is a remarkable collection of essays by an equally remarkable group of authors.

Unless otherwise indicated, all translationshere are the authors' own work. Biblical citations footnoted to the NJPS derive from the complete translation of Scripture first published under the title *Tanakh: The Holy Scriptures* by the Jewish Publication Society in Philadelphia in 1985.

I would like to take this opportunity to acknowledge the other senior editors of the Mesorah Matrix series, David Birnbaum and Benjamin Blech, as well as Saul J. Berman, our associate editor. They and our able staff have all supported me as I've labored to bring this volume to fruition and I am grateful to them all.

As always, I must also express my gratitude to the men and women, and particularly to the lay leadership, of the synagogue I serve as rabbi, the Shelter Rock Jewish Center in Roslyn, New York. Possessed of the unwavering conviction that their rabbi's book projects are part and parcel of his service to them—and, through them, to the larger community of those interested in learning about Judaism through the medium of the well-written word—they are remarkably supportive of my literary efforts as author and editor. I am in their debt, and I am pleased to acknowledge that debt formally here and whenever I publish my own work or the work of others.

Martin S. Cohen
Roslyn, New York
June 21, 2015/4 Tammuz 5775

Abbreviations

A.T. - *Arba·ah Turim*

B.   - Babylonian Talmud

M.   - Mishnah

M.T. - *Mishneh Torah*

T.   - Tosefta

Y.   - Yerushalmi

A Note from the Editors

Every effort has been made to retain a good level of consistency between the essays that appear here in terms of the translation and transliteration of Hebrew. Many of our decisions have, needs be, been arbitrary, but we have done our best to create a book that will be as accessible to newcomers to the study of Judaism as it is inspiring to cognoscenti. The four-letter name of God, left unpronounced by pious Jews as a sign of reverence, is mostly rendered in this volume as "the Eternal" or "the Eternal One," occasionally as "Lord" or "the Lord," or as YHVH. Other divine names are either transliterated or translated to create in English something akin to the way the text reads in Hebrew. All translations are their authors' unless otherwise indicated.

Essays

Mourner's Kaddish: A New Framing

Elie Kaunfer

The Mourner's Kaddish is seared in the minds of so many Jews as a familiar yet mysterious prayer that is taken with the utmost seriousness. In this essay, I will attempt to open up a broader interpretative field for the Mourner's Kaddish by examining three myths of the modern American experience of reciting the prayer.

Praise or Request?

In solemn testimony to that unbroken faith which links the generations one to another, let those who mourn now rise to magnify and sanctify God's holy name.

As a child growing up in Temple Emanuel in Providence, Rhode Island, I heard these words every week at the end of Shabbat morning services. The senior rabbi would intone this sentence with a deep sense of gravity and attention, cueing the recitation of the Mourner's Kaddish. The rabbi was quoting from Jacob Kohn's "Prayer before Kaddish" found in the 1960 edition of the *Sabbath and Festival Prayerbook* edited by Morris Silverman, known as the "Silverman Siddur" (altering the printed text slightly by changing "Thy holy name" to "God's holy name").[1]

This "Prayer before Kaddish" makes two claims. The first claim is that the Kaddish is a testimony to faith. More specifically, as developed in another reading by Silverman himself (also printed as an introduction to the Kaddish): "We express our undying faith in God's love and justice...."[2] The second claim is that the act of reciting the Kaddish is an act of "magnifying and sanctifying" God's name. Kaddish serves as a declaration about the state of God's "holy name," and even increases the glory given to that name. If one had to classify the Kaddish in one of the three main genres of Jewish prayer—praise, request, and thanks[3]—this framing clearly argues that Kaddish is praise.

This framing of the Kaddish resonates with other American *siddurim*[4] that precede and follow Silverman's. Julius Silberfeld, rabbi at Congregation B'nai Abraham in Newark, New Jersey, wrote, as part of the introduction to the Kaddish in a 1905 traditional prayerbook: "And may all the bereaved and mourners, in all their trials and tribulations, in all their disappointments and sorrows, be ever ready to rise and *sanctify Thy name*..."[5] Silverman's original *siddur*, published in 1936, offers introductions to the Kaddish in which mourners alternatively "rise to sanctify Thy name," "rise to acknowledge Thee," or "rise to hallow Thy name."[6] More recent publications invite mourners to "join in praise of God's name,"[7] "to recite God's praise,"[8] "to declare their faith in God, to magnify and sanctify God's holy name,"[9] or to "sanctify God's name."[10] The prayer has also been called "an elaborate praise of God."[11]

All of these introductions are relating to the first line of Kaddish: *yitgaddal v'yitkaddash sh'meih rabba*. Silberfeld's 1905 *siddur* translated this phrase as "Magnified and sanctifed be His great name," and many subsequent *siddurim* have followed in this same vein.[12] This is a somewhat ambiguous phrasing that nonetheless seems to indicate a description of God's state of being. But what is really being expressed through these four Aramaic words?

Prayers are better understand when recognized as part of a larger intertextual field, employing what I have called elsewhere "the literary-intertext method."[13] In Reuven Kimelman's words: "The meaning of the liturgy exists not so much in the liturgical text *per se* as in the interaction between the liturgical text and the biblical intertext. Meaning, in the mind of the reader, takes place between texts rather than within them."[14] In other words, a prayer text cannot fully be understood until one (a) recognizes which biblical text is being quoted in the prayer, and (b) examines the prayer in light of the biblical text referred to. In order to understand this opening declaration of the Kaddish, we must ask: "What are the biblical texts that lie behind it?"

Rabbi David Abudarham (14th century, Spain), who himself notes that almost all prayers are based on language from the Bible,[15] connects our phrase with Ezekiel 38:23.[16] Here is the relevant passage, with some of its surrounding context:[17]

On that day, when Gog sets foot on the soil of Israel—declares the LORD God—My raging anger shall flare up. For I have decreed in My indignation and in My blazing wrath: On that day, a terrible earthquake shall befall the land of Israel. The fish of the sea, the birds of the sky, the beasts of the field, all creeping things that move on the ground, and every human being on earth shall quake before Me. Mountains shall be overthrown, cliffs shall topple, and every wall shall crumble to the ground.

I will then summon the sword against him throughout My mountains—declares the LORD God—and every man's sword shall be turned against his brother. I will punish him with pestilence and with bloodshed; and I will pour torrential rain, hailstones, and sulfurous fire upon him and his hordes and the many peoples with him.

Thus will I manifest My greatness and My holiness (*v'hitgaddilti v'hitkaddishti*), and make Myself known in the sight of many nations. And they shall know that I am the LORD.

What is clear from this context is that God's name is not, according to the prophet, *currently* "magnified" or "sanctified." Rather, God *will* magnify and sanctify God's own name—and only at the end of this cataclysmic war with Gog. The Kaddish prayer, then, is not a praise of God's name as currently great and holy. It is a *request* for God to hasten the arrival of the end of time and make God's name holy, which will only be achieved when all nations recognize that God is the Supreme Being.

That the first line of Kaddish is a request rather than a form of praise is noted by early commentators on the prayer. I bring two examples below, one from Rav Hai Gaon (939-1038) and the other from the school of Rashi (1040-1105) :

> At first [in the Kaddish] one requests from God to hurry His promise, as He promised us through his prophet: "Thus will I manifest My greatness and My holiness, and make Myself known in the sight of many nations" (Ezekiel 38:23).[18]

> This is the meaning of "May God's name be magnified and sanctified." In the future His name should be made great and sanctified, as it is written: "And they will know that I am YHVH" (Ezekiel 38:23). For right now, He is not written as He is called. He is called Adonai, but He is written YHVH.[19]

Abudarham also notes that only in the future will God's name be great:

> "Magnified and sanctified"—based on the verse, "Thus will I manifest My greatness and My holiness, and make Myself known in the sight of many nations" (Ezekiel 38:23), as is said in connection with the war of Gog. For only then will God's name be holy, as it says: "Then the saviors will go up Mount. Zion to judge Mount Esau" (Obadiah 1:21) and it is written

afterward: "On that day YHVH will be one and His name one" (Zechariah 14:4).[20]

Jewish worshippers are familiar with this use of "magnify and sanctify" from another liturgical selection, which is clearly speaking about the future: a line in Kedushah of the Shabbat morning Amidah:

> From Your place, our Sovereign, appear! Save us and rule over us, for we await You! When will You rule over Zion? Soon, in our days and in our lives, may You dwell.[21] *May You be magnified and sanctified* in Jerusalem Your city, from generation to generation and forever and ever. May our eyes see Your sovereignty, as is said in the poems of Your strong one, from the mouth of David Your righteous Messiah: "May YHVH rule forever; Your God, O Zion, from generation to generation—Halleluyah!" (Psalm 146:10).[22]

In this poignant prayer, the worshipper notes that God is not yet sovereign in Jerusalem, and plaintively begs God to reveal how much longer we will have to wait for God's name to be magnified and sanctified forever.

It seems likely to me that mourners, "in all their trials and tribulations" (in Silberfeld's words) would identify less with a line that serves as testament to God's greatness *now*, than they would with the meaning of the prayer that is consonant with the context of the biblical verse that it is based on: praying for a different world, in which God—in an as yet unrealized future—will be recognized universally. This world is represented by the end of time, an epoch when death itself *will be* transformed.

The prevalent framing of the Kaddish as a praise of God—as opposed to a plea for God to become great (as evidenced by the commentaries on the *siddur*, adduced above)—has a deep impact on the worshippers' understanding of what the purpose of the prayer is. If the prayer is praise, it may be stoic praise—a declaration of faith—in the face of otherwise difficult emotions.[23] But if the prayer is request, it may resonate with the experience of mourning: of yearning for a different time, a new world.

The Mystery of the Kaddish Response

"While the Kaddish is recited in memory of the departed, it contains no reference to death. Rather, it is an avowal made in the midst of our sorrow that God is just, though we do not always comprehend His ways." This framing comment, also from the pen of Morris Silverman, notes one of the well-known oddities of the Mourner's Kaddish: the absence of any mention of death.[24] In this understanding, the Kaddish is an affirmation of the greatness of God despite our tragic state of mind. It is perhaps this aspect of "that unbroken faith" that Kohn makes reference to in the same prayerbook.

But there is another striking absence in the Kaddish: the absence of God's name. Why is God's name missing? God's name is rarely absent from the liturgy. In fact, Rav states explicitly that any blessing without God's name is not a blessing.[25] One proposed answer identifies the original Kaddish with a "study house" prayer, a locale in which the use of God's name was more circumspect than in the synagogue.[26] And yet, the question is heightened when taking note of the core line of the Kaddish: "May His great name be blessed forever and ever."

This line is often taken as a metonymy of the Kaddish as a whole. The Babylonian Talmud refers to the Kaddish prayer by this line (or similar variant).[27] And as we will explore below, it is a common response to the recitation of the name of God. How odd for a prayer to be built around a response to the name of God, without the name of God appearing in the prayer at all!

What might this line mean? Again we look to the Bible for intertexts to expand the field of potential meaning. The first intertext candidate comes from Daniel 2:17–20:

> Then Daniel went to his house and informed his companions, Ḥananiah, Mishael, and Azariah, of the matter, that they might implore the God of Heaven for help regarding this mystery, so that Daniel and his colleagues would not be put to death together with the other wise men of Babylon. The mystery was then revealed to Daniel in a night vision; *then Daniel blessed the God of Heaven. Daniel answered and said:* **"Let the name of God be blessed forever and ever,** *for wisdom and power are His."*[28]

In this scene, Daniel and his colleagues are under mortal threat from the Babylonian king. In this state of mind, Daniel beseeches God for protection—and his words invoking blessing on the name of God are framed as a request, rather than a description of reality (just as was the case in the passage from Ezekiel discussed above). But another aspect of the passage is striking as well: verse 20 coincides almost word for word with the line from Kaddish. The only difference is that in Daniel, God (called by the Aramaic word *elaha*) is mentioned directly. Why is God mentioned in the biblical text but missing in the prayer text?

A second biblical intertext for this line is found in Job 1:20–21:

> Then Job arose, tore his robe, cut off his hair, and threw himself on the ground and worshipped. He said: "Naked came I out of my mother's womb, and naked shall I return

there; *God has given, and God has taken away.* **Blessed be the name of God.**"[29]

Although death is not mentioned in the Kaddish, once the biblical intertext of Job is brought in, the context of mourning becomes clearer. Job, the quintessential biblical mourner, recites this line in the midst of his crippling loss. It might be that Job is stoically affirming the goodness and just actions of God.[30] However, Job seems to be quoting Psalm 113, critically leaving out the "now and forever" part of the blessing found there:

> Halleluyah! O servants of the LORD, give praise; praise the name of the LORD.
> **Let the name of the LORD be blessed now and forever.**[31]

Can Job perhaps not bear to quote the joyous line in its entirety?

These biblical intertexts help open up our phrase from the Kaddish to additional possible interpretations. But our focus on the missing name of God is only heightened by these texts. Note that in all of them—Daniel, Job, and Psalms—God's name appears. Again, we ask: why would the name of God be missing from a prayer that is so clearly influenced by these biblical texts that do mention God's name?

Before suggesting an answer, we note one other reason why we would expect to see God's name in the Kaddish. The phrase *y'hei sh'meih rabba* seems in fact to be one of many liturgical responses that are prompted by hearing the name of God spoken aloud. These include: *y'hi sheim Adonai m'vorakh mei-attah v'ad olam* ("let the name of Adonai be blessed from now until eternity"), and *kumu bar'khu et Adonai eloheikhem min ha-olam v'ad ha-olam* ("arise and bless Adonai your God forever and ever").[32]

All of these responses share the following components: blessed, name of God, and forever.[33] Thus, even if we didn't expect to see God's name in the response, we certainly would expect it to precede the phrase as a cue for the response. In other words, all of the above responses come *after* the mention of God's name. The case of Psalms, cited above, is most clear: "Praise the name of the LORD" is followed by "Let the name of the LORD be blessed now and forever."

This is also true of the phrase *barukh sheim k'vod malkhuto l'olam va-ed* ("blessed be the glorious name of His kingdom forever and ever"). This phrase is liturgically familiar as a response to the first line of the Shema (Deuteronomy 6:4). But it also is a response to the pronunciation of the name of God by the High Priest on Yom Kippur. When the priest uttered God's name, the people responded by falling prostrate and reciting these words.[34]

In his classic study on the Kaddish, David De Sola Pool notes this oddity in the prayer. He first states: "There is every reason to think that the response was often used in one form or another as an ejaculated praise at the mention of God's name."[35] He goes on to note: "There is no mention of God's Name in the Kaddish to occasion this response other than *yitgaddal v'yitkaddash sh'meih rabba*."[36]

I would like to propose one additional possible meaning to the absence of the name of God in the prayer, which nevertheless centers on a response to hearing God's name. This interpretation is based on one of the earliest mentions of the *y'hei sh'meih rabba* line in rabbinic literature:

> It is taught: Rabbi Yosi said: One time I was walking on the path, and I entered a ruin from one of the ruins of Jerusalem in order to pray. Elijah of blessed memory came and watched the doorway until I finished my prayer....He said to me..."Whenever the Israelites go into the synagogues and schoolhouses and respond: '**May His great name be blessed**,' God shakes His head and says: 'Happy is the king who is thus praised in his house! Woe[37] to the father who

had to banish his children, and woe to the children who had to be banished from the table of their father!'"[38]

This source offers another perspective on the meaning of *y'hei sh'meih*. On the one hand, when the phrase is recited by Israel in the synagogues and study houses, God is filled with happiness. But immediately following this statement of joy, God goes on to say: "Woe is Me and woe is Israel!" In other words, the source reflects the complex emotions that are embedded in the recitation of the line. This is a line that was associated with the presence of God; reciting it meant that God's name—the embodiment of God's immanence—was at hand. Yet it is recited not in the world of the Temple and the High Priest, but rather in a world in which Jerusalem is in ruins. The line has morphed from a reaction to God's presence to a painful reminder of God's absence. God is no longer available in this world in the way that God once was.

Significantly, the sufferer in this text is not limited to the "children"—that is, to Israel. Indeed, God is one of the suffering parties, along with Israel. Both experience woe. This is a far cry from the framing of Kaddish as a testimony to faith in a God whose actions cause us to suffer for reasons we can't understand. It is, rather, a prompt that reminds God of the brokenness of the world. By reciting this line, then, the mourner invites God into the emotional experience of remembering better times and of grief for the current, unredeemed state of the world.

Commenting on this passage in the Talmud, the *Eish Kodesh* (the rabbi of the Warsaw Ghetto) spells out clearly this view of God:

Now the Jew who is tormented by his afflictions thinks that he alone suffers, as if all his personal afflictions and those of all Israel do not affect [God] above, God forbid. Scripture states, however, "In all their troubles, He was troubled"

(Isaiah 63:9), and the Talmud states: When a person suffers, what does the Shekhinah say? "My head is too heavy for Me, My arm is too heavy for Me." Our sacred literature tells us that when a Jew is afflicted, God, blessed be He, suffers as it were much more than the person does.[39]

This opens one additional interpretative pathway in the Kaddish: the curious line that God is "above all the blessings and songs, praises and *consolations* (*neḥemata*) that we utter in the world." Why do we mention consolations in the middle of the praise list in the Kaddish? This passage clearly draws upon Nehemiah 9:5:

> The Levites Jeshua, Kadmiel, Bani, Hashabniah, Sherebiah, Hodiah, and Pethahiah said: "Rise, bless the LORD your God who is from eternity to eternity: 'May Your glorious name be blessed, exalted *though it is above every blessing and praise.*'"[40]

Interestingly, the source text in Nehemiah mentions both "blessing" and "praise"—which God is above—but does not mention any "consolation." To be clear: the phrase in the Kaddish indicates that whatever had been attempted by the worshipper is insufficient. The worshipper attempts to bless, even though God is above all blessing. But this also implies that by stating that God is above all consolation, the worshipper must have just attempted to console God. What consolation—*neḥamah*—could be offered here?[41] Or, in other words: consolation is something that is offered to a mourner; in what way is God mourning?

In the context of our broader understanding of the Kaddish, this comfort arrives in the recitation of the phrase *y'hei sh'meih rabba*. This phrase is both a consolation—reminding God about the happiness experienced in Temple times when the divine name was pronounced—and also a poignant reminder that things are not as they were once. The Kaddish, now, is not only about the personal and particular loss of the mourner's beloved. It is about the larger mourning that is occasioned by the state of a ruined world.[42]

In this understanding, the Kaddish is not a declaration of faith. It is a reminder to God of the old world that stands in ruins, and suggests the fellowship that the mourner might feel with God, as both grieve for a loss. The power of the words *y'hei sh'meih rabba* is grounded in their ability both to remind God of the Temple era, where intimacy prevailed, and—when recited in the ruins of our world—to offer stark commentary on the state of this broken world.

It is true that the Kaddish did not originate as a prayer for mourners.[43] But the language encoded in the prayer made it more than appropriate for mourning—both human mourning of loss, and divine mourning over the state of the world. It paints a very different picture of a God who is close and standing with us in mourning, rather than directing the world in inscrutable ways that require us to declare our blind faith despite our suffering.

The Magic of the Kaddish

The recitation of the Kaddish is often experienced as the most solemn moment in a given prayer service. It is then, in that moment of intoning the words of the prayer, that the congregation can focus on the loss to the mourner, and the mourner fulfills the obligation to recite the prayer on behalf of the departed.

But even this overarching context can be called into question. What is one doing when reciting the Kaddish, writ large? If one arrives at synagogue in time to say the Kaddish, but does nothing else, does this matter? If one can't make it to synagogue to recite Kaddish for a loved one, does it make sense to have someone else say Kaddish instead?

There are many complex psychological dimensions to the

commitment to say Kaddish, but they focus almost entirely on the saying of the words themselves, ignoring any larger context. I want to suggest here a wider scope of what it might mean to "say Kaddish."

The stories of the connection between the relief of the suffering of the dead and the words of the Kaddish appear in the Middle Ages. I will not rehearse the details of these stories in full; one can read more about them in other essays in this volume. I simply want to point out one common feature across all of these stories: the salve for the dead man is not limited to the recitation of the Kaddish by the son. Indeed, in the large number of stories about Rabbi Akiva (or, in some versions, Rabbi Yoḥanan ben Zakkai) and the dead father, the son is asked to do a number of activities, including: learning to lead the prayer service, reciting the Shema, reading Torah, having an *aliyah*, and leading the congregation in prayer. Reciting Kaddish only appears in some of these stories. Below are a number of versions of this part of the story:

...And teach him the Amidah; the Recitation of the Shema; three verses of the Torah, that he might take an *aliyah* and read from the Torah scroll, so that the congregation may answer after him: "Bless! Blessed is God, who is blessed."[44]

...Immediately God opened [the son's] heart and [Rabbi Akiva] taught him Torah, the Recitation of the Shema, and the Grace after Meals, and stood him before the congregation so that he said: "Bless!" And they answered after him: "Blessed is YHVH, who is blessed."[45]

They brought him and commanded him to be circumcised, and sat him to learn, and he did. They taught him the blessings for the Torah. On Shabbat, they commanded him to read from the Torah and say: "Blessed is YHVH who is blessed, etc, forever and ever."[46]

They stood him in the synagogue to bless for the congregation.[47]

He taught him Torah and the Recitation of the Shema and the Eighteen Blessings (Amidah) and the Grace after Meals, and they stood him before the congregation and he said: "Bless YHVH who is blessed!" And the congregration answered, "Blessed is YHVH who is blessed forever and ever. May [His name] be exalted…May His great name…"[48]

What becomes clear is that the recitation of the Kaddish is not the full picture of the responsibility of the child of the departed. In fact, in the various versions of this story, the more common thread is reading Torah and leading the congregation in prayer. To the extent that the Kaddish appears in this list, it is more accurately only one discrete component of a life committed to Torah study and prayer in general. Taken in total, these commitments indicate a form of resurrection:

It is taught: Rabbi Shimon ben Yoḥai said: Whoever has a son that toils in Torah, it is as if he has not died.[49]

The departed live on through their children. But they also live on through the commitments their children make. If the recitation of the Kaddish is divorced from a full life of Torah and *mitzvot*, it is in some ways missing the point. Instead, "Kaddish" in these texts seems to be a kind of shorthand, referring to the many different ways in which the children carry on the legacy of the deceased parent—a commitment to the highest values of a Jewish life. In this view, Kaddish is not a magical recitation that offers relief to the dead; rather, it is a capstone liturgical event that points to an entire way of life.

By broadening the literary context of the Kaddish, I have attempted to open up new potential pathways of understanding. As is clear from the framings of the Kaddish in twentieth-century *siddurim* (which themselves turned into a form of liturgy), the presentation of the Kaddish is critical to the experience of the Kaddish. My hope is that this essay will offer additional framings for a prayer recited by so many.

NOTES

[1] *Sabbath and Festival Prayerbook*, ed. Morris Silverman (1946; rpt. New York: Rabbinical Assembly of America, 1960), p. 159. The paragraph is attributed on p. 388 to Rabbi Jacob Kohn, who wrote it for his holiday prayerbook published in 1927. This sentence concludes a composition entitled "Prayer Before Kaddish." See Jacob Kohn, *Festival Prayer Book* (New York: United Synagogue of America, 1927), p. 18. This introduction is slightly reworded in *Siddur Sim Shalom for Shabbat, Festivals, and Weekdays*, ed. Jules Harlow (New York: Rabbinical Assembly, 1985), p. 324: "In solemn testimony to that unbroken faith which links our generations one to another, those observing Yahrzeit and those who mourn now rise to declare their faith in God, to magnify and sanctify God's holy name."

[2] Silverman, *Sabbath and Festival Prayerbook*, p. 159. We will deal with the issue of faith further below.

[3] See Rambam, M.T. Hilkhot Tefillah 1:2. Kimelman notes that this tripartite distinction is a late one; see Reuven Kimelman, "The Literary Structure of the Amidah and the Rhetoric of Redemption," in *Echoes of Many Texts: Reflections on Jewish and Christian Traditions: Essays in Honor of Lou H. Silberman*, eds. William Dever and J. Edward Wright (Missoula, MT: Scholars Press, 1997), pp. 171–230; the argument appears on pp. 177–178.

[4] The Hebrew word *siddur* (plural: *siddurim*) is used generally to denote the traditional prayerbook in its various permutations and innumerable editions.

[5] *The Sabbath Service*, ed. Julius Silberfeld (1905; rpt. New York: Bloch, 1916), p. 229; emphasis added.

[6] *Sabbath and Festival Services*, ed. Morris Silverman (Hartford, CT: Hartford Prayer Book Press, 1936), p. 278.

[7] *Siddur Sim Shalom for Shabbat and Festivals*, ed. Leonard Cahan (New York: Rabbinical Assembly, 1998), p. 51.

[8] *Siddur Lev Shalem for Shabbat and Festivals*, ed. Edward Feld (New York: Rabbinical Assembly, 2016), p. 30.

[9] *Sabbath and Festival Prayerbook*, ed. Silverman, p. 159.

[10] *Kol Haneshamah: Shabbat Vehagim*, ed. David Teutsch (Wyncote, PA: Reconstructionist Press, 1994), p. 129.

[11] *Mishkan T'filah: A Reform Siddur*, ed. Elyse Frishman (New York: Central Conference of American Rabbis, 2007), p. 46; and cf. p. 592.

[12] Compare the following comparable translations: "Exalted and sanctified be His great name" (*The Metsudah Siddur: Sabbath/Festival Prayers*, ed. Avrohom David [New York: Metsudah Publications, 1984], p. 85); "Exalted and hallowed be God's great name" (*Mishkan T'filah*, p. 532); "Let the glory of God be extolled, let His great name be hallowed" (*Gates of Prayer: The New Union Prayerbook*, ed. Chaim Stern [New York: Central Conference of American Rabbis, 1975], p.

629); and contrast these with the Artscroll translation: "May His great Name grow exalted and sanctified" (*The Artscroll Siddur*, ed. Nosson Scherman [1984; rpt. New York: Mesorah Publications, 2001], p. 57).

[13] Elie Kaunfer, *Interpreting Jewish Liturgy: The Literary-Intertext Method* (doctoral dissertation; New York: Jewish Theological Seminary, 2014), p. 16, available at http://www.mechonhadar.org/torah-resource/interpreting-jewish-liturgy. "Intertextuality" refers to the approach to reading in which "...a text cannot be studied in isolation. It belongs to a web of texts which are (partially) present whenever it is read or studied" (Steven Moyise, "Intertextuality and the Study of the Old Testament in the New Testament," in *The Old Testament in the New Testament: Essays in Honour of J. L. North*, ed. Steven Moyise [Sheffield, England: Sheffield Academic Press, 2000], pp. 14–41; the quote appears on pp. 15–16).

[14] Reuven Kimelman, "The Shema Liturgy: From Covenant Ceremony to Coronation," in *Kenishta: Studies of the Synagogue World* 1 (2001), pp. 9–105; the quote appears on p. 28.

[15] Abudarham writes: "You should know that the language of prayer is based on the language of Scripture. Therefore you will find written in this commentary on every word a verse like it or relating to its essence. There are a few words that did not have a biblical basis, and therefore I will bring for them a basis from the Talmud." See his *Sefer Abudarham Ha-Shaleim*, ed. Shlomo A. Wertheimer (Jerusalem: Usha, 1963), p. 6 and ed. Menahem Brown (Jerusalem: Or Ha-Sefer, 2001), p. 15.

[16] *Sefer Abudarham*, ed. Wertheimer, p. 66, and ed. Brown, p. 157.

[17] NJPS translation.

[18] Rav Hai Gaon in Louis Ginzberg, *Ginzei Schechter* (New York: Jewish Theological Seminary of America, 1929), vol. 2, p. 164.

[19] *Sefer Ha-Pardes* of Rashi; ed. H. L. Ehrenreich (Budapest: Katzburg Bros., 1924) p. 323. YHVH denotes the four Hebrew letters of the divine name, which are pronounced as "Adonai" (literally "my Lord," in the respectful plural).

[20] *Sefer Abudarham*, ed. Wertheimer, p. 66; ed. Brown, p. 157.

[21] Note that Daniel Goldschmidt argues that the word *tishkon* ("may You dwell") actually should be connected to the beginning of the following sentence, yielding: "May You dwell and be magnified and sanctified in Jerusalem..." See Daniel Goldschmidt, *Mahzor L'yamim Nora·im* (Jerusalem: Koren, 1970), vol. 1, p. 24, n. 37.

[22] This version of the text is taken from *Seder Rav Amram Gaon*, ed. Daniel Goldschmidt (Jerusalem: Mossad Harav Kook, 1972), p. 32, keeping in mind the concerns about the text of liturgy in this *siddur*, as outlined by Robert Brody and others; see Robert Brody, "L'hiddat Arikhato Shel Seder Rav Amram Gaon," in *K'nesset Ezra: Sifrut V'hayyim B'veit Ha-k'nesset*, eds. Shulamit Elizur, et al. (Jerusalem: Magnes Press, 1994), pp. 21–34. Note also the commentary of

the Rokei·aḥ (Rabbi Eleazar of Worms, c. 1176–1238) on this section of the prayers, in Moshe Hershler, *Peirushei Siddur Ha-t'fillah La-Rokei·aḥ* (Jerusalem: Makhon Hershler, 1992), p. 541, in which he connects this prayer to the future prophecy of the war with Gog.

[23] As Kohn wrote in his introduction to the Kaddish in 1927: "We accept the judgment of Thine inscrutable will…" *(Festival Prayer Book,* p. 18).

[24] *Sabbath and Festival Prayerbook*, p. 159. This interpretive direction is common in contemporary commentaries to the Kaddish. Cf., for example, the following comment of Yeruchem Eilfort in "Why Do Mourners Recite Kaddish" (available online at www.chabad.org): "Many find it intriguing that this prayer, the preeminent prayer said for those who have passed on, makes absolutely no mention of death, loss, or mourning. Nor is there mention of the person who died. Kaddish speaks of G-d's greatness. In fact, Kaddish is an affirmation of belief in the Almighty and His unlimited power. If one were to boil down the theme of Kaddish, it would be that G-d is great and everything comes from G-d, so everything that occurs is ultimately for the good." It is worth noting that in the first paragraph of the Kaddish, the word "life" appears twice.

[25] B. Berakhot 40b; cf. T. Berakhot 6:20.

[26] See Joseph Heinemann, *Ha-t'fillah Bi-t'kufat Ha-tanna·im V'ha-amora·im* (Jerusalem: Magnes Press, 1966), p. 163 and the literature cited there; and Avigdor Shinan's introductory essay in Yoram Verete and Yaron David, *Tom U-t'hom* (Tel Aviv: Oved Publishers, 2009), pp. 16–25.

[27] B. Sotah 49a; B. Shabbat 119b; B. Berakhot 21b; B. Berakhot 57a; B. Sukkah 38b–39a; B. Berakhot 3a (and we will return to this last source in more depth below). It is not entirely clear that the references to this line indicate the Kaddish as we know it, or a more general communal response of the same formulation. See further below.

[28] NJPS translation; emphasis added.

[29] NJPS translation; emphasis added.

[30] Cf. Job 2:10, where Job says to his wife: "Should we accept only good from God and not accept evil?"

[31] NJPS translation; emphasis added.

[32] Cf. Nehemiah 9:5 and T. Berakhot 6:22.

[33] David De Sola Pool, *The Kaddish* (Jerusalem: Sivan Press, 1964), p. 46; this work was originally published in 1909 as *The Old Jewish-Aramaic Prayer: The Kaddish*. See also Sifrei Devarim §306 (ed. Finkelstein, p. 342).

[34] See M. Yoma 3:8 and compare T. Taanit 1:11. This is also probably the case with the Shema, where the form of reciting Shema was call and response, and *barukh sheim* was a response to the uttering of God's name in the Shema itself. See T. Sotah 6:3 and B. Pesaḥim 56a. Earlier versions of the latter source conflate *barukh sheim* with *y'hei sh'meih*; see the Targumim (including Targum Yerushalmi and Neophyti) to Deuteronomy 6:4 and, generally, De Sola Pool, pp. 45–47.

35 De Sola Pool, p. 47.

36 Ibid., p. 50.

37 Note that while printed editions of the Talmud have the word *mah*, most manuscripts use the word *oy*. *Mah* seems to be a euphemism for *oy*, a substitution made by those uncomfortable with God experiencing woe. See Raphael Rabbinovicz, *Dikdukei Sofrim* (Munich, 1867), vol. 1, pp. 2b–3a; Moshe Benovitz, *Talmud Ha-iggud: Perek Rishon Mi-massekhet B'rakhot* (Jerusalem: Ha-iggud L'farshanut Ha-talmud, 2006), p. 98 and cf. p. 95, and n. 41.

38 B. Berakhot 3a.

39 *Eish Kodesh*, February 14, 1942, as translaed by Nehemia Polen in *The Holy Fire: The Teachings of Rabbi Kalonymus Kalman Shapira, the Rebbe of the Warsaw Ghetto* (Lanham, MD: Jason Aronson, 1999), p. 116. The talmudic passage cited is B. Sanhedrin 46a. The original source is at M. Sanhedrin 6:5.

40 NJPS translation; emphasis added.

41 For an extended analysis of the possible meanings of this word, see Moshe Bar-Asher, "*Al Ha-sheim 'Nehamata' B'Kaddish*," in *Sefer Zikkaron L'Moriah Lisbon*, eds. Aharon Meman and Rivka Bliboim (Jerusalem: Magnes Press, 2011), pp. 75–97. One of these approaches is discussed in the essay elsewhere in this volume by Martin I. Lockshin.

42 Compare the comment of the Levush (Rabbi Mordecai ben Avraham Yoffe, c. 1530–1612) to the Shulhan Arukh, Orah Hayyim 56:1, 3: "By manner of this praise, God is reminded of the destruction of the Temple and the exile of Israel…God is mourning our exile."

43 See Bar-Asher, "*Al Ha-sheim 'Nehamata' B'Kaddish*," p. 77, Heinemann, *Ha-t'fillah*, p. 163; Midrash Mishlei 14; Yalkut Shimoni *Mishlei* §951; Kohelet Rabbah 9:7; B. Sotah 49a.

44 This text derives from a fragment retrieved from the Cairo Genizah and currently preserved at Cambridge University under the file name T-S C.2., fol. 144c-d, as cited by Miron Bialik Lerner in his *Ma·aseh Ha-tanna V'ha-meit: Gilgulav Ha-sifrutiyim V'ha-hilkhatiyim*, in *Asufot* 2 (5748 [=1987/1988]), p. 69.

45 *Mahzor Vitry* §144 (ed. Shimon Horowitz; Nuremberg, 1923), p. 112.

46 Midrash of the 10 Commandments, ed. Adolph Jellenik, *Beit Ha-Midrasch* (Vienna, 1873), vol. 1, p. 81.

47 *Kallah Rabbati* 2 (*Massekhtot Kallah, V'hen Massekhet Kallah V'massekhet Kallah Rabbati*, ed. Michael Higger (New York: Debe Rabbanan, 1936), p. 202.

48 *Or Zarua*, pt. 2 §50.

49 Bereishit Rabbah 49:19, eds. Theodor-Albeck (1903; rpt. Jerusalem: Wahrmann, 1965), p. 503.

The Kaddish Is the Song of Songs

David Greenstein

Some eight hundred years ago a great rabbi, Rabbi Eleazar of Worms (c. 1165 - c. 1230), wrote: "The Kaddish is the Song of Songs."[1] What are some of the implications of this simple and startling statement? The Song of Songs is regarded by Jewish tradition as the greatest of love songs of the Jewish people. In what ways may we, following this rabbi's insight, regard the Kaddish as a love song, let alone as the greatest love song of the Jewish people? Of what sort of love does it sing? And how does the song fit the words?

"Love Is as Fierce as Death"[2]

It is a commonplace observation that the Mourner's Kaddish, identified since medieval times as the main Jewish prayer of mourning for the dead, never mentions death. Nevertheless, centuries of custom have melded this recitation, in our minds and hearts, to our confrontation with the tragedy and loss of death and to our ongoing grappling—emotionally, spiritually, intellectually, and socially—with the mourning process as we live it within the liturgical context of a Jewish community. Our experience of death and mortality suffuses the Kaddish, even as the word "death" is never spoken.[3]

Many find the silence of the Kaddish regarding death to be one of its most powerful features. The obvious presence of our pain and emotional wreckage needs no explicit expression. Instead, the prayer takes us places we might never go, were we to focus on the theme of death itself. Though never mentioned, death is ever present—coloring and, in turn, being colored by the ethereal words of the Kaddish. Similarly, the absence of the word "love" in the Kaddish does not necessarily indicate that love is not a central issue of the Kaddish. Just as we are expressing our mourning and working through it, by means of the phrases of this prayer, so may the Kaddish grant us the opportunity for giving voice, obliquely but profoundly, to our love— and thereby help us to redefine or grasp anew that love.

The Song of Songs is essentially a collection of love songs strung together into one composition. In its richness it celebrates love's joys and pleasures, its exhilaration and vitality. But its poets are also quite aware of the complex dynamics at play between lovers and within the hearts of lovers. Love is not just sweet. Like death, love can be hard and forceful, raw and painful. And it is during times of stress and hurt that love may become exposed and tested, deepened or strained. The time when the Kaddish is recited is a time of love's testing.

The Kaddish is recited within a communal liturgical setting, a *minyan*. The community is both witness to and participant in its recitation. It responds to three other players in this drama of love: the one saying Kaddish, the one for whom the Kaddish is being said (the deceased), and the One about whom the Kaddish is said: God. The person reciting the Kaddish and the community are present for each other. But just as the words "death" and "love" are both absent from the text of the Kaddish, so are both the deceased and God physically absent during its recitation.

Also hidden from the eyes and ears of the community is the inner drama that unfolds within the mind and heart of the one saying Kaddish. That drama varies from reciter to reciter and from recitation to recitation. Here is one scenario experienced by many: the absence of the deceased is, of course, the trigger for the recitation of the prayer; and yet often, as one experiences the enormity of one's loss, one feels the impossible yearning to reverse reality, to turn back time, to revive the dead—so that one might declare God's greatness in the company of one's loved one. After all, it is not some abstract numerical diminution of humanity at large that one mourns, but the specific loss of the possibility to give and receive love that was shared with this particular person. Why must this poem of praise require the loss of this life and this love, in order for it to be sung?

So it may happen that this prayer is sung as a love song, not sung to God, but *hurled at* God. In that case, it is not only the words "death" and "love" that are not said in the prayer, for the entire prayer is a substitute for the words that are not said: words of anguish, keening, affection, yearning, frustration, and anger.

The medieval sage who told us that the Kaddish is the Song of Songs knew of love's terrible loss firsthand. In 1196, his wife and children were slaughtered before his eyes by marauding Crusaders. Rabbi Eleazar of Worms, called the Rokei·aḥ (after one of his most important works), was a major scholar and leader of the German pietists.[4] He was heir to ancient Jewish esoteric traditions from the East as well as religious teachings from the school of Rashi, three generations before him.[5] Despite his suffering and struggles with God, prayer was his indispensable medium of expression. He composed his own dirges of sorrow.[6] But he also faithfully recited the words of the Kaddish. He composed one of the earliest extant commentaries on the prayerbook, in which he offers his own reworking of his inherited traditions about the meaning of the Kaddish.[7] But his characterization of the Kaddish as the Song of Songs seems to be his own contribution.

"I Sought Him but I Did Not Find Him"[8]

In Rabbi Eleazar's conception, the Kaddish is not simply a paean to God. It begins as an expression of yearning and ruefulness. For Rabbi Eleazar, the Kaddish opens with a recognition that God's "great Name" is actually a much diminished, broken name. The original, revealed name of God is the Tetragrammaton, the ineffable Name of Four Letters—spelled *yod-hei-vav-hei* (henceforth, YHVH). This name is found throughout our Torah, but traditional Jews, ever eager to avoid even the possibility of sacrilege, take care never to pronounce it. It is thus literally an unspoken presence. But Rabbi Eleazar explains that the start of the Kaddish, usually translated as "Magnified and sanctified be His great Name (*sh'meih rabba*)," should really be read as "Magnified and sanctified be the great 'Name YH' (*sheim YH*)."[9] In his reading, the 'Name YH' is a reference to God's name as truncated by God[10] when God acknowledged that the Divine Presence is not complete in this world as long as unmitigated evil exists. Our prayer is that the day may come when God's name, presently reduced by half, may once again be united with its other half and made whole.

Again, what is not mentioned is crucial, for ultimate evil, termed "Amalek"[11] in Jewish tradition, is not named. Nor is the final battle against evil, the battle of Gog and Magog (i.e., Armageddon) explicitly recalled. But, for Rabbi Eleazar, they are right there in our text and in our intent:

> *Yitgaddal v'yitkaddash*: This is based on Scripture, as it is written, "And I shall be magnified and sanctified and I shall become known in the eyes of [many] nations, and they shall know that I am God" (Ezekiel 38:23). The verse speaks of the war of Gog and Magog, [for then] the name of the blessed Holy One shall be enlarged, as it is written... "And God shall become Sovereign over the whole earth. On that day God shall be One and His name One"(Zechariah 14:9). That is to say:

the name of four letters that was split in two by the oath He took to fight against Amalek, as it is said, "A hand [swears] on the throne [*keis*] of Yah [YH] a war of God against Amalek from generation to generation" (Exodus 17:16).[12]

But if we specifically intend these matters, why don't we say them outright? We do not speak of these disturbing things because we do not wish to upset God any further. Our words are a loving attempt to console our defeated God with tender, supportive words of praise, eschewing any outright mention of the enemy's persistence and of God's continued impotence and frustration. Rabbi Eleazar describes the situation in this way:

This is like a parable of a king who redeemed his son from prison and the son was walking with his father. In the middle of the journey, a certain brigand met him and mortally beat him. When the king heard of this he was very enraged and he said, "The sufferings that my son suffered in prison were enough!" He placed him [the son] behind himself but the brigand set upon him. He placed him on his arms [safe from the brigand] but an eagle tried to kill him and eat him. The king stood up and threw his seal down and swore that his name would never be whole until he was avenged of that enemy and that His throne will not be whole until He is avenged of Amalek.[13]

This parable is Rabbi Eleazar's way of encapsulating the story of the exodus from Egypt and the subsequent travails of the Israelites in the wilderness immediately thereafter. He imagines Israel as a young prince, the son of the king who is, of course, God. God liberates the son from prison (Egypt) and they set out together into the wilderness, on the way to Mount Sinai. But the brigand (Egypt) comes and attacks Israel, despite God's attempts to shield the son (which is how the sages understood the maneuvers of the pillar of fire at the Sea of Reeds). However, after rescuing the son from the brigand, an eagle (Amalek) unexpectedly swoops down from above. This is too much for the king, who throws down his seal in an oath that his name will not be whole again until this outrage is avenged. By the last line of the parable the meaning is revealed plainly: the king has become the King (God) and the eagle has become Amalek.

The Kaddish is not a song of praise to God in order to console the human mourner. It is a song sung to God in order to console God, who has literally lost God's better half, the last letters of the divine name, through God's own failure to prevent innocent human suffering. We support the Divine by sweetening our words. We tell God that even God's half-name is still *rabba*, "abundantly great," because "it is not right to use the language of either diminution or smallness regarding anything Above that has been split or diminished."[14] And we console our God by assuring God that eventually God's name will be restored to completion. The opening words are meant to be as much a prediction as a plea.

A Wily Calculation

So far it seems that, in this reading of the text and its ritual recitation, our efforts are focused on helping God, who is in need of consolation that only a lover can bestow. But we are not being completely self-sacrificing in our tender care for God. We have something at stake here, as well: "It is concerning the name of four letters, that we say that it should become greater and become whole. And through that very aggrandizement and sanctification our redemption will eventually come."[15]

Our salvation hinges on the reconstitution of the divine name. The union of the separated letters of God's name will also mean that we will be joined together in loving union with our God. Our present exile and estrangement, physically and emotionally, will cease.

But here a paradox develops. In order to motivate God, to bestir a deity immersed in feelings of impotence and futility in the face of ongoing human evil, we sing soothing words of encouragement. We consciously avoid mentioning the negative elements of reality, but lovingly sing to God of the realization of God's dream of wholeness restored—because we wish to raise God's spirits and bestir God's redemptive energies, by expressing our inextinguishable love. Yet, precisely because God is overtaken by our loving words, God is overcome with sorrow and regret for having exiled such loving children. God can see right through our subterfuge and understands that we have adapted and censored our song, out of our undying sensitivity and care for our Beloved. God understands that, out of our love and concern, we are thinking more than we are saying, singing a song of praise while keeping silent about our awareness of the problems that make such a consoling song necessary.

> Rabbi Eleazar continues:
> And when the blessed Holy One hears that Israel, in wily calculation, think in their hearts of the oath that He took about Amalek, to destroy their memory, and they pray these four words with all their strength—*y'hei sh'meih rabba m'varakh*, corresponding to the four letters of the Name—so as to enlarge His name of four letters, He says, "Woe to the sons who have been exiled from their father's table, and woe to the father who is praised this way by his sons while he has sent them far away from his table." Therefore there is great sadness in heaven.[16]

Thus, just when we prove our selfless love by offering the defeated God our words of solace and encouragement, and just as we do our very best to prevent our discouraged Redeemer from losing heart by shrewdly spinning our song away from dark allusions, God's mood darkens in contemplating the tragedy of this great love that has been thwarted by divine decree. God's impotence is debilitating and paralyzing. God is unable to defeat evil, and is thus demoralized. Though identified in the midrash as an authoritative Father, God is unable to overrule past decisions. The person reciting Kaddish may wish that time could be overturned and reversed, that the deceased loved one might be found alive, his or her death annulled. But Rabbi Eleazar's dramatic reading of the Kaddish tells us that God is just as bound by the past as we are. God cannot reverse time for the individual, for the people, or for God's own sake.

Singing in a Foreign Language

Have we, then, failed, despite our own wily calculations? Not yet. We know that our song will have this effect on our Beloved. But we are not ready to give up. We are not only careful about what we say and what we do not say; we are also careful about what language we use to say it.

It is a commonplace observation that the Kaddish is composed in Aramaic, not Hebrew. This lends its words a strange, alien feel, even to literate Jews, and gives its recitation an exotic, formal quality. We pronounce the rhythmic, poetic, and foreign prayer uncomprehendingly, hoping that this very incomprehensibility will enhance its spiritual potency in the heavens above or in our own hearts. But two thousand years ago Aramaic was the vernacular of Jews. Perhaps, back then, the Kaddish was the most easily comprehended of the prayers, precisely because it was recited in Aramaic.

But this common knowledge is only half-right. Actually, the Kaddish zigzags between Hebrew and Aramaic. It begins in Hebrew and then moves into Aramaic. After the communal response of *y'hei sh'meih rabba m'varakh* in Aramaic, the prayer again uses eight Hebrew words of praise (*yitbarakh v'yishtabbaḥ...*), only to then change back to Aramaic once more. And Hebrew must wait to reappear until the last line, *oseh shalom*, "May the One who makes peace...." Why this alternation?

Rabbi Eleazar adopts the explanation that it is necessary in order to befuddle the heavenly hosts.[17] Usually our prayers are presented to God by the ministering angels. But they love God so much that they cannot abide seeing God upset and saddened. Were they to hear that Israel's Kaddish song was causing God sorrow and remorse, they would promptly intervene and prevent God from hearing our prayer! How can we move beyond the angels, who might try their best to obstruct our prayers? If we are creative about it we can outwit them, for, according to ancient tradition, angels understand Hebrew but they do not understand Aramaic. Rabbi Eleazar explains:

And when the ministering angels hear and see the sadness that befalls the blessed Holy One, they are shocked and they tremble because, not understanding Aramaic, they do not know what the sadness is about. When we begin Kaddish, *yitgaddal v'yitkaddash*, this is the Hebrew language....But from the third [and fourth] word[s] on, which are *sh'meih rabba*, this is Aramaic. And had we said *sh'meih rabba* in Hebrew...the angels would understand...and then confuse the prayer of the Kaddish so that it could not ascend above, and Israel would not be able to utter such an excellent praise as this, and the Kaddish would be nullified. Therefore we say it from *sh'meih rabba* onwards in Aramaic, so that the angels will not understand what the sadness is about.[18]

How is it possible that the angels do not know Aramaic? And how could they dare to prevent our prayers from ascending heavenward? There is one answer to both these questions. The ancient tradition that the angels do not understand Aramaic is based precisely upon the idea that it is the vernacular. Angels do not and cannot understand human beings. They are incapable of fathoming the complexities of human nature and the messiness of human relationships. Thus, it should not be surprising that they can only understand the original, holy tongue of God—Hebrew—but that they cannot understand everyday human speech in a language like Aramaic. They understand only the pure holiness of praise and servitude to God's majesty and they accept humanity only insofar as we attempt to imitate angelic singleness of purpose and purity of mission.

This is what differentiates our all-too-human love for God from the love of the angels above. The angels also love God; however, because they cannot understand the human being, they cannot understand the loving relationship that pulsates between God and human beings. And their concept of God's love is as inhuman as is their own. In their pure, simple love of God they seek only to guard God from any wound or sorrow, for a failure to do so would be a shattering attack upon God's perfection. The angels know only the present. They cannot know the regret that comes from remembering a lost past. They do not have an inkling of the anxiety or yearning that springs from picturing a more blessed future. Their love is one-dimensional. They know only that they must continuously serve and please God by placing hymns of praise before the heavenly throne, celebrating God's power and might.

But our love for God is deeper and more encompassing than the love of the angels, because our love is bound up in faith in God's future. Our love is not afraid of embracing death, despair, and impotent regret, of embracing them and moving beyond them. But, in order to believe that we can overcome failure, pain, and death, we must first be able to believe that God can overcome them, as well. That is our mission in reciting this prayer. We sing of a mature love that is well aware of disappointment and weakness, but that firmly holds to a shared dream of recuperation, reconciliation, and sweet consummation.

So, if we are to succeed in our purpose in reciting the Kaddish, if we are to succeed in singing this prayer as the love song God needs to hear, we must exhaust every ounce of our crafty resourcefulness. The angels will try to mix up our prayer in order to nullify it. Therefore we must mix up our words, zigzagging between sacred words and human speech, to throw the angels off their misconceived guard. So, spurred on by our intuition of how much our Beloved needs us, we create an elaborate stratagem to make sure that our prayer overcomes these anticipated difficulties and pushes toward its goal of restoring strength to God.

"I Sought Him but I Did Not Find Him; I Called to Him but He Did Not Answer Me"[19]

Love is hard and fierce. It does not give up immediately when the beloved has disappeared or turned silent. God needs us and we will respond, because we must. We do not say what we *could* say, in order to be able to say what we *must*. But such a controlled approach to our words demands extraordinary focus and discipline. To maintain our earthly (Aramaic) lyrics requires an exhausting amount of concentration. The eight Hebrew words serve as a spiritual respite from this demanding aria. Says Rabbi Eleazar:

Then immediately the congregation returns from this praise to the Hebrew language and says *yitbarakh v'yishtabbah*...and we must draw all of the[se praises] out in order to beautify the praise and its melody. For in these praises there is not any word that has any hint that any creature could detect about what causes the sadness above.[20]

For a moment we allow ourselves to forget the sadness through the beauty and melody of the words. We let our consciousness take a breath, as it were. We float temporarily in the oblivion of "not any word," "not any hint," "not any creature," "not any sadness." But we cannot tarry there for long. With this brief pause we gather enough strength to try to raise God above all songs, praises, and consolations. The challenge is not to forget the sadness, but to sing through it.

This is a love song, for what it does not say and for what it says and for how it balances between the saying and the silence. To fully realize itself as the greatest love song, the Mourner's Kaddish takes the overall compositional strategy of the Full Kaddish one step further. It is identical to the Full Kaddish except that, in addition to all the unsaid allusions—unsaid but understood between lovers—the Mourner's Kaddish leaves out one more stanza from the established text.

That stanza is the line in the longer Kaddish that begins with the words *titkabbeil tz'lot'hon* ("May the prayers and entreaties of the whole House of Israel be accepted before our Father in heaven"). It is striking that, after all the wily calculations we have expended in formulating a song that the angels will not be able to block—a song that will surely, directly, reach our heavenly Father—we now desist from praying for its acceptance. Is it because we are so confident in our plan? Hardly. It is because we are singing this song after a painful loss, after we and others have poured out our hearts in prayer and supplication—but our prayers were not answered. Just as we do not remind God of God's failure to eradicate evil from this world, we also do not remind God of God's failure to answer us in our distress. Why not? Because despite the hardships and disappointments, "many waters cannot extinguish love and rivers cannot wash it away."[21] Love does not arise and is not established through an arrangement of quid pro quo. "Were a person to offer all the fortunes of his house for love, all would dismiss him with contempt."[22]

"Its Fevers Are Fiery Fevers, Flame of *Yah*"[23]

We live a love affair that the angels cannot understand. They cannot grasp a God in love with imperfect human beings; they cannot grasp a love that is complete only when it encompasses imperfection. When we fail to understand the possibility of such a love, we unwittingly fall into the trap of trying to imitate the angels rather than being who we are. The Kaddish asks us to sing out that love. This is why the Kaddish is the Song of Songs. It is a love song sung because our love will not subside or disappear. Our song is a song of words unsung as well as words sung, because our love endures through the presence and absence of the Beloved—just as we wish for our Beloved to cherish us whether we are present or absent, in our own moments of tender response and even in our moments of stony silence. As we recite the Kaddish we embrace the fullness of this elusive love and this elusive Lover. In the last verse of Song of Songs, one lover gives to her beloved a joyful, if rueful, release: to run off, even far away; perhaps, even, to temporarily disappear. Does she hope for their eventual sweet reunion? Because it is a song of love, the Song ends with that hope unspoken: "Flee my beloved, and be like a gazelle or the young stags, upon the fragrant mountains."[24]

NOTES

[1] Rabbi Eleazar of Worms, *Peirushei Siddur Ha-t'fillah La-rokei·aḥ* (Jerusalem: Makhon Ha-rav Hershler, 1992), vol. 1, p. 242.

[2] Song of Songs 8:6.

[3] Of course, the Kaddish is routinely recited at various points in the traditional service without any linkage to death and dying. Still, I am here describing the phenomenology of the recitation of the Mourner's Kaddish specifically.

[4] The German pietists, called in Hebrew Ḥasidei Ashkenaz, were a small group of Jews living in the Rhineland during the twelfth and thirteenth centuries. They strove to imbue their everyday lives with the scrupulous intensity of mystical consciousness and devotion.

[5] Rashi's teachings were collected and expanded upon in a number of works. One important repository of teachings from Rashi and his school is called *Maḥzor Vitry*, a miscellany of commentaries, rulings, rabbinic texts, and poems first compiled by as student of Rashi in the late eleventh century and augmented thereafter in the following few centuries. The standard printed text was edited by S. Hurwitz and published in 1923 in Nuremberg, then reprinted in 1988 in Jerusalem.

[6] Little of his work in this genre is available in English. For one small excerpt, see *The Penguin Book of Hebrew Verse*, ed. T. Carmi (New York: Viking Press, 1981), pp. 387–388.

[7] For some selections and discussion of his teachings on this subject and the traditions they draw from, see Leon Wieseltier, *Kaddish* (New York: Knopf, 1998), pp. 422–432.

[8] Song of Songs 3:1.

[9] The word *sh'meih* is written with four letters: *shin-mem-yod-hei*. Rabbi Eleazar reads this word as comprising two words put together: the first two letters, *shin-mem*, spell the word *sheim*, meaning "name." The last two letters, *yod-hei*, are the same two letters found at the start of God's Tetragrammaton, often pronounced as *yah*. Rabbi Eleazar reads those remaining two letters as referring to God's name.

[10] The last two of the four letters of the Name—*vav and hei*—are missing. The phrase "God's name" refers to more than a linguistic or textual term. It traditionally alludes to the Divine Presence as experienced and spoken about in this world, as distinct from any additional transcendent, ungraspable, and unnamable divine reality. Thus, to speak of a full name of God would refer to God's Presence as fully manifest in this world. If only half of God's name is mentioned, this refers to a weakened or diminished sense of God's Presence.

[11] Amalek became the symbol of pure evil after it attacked the Israelites right after God had liberated them from Egypt. Israel was frail and vulnerable and Amalek, unprovoked, launched an attack specifically targeting the weak and defenseless of the people. See Exodus 17:8–16.

[12] Rabbi Eleazar of Worms, *Peirushei Siddur Ha-t'fillah*, vol. 1, p. 251.

[13] Ibid.

[14] Ibid.

[15] Ibid.

[16] Ibid., p. 252, referencing B. Berakhot 3a. See Wieseltier, *Kaddish*, p. 428, who offers a similar text and attributes it to the *Maḥzor Vitry* (see note 5 above). But I have not found this key element—that Israel uses "wily calculation" in its formulation of the Kaddish—in that version. To be "wily in one's reverence for God" is a particular concern of the German pietists.

[17] See *Maḥzor Vitry*, pp. 54–55.

[18] Rabbi Eleazar of Worms, *Peirushei Siddur Ha-t'fillah*, vol. 1, p. 252. This text has a parallel in *Maḥzor Vitry*, p. 54.

[19] Song of Songs 5:6.

[20] Rabbi Eleazar of Worms, *Peirushei Siddur Ha-t'fillah*, vol. 1, p. 253.

[21] Song of Songs 8:7.

[23] Song of Songs 8:6.

[24] Ibid. 8:14.

For a God Who Mourns

Noah Zvi Farkas

Jews Pray Our Stories

As a pulpit rabbi, I hear the pain in the voices of those who can muster enough strength to stand over the grave of a loved one and recite the Kaddish. I hear it voiced again, ringing through the halls of houses of mourning. I am always moved by the mourner's ability to rise and declare God's greatness in the face of death. It takes bravery to mourn, and it takes strength to mourn. Kaddish is recited as a memorial prayer, and it requires all of our courage to be singled out publicly as bereaved and to tell the story of those who died. The very difficult task of remembering through prayer binds together two modes of thought, which creates the tapestry of life. The first mode of thinking is our story, the collected pearls of actions that make up our unique human narrative. While others in our lives might share in our story as partners, friends, and family, the phenomena of life we experience are irrefragably our own. We cannot compare our lives to the lives of others, nor can we say that our lives belong to someone else. The actions we take are ours, as are our successes and our failures. The story of Rabbi Zusya of Hanipol comes to mind. Rabbi Zusya was the younger brother of Elimelekh of Lizhensk, one of the greatest rabbinic luminaries of his generation. Rabbi Zusya was worried that at the end of his days, he would be seen as a failure compared to his scholarly brother. His worries were abated when he came to the realization that he had his own unique story and gifts to contribute to the world. God would not ask Rabbi Zusya why he was not his brother, nor even the great prophet Moses. God would ask, "Zusya, why were you not Zusya?"[1] Why did you not own your own story? Why did you not act as the very best version of yourself? Each of our life-stories is unique, and they are incomparable.

The story of a person's life is, by nature, never *solely* a narrative; there are always unspoken foundations of emotion and philosophy beneath the tale of one's experience. The rabbis say, "Do not let stories be light in your eyes, because it is with stories that a person can stand with the knowledge of the Torah."[2] Through the stories of our lives, we come to know our truth: Who am I? What do I believe? What wisdom do I garner? Beyond our biographies, we embody values that can be shared with others. It is often our values, more than our deeds, that remain with our loved ones after we die. When I sit with families preparing for a funeral, the conversation quickly moves from what the deceased *did* in life, to who they *were* in life. When I walk past the headstones of the thousands of graves in the Jewish cemetery, I rarely read words like "salesman" or "lawyer" engraved into the stone. Instead I often read words like "kind," "just," or "friend." Our stories can be winnowed away in death like chaff. What remains are the seeds of wisdom, our personal Torah that can be shared with our posterity. When we rise to mourn for the dead by reciting Kaddish, we bring together these two modes of thought—the threads of the biography of a life that is now expired, and the threads of what we can learn from their personal Torah. When we remember, through the rituals of burial and Kaddish, we entwine warp and woof, deed and thought, into a single narrative of life.

As Jews, we pray our stories. The words of the liturgy weave together our sense of being in the world and our relationship to God, interlaced with elements of our most sacred narratives. When we address God as the "God of our ancestors, of Abraham, Isaac, and Jacob; of Sarah

Rebecca, Rachel, and Leah," we allude to the life-stories of our ancient mothers and fathers. Morning and night we retell the story of the Exodus in the words of the liturgy. On a personal level, we may find ourselves beneath the surface of those prayers, as our unique life-narratives resonate with their ancient words. As we pray for health, we think of those who are sick. As we pray for peace, we think of those who need peace. As we express gratitude for each day, we are reminded of the awe and majesty that the world presents to us. We pray our stories, and our stories are our prayers.

With this in mind, we ask: What story does the Mourner's Kaddish tell? Other essays in this volume explore the history and grammatical nuances of the Kaddish, and its liturgical role in the broader context of Jewish liturgy. My purpose is wholly different. As a student of philosophy and theology, I seek to tell the story of the Kaddish from a theological perspective, and to open a door of meaning for those who find themselves in a place to recite it. As a rabbi who serves a community, I seek to tell the story of the Kaddish that will give comfort to the bereaved. Therefore, I will here read the Kaddish theologically to try to describe the character of God in the moment of remembrance, and to draw out a sense of comfort that will give solace to those who mourn.

The Special Pathos of Death

To help us to understand the Kaddish as a memorial prayer, we must understand more about the nature of death. To speak theologically about death is to distinguish between the terminus of the biological, psychological part of ourselves and the unending transcendent part. It is a fact that we will all die. The heart will cease to pump blood through our arteries and our brains will cease to create waves of activity. Biological death is utterly common and universal. There is not a living creature in this world that will not come to its own demise. Death, however, is more than biological; it is also the end of our psychological selves. The moment we cease to be, our aspirations, our egos, our existential ruminations come to their end as well. There is neither regret nor pride in death. We cannot remember our successes or failures; we can neither hope nor dream. In death, all self-understanding is eliminated. The psalmist teaches, "The dead cannot sing praises to God, nor those who lay down in silence" (Psalm 115:17). Death silences the living.

It is a traditional Jewish belief that something exists after the extinguishing of life, just as many people harbor different beliefs about what constitutes the afterlife. What they share is the idea that death is not so much a final destination but a waypoint of transformation. Beyond biology and beyond psychology, death in a theological perspective is only part of a larger schema of life. When we die our body fails, but our soul does not. It becomes part of a larger collective, in one way or another. Life never ceases, even in death. Life enfolds around death. Life is everlasting; death is a significant part of life, but one that can never entirely destroy life itself. Theologically, the idea of death is twofold: death is both the destruction of life and part of a greater life.

I am led to understand death in still further dimensions precisely because of death's manifold dimensions, including biological, psychological, and theological. The phenomenon of death references the biography of life, but it also carries with it its own kind of experience, which affects the living. The experience of death creates a multifaceted pathos that is at once unique and common. We *feel* that every death is unique. Every death is the end of a unique story. We miss the departed for who they were and what they taught us. Yet the pathos of death is something we all share. Death occurs all the time, everywhere. The absolute dignity embedded in each of our lives as deontological beings gives rise to the ethical standard, "To save a life is to save the whole world."[3] Could we not say therefore that when a life is *not* saved, when death occurs, it is as if the whole world dies? The pathos of death rings out universally through all of life, present and future. When Cain is accused by God of fratricide, God says, "What have you done? The blood of your brother cries out to Me!" (Genesis 4:10). The rabbis comment, "It is not just the blood of Abel that is crying out, but the blood of his future descendants that is also crying out."[4] The pathos is a cry of all that could be. Cain stands accused not just of one murder, but of all murder—present and future. Like ripples on the glassy surface of a lake, the pathos of death stretches through time and space. Death is a universal world-ender. Its pathos affects not only the dying, but all who live and all who will live. If death is both unique and universal, if the pathos of death is both immanent and transcendent, then it affects everything, including the Universal itself—and by that I mean God.

A God Who Mourns

If, theologically, the pathos of death ends a world and thus affects all who are involved with life, then it must especially affect the Creator of the world. When recited as a mourner's prayer, the Kaddish begins with this very theme. By looking at the doxology of death, we may gain insight into this special category of universal pathos and its relationship to God. The first line of the Kaddish states: *yitgaddal v'yitkaddash sh'meih rabba*, "May God's name become magnified and sanctified." It continues: *b'alma di-v'ra khi-re'uteih*, "in the world that God created according to the divine will." The image of God brought to mind at the beginning of the Kaddish is the only image of God that we have in the entirety of the prayer. God's other major roles in the Bible—as Judge, Miracle Worker, or Deliverer of the people—are absent in Kaddish. It is only God the Creator, the Giver of Life, that is the focus here. What do we learn from this singular image of the God of life, when we are faced with the world-ending pathos of death?

This question brings to mind the classic theological questions of God's justice as Creator, called "theodicy" by philosophers and theologians. Why would God, the Font of Life, allow for death? Could it not seem offensive, or at least insensitive, to speak of life at the time when we are experiencing death? Why did a prayer whose only description of God is that of Creator become the quintessential prayer recited by those who mourn the dead?

To begin to search for answers to these theological questions, we must first peer deeper into the particular theological underpinnings of the Kaddish. In the midrash,[5] God's power of creation, by animating the dust of the earth to fashion life, includes the creation of death as well. After each day of creation when God saw all that was made, the midrash rightly points out that God remarked, "It is good." On the eve of the sixth day, however, God's words changed, saying: "And behold, it is *very* good" (*tov me'od*; Genesis 1:31). For the midrash, the insertion of the word "very" upon the completion of the sixth day gives rise to question: what changed in the world to warrant the superlative comment? The rabbis in the midrash claim that the extra word "very" refers to the Angel of Death, thus asserting that God created death alongside the world—as a separate but integral part of life, which adds goodness to creation in some way. When the homily was taught in the academy, the students present stood up and exclaimed, "How can the angel of death ever be good?" Death is the end of life! Death brings suffering and pain! Death leaves sorrow in its wake! The rabbis responded by asserting that goodness has no meaning without the Angel of Death. One cannot know what it means to be good, if one has no fear. Fear comes from the sense of mortality that each of us shares. Death is indeed very good, say the rabbis, because it becomes God's uneasy dance partner, completing creation by introducing moral balance into the consciousness of the world, through the fear of our own mortality.

Morality, this sense of moral balance, cannot be the singular reason for death. It is a weak moral purchase to receive the blessings of goodness solely in exchange for mortal fear. Stronger is the claim that the rewards for deeds are the deeds themselves.[6] Even if death gives us a sense of morality as part of the larger schema of life, why does death seem to be outside of God's direct control? We find death as a nearly uncontrollable force in a number of texts in the Torah—for example, in the narrative where the Israelites must paint their doorposts and with the blood of the paschal lamb so that they will be saved from death's unbridled power (Exodus 12).[7] The God of the Bible appears to have a relationship to death, creating it, using it to help fashion moral human lives, even occasionally revoking its terrible power. For the students in the academy and for us, there still seems to be a power dynamic that makes us uneasy between World-Creator and World-Ender.

Here, we return to the notion that death is both the end of life and part of the greater schema of life. The transcendence of life beyond death in fact points to God's transcendence. Understanding the theology of the Kaddish, we look to God—the immortal Universal that encompasses all of life, including death. God is absolute, and therefore bears witness to death, as do the mourners. God's utter uniqueness is that God experiences the special pathos of all of death. While mortality is a price we pay for living in a finite world where things begin and end both spatially and temporally, God—who is infinite and transcendent—cannot die. God alone bears witness to the unceasing universality of death within all of existence. God alone knows the true extent of death's ubiquity, from the expiration of a single bacterium to the wailing of a mother over the loss of her child. Every death throughout all of history is experienced by the

Universal. Thus, there is none more affected by death's pathos than the Creator of life.

That God is affected by the pathos of death might be a provocative claim, but I find it equally provocative to claim that God is so disentangled from the world as to let life expire without concern either way. A God who does not feel compassion, who does not feel attached to the events of the world, is not the God of the Torah. The Bible is the story of God and humanity working out their mutual attachment to each other. For millennia we have envisioned God as caring about our lives. Our lives are precious to God, for God created all of us in the divine image. On the banks of the Sea of Reeds, at the opening moment of Israel's freedom, as the people were dancing and singing with timbrel in hand, the Talmud envisions God chastening them, saying: "How can you sing as the works of My hand are drowning in the sea?"[8] All life is precious, even those who are seen as enemies.

Our lives are interdependent with God's. We are bound to God's world and God to ours. In the words of Rabbi Abraham Joshua Heschel, "The essence of Judaism is the awareness of the reciprocity of God and man, of man's togetherness with Him who abides in eternal otherness. For the task of living is His and ours, and so is the responsibility."[9] Heschel echoes a much more ancient rabbinic teaching based on the Book of Isaiah, "You are My witnesses, says the Eternal...that I am God; before Me there was no God, neither shall any exist after me" (43:10). And to that, Rabbi Shimon bar Yoḥai explained: "If you are My witnesses, then I am God....But if you are not My witnesses, then I am not, as it were, God."[10]

God's interdependence with humanity becomes intelligible to us through our collected wisdom. The language of the Torah is written in human idioms. As such, our intelligible perception of God is that of God *in the world*, entangled in human affairs and therefore vulnerable to the crests and valleys of the human experience. We see this theme again in the Talmud:

> Rabbi Yosi said: I was once traveling on the road, when I entered into one of the ruins of Jerusalem in order to pray. Elijah the prophet, of blessed memory, came and guarded the door for me while I prayed. Once I finished he asked me, "My son, why did you enter this ruin?"…I replied, "I heard the divine voice, cooing like a dove, saying, 'Woe to Me, that razed My house, burned My Temple, and exiled My children among the nations!'" [Elijah] said to me…"It is not only now that God cries this way; God does this three times a day!"[11]

Our God, in Rabbi Yosi's words, is a God who mourns as we mourn. Our joy becomes God's joy. Our pain becomes God's pain. It is not a theological stretch, then, to imagine God—whose greatness is embedded with God's role as Creator—feeling the diminution of greatness, affected by the grim pathos of death. When we recite the Kaddish, we bring the image of a mourning God to mind. We dare to say that our pain, which is our own, also belongs to God. In the face of death, God's greatness becomes diminished. All of death cries out to God and God cries with them all. The goal of the recitation of Kaddish, as we shall see, is to be with God in our mourning and to ask God to return to greatness again by bringing life back into a world affronted by death.

Making a Heavenly *Shiva* Call

When Jews mourn, we gather together in each other's homes to sit with the bereaved, to comfort them. The traditional seven-day mourning period is called *shiva*, which literally means "seven." It is a week of sadness, but also a week filled with love. Friends fill the homes of the mourners with food and warm faces of caring, which express both their love for the deceased and their love for the mourner. It is an ancient understanding that the potency of love is the antidote to the pathos of death.[12] Through our love, we bring comfort to the mourner and give them strength to come back into the community again. It is through our love that we know we can share the burden of death's pathos. It is through our love that we bring life back to the world. Mourning must, eventually, come to an end. The mourners are commanded to come out of their isolation and walk back into the world. It is through love that life is given back, in a spiritual movement from comfort to strength and renewal. It is this story that rest of Kaddish seeks to tell.

The opening phrase of the Kaddish, *yitgaddal v'yitkaddash sh'meih rabba* ("may God's name become magnified and sanctified") is based on the prophet Ezekiel's vision of the apocalypse, in which he imagines God saying, "Thus will I magnify Myself (*v'hitgaddilti*) and sanctify Myself (*v'hitkaddishti*), and I will make Myself known in the eyes of many nations; and they shall know that I am the Eternal" (Ezekiel 38:23). Ezekiel's prophecy is of a God whose holiness is based in the divine–human partnership. God acquires greatness in the prophecy through the witnessing of the global polity. The verbs *hitgaddilti* and *hitkaddishti* in Ezekiel's prophecy are changed, dramatically, to *yitgaddal* and *yitkaddash* in the Kaddish. In the Kaddish, *God is not the singular agent of sanctification*. Where Ezekiel's vision imagines God saying "I will magnify Myself," the first chapter of the story that the Kaddish tells reformulates the partnership between God and humanity into one that depends on humanity to bring holiness to fruition. For God's greatness to become manifest, a relationship of mutual comfort and interdependence is required between God and the mourner.

Thus, the story of the Kaddish opens with a radical statement of theology. God, the Creator of the world, loves life and is saddened and diminished by the special pathos of death. The responsibility of returning sanctity and greatness to God rests not within the thundering pronouncements of God's prophet, but rather in the hushed recitation of the Kaddish by those who know the pain of death. It is the mourner whose life is torn asunder. It is the mourner who is traveling in death's shadow. It is the mourner who feels his or her strength sapped by death's vacuous inexplicability. It is the mourner who feels death's power as both transitive and transcendent, reaching into the cosmos. God not only knows the mourner's pain, but becomes diminished—as does the mourner—by the pathos of death itself. God and the mourner share in the experience of death. And thus it is the mourner who is given the privilege and responsibility to restore greatness to God as well as to him or herself. It is through this prayer that the mourner's courage becomes clear: it is courageous to rise in the face of death and to affirm solidarity with the God who needs us to gather in community and say, "May Your name be great."

How do we give comfort to God through Kaddish? What is our approach to a God who mourns? To find the answers to these questions and see the continuation of the story of the Kaddish, we must look to its second paragraph. There are eight verbs of praise in this stanza: *yitbarakh v'yishtabbaḥ v'yitpa·ar v'yitromam v'yitnasei, v'yit·haddar v'yitalleh v'yit·hallal sh'meih d'kudsha, b'rikh hu,* "blessed and praised; adorned, exalted, and lifted up; beautified, adored, and lauded—be the name of the blessed Holy One!" This bouquet of blessings could be a simple litany, a beautiful heap of blessings layered upon each other to give focus to the holiness of God. However, I would like to propose a different reading, in which these eight verbs describe a path of ascension that culminates with an encounter with God. Taken as a whole, my reading makes the argument that the mourner, along with the community, is making a "*shiva* call" in heaven, for a God who is in deep mourning.

To make the case, we must look at these verbs both from a grammatical and literary perspective. To do that, we can divide these eight verbs of praise into three sections, each focusing on a different type of praising, from lowest to highest. The breakdown is as follows:

1. *yitbarakh v'yishtabbaḥ*, "blessed and praised"
2. *v'yitpa·ar v'yitromam v'yitnassei*, "adorned, exalted, and lifted up"
3. *v'yit·haddar v'yitalleh v'yit·hallal*, "beautified, adored, and lauded"

Yitbarakh v'yishtabbah, "blessed and praised." Once we pair the first two words together, we see that both verbs share a sense of praise that is most readily associated with the act of prayer itself. *Yitbarakh* uses the root letters *bet-resh-kaf*, which can allude to the act of bowing at the knee, as in the line from Isaiah: "Unto Me every knee (*berekh*) shall bow, every tongue shall swear" (45:23). The image in Isaiah is of the global acknowledgment of God's universal oneness, but in the Kaddish the tone is different. *Yitbarakh* (along with the seven other verbs) points to the future, indicating that God *will* be bowed to with the knee—that is to say that the initial approach to God is embarked upon by bowing low in humility. *Yishtabbah* carries a similar depiction of the worshipper in a lower position, while God remains high up. In this regard, it is instructive to read the midrash that envisions the angels who approach the seated Abraham, as he recovers from his circumcision:

"As he [Abraham] sat (*yosheiv*) at the opening to the tent in the heat of the day" (Genesis 18:1). Rabbi Berekhiah said in Rabbi Levi's name: [The word written here could just as easily be read as] *yashav* ("he sat"), to suggest that] Abraham had wished to rise, but God said to him: "Sit, for you are a symbol for your posterity: just as you sit while God's Presence stands before you, so will your children sit as God's Presence comes before them, as it says: "God stands (*nitzav*) in the congregation of God" (Psalms 82:1)....

Rabbi Samuel bar Rabbi Ḥiyya and Rabbi Yudan in Rabbi Ḥanina's name said: Every time that Israel heaps praises (*shevah va-shevah*) upon the blessed Holy One, God's Presence comes to rest upon them. What is the proof of this? [It is the verse from the Psalms that reads, regarding God,] "You are holy, You who sit (*yosheiv*) upon the praises of Israel" (Psalms 22:4).[13]

The midrash uses a poetic structure of sitting and standing. In the beginning, it is Abraham who sits while God's Presence stands. Note, however, that the midrash never imagines the worshippers standing: God sits on high, while we, down below, sit. The thrust of this idea in the Kaddish is that when we embark on our journey to heaven we begin seated, in a low position, and then we rise to meet God.

V'yitpa·ar v'yitromam v'yit·hassei, "adorned, exalted, and lifted up." In this next phase of movement, the direction is clearly upward. The root of the word *yitpa·ar* (*pei-alef-resh*) normally generates words related to the concept of adornment, like a headdress or crown.[14] We thus engender the feeling of direct address to God, who becomes glorified as Sovereign through the partnership with the people Israel (Isaiah 44:23). *Yitromam* and *yitnassei* are clearly verbs of praising in an upwardly direction. They are paired in the verse, "Now I will arise, says the Eternal; now I will exalt Myself (*eiromam*), raise Myself high (*ennasei*)" (Isaiah 33:10). Again, note the difference between the prophecy and the prayer: in Isaiah, God is the actor; in the Kaddish, the mourners are the actors, who effect the raising and exalting of

God. These words take us from the lowly plain to the celestial, as if we are taking a step toward our encounter with God—which is the focus of the last section.

V'yit·haddar v'yitalleh v'yit¬hallal, "beautified, adored, and lauded." *Yit·haddar* is generated from the verbal root *hei-dalet-resh,* which usually yields words related to the concept of splendor or beauty. It is a word used to describe an encounter with an elder (Leviticus 19:32), as well as God's majestic holiness (Psalm 29:2). The word *v'yitalleh* shares its root with the words meaning "ascent." It is used to describe the rising of the sun and the breaking of dawn (Genesis 32:25), the ascent to Mount Sinai (Exodus 19:12), and the travels of the Israelites out of Egypt and into the Promised Land (Judges 19:29). The word *olah* (derived from the same verbal root) itself describes the burnt offering, whose purpose is to draw close to God through the ascension of the smoke and savory smell of the sacrifice (Leviticus 6:2). *Yit·hallal* comes from the root *hei-lamed-lamed* and is the word for praising in ecstasy, as in the word *halleluyah* found repeatedly in the Book of Psalms.[15] All three of these final words of praise share the sense of a direct encounter with God's Presence. Taken together, these last three verbs envision the beauty and splendor of seeing God's Presence.

As a whole, the eight words of praising are a journey, where the worshipper rises above the sky into the celestial plane where God's name and light are seen in a vision of ecstasy. The first section begins with the worshipper in a lowly position of being seated or bowing at the knee. The movement reminds us of our humility, and despondency through mourning. In an act of courage, the second section takes the mourner upward from the plane of his or her life to the celestial plane. The third section takes the mourner still higher, until finally coming upon God's splendor. At this point the gathered community recites the name of God, in whose presence the mourner now stands: *kudsha b'rikh hu,* the blessed Holy One!

When we add this chapter of the story of Kaddish to its first chapter, the theology of Kaddish begins to emerge. We see, first, the cosmic nature of death that affects all living things, including God. We can find comfort in the knowledge that our pain is not only our own, because God feels our pain and in fact mourns with us. We also feel our deeply entwined partnership with God, and come to know the responsibility we have to support each other in our mutual pain. Through the ascent to heaven, we eventually come face to face with God, in our reciprocity of spirit.

What Can We Really Say to Bring Comfort to God?

Once we climb the ladder of the eight verbs of praise to pay God our respects in our celestial bereavement call, what does one say to God? For that matter, what does one say to anyone who has experienced loss? One way to approach this moment is to compare the Kaddish to other moments in the liturgy when we encounter God directly. Perhaps what is said in those moments can be of some help.

One example of a God-encounter in the liturgy is found in the Kedushah, a prayer centered on the holiness of God in concert with the angelic hosts. The Kedushah is a collection of poetry and verses from Isaiah and Ezekiel (the prophets upon whose words the Kaddish most heavily leans). In the Bible, Isaiah ascends to heaven to receive his commission, and as he passes through the heights of heaven he sees God, seated in majesty on the heavenly throne and surrounded by a host of fiery angels singing out to each other, "Holy, holy, holy, is the Eternal One of Hosts, whose aura fills the world with glory!" (Isaiah 6:3). Isaiah is filled with dread and awe of God's power. During the Kedushah, worshippers recite the verse from Isaiah—thereby placing themselves in the role of the angels, as they flutter up and down on their toes while singing aloud. The theological underpinnings of the Kedushah are a communion with God at the peak of greatness and glory. In fact, the verbs *titgaddal v'titkaddash* ("You make Yourself great and holy")—which are similar to the Kaddish's *yitgaddal v'yitkaddash*—appear in the second paragraph of the Kedushah[16] as an encouragement for God to return to Jerusalem to redeem the world. Note again the verbal structure: in both the Kedushah and the Kaddish, it is God who becomes great and holy, through our role as God's partners. The Kedushah is similar to the Kaddish, insofar as both prayers have as their goal a direct encounter between the worshipper and God.

A second communion of sorts is found in the liturgy for Rosh Hashanah and Yom Kippur in the U-netaneh Tokef prayer. In this liturgical poem that introduces the Kedushah of the Musaf service, we imagine God sitting as a sovereign on high, with the Book of Remembrances of our lives open and ready. Like the Kedushah, the U-netaneh Tokef allows the worshipper a peek into heaven. At this moment, however, angels are not singing songs of holiness but are instead trembling with fear, for the Day of Judgment has come. Worshippers enter this celestial vision one by one and pass under the divine gaze, as God takes note of their deeds and marks them for either life or death in the coming year. This encounter with God is full of awe and dread, as worshippers are reminded of their misgivings and their mortality before a God who is everlasting. The U-netaneh Tokef is the prayer that has come to epitomize the High Holy Days, during which we each reflect on our lives and look for the opportunities of repentance that can give us life in the year to come. Unlike the Kedushah, the focus in the U-netaneh Tokef is not so much on God's sovereignty and majesty, but rather on God's judgment. In each, the heavenly throneroom is filled with angels, singing or trembling (depending on God's mood), and the worshipper is there to take in the scene and to be humbled by God's unfurled glory and power.

The Kaddish, I argue, is an encounter with God similar to both the Kedushah and the U-netaneh Tokef, in which the mourner goes to heaven to see God on the divine throne. All three prayers draw on images from the prophets Isaiah and Ezekiel. The Kedushah, as noted earlier, uses language similar to that of the Kaddish. The Kaddish differs significantly from both the Kedushah and the U-netaneh Tokef, however, regarding the nature of the celestial encounter. In the Kedushah and the U-netaneh Tokef, God is envisioned as seated on the heavenly throne, as divine splendor and glory fill the whole earth. In the Kaddish, we see a different image of God. No longer are the angels singing or trembling. Instead of a chamber with the noise of the chorus or the sound of the great *shofar*, we hear nothing. Where are the angels fluttering about? Where is the drama of the great pageant? In the Kaddish, the scene is quieter, the music turned off, the angels absent. The power of the moment is etiolated. God is alone, in mourning, and waiting for us to reach out in partnership. Where the Kedushah focuses on power and glory, the Kaddish focuses on love and praise. Where the U-netaneh Tokef centers on judgment, the Kaddish centers on interdependence. Our ascension to heaven rides not on words of awe or power, but on verses of praise that try to bring comfort to God. Unlike the Kedushah and the U-netaneh Tokef, the Kaddish approaches God without glory and song, and without fear. The power dynamic has shifted, and we come before God not in awe or dread, but in love.

What does one say to God who is in mourning? I believe the Kaddish gives us the answer in the next phrase: *l'eilla min kol birkhata v'shirata, tushb'hata v'nehemata, da-amiran b'alma*, "higher than any blessing or song, praise or consolation, that are uttered the world over." There are often no words that can truly express the depth of grief that one feels in the face the death. Death as the ultimate privation defies our categories of understanding, because it is the terminus of understanding itself. Every death is different, and yet we will all share in the same experience. I am reminded of the words of Shakespeare: "Well, everyone can master a grief but he that has it."[17] Many times, no words will give comfort to the bereaved. When sitting with a friend who has lost a loved one, our presence is more important than our words. When we do speak, we might slip into a kind of judgment by saying, "Maybe you should have done this…" or a kind of justification by saying, "It's for the best that she died…"— when it would be far better to live in the terrible moment without any words at all. This is precisely the mood the Kaddish attempts to create. Therefore, the only words of comfort we can give to a mourning God is to say that our presence is higher than "any blessing, song, praise, or consolation that is uttered the world over."[18] These words give God heart, because they recognize that there are no words that can truly give comfort to those who encounter death. It is fitting, then, that the community adds its affirmation of love for the mourner and for God by saying "Amen." For there is nothing can be said to buttress the truth that presence can be ultimately a greater comfort than the words themselves.

Come Back to Life

As the rites of *shiva* draw to a close we must rise from our stools, uncover the mirrors, and return to the world again. We cannot mourn for too long. Life must move on, and so must we in our journey without those who have died. The story of the Kaddish traces this movement as well. We have ascended to the heavenly court and sat face-to-face with a God who mourns. We give comfort through praise and presence, but we know the story must continue; life must be returned to life. So we dare to ask of God: *y'hei sh'lama rabba min sh'mayya, v'hayyim aleinu v'al kol yisrael,* "may abundant peace and life flow down from heaven to us and the people of Israel." In the shadow of death, when all seems turned upside down, we ask for an overflowing peace to come back from heaven. We ask, most boldly, for the Giver of Life to bring life back upon the world, and us.

Theologically, our partnership with God comes to this very moment, where mourning must stop and living must begin again. In perhaps the most daring move, we allude to the beginning of the Kaddish, by reminding God of God's role as Creator. We ask God to come back with us, to bring life and peace to a world ravaged by death. It is as if we go up to heaven to console a mourning God, and then use our own strong hands and outstretched arms to bring God's peace and God's life-force back down to earth. The redeemed become the redeemers. In partnership, we can make goodness happen in the world again. Through the mutual love and regard, God and humanity can create new life, new worlds, and bring harmony back to the world. The Kaddish reinforces this movement away from heaven with peace and life in hand, in the final line: *oseh shalom bi-m'romav, hu ya·aseh shalom aleinu v'al kol yisrael,* "may the One who makes peace on high, make peace for us and for all of Israel." We come back to earth, knowing that in the wake of death our responsibility is to live in peace with ourselves and with death. And the community affirms life, by saying "Amen."

The Kaddish tells the story of life and death. It is a reflection of our own story of mourning and comfort in a community. We weave the prayer back together, to find a journey into holiness through mutual need and empathy. The constancy of death in life is a phenomenon that all of us must confront, including God. The Kaddish is a journey where we rise from our own seats of mourning to ascend to heaven and find God seated on the throne—not in judgment or in glory, as in the Kedushah or the U-netaneh Tokef, but seated in mourning, experiencing the loss of a world, a precious life. God mourns as we mourn, and in our interdependence we can find comfort in a God who feels our pain deeply, and needs our prayers—just as we need God's grace. Through the story of the Kaddish we can come back to ourselves with God's partnership, to return to the task of making life again by drawing down, to our life in this world, the hope for peace and love. We move from death to life, and turn the tragedy of mourning into the sweetness of memory.

NOTES

[1] Based on Martin Buber, *Tales of the Hasidim: Early Masters,* trans. Olga Marx (New York: Schocken, 1947), p. 252.

[2] Shir Hashirim Rabbah 1:8.

[3] Cf. M. Sanhedrin 4:5.

[4] See B. Sanhedrin 37a.

[5] Bereishit Rabbah 9:10.

[6] Pirkei Avot 4:2.

[7] Many other texts likewise seem to assume that God is powerless in the face of death's own separate powers; see, e.g., B. Mo·eid Katan 28a, Bemidbar Rabbah 17:24, Devarim Rabbah 11:5, and cf. Zohar I 35b and 63a.

[8] B. Megillah 10b.

[9] Abraham Joshua Heschel, *Man Is Not Alone: A Philosophy of Judaism* (New York: Farrar, Strauss and Giroux, 1951), p. 241.

[10] Peskita D'rav Kahana 12:6.

[11] B. Berakhot 3a.

[12] Cf. Song of Songs 8:6.

[13] Bereishit Rabbah 48:7.

[14] See, e.g., Isaiah 61:10 and Ezekiel 24:17.

[15] See Psalm 150, for example, where words formed from the root *hei-lamed-lamed* (including *halleluyah*) appear eleven times.

[16] These words appear in the second paragraph of the version of the Kedushah recited during the Shaḥarit service on Shabbat and festivals; they are absent from the daily version of the Kedushah.

[17] William Shakespeare, *Much Ado About Nothing*, Act III, scene 2.

[18] It is important to note briefly the word *neḥemata*, "consolation." The inclusion of this phrase is vitally important for my reading of the Kaddish. The idea of adding words of consolation at the moment that God is encountered bolsters the idea that both the community of Israel and God *need* consolation. I admit the reference here is oblique, as I have not found any phrases in the Bible where this word is used to give comfort to God. But, given the general theological stance I am taking—that God, too, is in mourning—the utilization of the word *neḥemata* seems appropriate.

Death Is But a Dream

Martin S. Cohen

The custom of mourners rising in synagogue to recite the Kaddish prayer for their lost loved ones exerts a hold on the popular Jewish imagination that is almost without parallel.[1] Indeed, any rabbi like myself who works in the congregational world will be familiar with the experience of people who are fairly negligent with respect to the exigencies of Jewish ritual in many other ways nevertheless feeling eager and willing to come to synagogue to recite Kaddish after suffering a keenly felt loss—and to do so daily for many months. In a sense, it is not that difficult a phenomenon to explain: most aspects of religious observance involve some combination of obligation, restriction, and self-denial, but embedded in the concept of reciting a prayer "for" someone who has passed away is the siren notion, all the more powerful for being left formally unstated, that the decedent in question is not quite gone from the world, that the individual for whom Kaddish is being said is still somewhere in the accessible universe, still somehow in need of the succor (if that is the right word) that comes from being the object of another's prayers.

In turn, that notion—that death is a threshold over which all must eventually pass on their way to the next phase of their existence, rather than an end that none may avoid but beyond which lies nothing at all—becomes a great source of comfort for many. Indeed, what draws people to synagogue to recite Kaddish is precisely the much-wished-for solace that inheres in that specific complex of theories about death.

There are two related, but also distinct, notions that serve as the ideational foundation of that complex: first, that the dead live on somewhere, somehow, in some mostly inaccessible but still fully real realm of being; and second, that the living, acting unilaterally and possessed solely of the spiritual force of their personal desire to pierce the veil that separates this world from the next, can create some sort of link to the realm of posthumous existence that the dead inhabit in order to exert some sort of salutary effect on its inhabitants. The recitation of Kaddish thus fosters the idea that the dead are absent in the world but not truly gone from it. Indeed, saying Kaddish implies that the dead are only absent from the world in the gross, physical sense...but nevertheless continue to exist in some discernible and meaningful way.

Death as a Journey

I would like to present a legend that speaks directly to the second notion mentioned above, but I would like to make some brief points about the first as well. The notion that death is a "journey toward" as much as a "journey from" is ancient. There are those who argue that humans as early as Neanderthal times believed that life somehow continued beyond the grave.[2] The Egyptians imagined the souls of the deceased living on in the Fields of Aaru.[3] The Greeks imagined Hades, as did the Romans.[4] The Teutons imagined Hel.[5] The ancient Hebrews imagined Sheol, the biblical conception of a dank netherworld to which human souls descend at death, that was eventually replaced in rabbinic times by Gehenna.[6] In their own category are the stories in the Talmud about the spirits of the dead flitting back to earth *mei-aḥorei ha-pargod* (literally, "from behind the curtain"—that is, the great drape that separates the abode of the disembodied souls of the dead from the world they departed) and sharing some detail or another with those they left behind in the land of the living.[7]

The idea, therefore, that death is a gate rather than a wall—and the corollary notion that life, therefore, is a journey that continues beyond the grave—is so much part and parcel of human culture that it would be difficult to come up with the name of a culture or a religious tradition that totally denies the possibility of life after death.[8] Nor is this purely a religious phenomenon in our day: even so-called secularists seem caught up in the possibility of posthumous existence, as convincingly witness the proliferation of books brought out by non-religious publishers in recent years about so-called "near-death experiences," works that almost invariably feature the stories of people who purportedly died, took a good look at what lies beyond, and then returned to earth to write, usually breathlessly, all about it.[9]

It is, however, the second notion—the one that posits not solely that the realm of the "living dead" exists, but that the still-living can affect the fate of their dear ones who have moved on to life *mei-ahorei ha-pargod* by reciting prayers for them—that draws me more powerfully. Perhaps I should add that I speak from personal experience in this regard: my father outlived my mother by almost twenty years, but my personal experience saying Kaddish for them was not that different. (I myself was quite different at forty-six than I was at twenty-six. But it was the longing embedded in the experience that I recall now as having been quite similar: there was greater consolation for me in reciting Kaddish—and in so doing simultaneously to be embracing the core concept that the lot of the dead can be ameliorated through the efforts of the living, which only makes sense if the departed live on in at least some sense— there was more comfort for me personally in that than in any of the other requisite rituals of formal bereavement. Tearing my shirt in the chapel before the service felt like shutting a door; saying Kaddish felt more like opening one…at least little, a crack.)

An Ancient Story

Floating through the corpus of ancient and medieval Jewish literature is a story that is widely told, but never with all the same details. When read in the context of one of the books in which it appears, it feels like a legend cast as a kind of a quasi-historical account. But when followed through all the books in which it appears, it takes on a dream-like aura as details shift and the storyline moves forward in fits and starts toward essentially the same destination but not at all along the same path. Some of the sources even go so far as to present the story as having originated *within* a dream—and, indeed, as the tale travels from antiquity through medieval halakhic and kabbalistic sources into the modern books that retell it, one absolutely does get the sense that one is following a recurring dream from night to night as it morphs forward into various iterations without any discernible pattern. And yet, for all the dissimilarity, the texts at hand clearly are all telling the same story.

The versions of our story fall largely into three basic groups: two featured in ancient rabbinic sources and one that derives from the kabbalistic milieu that produced the Zohar and its ancillary works. The history of these various versions—and even the question of whether they are all derived from a single original source—is extremely complex and has been the subject of several thoughtful scholarly essays.[10] My purpose here is neither to evaluate those efforts nor even to express a formal opinion of my own, but simply to present the tale to my own readers in a spiritual and literary (rather than historical) way, as a way of stimulating the thoughtful evaluation of its details without becoming overwhelmed by the intricacies of its transmission through the generations.

The First Group

The first group features overlays of a story that appears first in the ancient rabbinic work called *Kallah Rabbati*. (When the book was written and by whom is not known, but it clearly contains material from many different sources.) And there, in the second section of the eighth chapter, we find the earliest version of the tale I want to tell.[11]

The passage begins by asking if children can atone for their parents' sins. (What a good question!) And then, using the talmudic turn of phrase "come and hear" to introduce a passage that does not actually appear in any ancient rabbinic source, our story begins. I translate loosely, adding here and there words I hear suggested, if left unsaid, in the original:

> Rabbi Akiva was once on his way walking somewhere when he came across a man carrying a burden on his shoulders so large that he could barely manage to walk at all. Nor was he bearing his burden silently but, instead, was groaning and moaning as he struggled to carry it successfully. Rabbi Akiva, sensing that there was more here than met the eye, asked the man to tell him his story, whereupon the man obliged. "There is no prohibition in the world that I did not transgress," he said, "and now I have these heavenly guards assigned to me who refuse to allow me even a moment's rest."
>
> Rabbi Akiva, suddenly realizing he was chatting with a dead man, asked if the man by any chance had left behind a son. "I swear that you mustn't hold me up with questions," the man retorted, "because I am terrified that the angel assigned to me will come and beat me with lashes made of fire while asking why I'm not worker faster."[12] Undaunted, Rabbi Akiva asked the man who it was that he had left behind in the world, and the man answered that he had left behind a pregnant wife.

Hearing this, Rabbi Akiva immediately went to that man's city and asked for the whereabouts of the man's wife. The response was unkind: "May that man's name be uprooted from society," the citizens answered, "and may his bones be ground up." Rabbi Akiva asked why they felt so strongly, whereupon they replied: "The man was a thief. And a cannibal. And he caused nothing but misery to everybody around here. And not only that, but he once violated a betrothed woman on Yom Kippur."

Having heard enough, Rabbi Akiva then went to the man's home and found his wife pregnant. Doing nothing precipitous, he merely waited for her give birth, then personally undertook to circumcise the child. And when the child grew up, he personally took him to the synagogue so that he could say his blessings in public. That did the trick—the next time Rabbi Akiva passed by that place in which he first met the boy's father, he saw him again. "You can set your mind to rest," the man said, "for you have surely set mine at rest for me."[13]

It is, by all accounts, a remarkable story and one surprisingly well told.

Other versions of the tale both sharpen and weaken the focus. The version that appears in the great *Or Zarua* of Rabbi Isaac of Vienna (c. 1200–c. 1270), for example, adds the details that the skin of the man Rabbi Akiva came across was so singed that it appeared as black as coal, and that he was totally naked. And that text also adds that he was not just racing around when Rabbi Akiva first spied him, but was running as fast as a horse.[14] (There is no way to know if these are new details that Rabbi Isaac added to his story to enhance its texture and bring color to the tableau he was presenting to his readers, or if he simply was copying from a different text than the one that we find in our editions of *Kallah Rabbati* today.) And Rabbi Isaac's version also features a different set of sins—indicting the dead man of having once been a crooked tax collector who unfairly favored the rich and treated the poor wretchedly, rather than of cannibalism. Other details in this version fill in the picture even more deftly. The sinner here is required daily to gather the wood for daily immolation on his self-made pyre. And his name too is revealed: the sinner here is—oddly, but also deeply suggestively—Akiva, just the same as his savior. (Aren't we all destined in the end to save ourselves, or not to?) His wife's name is Shishkhiya. Their town is Ludkiya.

Most important of all is the section of Rabbi Isaac's version that reveals the only avenue of escape from the fires of hell. In the *Kallah Rabbati* version, Rabbi Akiva somehow intuitively knows what must be done. But in the *Or Zarua*, the story reads entirely differently as, after sinner-Akiva tells savior-Akiva not to hold him up, he adds something that he heard his tormentors mention (presumably when chatting among themselves) something that he himself qualifies as unbelievable: that if a tormented soul were to have left behind in the land of the living a son who were to lead the synagogue service by reciting the Bar'khu[16] or the Yitgaddal,[17] then that lad's father would instantly be released from the torments of hell. It is hard to say whether the reference to Kaddish is a kind of commentary on what the earlier text meant by someone coming to synagogue to say, or perhaps to elicit, the blessing of God in public, or if Rabbi Isaac simply had a different text before him. But the bottom line is that it was through Rabbi Isaac's book that the legend was passed on to future generations.[18]

The Second Group

A similar progression of ideas informs the second version of the story, which first appears in the obscure midrashic work called, the

Tanna D'vei Eliyahu.[19] Here the protagonist is not Rabbi Akiva but Rabbi Yoḥanan ben Zakkai, an even earlier figure who lived in the first century C.E.[20] He too is out for a walk and comes upon a man, but this one is not carrying a huge burden on his shoulders but rather is gathering sticks. Yoḥanan ben Zakkai approaches him, but the man remains silent at first and only after a while speaks up. "Rabbi," he says, "I am a dead man, not a living one." And now we can listen to Rabbi Yoḥanan narrate his own tale:

> So I said to him, "If you are dead, what do you need with all that wood?" He responded, "Rabbi, listen carefully to what I am about to tell you. When I was still alive, my friend and I committed *the* sin in my villa and when we came to this place, *they* delivered against us the verdict of immolation. And this is how it works: first I gather the wood and they burn my friend, then he gathers the wood and they burn me." Aghast, I asked, "How long does this sentence last?" And he said to me, "When I came here, I left behind a pregnant wife and I know for a fact she is going to have a boy. Therefore, I implore you, watch over that lad from the moment of his birth until he is five years old, then take him personally and enroll him in elementary school because as soon as he learns to say [the Bar'khu] my term in hell will be ended."[21]

So many questions to ask from one short text. Did five-year-olds lead the prayer service in the author's day? Or is the idea for the boy to start school at age five so that he will be capable of leading the prayer service when he turns thirteen and can first be counted in the quorum?[22] And what exactly was *the* sin that this unfortunate and his fellow committed?[23] The word translated as "villa" above is *palt'rin*, which usually designates a palace of some kind. Is our prisoner a former king of his own country? Odd, then, not to mention that…but also odd to include the *palt'rin* reference if the intent was to obfuscate. And who exactly is the *they* who sentenced our unfortunate to hell? To none of these questions do any ready answers present themselves.

But it is the later, medieval iterations of this version of the story—clearly cousins of the *Kallah Rabbati* story, if not quite siblings—that are of interest to me, because they follow the same pattern I noted above of taking a story that is originally about the Barkhu and making it also about the Kaddish.[24] And, indeed, the medieval versions of the story do just that. Just as the *Kallah Rabbati* stories are all about a man attempting to carry an insupportable burden on his back, these Tanna D'vei Eliyahu stories are all about a man gathering sticks.[25] The *Kol Bo*, for example, is a mysterious work in its own right, clearly the work of a medieval rabbi, and its version of the story clearly matches the story's source, albeit not precisely.[26] Here, for example, the dead man is gathering brambles, not wood.[27] But far more important is the solution to the man's problem: in the *Kol Bo*, the way to escape from the fiery torments to which he in the interim must submit is to have a son either say Kaddish or come to synagogue to recite a *haftarah*.[28] And this remedy is repeated throughout the literature, noticeably in the *Orḥot Ḥayyim* of Rabbi Aaron ben Jacob Hakohen of Lunel (fl. 14th century),[29] in a responsum on the topic by Rabbi Isaac ben Sheshet (1326–1408, known by his acronym as the Rivash),[30] and in the famous *Beit Yosef* commentary of Rabbi Joseph Karo (1488–1575) on the *Arba·ah Turim* of Rabbi Jacob ben Asher.[31] And so we see a pattern emerging: as the Kaddish established itself as the prayer par excellence for the dead, the legend was reworked just slightly to incorporate in its ancient detail the thought that reciting Kaddish can save the dead from their postmortem agonies.

The Third Group

In their own category are the versions of the story that appears in the larger Zoharic literary corpus. An introduction to the Zohar and to modern-day scholarship regarding the Zohar would be impossible to undertake even cursorily in an essay such as this,[32] but it should suffice here to note that the Zohar is more of an anthology than a single work and that scholars are not at all in agreement about the relationship of its many parts.[33] Part of the discussion regarding the relationship of these constituent elements has to do with material that appears in several of them, but not in precisely the same format or text. And that is just what we have with the kabbalistic version of the tale under discussion: both appear in the Zoharic tome called the *Zohar Ḥadash*, one in a section labelled *Sitrei Torah* (literally, "Secrets of the Torah") and the other under the vague title *Midrash Ruth*.[34] Both are clearly versions of the same story. But they differ as well, and in interesting, meaningful ways.

The passage from *Midrash Ruth* features most of the same details we have already seen. A rabbi (in this passage, an otherwise unknown Rabbi Zemira) is out on a walk, just as were the others.[35] He arrives in a place called Ḥakal Oni, where he notes flames shooting out of the ground. Intrigued, he puts his ear to the ground and hears—to his surprise—voices, whereupon a local Arab appears and invites him to a different section of terrain, where he sees even more flames shooting up from the ground and even louder voices of people moaning and groaning. Realizing he must have come across one of the "air vents" of hell—in this version of the tale, Gehenna, like its biblical predecessor Sheol, is an underground city of the dead—Rabbi Zemira turns to thank his guide for showing him such a remarkable sight, but the Arab has vanished and Rabbi Zemira is totally alone.

And now the story begins in earnest. While present in that place, Rabbi Zemira comes across a man—clearly one above ground—who is groaning and wailing. But as Rabbi Zemira watches from afar, "they" suddenly arrive and drag the man back underground so that he can no longer be seen. Suddenly exhausted, Rabbi Zemira lies down and instantly falls asleep, then begins to dream. In his dream, he sees that very man whom "they" had pulled back to Gehenna. He asks him, "Who are you?" The man responds, "A Jew…but a wicked one, for I did not leave one evil deed of sin in the world undone." Within his dream, Rabbi Zemira pursues his questioning: "But what is your name?" he asks. "I have no idea," the man replies openly, "for one of the punishments of the wicked in hell is that they cannot remember their own names."[36] "Well, then," Rabbi Zemira continues, "where are you from?" That question, the man could answer easily: "In life, I was a butcher in the Upper Galilee," he says, "but now, because of my wickedness, I am judged three times every day and three times each night as well."[37] Finally, Rabbi Zemira asks if the dead man left behind any sons and the man responds that he did.

Upon awakening, the rabbi departs immediately for the Upper Galilee. But where to find the child? Fortunately, he stumbles across a child almost as soon as he arrives who greets him with a verse from Proverbs regarding the search for wisdom: "If you seek her like silver and search for her as though for hidden treasures, then shall you understand what it means to fear the Eternal…" (Proverbs 2:4–5). Taking the verse to mean that he should seek the dead man's child in a school, he proceeds to a local study hall where he finds another precocious child with a verse to assist him in his search: "Seek justice and cultivate humility, and perhaps as a result shall you be hidden on the day of the Eternal's wrath" (Zephaniah 2:3). Taking this second verse as a suggestion that he would do better humbly just to ask for the boy, he stops a third child and asks where the man had lived in life. The child does not respond kindly, however. "Damn that man," he says, "for he did not leave even one wicked act or sin undone, and the same goes for the wet nurse that once suckled him at her breast." Ignoring the vituperation, Rabbi Zemira now asks one final question, inquiring if the man left behind a son. "Yes, he did," the boy responds, "and he's as bad as his father and just spends his days hanging around his father's old butcher shop."

Rabbi Zemira has heard enough. He goes and finds the boy, undertakes personally to serve as his teacher, and does not desist until the boy knows some Bible and can say his prayers and recite the Shema. And then the lad's education begins in earnest as Rabbi Zemira undertakes to teach him Mishnah, Talmud, and various other Jewish texts. Eventually, the butcher's boy becomes wise and attains rabbinic ordination. Now the boy's name was Naḥum, but as a man he became known as Rabbi Naḥum Ha-pakuli, this latter sobriquet being derived from a wordplay on Isaiah 28:7 and taken to imply that he managed through his pious efforts to free his father from the torment of hell. And the name stuck, we learn, and future generations were called by that name as well in honor of the son's success in alleviating his father's posthumous suffering.

Later on, the dead man came again to Rabbi Zemira in a dream and said to him, "May God grant you the comfort you have brought to me, for with each incremental step he took forward in his learning, my son brought me closer and closer to freedom from the misery of Gehenna." And then the text wraps up the whole story by enthusing about how happy one who leaves behind a child in the world who studies Torah should be and then, as a closing comment, by also recalling that a similar incident once happened to Rabbi Akiba![38]

The other Zoharic source tells a similar story. A man is walking in the mythical mountains of Kardunia, but in this version of the story he is not alone and has two traveling companions. Like in the other story, they come across a field of fissures in the ground from which are shooting flames and billowing smoke and, as in the other version, once they hear subterranean groaning they realize that they are walking on the roof of hell. The man falls asleep—perhaps they all do—and in his dream he sees the man we have been reading about. The dead man has a huge bundle of brambles on his back and, as our traveler looks on, two angelic overseers ignite the brambles and immolate the man bearing them. He screams, but the overseers are unimpressed and merely pause to remind the man that he is the author of his own misfortune. Of course, being dead, he can't die. And so we begin to understand what it means to burn in hell—being unable to die, you simply face execution every single day…and by the most terrifying and painful means possible.

As above, our traveler asks the man who he is and he gets the same answer, except that the man reports that he faces torture not six times a day but only five: three times by day and twice by night. The text then embarks on a complicated excursus about the human soul, then returns to the topic at hand. The traveler wakes up from his sleep and heads off for the Upper Galilee. He meets one of the wonder children, hears him recite a helpful verse, then uses it as a clue to locate the boy he is seeking at his father's butcher shop where he is at play with some other boys. He takes the boy away, dresses him in decent clothing, and hands him off to a local rabbi who undertakes to teach him to read. Eventually, the boy becomes learned enough to read a *haftarah* in the synagogue, then continues on to learn how to lead the prayer service. Eventually, he becomes a rabbi. His name is not revealed, but eventually his father comes to visit his son's savior in a dream. The dead man blesses the living one with God's comfort, then explains how this actually works:

> When my son read the *haftarah* in synagogue, I was relieved from the [torments associated with my] judgment. When he led the prayer service *and recited Kaddish*, the judgment

itself was retracted. When he grew truly wise, I was awarded my place in paradise—and that place in Eden is precisely the "portion" referenced in the expression "a portion of the World to Come," i.e., the portion awarded personally to every righteous individual—and brought up to be seated in the company of the righteous.[39]

The passage then wraps up much as did the other.

Most of the differences between the versions of the tale are negligible; some are interesting. But what interests me the most has to do with the way that children can save their parents from the torments of hell: in the first Zoharic story what counted was Torah study alone; as the boy learned first to read, then to say the Shema, then was ordained and deemed a master of rabbinics, his father was freed from each successive torment. But in the second story, reminiscent of one subset of the texts cited above, the key to relief lies in the child reading the *haftarah* and saying Kaddish.

Conclusion

And so the idea that Kaddish alleviates the misery of the dead as they suffer through the punishment for their earthly sins on their way to personal redemption in paradise percolates its way through the sources, as one basic legend takes on a dozen different guises and eventually leads to the sense so many have today—including many who would balk mightily at explaining themselves with reference to belief in an actual hell or a physically real heaven—that the Kaddish is capable not merely of soothing the bereaved, but actually of having an salutary effect on the dead.

To what extent can moderns embrace the concept that lies beneath the ritual recitation of Kaddish for the dead? The notion itself of reciting a prayer "for" a deceased individual, after all, inescapably implies the reality of some sort of posthumous existence. (What else could it possibly mean to recite a prayer "for" an individual who no longer exists? How could a prayer help such a non-person?) And there are books out there—many of them—that recommend the Kaddish for that specific reason, and that do so unabashedly and without complicated argumentation. One author, who lived about a century ago, wrote that what we learn from all these texts is that "the Kaddish and the Bar'khu that someone recites for a parent have a greatly beneficent effect on the soul of the deceased individual in question."[40] Another author, Zev Aryeh Rabiner, seeks to anchor in Scripture the theory that the living can exert a salutary effect on the dead through the medium of daily prayer, including the daily recitation of Kaddish. He finds a reference to the Kaddish both in Balaam's reference to his wish to die the death of the righteous (the word for "righteous" in this verse, y'sharim, is taken as an acronym for the public response during Kaddish that begins with the words y'hei shmeih rabba m'varakh), but also, and far more impressively, in the Torah's promise that parents shall not be responsible for their children's deeds (Deuteronomy 24:16). "This," Rabbi Rabbiner writes candidly, "implies that the souls of parents will not die *if* they are rescued [i.e., from oblivion] by their children…and it is herein that lies the power of the Kaddish."[41]

A third author I'd like to mention, Aaron Mendel Cohen (1866–1927), devotes a full chapter in his *Sefer Ha-n'shamah V'ha-kaddish* to exploring the effect that Kaddish can have on the souls of the departed. It is a magical chapter, one I have now read many times in the course of just a few months. To my readers who can read Hebrew, I recommend the entire book—and particularly the closing chapter—as an example of spiritually uplifting writing at its finest. I will close here merely by citing a single passage of this work. Playing on the talmudic turn of phrase *bara m'zakkei abba* ("a son can grant merit to a father"), Cohen writes: "Our sages of blessed memory wrote that a son can grant merit to a father, and, indeed, all Jewish people believe that a son can indeed grant merit to his father to the extent actually of freeing his father from the torments of hell through the recitation of the Kaddish and elevating his father's soul to its celestial source."[42]

There are many more books that say the same, albeit most of them far less elegantly than Cohen does. Whether Jews today can embrace this aspect of the Kaddish and what it implies about the nature of death—*that* is the question to ponder, the one tacitly posed by each individual who comes to synagogue to say Kaddish for a parent or for some other late relation or friend. The question is admittedly a bit overwhelming even to ask out loud. But that the Jewish people—including many who would describe themselves as fully rational—have answered not with words but by voting with their feet as they make their way to synagogue to pray for the souls of those whom they have lost—that should be a source of comfort and solace for Jews everywhere, both those who have known bereavement personally and those lucky few who know death only from a distance.

NOTES

[1] The oldest reference to Kaddish being a prayer connected with mourning is a passage in the extra-talmudic tractate Sofrim that instructs the *ḥazzan* to leave the pulpit and "find" mourners and their families gathered outside the synagogue so that he might offer them consolation by reciting a special blessing called Birkat Aveilim (literally "the mourners' blessing") and Kaddish on their behalf. See Sofrim 19:9, ed. Michael Higger (New York: Hotzaat D'vei Rabbanan, 1937), p. 336; in some editions, this text appears as 19:12. Another ancient book of uncertain provenance, the *Otiyyot D'rabbi Akiva*, imagines that the great resurrection of the dead that will be part of the (Jewishly-conceived) eschaton will be heralded by Zerubbabel, the ancient governor of Judah in the fifth century B.C.E., rising up before God in heaven and pronouncing the Kaddish, whereupon the gates of Gehenna, all 40,000 of them, will open and those imprisoned there will be free to re-enter the world. (There is no authoritative edition of the text, but readers may consult the version presented by J. D. Eisenstein in his *Otzar Midrashim* [New York: Eisenstein, 1915], p. 84.) But it was only later on, in the medieval period, that the custom is first mentioned that the mourners themselves should recite the Kaddish for their own dead.

[2] For the latest thinking on Neanderthal life and culture, see Dimitra Papagianni and Michael A. Morse, *The Neanderthals Rediscovered: How Modern Science Is Rewriting Their Story* (London: Thames and Hudson, 2013).

[3] See, e.g., Allesandro della Seta, *Religion and Art: A Study in the Evolution of Sculpture, Painting, and Architecture*, trans. Marion C. Harrison (New York: Scribner's, 1914), pp. 90–91.

[4] See, e.g., Franz Cumont, *After Life in Roman Paganism* (New Haven: Yale University Press, 1922), pp. 70–90.

[5] See, e.g., P. D. Chantepie de la Saussaye, *The Religion of the Teutons*, trans. Bert J. Vos (Boston and London: Ginn & Co., 1902), pp. 291–292.

[6] See, e.g., Laurentino Jose Afonso and Batya Kedar's essay, "Netherworld," in *Encyclopaedia Judaica*, ed. Michael Berenbaum and Fred Skolnik, 2nd ed. (Detroit: Macmillan Reference USA, 2007), vol. 15, pp. 110–112. Gehenna is the anglicization of the Hebrew *geihinnom*, a regular designation for hell in rabbinic literature.

[7] These stories are gathered together in the Babylonian Talmud at B. Berakhot 18b, and cf. the parallel usage of the term *mei-aḥarei ha-pargod* at B. Yoma 77a, Ḥagigah 15a, Sotah 49a, Bava Metzia 59a, and Sanhedrin 89b.

[8] In this regard, see Alan F. Segal's book, *Life After Death: A History of the Afterlife in Western Religion* (New York, London, Toronto, Sydney, and Auckland: Doubleday, 2010).

[9] See, e.g., Dr. Eben Alexander III's bestselling book, *Proof of Heaven: A Neurosurgeon's Journey into the Afterlife* (New York: Simon and Schuster,

2012) or Todd Burpo's *Heaven Is for Real: A Little Boy's Astounding Story of His Trip to Heaven and Back*, published by Thomas Nelson in 2010, which at the time I am writing this has been on the *New York Times*' paperback non-fiction bestseller list for an astounding 194 weeks, 101 weeks longer than Eben Alexander's book.

[10] I do not know of any serious studies of the tale in English, but Hebrew readers will profit from reading Miron Bialik Lerner's very detailed essay, "*Ma·aseh Ha-tanna V'ha-meit: Gilgulav Ha-sifrutiyim V'ha-hilkhatiyim*, published in the Israeli journal *Asufot* 2 (5748 [1987/1988]), pp. 29–70, as well as Yehudit Weiss's article, "*Sh'tei Girsa·ot Ha-zohar L'aggadat 'Ha-tanna V'ha-meit,'*" published in *Tarbiz* 78 (5769 [2008/2009]), pp. 521–554. And cf. also the comments of Relah Kushelevski in the *Entziklopeida shel Ha-sippur Ha-ivri*, eds. Yoav Elshtein, Avidav Lipsker, and Relah Kushelevski (Ramat Gan: Bar Ilan University Press, 5765 [2004/2005]), pp. 281–296.

[11] Victor Aptowitzer tentatively suggested an origin in the rabbinic academy at Sura in mid-eighth-century C.E. Iraq; see his "*Le traité de 'Kallah,'*" *Revue des Etudes Juives* 57 (1909), pp. 239–244. Other scholars imagine it to be a much older work; cf., e.g., David Brodsky, *A Bride Without a Blessing* (Tübingen: Mohr Siebeck, 2006), pp. 34–40.

[12] The term *pulsa d'nura* literally means "rings of fire" and probably denotes a kind of lash that had rings made of heated metal at the end of each lash. See the comment of Marcus Jastrow in his *A Dictionary of the Targumim, the Talmud Babli and Yerushalmi, and the Midrashic Literature* (1903; rpt. New York: Judaica Press, 1996), p. 1142, s.v. *pulsa*.

[13] *Kallah Rabbati* 2:9 as printed in *Massekhtot Kallah*, ed. Michael Higger, pp. 202–203, and cf. the editor's own comments on pp. 68–72, to which may be compared the remarks of Louis Ginzberg in the first volume of his *Ginzei Schechter* (New York: Jewish Theological Seminary, 5688 [1927/1928]), pp. 235–237, regarding the very early version of the story that survived in the Cairo Genizah. Ginzberg himself imagines that the original version of the story (of which the other extant versions are mere iterations) is in the book *Ḥibbur Yafeh Mei-ha-y'shu·ah* of Rav Nissim ben Yaakov Gaon (990–1062), more correctly called by its full name *Sefer Ma·asiyyot Ha-ḥakhamim v'hu Ḥibbur Yafeh Mei-ha-y'shu·ah*, a collection of sixty or so talmudic tales intended to provide solace and comfort to its readers. The *Ḥibbur Yafeh* version can be found in the Warsaw 5646 [1885/1886] edition of that book, pp. 84–85, or in William M. Brinner's fine translation, *An Elegant Composition Regarding Relief After Adversity* (New Haven: Yale Judaica Series, 1977). For an interesting glimpse into medieval Christian sources relating to the possibility of a sinful decedent gaining release from a place of posthumous punishment through the medium of a living relation's prayers, see Jacques Le Goff's magisterial *The Birth of Purgatory*, trans. Arthur Goldhammer (Chicago: University of Chicago Press,

1984), pp. 293–294 and 350–352.

[14] Isaac of Vienna, *Sefer Or Zarua* (ed. Zhitomir, 1862), part 2, p. 11b. And cf. also the version that appears in the *Maḥzor Vitry*, a compendium of halakhic decisions published by Rabbi Simḥah of Vitry (d. 1105), ed. S. Hurwitz (Nuremberg, 1923), pp. 112–113.

[15] The text of the *Or Zarua* says that he "killed the poor," presumably taking the reference to cannibalism in *Kallah Rabbati* metaphorically.

[16] That is, the call to prayer, recited in both the morning and evening services, that invites the assembled to bless God and elicits the response "Blessed be blessed God for all time."

[17] That is, the Kaddish, which elicits the response, "May the great name of God be blessed from this time on and forever."

[18] There are long-standing scholarly debates about the precise meaning of these terms, mostly centering around the question of whether the *yitgaddal* line—which moderns know solely from the Kaddish—was possibly in earlier times also used as a response to the Bar'khu. See in this regard Israel Ta-Shma's essay, "*K'tzat Inyanei Kaddish Yatom U-minhagav,*" *Tarbiz* 53(5744 [1983/1984]), pp. 557–568, or his book *Minhag Ashk'naz Ha-kadum* (Jerusalem: Magnes Press, 1992), pp. 299–310, and also the essay of Avraham Naftali Tzvi Roth, "*Azkarah V'haftarah V'kaddish Yatom,*" *Talpiyyot* 7 (5761 [1960/1961]), pp. 369–381.

[19] Scholars have not fixed an agreed-upon date for the Tanna D'vei Eliyahu, which is almost definitely not the work of that name mentioned several times in the Talmud. See Jacob Elbaum's comments in his article on the book in the *Encyclopaedia Judaica*, vol. 19, p. 508.

[20] Tanna D'vei Eliyahu 17:18 (ed. Jerusalem, 1994), p. 498.

[21] Ibid.

[22] The question of how old the son in the story was and the halakhic implications of that detail are presented at length by Miron Lerner in his essay referenced above in note 10, pp. 63–64.

[23] Louis Ginzberg, writing in *Ginzei Schechter*, vol. 1, p. 236, suggests that they were involved in homosexual intercourse, a conclusion he derives by taking the words denoting the specific sin for which they were being punished as a corruption of the Hebrew version of the Greek *paiderastia*, which he takes not to have the same meaning as its latter-day English version but rather to refer to sexual relations among adult men, a conclusion that was rejected by Saul Lieberman in his essay "*Eser Millin,*" published in *Eshkolot* 3 (5719 [1958/1959]), p. 86. Michael Higger's suggestion in his introduction to *Kallah Rabbati*, p. 71, that the men were secret worshippers of Jesus, has also been firmly rejected (cf. Miron Lerner's comments in the essay referenced above in note 10, p. 37). For his part, Lerner emends the text to yield the conclusion that the men were armed robbers.

[24] See Avraham Naftali Tzvi Roth's essay referenced above in note 18 for a longer discussion of this idea of how the tale developed.

[25] See Miron Lerner's comments in his essay referenced above in note 10, p. 33.

[26] Rabbi Joseph Karo took it to be an abridgement of the much longer *Sefer Orhot Ḥayyim* of Rabbi Aaron ben Jacob Hakohen of Lunel, but there are many other theories and opinions afloat. Cf. the comments of Cyrus Adler and Max Seligsohn in their essay on the book in the *Jewish Encyclopedia* (New York: Funk and Wagnalls, 1906), vol. 7, pp. 538–539, and also the comments of Moshe Schlesinger in his introduction to his critical edition of Rabbi Aaron's book published in Berlin in 1902, pp. xxiv–xxviii.

[27] The Hebrew *kotzim* ("brambles") could be dismissed simply as a misreading of the original *eitzim* ("wood"), but I do not believe that is the correct explanation. See below.

[28] The term *haftarah* is used in the lectionary cycle of the synagogue to denote the lesson from the Prophets chanted immediately after the Torah is read aloud.

[29] Aaron ben Jacob Hakohen of Lunel, *Sefer Orhot Ḥayyim*, pt. 2, ed. Moshe Elyakim Schlesinger (Berlin: Tzvi Hirsch Itzkowsky, 1902), p. 601.

[30] *She'eilot U-t'shuvot Riva"sh* (ed. Jerusalem, 1975), responsum no. 115, p. 46.

[31] Rabbi Joseph Karo, *Beit Yosef* to the Arba·ah Turim, Yoreh Dei·ah 376, s.v. *katav ha-kolbo*.

[32] Of introductions to the Zohar the world has also produced no end. Readers new to the work can get off to a good start with Arthur Green's *A Guide to the Zohar* (Stanford: Stanford University Press, 2004), Nathan Wolski's *A Journey into the Zohar* (Albany: State University of New York Press, 2010), and Melila Hellner-Eshed's A River *Flows from Eden: The Language of Mystic Experience in the Zohar*, trans. Nathan Wolski (Stanford: Stanford University Press, 2009).

[33] A list of those parts may conveniently be found in the encyclopedia entry "Zohar" by Gershom Scholem and Melila Hellner-Eshed in the *Encyclopaedia Judaica*, vol. 21, pp. 648–650.

[34] The larger questions connected to the specific place of this story in the larger Zoharic corpus are discussed in detail by Yehudit Weiss in her essay referenced above in note 10.

[35] Rabbis out for walks is a recurrent motif throughout the Zohar and its ancillary works. See in this regard most recently David Greenstein's remarkable *Roads to Utopia: The Walking Stories of the Zohar* (Stanford: Stanford University Press, 2014).

[36] Is this what it meant in the other story when the dead man told Rabbi Akiva that his name too was Akiva, that he was just offering the first name that came to mind as his own since he could not actually recall his own name?

[37] *Zohar Ḥadash*, ed. Reuven Margoliot (Jerusalem: Mossad Harav Kook, 1978), p. 84c.

[38] Ibid. This is a loose translation that departs from literality in some places for

the sake of smoothing out the narrative for the reader in translation.

[39] *Zohar Ḥadash*, ed. cit., p. 49a–b, my emphasis.

[40] Aaron Mendel Cohen, *Ha-kaddish: M'koro V'to·alto V'nusha·otav, Dinav, U-minhagav* (Cairo: Reuven Moscovitch, 1919), p. 46. Cohen was the head of the rabbinic court and rabbi of the Ashkenazic community of Jews in Cairo in the first decades of the twentieth century.

[41] Zev Aryeh Rabbiner, *Raza D'ḥayyei* (Tel Aviv: Privately Printed with the assistance of Mossad Harav Kook, 1953), p. 165.

[42] Aaron Mendel Cohen, *Sefer Ha-n'shamah V'ha-kaddish* (Jerusalem: D'fus Levi, 1921), p. 60a. The expression *bara m'zakkei abba* appears in the Talmud at B. Sanhedrin 104a in a discussion regarding the relative merits of the kings of ancient Judah.

Do We Expect Too Much from Kaddish…Or Not Enough?

Reuven P. Bulka

Like many of my colleagues, I have spent a career in the rabbinate observing the impact of Kaddish on mourners. But embedded in that impact is a challenge and also a kind of a mystery. I invite you, my readers, to ride along with me as I probe that mystery, and thus also attempt to meet the challenge posed by the power of Kaddish.

Is It Magic?

Kaddish is magical. It gets people to do things they never did before, or rarely did before—like joining a *minyan*, putting on *t'fillin*, and becoming ensconced in synagogue life.

That is Kaddish at its magical best. But not everyone feels the magic. Too often I have had people who start saying Kaddish ask me why it is not working, why they feel nothing when they say it, why— and with this they finally get to the point—why it does nothing at all for them.

Mystically, we are assured that Kaddish elevates the soul of the deceased. In this regard, Hebrew readers can profit from considering the wide-ranging discussion on this topic in Rabbi Yeḥiel Mikhel Tukachinsky's volume of relatively recent vintage, his *Gesher Ha-ḥayyim*.[1] But centuries earlier, Rabbi Moshe Isserles (1520–1572) already states quite explicitly that "when the son prays and sanctifies (i.e., recites Kaddish) in public, he redeems his father and mother from Gehenna."[2]

How that works is probably beyond our grasp; much like so many elements of faith.[3] Take, for example, something relatively simple, such as the idea of receiving a reward for fulfillment of the commandments. Traditional Jews speak about it all the time,[4] but does anyone really know how this "credit system" works? Is it a point system, based on degree of difficulty? Does it vary from *mitzvah* to *mitzvah*, or from person to person? How many points does a person have to accrue in order to "make it"? And what exactly does "making it" mean? Can one blockbuster *mitzvah* erase a large *mitzvah* deficit? Can one blockbuster sin erase a lifetime of good deeds? The truth is that as much as we talk about the concept of reward and punishment, we really do not know anything at all about it with certainty. And that is a good thing, because if we knew with certainty which of our good deeds are rewarded and in what specific way, all our actions would be focused on making it, on getting the points. But in doing so, we would almost entirely be missing the point.

A Disconnect

Back to Kaddish. In a famous talmudic passage, we read that the soul wanders between heaven and earth in the protective cover of the body throughout the twelve months following death:

> For all of the twelve months [after death], one's body is intact and one's soul rises and descends. After twelve months, [however], one's body is no longer intact and one's soul rises and cannot be forced to descend.[5]

This ostensibly is what we refer to when speaking about the elevation of the soul, a concept that is simple enough to express but exceedingly difficult to explain.

Even if we were able to truly define what "elevating the soul" means, we would still need to explain the dynamics of the process, and then to say clearly what precisely it is that we think saying Kaddish achieves. Does every recitation of Kaddish actually improve or elevate the soul of the deceased? Does it make a difference who is saying Kaddish for the deceased? Is a child saying Kaddish for a parent a more potent soul-elevator, or for that matter soul-escalator, than a stranger saying Kaddish for an unknown decedent? How does that really work, and why? For all that we ponder the Kaddish issue, however, there remains something elusive about the entire matter— and particularly about the reasons that this particular prayer has exerted such a hold on the Jewish people throughout the generations. It is so clear that Kaddish has nothing obvious to do with death and bereavement that we dare not ignore this glaring perplexity. And so I begin by asking the simplest questions: why Kaddish, of all prayers? And how did it ever get so intimately enmeshed into the struggle to extricate oneself from grief? For generations, mourning without Kaddish has simply been inconceivable. Yet we remain at a loss to explain how, and why, this has been the case.

The perplexing connection between Kaddish and mourning is comparable to suggesting that one can alleviate hunger by reading short stories and allowing oneself to be distracted by them. Some people who read may actually have their hunger alleviated, but there is no real cause-and-effect relationship. We can explain it along psychological lines: namely, that by focusing on things other than one's hunger, one would no longer feel the hunger, although it is still there. It is thus something of a mental trick. But can someone who is hungry, and who then does something as a result of which his or her attention is deflected from that hunger, truly be said to no longer be hungry?

Is the case of Kaddish analogous—that is, that by concentrating on one thing (namely, the prayer), is the mind deflected from thinking incessantly about something else (namely, the deceased, and one's grief)? Somehow, that does not seem to "click" as an explanation for why Kaddish "works." There must be a more purposeful agenda here, more than just getting the mind off mourning.

There have been many attempts to explain the connection between the Kaddish and the grieving process, but none has adequately explained the magic—for want of a better word—inherent in the larger enterprise of saying Kaddish repeatedly, over the course of a month or a year. The attempts are noble, sometimes even eloquent. But they still leave one wondering how this all came to be. It seems as if Kaddish came out of nowhere, and all the explanations are by way of after-the-fact justifications.

Purposeful Diversion

I would like to humbly suggest what may seem—indeed, what may be—a preposterous proposal: that Kaddish has nothing to do with death and bereavement, and that this is *precisely* the reason that it works so well. It is the purposeful, deliberate, intentional disconnect that makes the prayer work so effectively, if also paradoxically and even illogically.

Kaddish is a diversion from death and a counterpoint to bereavement; it is an antithesis to the thesis of loss, a purposeful radical departure from the logical process of putting salve on a wound to ease the pain. That purposefulness, I suggest, yields its desired result when people focus on life-matters at the very time that they are mired in sorrow. And indeed, at the very time that mourners are turned inward, the Kaddish turns them outward. It yanks them away from their internal concern of "How will I endure this misery?" to an external concern of "How will I make the world a better place?"

There is a story ascribed to Alfred Adler, the founding father of Individual Therapy. To someone who complained to him about being depressed, Adler reportedly offered advice along the lines of: "For the next two weeks, spend the first half hour after you awaken thinking about what you can do to help others. Your depression is sure to disappear." Clearly, this approach will not address all depressions. There simply is no magic bullet that can rectify all depressions, because depressions come in different sizes and shapes. But there are some depressions that are rooted in excessive focus on the self, on living in a closed-in world in which only the "me" matters. And it was to people suffering from that variety of depression that Adler was offering his good counsel.

A world in which only the "me" matters is a world with high walls, a world in which the light has difficulty shining, a world which can—and often does—become bleak and dark. It was to this reality that Adler addressed himself by suggesting that a tincture dose of self-transcendence, of going beyond one's self, of concentrating for a few brief moments on the plight of others, will perforce raise the depressed person out of the "me only" doldrums.

In my experience, sometimes a simple attitude shift is all it takes to extricate oneself from the gloom of both warranted and unwarranted sadness. That is what Adler was proposing, for what he undoubtedly thought was an attitudinally-based depression. Could it be that this Adlerian insight was at work when Kaddish so subtly entered into the mourner's repertoire of responses to loss? I say "subtly" because, to this day, we really do not know precisely when, how, or why Kaddish became the mourner's anthem.

Perhaps, just perhaps, the rabbis of yesteryear recognized that people were going about their mourning in a less than optimally effective way. They were trying to creep out of the mourning as best they could, but were only getting themselves deeper and deeper into their misery—somewhat like people struggling to climb out of a pit of quicksand who only become mired ever more deeply. What better way to avoid this almost inevitable trap than by deflecting the mourner's natural inward gaze, via a prayerful expression that obliges the bereaved to look out into the world?

But then, a funny strange thing happened: the very instrument of movement *away from* mourning itself became the vehicle *to express* mourning grief. What may have happened is that the magic elixir of self-transcendence that is the essence of Kaddish worked so well that people ascribed to it magical powers—or surely, at the very least, a psychologically powerful antidote to mourning.

People thought it was "working" but did not realize *why* it was working. They thought it was something inherent to the Kaddish itself that alleviated their grief, when in fact it was what the Kaddish gently achieved—the successful movement away from mourning and potential self-absorption, which leads almost inevitably to depression and its attendant ills—that had led to the amelioration of their grief, and the lessening of the weight of their loss.

Kaddish for Whom?

One of the earliest references to Kaddish, found in tractate Sofrim, offers an interesting perspective to the Kaddish:

> When the Holy Sanctuary was destroyed, the sages enacted that bridegrooms and mourners go to the synagogue in order [that others may] bestow kindness on them. Bridegrooms [go so that others may] praise them and [then] escort them to their homes. As for mourners, the *hazzan* [i.e., prayer

leader], after concluding the Musaf prayer, would move beyond the back doors of the synagogue...and there meet the mourners and all their relatives to recite for them the [Mourners'] Blessing and to recite Kaddish....⁶

This act of kindness to mourners took place on the Shabbat, when public displays of mourning were suspended. The gesture itself was apparently not considered a breach of the protocol proscribing public mourning on the Shabbat. Furthermore, the mourners were comforted via the Kaddish recited in Aramaic, the vernacular of the day. By using the spoken language of the day, the prayer leader ensured that the mourners understood the words. It is somewhat ironic that the vernacular of yesteryear is today so forgotten that the Kaddish is difficult for many to pronounce, let alone to understand.

Think about the mourner for a moment. Would a mourner be in the mood to hear this Kaddish, which had to be unwelcome in the days immediately following a devastating loss—even if it was a Shabbat? My guess is that most of the words probably fell on deaf ears, because the mourners were *not* in the right frame of mind to absorb the essence of the Kaddish message. Remember too that if the message was in Aramaic, it is quite likely precisely because the mourners were not regular attendees at prayer services and could not be expected to be well-versed in liturgical intricacies. If that is the case, then speaking to them in their usual language made eminent sense, in that it increased the chance that the Kaddish message would get through.

Concerning the assumption that mourners may not have been regular synagogue attendees, consider the observation of Naḥmanides, commenting on the end of the Sofrim passage quoted above. There, the text of Sofrim notes that it is the regular Kaddish that is recited by the *ḥazzan* for the mourners, not the Kaddish that refers to the World to Come.⁷ Regarding this, Nahmanides writes: "The reason for this is that we do not mention the new world (i.e., the World to Come) except for one whose deeds clearly indicate that such person is worthy of being resurrected (i.e., in the new world); but for ordinary people, we do not [mention it]."[8]

Moreover, in explaining why the Kaddish is in Aramaic, we are told that there were ignorant people who were not all conversant in the holy tongue, Hebrew; therefore, the recitation of the Kaddish was instituted in Aramaic so that all could understand, as that was the common language.[9] This all adds up to the fascinating conclusion that Kaddish—at the very least, the text and the language (Aramaic) of the text—was directed at the less-than-fully involved members of the community.

The Impact of Kaddish

But why even the regular Kaddish? As noted, tractate Sofrim teaches us that it was not the mourners who recited the Kaddish; it was the *ḥazzan*. And a further point to ponder is: what about Kaddish, if anything, would have resonated with the mourners at all, to the extent that the practice of the *ḥazzan* going immediately outside the synagogue to meet the mourners was introduced? And: what, of what they would have heard, would have impacted them so meaningfully that their grief would be assuaged, at least somewhat, by the experience?

Although I do not have a source to cite to support my answer, my hunch is that the second word of the Kaddish, *v'yitkaddash*—from which word the "Kaddish" derives its name as well—perhaps that was the word that pierced the souls of the mourners. And so did the progression begin in their minds: from *yitkaddash* to *kadosh* (literally "holy," but also a common designation of God, the Holy One), to *kiddush ha-sheim* (literally "the sanctification of the name [i.e., of God]," and generally the usual Jewish term for martyrdom, but more simply the name of the commandment to sanctify God in the world that God created, of which martyrdom is merely the ultimate example). And so, if I am correct, the leader of the prayers was asking the mourners to engage in *kiddush ha-sheim*, sanctification of God's name. This was more than simply hoping and praying that God's name be sanctified; it was a call to action. When the leader went to the mourners and expressed this wish, the latter could not help but think that they were being drafted into this endeavor. The mourners' loud, resonant "Amen" was then nothing other than a ringing endorsement of the proposal thus put to them. (Kaddish today is recited by the mourners, not *for* them, so the sense of being called to a higher duty is not as clear.)

The community was requesting that the mourners respond to loss by rededicating themselves to the great *mitzvah* of *kiddush ha-sheim*, rejoining the community that they had left behind. This may originally have happened spontaneously, as the established community seized the opportunity to draw the mourners in their midst back to life, by calling them to perform the most noble of all tasks: sanctifying God's name.

Although it sounds cogent, I doubt that this theory is fully correct. Surely the time could not have been right for recruitment even for a noble goal. It was probably not recruitment at all, therefore, that was behind the Kaddish initiative (even though a recruitment, of sorts, did result as a by-product).

A Kindness Custom

What if the community leaders of the day, seeing mourners mired in grief, sought something to help them in their moments of intense travail...and came up with the anti-depressant that was to become known as the Kaddish?

From the text in Sofrim, it seems that the institution of Kaddish is an extension of the insight that once inspired King Solomon who, apprehending the power of kindness, built special "kindness gates" in the Temple: one for bridegrooms and one for mourners, one gate for the people to interact kindly with the bridegrooms and the other gate to interact kindly with the mourners.[10]

The custom described above, of the *ḥazzan* going to the mourners to recite the blessing and then the Kaddish, was designed as a carryover from the practice instituted by Solomon in Temple times concerning the acts of kindness for [grooms and] mourners at the Temple gates. The Kaddish may thus be interpreted as a ritual designed to permit the congregation to show kindness to the mourners in their midst. But this Kaddish, according to tractate Sofrim, was said *to* the mourners, not *by* the mourners. How exactly did that work? What elevation of the soul was thereby achieved?

The kindness shown to the mourners by reciting Kaddish *to* them was not so much to effect the elevation of the soul of the deceased, as much as it was to effect the elevation of the mood of the mourners from the depths of despair to the heights of opportunity. It took place on Shabbat, on the very day when the tight constraints of mourning are loosened somewhat and mourners may thus licitly catch a glimpse of the life of meaning that still awaited them. And why was this done on the day when public mourning is proscribed, on Shabbat, if not precisely because this was specifically *not* an exercise in mourning? Indeed, it was just the opposite: it was an exercise in going beyond mourning and despair. It was an act of communal kindness.

If all that has been suggested herein is correct, it puts an entirely different slant on the Kaddish. We dare not deny the mystical component to Kaddish, the impact that the Kaddish is intended to have on the soul of the deceased. But what I am suggesting is that the Kaddish is a multi-faceted expression, one with potential impact both on the soul of the deceased and also on the emotional and spiritual well-being of the mourner.

Mourners as Sanctifiers

How, indeed, does God's great name become sanctified? By people behaving in an exemplary manner, thereby inspiring others to acknowledge God and to affirm God's majesty. But what does this have to do with mourning? The immediate connection to the mourners is that with the death of their loved one, there is one less person in the world able to sanctify God's name. The mourners are called upon to redouble their efforts in this regard, and thus personally to address the deficit by becoming public sanctifiers of God's name.

This at once helps them out of despair by giving them a meaning-oriented outlook toward the outer world just when they are prone to be focused most intensely inward. By sanctifying God's great name through their deeds, mourners elevate the souls of the deceased by elevating God in the eyes of humankind. The Kaddish, though recited in the synagogue, thus becomes a call to mourners to go beyond the synagogue, to immerse themselves in the great effort of *tikkun olam*, of making God's world more worthy of its divine Creator.

Admittedly, this may be a far cry from what most think Kaddish to be about. But it is not as preposterous as it may seem. Consider the following words by Rabbi Tukachinsky:

> With the recitation of the Kaddish, one should not imagine oneself to be saying it [i.e., the Kaddish] in order to shield the deceased [from posthumous punishment]; rather the entire intent should be to sanctify God's great and blessed

name, [secure in the knowledge that by virtue of that] merit [i.e., the merit earned through the recitation of the Kaddish as an act of sanctifying God's holy name], the deceased will be saved from the judgment of Gehenna."[11]

This is the same Rabbi Tukachinsky who fully endorses the mystical notion of elevation of souls, of saving souls from hell via the recitation of Kaddish. Yet he speaks at the very same time about the sanctifying of God's great name as the *fundamental* intent of the Kaddish, as the act by means of which the elevation of the soul (or its rescue from hell) is achieved.

Critical in all this is having the proper intention. According to Rabbi Tukachinsky, the proper intention that we should bring to the recitation of Kaddish is that this practice is to help us sanctify God's name in the world—and not simply to shield, save, or elevate the soul of the deceased. Nor is it irrelevant that he presents this notion not as a personal opinion, but as an obvious truth.

One may wonder what exactly would be wrong with people reciting the Kaddish simply in order to elevate the souls of their departed loved ones. Is that not what most people, including learned individuals, intend when they recite the Kaddish? Would any rabbi tell those reciting Kaddish for that reason that they are in error? Yet having only this specific intention in mind while reciting the prayer reduces Kaddish to the level of magical incantation, by setting it atop the truly preposterous notion that merely by mouthing words—even the nicest ones—we cause the soul of the deceased to be saved or elevated. This makes little sense. Further, it reduces the potential for a profound connection with God *and* with the deceased to a push-button, cause-and-effect exercise empty of any real meaning. The Kaddish gains its most significant meaning when it is understood as a call to action, and when that call is answered in a sanctifying way.

An Inspiring Irony

It is more than ironic that those who bemoan Kaddish because it does nothing for them are in their own way echoing the view of Rabbi Tukachinsky—or, more precisely, the logical view that Rabbi Tukachinsky articulates so clearly—to the effect that making Kaddish into a causal expression is ultimately a distortion of what Kaddish is all about. It is more than ironic because the bemoaners are more likely to be among those Jews who do not frequent the synagogue—the very people for whom Kaddish was probably initiated as a mourning protocol practice, beyond the central role of Kaddish in congregational prayer.

Perhaps we have come full circle, and now those for whom Kaddish was originally intended are reminding us of what Kaddish is not. But even more importantly, they are reminding us of what Kaddish *should* be: a wake-up call to infuse life with good deeds, deeds that sanctify God in the minds and hearts of others and thus elevate both the living and the departed.

What started off sounding like a far-out idea—namely, Kaddish as essentially purposeful diversion—now seems almost self-evident. But if the idea sounds cogent and reasonable, its actual application would signal a radical change in how Kaddish is understood by most.

How many people come away from recitation of Kaddish imbued with the responsibility actually to go out and sanctify God's name? Not many! Yet I would argue that this is the great secret of the Kaddish…albeit one lost in the translation over the years, and to the detriment of those who vainly search for the magic in Kaddish.

The Kaddish has "helped" so many over the course of past generations, because people then understood what Kaddish was telling them, what it was *asking* of them. Over time, people heard the Kaddish and saw the impact it could have, but missed the connection between saying and impact. They did not see the deeds done by the mourners as a response to the call of the Kaddish. And in missing this step, they jumped to the wrong conclusion about Kaddish—a serious misunderstanding that beckons to be fixed.

This is somewhat reminiscent of a story I heard years ago regarding the Chelmite who saw the seemingly magical effect that sounding an alarm had on the men of the fire brigade of a neighboring village, who came to put out a fire almost immediately upon hearing the alarm. He came back to his community excited that he had discovered an inexpensive way to put out fires: all you need to do, he explained, is buy an alarm bell. Then, when there is a fire, all anyone has to do is sound it and the fire will be doused instantaneously. The community was delighted by this new discovery, confident they were now as good as fire-proof. And, indeed, when a fire broke out, they ran to sound the alarm. There was lots of noise, of course, but no fire wagons, no water, and no fire fighters. Instead, the fire caused serious damage to community buildings. The Chelmites were obviously upset and angry, and so they sent a delegation to the city where the system actually worked. They were shocked to learn that there was no magic to the bell. The bell simply sounded a call to action, as there was a fire brigade already set up and poised to react when the alarm was heard. But a fire alarm system with no fire brigade in place to react is absolutely useless.[12]

Where We Go from Here

There are many who think they have captured the "magic" of Kaddish, only to be mistaken in their presumption. Think of how much better they would actually feel, if they saw the full import of the Kaddish for mourners!

The approach I am suggesting for the Mourner's Kaddish is no less pertinent for non-mourners who attend prayer servers on a regular (or even a less-than-regular) basis. The Kaddish for them too is a call to action, a call to sanctify God via their deeds. But it was mourners to whom a special, laser-precision directive, was originally addressed.

In the end, the magic of Kaddish inheres in the fact that it is not magic at all—in the fact, in fact, that it is anti-magic. We simply need to rediscover its profound purpose. That can be attained by recognizing the fundamental idea that we must magnifiy God's glory in the world—an idea that pertains not only to Kaddish but to all entreaties, liturgical and otherwise. Prayer itself will never be enough, as long as it remains inner-focused. For example, praying to God for good health without doing our part to care for our health misses a key point. Similarly, asking, hoping, or praying that God be sanctified—as encapsulated in the word that gave its name to the Kaddish itself, *yitkaddash*—is sorely deficient if we are not inspired enough to *do* what we can to make that happen.

Those who heed the call of Kaddish, who translate that call into sanctifying deeds, make the original rabbinic intent behind the establishment of Kaddish as a prayer for mourners become a vibrant reality. And mourners, through making the world a better place, highlight and answer the question with which I began: Why Kaddish?

The implicit hope in this approach is that the mourners will, in the process of this call to look out at the world, find comfort in the interior chambers of their own hearts—and that is, of course, slightly ironic. But mourners, who may well have been obsessively involved in the vanities of life and the pursuit of material gain, will understand the impact of death as proof that wasting time on empty pursuits is not what life is all about. The Kaddish steps in when death crashes into the pattern of the mourners, offering the chance to redirect one's energies to endeavors that will have lasting value, endeavors that express godly values. Kaddish, in its most familiar iteration as a prayer "for" mourners, is designed to do something beneficial for everyone.

NOTES

[1] Yeḥiel Mikhel Tukachinsky, *Gesher Ha-ḥayyim* (Jerusalem: Salmon Press, 1960), vol. 1, pp. 313–318, and particularly pp. 315–316 regarding the "redemption" of the deceased.

[2] S.A. Yoreh Dei·ah 376:4. Gehenna is the anglicization of the Hebrew *geihinnom*, a regular designation for hell in rabbinic literature.

[3] Regarding this notion of the redemption of the soul of the deceased, see several other essays in this volume, particularly the ones by Martin S. Cohen, Ruth Walfish, and Orna Triguboff.

[4] See Deuteronomy 11:13–21, particularly the last verse. The regular way people talk about "doing" a *mitzvah* and getting "credit" for having fulfilled a *mitzvah* implicitly refer to this system.

[5] B. Shabbat 152b. My translation follows the interpretation of Tosafot as given on B. Shabbat 153a, s.v. *v'nishmato olah v'shuv einah yoredet.*

[6] Sofrim 19:9, ed. Michael Higger (New York: Hotza·at D'vei Rabbanan, 5697 [1936/1937]), p. 336. The "Mourner's Blessing" is referenced in the Talmud (see, e.g., the text at B. Megillah 23b) and is a text intended to comfort that concludes with a reference to God as the "Comforter of the bereaved."

[7] Cf. Sofrim 19:12.

[8] Naḥmanides, *Sefer Torat Ha-adam*, published in *Kitvei Rabbeinu Mosheh ben Naḥman* (5728 [1967/1968]; rpt. Jerusalem: Mossad Harav Kook, 2006), p. 155.

[9] This is the opinion of the Tosafot as set forth at B. Berakhot 3a, s.v. *hayah l'kha l'hitpalleil t'fillah k'tzarah.*

[10] Sofrim 19:12 (beginning).

[11] Tukachinsky, *Gesher Ha-ḥayyim*, vol. 1, p. 316, note 2.

[12] A majority of the residents of Chełm, a city in eastern Poland near Lublin, were Jewish, until the community was annihilated during the Shoah. In Eastern European Jewish folk-tradition, the residents of the town were thought of as fools and many folktales about them and their foolishness were widely known. Where this specific story has its origin, I cannot say.

Kaddish and the Red Heifer

Benjamin Blech

Death is more than a personal tragedy. In a profound sense it is a test of faith. It makes us question the meaning of life as well as the existence of a just and divine Ruler of the universe. It challenges us with the fear of ultimate extinction. It makes us uncertain if we are indeed created in the image of God.

Mortality seems to deny our unique place in the scheme of creation. It drives us to adopt existentialism as our credo. Since life will lead us only to the grave, life is meaningless and nothing less than absurd—a tale, as Shakespeare put it, "told by an idiot, full of sound and fury, signifying nothing."[1]

That is why death requires a religious response.

In Torah law, direct contact with death—even with a corpse, even of a person with whom one had no familial relationship—is considered a source of *tumah*, a word that is almost impossible to define in English. Standard translations render it as "uncleanness," making it erroneously appear as if it had something to do with hygienic practice. Jewish commentators are clear that *tumah* refers to a kind of spiritual impurity, an impurity whose effect is not on the body but on the soul of the person who has been physically exposed to death.

Somehow, getting too close to death diminishes our potential to experience sanctity. The Talmud connects the word *tumah* to the word *timtum*, "confusion."[2] We experience confusion about life and its purpose, even as we question our spiritual values, in a confrontation with the reality of death. Samson Raphael Hirsch, in his commentary on Numbers 19:13, explains that "every dead human body represents the mortality of human beings, and the danger is very near to lead to thinking of this physical lack of freedom which death demonstrates as extending also to the cyclical nature of man in its connection with the physical during life."[3] As human beings, we are meant to understand our unique capability as free-willed agents to choose between right and wrong, between good and evil. Contact with death momentarily diminishes this awareness within us. Mordechai Becher summed this up well:

> When we see a corpse, we confront physical forces overpowering the spiritual; we can perceive only the material side of the human being, and we become confused and depressed. That which we thought was lofty and eternal seems to be merely decaying flesh. In reality, the essence of the deceased person lives on, but the impression formed by our senses is so overwhelming that we momentarily forget this truth and focus instead on death as the ultimate end, the final victory of earth over heaven. This confusion lies at the heart of the concept of impurity, *tumah*.[4]

In general, the sources of *tumah* other than direct contact with a corpse—such as someone stricken with a form of skin disease biblically called *tzara·at*, for example—are in some way associated with death (or a missed chance for potential life), and the spiritual correlate to *tumah* is depression or despair. Death, Jewish law makes clear, is *avi avot ha-tumah*, the primary source of religious impurity. Conversely, the purification process invariably involves some type of reaffirmation of life.

It is from this perspective that we must come to analyze the remarkable ritual of the red heifer (*parah adummah*), the seemingly incomprehensible set of laws meant to "cleanse" those who have become impure by contact with a dead body. It is certainly noteworthy, and no small irony, that the Torah's response to the enigma of death is the most perplexing of all biblical laws. We read, in Numbers 19:2: "This is the statute [*hukkat*]of the law that the Eternal has commanded." The elaboration of the detailed laws regarding the red heifer that follows represents the paradigmatic *hok*: inexplicable, seemingly irrational, and perhaps even self-contradictory.[6]

Death and the law of the *parah adummah* share in their inscrutability. Much as we try, both appear to be beyond our comprehension. Yet if we are to retain faith, we need to seek at least some level of explanation.

Searching for Explanations

There are a number of instances in the Torah of laws described specifically as *hukkim*[7] ("statutes"). Midrash Tanḥuma points out that four of them not only have no apparent reason but in fact seem eminently unreasonable;[8] about them "the evil inclination" may well argue. The midrash states:

> It is written, "You shall not uncover the nakedness of your brother's wife; it is your brother's nakedness" (Leviticus 18:16). And yet it is also written: "If brothers dwell together and one of them dies, having no child, the wife of the dead shall not be married abroad unto one not of his kin; her husband's brother shall go in to her, and take her to him to wife, and perform the duty of a husband's brother to her" (Deuteronomy 25:5).

So too, the midrash points out, a mixture of wool and linen is forbidden (Leviticus 19:19, Deuteronomy 22:11)—and yet for the *mitzvah* of *tzitzit*, the fringes biblically required to be attached to a four-cornered garment (Numbers 15:37–41), it is permissible. In the Yom Kippur ceremony of the two goats, the one in charge of the goat that is to be sent to its death in Azazel becomes unclean and must wash his clothes and bathe his flesh (Leviticus 16:26), and yet he himself effects atonement for others (Leviticus 16:22). And, finally, the red heifer renders impure the garments of all those involved in its preparations, and yet its ashes serve as the source of purification for someone who has come into contact with a corpse.[9]

Each one of these cases transcends our ability to rationalize or to comprehend. Each one illustrates the category of *ḥok*. And yet it is the law of the red heifer alone that is prefaced with the words, "*This is the statute of the Torah*" (*zot ḥukkat ha-torah*). This is the one law that stands at the apex of the suprarational category. It is the most paradoxical of all—and it is the one designated by God as the biblical response to our mortality, the greatest mystery of our existence.

The midrash underscores the unique place that the law of the red heifer occupies in the category of *ḥukkim* when it points out that King Solomon, the wisest of all men, was able to penetrate the secrets of the other statutes—but when faced with the law of the red heifer, he had to admit that its logic was beyond him. Even he remained humbled by the limitations of human intelligence when it came to understanding the biblical rituals surrounding death and the ways we are to respond to our inevitable encounters with it.[10]

Yet we are not to assume that this proves that the *parah adummah* defied understanding precisely because it is in fact not intelligible—a law with no logic, decreed solely as a test of our willingness to obey even what is not reasonable simply because it represents the will of God. The midrash elsewhere makes clear that although Solomon was unable to understand this enigmatic statute, that doesn't imply that there isn't a divine secret concealed within it. Indeed, what Solomon could not grasp *was* revealed to Moses:

> Said Rabbi Yosi son of Rabbi Ḥanina: The blessed Holy One said to Moses, "To you I reveal the rationale of the red heifer, but to others it shall remain simply as statute (*ḥok*)."[11]

This *ḥok*, like the others, is not irrational but suprarational. Its deepest meaning may have escaped even Solomon, but it was entrusted to Moses. The man charged with teaching it to the Jewish people needed to feel confident about transmitting only those laws that he understood to be consistent with some standard of logic and truth.

For this reason, many commentators rightly felt hesitant about offering their own interpretations of this paradigmatic *ḥok*. If God intentionally revealed the secret of the *parah adummah* only to Moses, perhaps it was meant to remain an unsolved mystery for the rest of us.

The *Sefer Ha-ḥinnukh*, attributed to the renowned Rabbi Aharon Halevi of Barcelona, was written with the stated goal of explaining the 613 *mitzvot*.[12] To that end, it offers many illuminating insights and explanations for Torah laws. Yet in the section on the red heifer, Rabbi Aharon Halevi writes that although he justified his efforts to put forth reasons for biblical laws as a way to teach and inspire his son and friends, when he came to this *mitzvah* his "hands weakened."[13] He was unable to offer interpretations for a law about which even King Solomon admitted his ignorance; indeed, God had told Moses that its reason would be revealed only to him. We might very well then conclude that any discussion about the meaning of the mysterious law of the red heifer is inappropriate.

And yet, remarkably enough, the Torah commentary of Rashi (1040–1105) seems to attempt precisely that task. At the very outset of his commentary on Numbers 19, Rashi's approach appears to echo the warning against any efforts to rationalize the laws of the red heifer:

> *This is the statute of the Torah:* Because Satan and the nations of the world taunt Israel, saying, "What is this commandment, and what purpose does it have?" Therefore, the Torah uses the term "statute" (*ḥok*). I have decreed it; you have no right to challenge it.[14]

Both Satan and the nations of the world are cited as being particularly troubled by this *mitzvah*, with the plaint that it has no discernible explanation.[15] Precisely for that reason the Torah refers to it as a *ḥok*: it is a decree from God, and humans are not to question it.

In a somewhat unusual format, Rashi continues to offer concise comments on the text of Numbers 19 until he reaches verse 22, the end of the pericope dealing with the red heifer. But at that point he takes us back again to the very beginning of the chapter in order to introduce a totally different approach to *parah adummah* that offers a rationale for its laws.[16] In this approach, the response to Satan and the nations of the world is not simply to claim legitimacy for the laws of the red heifer as a divine decree that neither requires nor allows for human understanding. In a seemingly radical departure from his opening statement ("I have decreed it; you have no right to challenge it"), Rashi concludes his commentary with an approach that links rituals with symbolic meaning, imbuing them with comprehensible purpose.

In this approach, Rashi suggests that the *mitzvah* of the red heifer (*parah adummah*) is to be understood in conjunction with the sin of the golden calf (*eigel ha-zahav*), narrated in Exodus 32. Rashi draws out the following points of comparison between the two:[17]

> 1. Just as the Jews took their golden jewelry to build an idol in the form of an *eigel* (Exodus 32:3), they must now show

their willingness to offer a rare and costly *parah* as an act of atonement.[18]

2. The *parah* is to be red (Numbers 19:2), because that is the color that symbolizes sin (Isaiah 1:18).

3. The *parah* is to be "perfect" (*t'mimah*, Numbers 19:2); prior to the *eigel* the Jews had been "perfect," but they became blemished through the sin of the golden calf and so they now need to be restored to their original purity.

4. The red heifer must be one that never had a yoke placed upon it (Numbers 19:2), symbolic of the people's sin in throwing off the "yoke of heaven."

5. Just as the Jews surrounded Aaron, the high priest, and forced him to make the golden calf (Exodus 32:1), the ritual of the red heifer was to be performed by a priest. However, the ritual of the red heifer was to be performed by Aaron's son, Eleazar (Numbers 19:3), because of the principle that *ein kateigor na·aseh saneigor* ("the prosecution cannot also serve as the defense"):[19] since Aaron had made the golden calf, he is not allowed to play a part in the process of atonement for that sin.

6. The *parah* must be burnt (Numbers 19:5), to correspond to the fate of the molten *eigel* (Exodus 32:20).

7. The three materials mentioned in conjunction with the red heifer—cedar, hyssop, and scarlet yarn (Numbers 19:6)—correspond to the 3000 men who perished as a result of their role in the sin of the golden calf (Exodus 32:28). Moreover, the cedar is the tallest of trees and the hyssop the lowest; their inclusion in the ritual was meant as a sign that the loftiest, whose pride caused them to sin, must lower themselves in order to gain forgiveness.

8. Just as the guilt for the sin of the golden calf would be remembered for generations,[20] so too is this law of the red heifer meant as an eternal reminder of our mortality (Numbers 19:9).

9. And finally, just as the golden calf rendered impure all

those who were involved with it, so too did the red heifer;[21] and just as the ashes of the golden calf served to purify sinners, so did the ashes of the red heifer serve the same purpose (Numbers 19:17–19).[22]

The thematic connections between *eigel* and *parah* are striking, adding a totally new dimension to what we had assumed was simply *hok*—senseless, irrational, and devoid of meaning. The laws of the red heifer, according to this analysis, are all comprehensible as allusions to another major event of our past, a linkage with lasting messages crucial to the preservation of our people's spiritual purity.

We are left to wonder: if these insights are indeed legitimate, why then were they beyond the ability of King Solomon to fathom? And if, as the midrash claims, God chose to reveal only to Moses the esoteric meanings of the rite, then how could a medieval commentator such as Rashi feel justified in exploring its deeper meaning? Rabbi Menaḥem Recanati, the thirteenth-century Italian scholar famous for his kabbalistic commentary on the Torah, offered an interesting answer to this question:

> The intent of the midrash which taught that God desired to reveal the reason for the red heifer only to Moses never meant to suggest that *all* of its laws were to be sealed from our comprehension; only one small specific aspect was designated as secret information. What even King Solomon was unable to explain was why the one who was sprinkled with the ashes became pure, even as the person performing the sprinkling was rendered impure. That, and that alone, is the inexplicable *hok*. The rest of the ritual contains many messages that we are not only permitted, but perhaps even duty-bound, to understand.[23]

That is why the symbolism associated with the red heifer deserves our careful attention and study. It is the Torah's response to death. And while we no longer have the ability to fulfill the procedure of the *parah adummah* as biblically commanded, we surely have much to gain from an analysis of the ideas associated with the ritual we were meant to enact in the aftermath of our contact with the dead.

As we discussed at the outset, death frightens us. Death forces us to question our belief in the goodness of God. Death makes us wonder if the world is governed by a truly just and divine Ruler. Death is perhaps the greatest challenge to our faith. In spiritual terms, death is the key source of *tumah*, an impurity that threatens our continued relationship with the Almighty. How were the laws of the red heifer meant to help us cope in the aftermath of our confrontation with mortality? And how, at a time of great spiritual weakness, could its message return us to purity? The answer, I believe, can be found in the fascinating link of the *parah adummah* with two biblical narratives: the story of Jacob and Esau and the birthright, and the story of the golden calf.

The Color Red and Death

Clearly, the most striking feature of the *parah adummah* is its color. That is what made it so difficult to obtain. And, indeed, improper color constituted the most important reason to proclaim the animal unfit: the heifer had to be completely red and was disqualified if there were even two black hairs on it.[24] What is this requirement meant to teach us?

I was blessed to hear Rabbi Soloveitchik develop the thesis that when biblical laws are couched in symbolic language, their true message and meaning can always be discovered in earlier Torah stories.

If the color red plays such a prominent role in a law that deals with our response to death, it must have a prequel in a different biblical passage in which red is featured and the focus is on a similar theme.

It is simple enough to identify the Torah story that fulfills this requirement: it is the transaction in which Jacob buys Esau's birthright for a bowl of lentil stew (Genesis 25:27–34). It is a seminal moment in the life of one of our patriarchs, one which was to determine both the history and destiny of the Jewish people—guaranteeing that Jacob and his descendants, rather than Esau, were to be the recipients of Isaac's spiritual patrimony. And although not emphasized in the text, rabbinic commentary makes clear that death (and the way in which we respond to it) is key to understanding this narrative.

On the surface, the incident seems rather prosaic. While Esau is out hunting, Jacob is cooking soup. When the older brother comes in from the field, he begs, "Pour me please, I pray, some of this red, red pottage; for I am faint" (verse 30). Two times, remarkably enough, we are told the color of the soup, seemingly to further emphasize it.[25] Yet even that apparently isn't sufficient. After the request for the red soup, the Torah immediately adds, "Therefore was his name called Edom/Red" (verse 30). In exchange for the soup, Jacob insists that Esau sell him the birthright. Esau replies, "Behold I am going to die, and what need have I for the birthright?!" (verse 32)—a response, as we will see from the midrash, with a deep and profound meaning. At this moment, Esau "despised his birthright" and sold it for a mess of red pottage, and it was then that he got the name that would forevermore identify his people by way of the color red, Edom.

What is the subtext of this story, that allows a pot of soup to play such a prominent role in Jewish history? And what does all this have to do with death?

Obviously this was no ordinary soup. It had ritual significance, which is the reason it was important enough to be mentioned:

Jacob had just heard of the death of his grandfather, Abraham. As was customary even then, he prepared the mourner's meal for his father—a soup with lentils, whose rounded shape is meant to suggest the eternal cycle of life and death.[26] When Esau came back from the field he did not yet know what had happened to his grandfather. Jacob shared the sad news, as he explained the reason for his cooking preparations. Esau was stunned: "My loved ones and my enemies share the same fate?! Abraham dies and Nimrod dies?!" His response to the news of the death of the righteous was the loss of his faith.[27]

Another midrash clarifies Esau's reaction even further:

And Jacob was cooking a soup: He [Esau] said to him [Jacob]: "What is the nature of this soup? [I.e., why are you making it?]" He [Jacob] said to him [Esau]: "Because that elder [i.e., Abraham] died." He [Esau] said, "That elder was accosted by the attribute of strict justice?" He [Jacob] responded, "Yes." He [Esau] then said, "If so, there is no granting of reward; neither is there resurrection of the dead."[28]

Overwhelmed by the realization that even someone as holy as his grandfather was mortal, Esau saw in the red color of the soup the color of blood[29]—an affirmation of his conviction that human beings are no more than flesh and blood. Red is the ultimate reality of our existence. Red is who we are, defined by our physical nature and ultimately doomed by our corporeality. We may as well eat, drink, and be merry, for it is our certain fate that tomorrow we too shall die, with no hope for any other future.

Contact with death caused Esau to become spiritually impure. He denied the doctrine of the resurrection of the dead, which rabbinic Judaism considered a fundamental belief.[30] He was willing to barter away the birthright so cheaply, because it no longer meant anything to him. "Behold I'm going to die"—and if the end of every human being is death, then it is absurd to be concerned with the privileges and blessings that are the legacy of the birthright.

It is fascinating to note that there appears to be a profound psychological link between Esau's character and his strong attraction to the color red.[31] The Lüscher Color Test is a psychological quiz invented by Dr. Max Lüscher (b.1923) in Basel, Switzerland.[32] Lüscher believed that sensory perception of color is objective and universally shared by all, but that color preferences are subjective—and that this distinction allows subjective states to be objectively measured by using test colors. Lüscher posited that because the color selections in the test are guided in an unconscious manner, they reveal people as they really are, not as they perceive themselves or would like to be perceived. Many doctors, psychologists, government agencies, and universities (particularly in Europe) use the Lüscher color test to screen candidates. Some psychologists (again, particularly in Europe) use the Lüscher color test to assist in helping to identify personality traits, as well to yield information about a patient's physical, mental, and emotional state.[33]

With regard to the color red, Lüscher writes:

> To primitive man, activity as a rule took one of two forms—either he was hunting and attacking, or he was being hunted and defending himself against attack: activity directed towards conquest and acquisition or activity directed towards self-preservation. The outgoing actions of attack and conquest are universally represented by the color red; self-preservation by its complement, green.
> Since his actions, whether of attack (red) or defense (green) were at least under his control, these factors and colors are described as "autonomous," or self-regulating. On the other hand, attack being an acquisitive and outgoing action is considered to be "active," while defense, being concerned only with self-preservation, is considered to be "passive."[34]

How fitting that Esau, introduced to us as *ish yodei·a tzayid ish sadeh* ("a cunning hunter, a man of the field," Genesis 25:27) had the perfect psychological profile of Edom the Red!

A summary of a red-color-preference person includes the following:

Above all else, red values freedom of expression. It wants to do what it wants, when it wants, to whom it wants, and nobody can tell it otherwise. It believes that life would be much more fun if everyone stopped caring about rules, laws, and personal appearances and just spent their time indulging their desires. This leads into red's other core value: chaos. Red sees order of any kind as pointlessly inhibiting, believing that only through embracing anarchy could everyone really be free to enjoy life to the fullest. Finally, red is the color of immediate action and immediate gratification. If it wants something it will act on its impulses and take it, regardless of what the consequences may be.[35]

Esau wanted the soup *now* and forfeited the future.[36] Immediate gratification was his lifestyle. Red was his other name; red was the color of the soup he could not resist. His name, thus, was both descriptive of his appearance...and his essence.

Unfortunately the Torah doesn't reveal to us Jacob's color preference. We do know, though, from this story that Jacob responded to death in a totally different manner. Instead of losing his faith, he chose this moment to fulfill the *mitzvah* of preparing a mourner's meal and then to secure a spiritual blessing. Death spurred him to greater piety, even as it destroyed his sibling's belief.

How was that possible? Simply because *the very same experience that has the power to render a person impure incredibly enough brings with it the exact opposite potential as well: the ability to engender even greater purity.*

In Pirkei Avot, we are taught the ideal way to combat our inclination to sin:

> Akaviah the son of Mahalalel would say: Reflect upon three things and you will not come to the hands of transgression. Know from where you came, where you are going, and before whom you are destined to give a judgment and accounting. From where you came—from a putrid drop; where you are going—to a place of dust, maggots, and worms; and before whom you are destined to give a judgment and accounting—before the supreme Sovereign of sovereigns, the blessed Holy One. (Pirkei Avot 3:1)

The recognition of our mortality, far from ensuring a loss of faith, can inspire us to make the most of our limited time here on earth. Instead of encouraging us to adopt a hedonistic lifestyle, it can lead us to realize that the judgment of eternity is far more meaningful than any temporal pleasures. Knowing that we will die can be the most powerful motivation to teach us how to live.

Elisabeth Kübler-Ross, the famous pioneer of near-death studies, put it well: "It's only when we truly know and understand that we have a limited time on earth—and that we have no way of knowing when our time is up—that we will begin to live each day to the fullest, as if it was the only one we had."[37] So too, Jacob's response to death was to choose spiritual privilege over red pottage. As a result of this decision, the children of Israel were blessed to be entrusted with spreading Abraham's message of monotheism to the rest of the world.

The color red emphasized by the ritual of the *parah adummah* links us to a seminal moment of our history: a moment of response to death that had the seemingly paradoxical effect, at one and the same time, of creating both purity and impurity. It was the very same spiritual challenge to faith faced by Esau and Jacob as they confronted the death of their righteous grandfather Abraham.

For Esau, death confirmed our finite existence. It "proved" that we are no more than flesh and blood. It strengthened his resolve to live life in the moment; to grab immediate pleasure over long-term privilege; to be guided by the traits of the "red personality" and to forsake belief in God. "Eat, drink, and be merry, for tomorrow we will die" was his maxim, centuries before Epicurus made it the primary focus of his Epicurean philosophy—even as it would come to identify a heretic as an *epikoros*.

For Jacob, contemplating death brought him to a higher level for comprehending life's purpose. Recognizing the brevity of our years on earth made him all the more sensitive to the need to endow them with spiritual meaning. Acknowledging mortality provided him with greater wisdom and idealism.

This dichotomy of reaction to death resonates powerfully with us as well. Esau's conclusion continues to echo among many grieving mourners to this day. Confronting the reality of the death of loved ones, they simply cannot believe that a just God could allow the righteous to perish. "If this is so," they conclude with Esau, "then there is no reward and I can no longer believe in God."

We need to choose—intellectually and emotionally—between the reactions of Esau and Jacob. The red of the heifer reminds us of the biblical test of soup versus birthright.

Remembering the story of Jacob and Esau, and the red pottage, is a powerful reminder that death need not destroy our relationship with God; quite the reverse, it may strengthen our bond with God and inspire us to live life in a way that proclaims *yitgaddal v'yitkaddash sh'meih rabba*, "May God's great name be glorified and sanctified."

The Golden Calf and Death

The story in Genesis, however, is not the sole biblical text that resonates with the law of the red heifer. That biblical commandment also draws us to another pivotal moment of Jewish history. Focusing on the "red" of the *parah adummah* reminds us of the story of Jacob and Esau, but focusing on the "heifer" directs our attention to a different biblical story involving a bovine: the scene shortly after Moses ascended Mount Sinai to receive the two tablets of stone and the Ten Commandments: the story of the golden calf. Making and worshipping the golden calf was a sin of incredible magnitude; coming so soon after the experience of revelation, it seems in retrospect almost unimaginable. How could a people who had personally heard the voice of the Almighty become guilty of the crime of idolatry? And yet the text tells us, "When the people saw that Moses delayed to come down from the mountain, they gathered themselves together unto Aaron, and said to him, 'Make for us a god who can go before us—for as regards this Moses, the man that brought us up out of the land of Egypt, we do not know what has become of him'" (Exodus 32:1).

Here too, the subtext of the biblical narrative has to do with death. Moses had gone up the mountain to meet with God, and promised to return after forty days. The people miscalculated the length of his absence and when Moses failed to appear at what they assumed to be the appointed time, their cry—as instigated by Satan—was "Moses died."[38]

Just as Esau had been incapable of coping with the death of Abraham, the Jewish people found themselves devastated by the assumption that their leader, Moses, had perished. But of course, they were wrong—not just because they miscalculated the time of Moses' return, but because they failed to understand what death, whenever it might come to their leader, would mean.

In a striking passage in the Talmud, the rabbis ascribe eternal life to Moses, claiming *lo meit moshe*, Moses did not die:

> Moses did not die [based on the following exegesis]. In one place it is written, "And he died *there*" [in the land of Moab] (Deuteronomy 34:5)]; in another place it is written, "And he was *there* [on Mount Sinai] with God [for forty days and forty nights]" (Exodus 34:28). Just as he was standing [before God and serving Him; although utterly removed from worldly concerns such as eating and drinking, Moses still was not dead] at Mount Sinai, so too was he standing here [at the end of Moses' one hundred twenty years of life], standing and serving.[39]

In truth, Moses would never die. His legacy would live on forever, and in that sense he is still alive today. Moreover, the righteous do not really perish; they live on in the World to Come, in the presence of God. Even had Moses not returned to the people, their response was not only repugnant but foolish as well. Thus, the story of the sin of the golden calf is yet another example of a misguided response to death—albeit in this case to a death that didn't actually happen.

The law of the red heifer implies that we must continually atone for that specific sin—a linkage we have noted above in the commentary of Rashi and in the midrash. We are urged to recognize that death is not what it appears to be. It is not an end, but a new beginning. It is not the conclusion of the story of a body brought to lasting internment, as much as it is the commencement of the journey of the soul to its heavenly reward. It is a fulfillment of the biblical verse that "The dust returns to the earth from whence it came, but the spirit returns unto God who gave it" (Kohelet 12:7).

As the hasidic Rabbi Mendel of Kotzk so beautifully put it, "Death is simply a matter of going from one room to another, a room that is in fact far more beautiful."[40]

Kaddish as a Substitute for the *Parah Adummah*

According to the Mishnah,[41] only eight red heifers were actually slaughtered in the period from Moses to the destruction of the Second Temple. To this day, in the absence of the Temple, we are still unable to use the biblical ritual for effecting purification after contact with death.

But even if we are unable to perform the ritual physically, we may still gain a measure of its effectiveness by concentrating on its symbolic message. And that message resonates with us as we recite the remarkable words of the Kaddish—for the very same symbolic ideas that were implicit in the ritual of the red heifer were, much later in Jewish history, given verbal expression in the mourners' recitation of the Kaddish.

There is ample precedent for the role of Kaddish as replacement, through prayer, for a sacrificial process that could no longer be practiced in the absence of the Temple. Indeed, the very source of prayer is the sacrificial system, as made clear by the prophet Hosea: "Take with you words, and turn to the Eternal. Say to Him: forgive all iniquity and receive us graciously, so we will offer the words of our lips instead of heifers" (14:3). So, too, the Talmud teaches that prayer takes the place of sacrifice, *t'fillah bi-m'kom korban*.[42]

In the same manner, the Kaddish serves as mourners' religious response to the loss of their loved ones. What once was expressed through animal offerings comes now from our hearts, by way of our lips; what once was the perplexing law of the red heifer is now the powerful prayer that offers mourners comfort and consolation to cope with their grief in the aftermath of their personal confrontation with death:

> Magnified and sanctified be His great name in the world that [God] has created according to the divine will.

> May [God] establish His kingdom during your life and
> during your days, and during the life of all the house of
> Israel, even speedily and at a near time; and say: *Amen.*
> Let [God's] great name be blessed for ever and ever and for
> all eternity.

Strikingly enough, nowhere in this prayer is there any mention of death. Instead, it is a powerful reaffirmation of faith. It proclaims that throughout all the changing conditions of time and place, the universal recognition of God's name in its undiminished grandeur will be achieved in a world that the Almighty has created according to the divine will.

Why are these words religiously mandated as the most appropriate response to death? Because, as Rabbi Elie Munk put it:

> The significance of the Kaddish is that all the apparent
> shortcomings and deficiencies of this world [even death]
> cannot prevent the goal from being attained, nay, they are
> in themselves but the means to attain it. For the Almighty
> could surely have created a different world if this would have
> better suited His purpose. The Kaddish emphasizes at every
> turning point of the prayer the unwavering faith of Israel
> in the ultimate realization of this aim during our lifetime
> and in the lifetime of all Israel, as the reader proclaims. The
> congregation responds to it with *amen*, making this ardent
> and confident faith their own. They add the wish in the hope
> that the recognition of His great name be spread through all
> eternity and brought to full realization on earth. And to this
> affirmation the congregation responds with *amen*.[43]

The Kaddish was composed in the period following the destruction of the First Temple, during Israel's exile, and its wording is culled from the prophet Ezekiel 38:23.[44] Its major theme—the striving for the restoration of the great name of God to its full glory—was based on the prophetic response to a national tragedy. The members of the council referenced in ancient Jewish literature as "the Great Assembly" daringly compared personal loss to national catastrophe: both challenge belief; both make us question God and God's ways; both present us with comparable tests—and both demand that we affirm that our faith is stronger than the challenges posed by our misfortune.

Kaddish was the response to the destruction of the Temple, and Kaddish is the response to the death of our loved ones. Reciting Kaddish proclaims that we have passed the test that Esau failed when he could not cope with the death of his grandfather Abraham and therefore sold his birthright for a mess of pottage. And reciting Kaddish proclaims that we have passed the test that the Jewish people failed, when they presumed the death of Moses and therefore sinned by worshipping the golden calf.

With the words of the Kaddish, we assert the sacredness of life and the eternal legacy of the righteous who preceded us. We declare that we have not been overwhelmed by the spirit of impurity and *tumah* that death brings in its wake. We affirm that, even without the ashes of the red heifer, we have been able to incorporate into our psyches the messages it was intended to teach us—and for that, most of all, we give thanks.

NOTES

[1] *Macbeth*, Act 5, scene 5, lines 27–28.

[2] B. Yoma 35a.

[3] Samson Raphael Hirsch, *The Pentateuch Translated and Explained*, trans. Isaac Levy (ed. London, 1964), vol. 4, p. 337. Hirsch was a German rabbi best known as the intellectual founder of the "*torah im derekh eretz*" school of contemporary Orthodox Judaism.

[4] Mordechai Becher, *Gateway To Judaism: The What, How, and Why of Jewish Life* (Brooklyn, NY: Shaar Press, 2005), p. 64.

[5] Cf. Rashi to Numbers 19:22, s.v. *titma ad ha-arev*, cf. M. Keilim 1:4.

[6] The classical Hebrew word *ḥok* means "law." A variant of of *ḥok* is *ḥukkah*, from which derives the form found in Numbers 19:2 (*ḥukkat*).

[7] *Ḥukkim* is the plural of *ḥok*.

[8] Midrash Tanḥuma, *Ḥukkat* §7.

[9] For a different list of those laws that serve to raise the objections of Satan as well as the nations of the world, see B. Yoma 67b.

[10] See Bemidbar Rabbah 19:3.

[11] Bemidbar Rabbah 19:6.

[12] *Sefer Ha-ḥinnukh* was first published in Venice in 1523.

[13] *Sefer Ha-ḥinnukh*, ed. Chaim Chavel (Jerusalem: Mossad Harav Kook, 1960), *mitzvah* 397, p. 504.

[14] Rashi on Numbers 19:2, s.v. *zot ḥukkat ha-torah*.

[15] For more on this concept of Satan's taunts to Israel, see B. Yoma 67b.

[16] Rashi on Numbers 19:22, s.v. *titma ad ha-arev*.

[17] See the *Ba·al Ha-turim* commentary of Rabbi Jacob ben Asher (c. 1269–c.1343) to Numbers 19:2, s.v. *zot ḥukkat ha-torah*, who finds a connection between *parah adummah* and the expression *al avon eigel* ("for the sin of the golden calf"), both of which have the same numerological value.

[18] For a talmudic source relating to the costliness of the *parah adummah* and the sages' willingness to go to any extreme to procure one, see B. Kiddushin 31a.

[19] B. Rosh Hashanah 26a.

[20] Cf. Rashi's comment to Exodus 32:34, s.v. *u–v'yom pokdi*.

[21] Cf. Rashi's comment to Numbers 19:22, s.v. *titma ad ha-arev*.

[22] Ibid.

[23] Commentary of Menaḥem Recanati to Numbers 19:2, ed. Venice, 1523, p. 254a–b, s.v. *zot ḥukkat ha-torah*.

[24] Rashi to Numbers 19:2, s.v. *adummah t'mimah*, referencing M. Parah 2:5, cf. T. Parah 2:5.

[25] A fascinating variant translation is that of the *Da·at Z'keinim* commentary on Genesis 25:30 (ed. Livorno, 1783, p. 13a), s.v. *ḥaliteini na*: "Pour some of this red pottage to me, who is [similarly] red." *Da·at Z'keinim* is a compendium

of comments on the text of the Torah attributed to the Tosafists of medieval France and Germany, the earliest of whom were disciples of Rashi.

[26] Cf. Rashi's comment to that verse, s.v. *min ha-adom ha-adom.*

[27] Midrash Tanḥuma (ed. S. Buber), *Toldot* §3.

[28] Bereishit Rabbah 63:11.

[29] Note that the letters *dalet* and *mem*, which together spell out the Hebrew word for blood, *dam*, are part of the name Edom as well.

[30] M. Sanhedrin 10:1 lists those who have no share in the World to Come, and those mentioned first are those who reject belief in the ultimate resurrection of the dead—the very sin ascribed here to Esau.

[31] See the *K'li Yakar* commentary of Rabbi Solomon Ephraim ben Aaron of Luntschitz (1550–1619) to Genesis 25:30 (ed. Piotrków, 1889, p. 39a), s.v. *al kein kara sh'mo edom*, and the way he uses the science of his day to explain Esau's obsession with the soup as having to do not with its flavor or texture, but rather with its color: "*And for that reason was he called Edom.* And why was it that he was not called 'Edom' immediately after his birth, given that Scripture relates that 'when the first child emerged he was ruddy' (Genesis 25:25)? Because there was nothing unusual in that occurrence; as noted by Rabbi Nathan in the Talmud (at B. Shabbat 134a); many children are born with ruddy complexions because their blood has not yet been [fully] absorbed. The appearance of such children eventually changes, so [Esau's] parents thought that he was possibly ruddy in that temporary sense and not in a permanent way. But once he said the words 'Give me to eat of that red, red pottage' (Genesis 25:30) and it struck them as odd that he didn't just call the lentil stew by its more normal name, they realized that he was not drawn to the porridge because of its taste, but because of its red appearance. And that realization led them to understand that his nature was drawn to 'redness,' because red bile dominated the mixture of his inner humors, and that it was for that reason that he was drawn to all things that derived from that aspect of his nature—that is, to every red thing, and it was for *that* reason—once it became obvious that his inmost nature itself was 'red'—that he was called Edom."

[32] Max Lüscher, *The Lüscher Color Test: Remarkable Test That Reveals Your Personality Through Color*, trans. E.A. Cohen and Susan Guarmati (New York: Washington Square Books), 1971.

[33] For additional studies see: Bruce M. Burdick, et al., "The Relationship between Color Preference and Psychiatric Disorders," in *Journal of Clinical Psychology* 41:6 (1985), pp. 746–749; James C. Carmer, Ray A. Craddick, and Edward W. L. Smith, "An Investigation of the Lüscher Color Test Personality Descriptions," in *International Journal of Symbology* 5:2 (1974), pp. 1–6.

[34] Lüscher, *The Lüscher Color Test*, pp. 11–12.

[35] Ibid.

[36] The element of haste in Esau's request resolves a question that, strangely

enough, seems not to have been asked by the commentators. Anyone familiar with cooking lentils will confirm that there is no such thing as a red lentil soup; even the reddest of lentils always turns golden when cooked. Gil Marks, author of the *Encyclopedia of Jewish Food* (Hoboken, NJ: John Wiley & Sons, 2010), offered this observation in an internet-based Torah commentary (available online at www.w.ouradio.org/shabbat/recipes/toldot62.htm): "There is something unexpected in Esau's request, for despite his evident hurry and bluntness, he says '*na.*' This term, like many things in this *parshah*, can be taken two ways: it usually means 'please,' but can also translate as 'raw' (cf. Exodus 12:9). In other words, Esau wanted the stew before it was even fully cooked, which for red lentils is a relatively short time, in as little as ten minutes once the water is boiling. This corresponds to the tenor of the rest of Esau's demand to literally 'pour the red stuff down his throat,' not even taking time to chew or savor it. And, in fact, since red lentils tend to turn pink or golden as they cook, a red hue would seem to indicate an underdone state. Thus Esau was certainly no gourmand, practically begging to wolf down an undercooked, unsophisticated dish. It was an act of animalistic gratification, far from a spiritual expression and not even a matter of enjoyment."

[37] See www.ekrfoundation.org/quotes.

[38] B. Shabbat 89a.

[39] B. Sotah 13b.

[40] Rabbi Mendel of Kotzk, as cited in Yisroel Artin, *Emet Ve-emunah* (ed. Jerusalem, 1940), p. 30.

[41] M. Parah 3:5.

[42] B. Berakhot 26a.

[43] Elie Munk, *The World Of Prayer: Commentary And Translation of the Daily Prayers*, trans. Henry Bieberfeld and Leonard Oschry (New York: Phillip Feldheim, Inc., 1961), vol. 1, pp. 184–185.

[44] Ibid., p. 88.

Is the Kaddish About You and Me...or God?

Avi S. Olitzky

In our dark world, plagued by disease, war, and death, we must force ourselves to derive light from whatever holiness we come across. The life of every person will eventually come to an end, and likewise most will eventually mourn the loss of a loved one. Judaism offers the Mourner's Kaddish as a vehicle for holiness and comfort during those heartrending times. Kaddish Yatom is recited antiphonally, as a kind of liturgical duet between the mourner and the congregation. Both take part, but the prayer feels as though it is "about" the mourner —and the congregation is just the chorus shoring up the "real" participant. In light of that, is it better to be the one responding *amen* and *y'hei sh'meih* to the Mourner's Kaddish, or the one reciting it *in toto*?

It is important to first explore the content of the Mourner's Kaddish—a prayer interestingly without any mention of death— in order to begin to understand the relationship between the one reciting the Mourner's Kaddish and the one (or ones) responding to it. The Mourner's Kaddish is comprised of five sections. The first two relate praise for the *sh'meih rabba*, God's great name. The third section (along with the "amens" throughout—the core of the response) is similar to the first two, but relates praise for the *sh'meih d'kudsha b'rikh hu*, the name of the blessed Holy One. This is the same God and the same great name, but the nuance is slightly different. Nevertheless, we might group the first three paragraphs together under the heading "The Greatness of the Blessed Holy One's Name." The fourth and fifth sections of the Mourner's Kaddish are about peace (or, better, completeness).[1] More specifically, these final two sections are: first, an Aramaic plea for peace and life for all Israel; and second, a Hebrew plea for peace and harmony for "us" (i.e., the congregation) and, by extension, all of Israel.

Unfortunately, many Jews have their first intimate encounter with the Mourner's Kaddish as they stumble over the words during the initial days of mourning. One would hope that these mourners are not reciting the Kaddish alone, since the Mourner's Kaddish may not be recited without the presence of a *minyan*.[2] Moreover, the Mourner's Kaddish is meant to be recited in community, exemplary of this prayerful back-and-forth of praise (*shevaḥ*) and supplication (*bakkashah*).

This communal context might lead us to conclude that the recitation of the Mourner's Kaddish is not necessarily for the benefit of the one reciting it, but instead for those present who are ready and willing to respond. In fact, according to Rabbi Joshua ben Levi, it would seem that the Kaddish is recited specifically for the benefit of the individual *responding* to the Kaddish and not for the one saying it at all—or, at least, not exclusively or mainly for that individual. The rabbi teaches, concerning those who say "*amen y'hei sh'meih rabba m'varakh*" (the communal response) with supreme might (*b'khol koḥo*)," that whatever edicts may have been enacted against them, presumably in the heavenly court, are immediately torn up.[3] Though Rashi and most of the Tosafot understand *b'khol koḥo* to mean "with all of one's might" (read: full intentionality), one French tosafist, the twelfth-century Rabbi Yitzḥak ben Shmuel, refers to the tale of Rabbi Ishmael ben Elisha, which teaches that one is to recite the *y'hei sh'meih* line when entering the synagogue in a *kol ram*—a loud voice—and that it nullifies the harsh decree (*m'vat'lim g'zeirot kashot*). Rabbi Ḥiyya bar Abba adds greater weight to the equation, teaching in the name of Rabbi Yoḥanan that even idolaters are forgiven for their sins, upon reciting *y'hei sh'meih rabba m'varakh*.[4] We further learn that the one who recites *y'hei sh'meih rabba m'vorakh* in a dream merits a portion in the age to come.[5] Granted, in our liturgical tradition, the *y'hei sh'meih* response—often referred to as a doxology—likely constituted, in an earlier period, the totality of the Kaddish prayer; but for our purposes, it is the congregational response to the mourner's recitation of Kaddish. Nevertheless, the call-and-response power of the Kaddish may exert even more of a pull on the general *minyan* attendee than on the mourner him or herself.

Rabbi Joshua ben Levi suggests that the community responds to the Kaddish as a vehicle for self-benefit in order that they might improve their "sin-rating," serving as a vehicle for doing *t'shuvah* and thus effecting *m'ḥilah*.[6] Still, even before Rabbi Joshua ben Levi made the case that the Kaddish was beneficial to those who responded to it (even for those who had not personally suffered a loss), insofar as it served as a vehicle for the absolution of sin (or at least for the cancellation of the harsh punishment that it might have triggered), Jewish lore suggested that the Kaddish and *t'shuvah* have a powerful relationship, suspending the punishment of the responder. The idea of whether or not children can atone for the sins of their parents is developed in an obscure story recorded in tractate Kallah.[7] The core of the story is that Rabbi Akiva encounters a dead man in a cemetery, who seems to be eternally damned for having essentially transgressed every prohibition in the Torah. Rabbi Akiva seeks out the man's son (after the latter is born and grows to the proper age) and brings him to the synagogue *li-v'rukhei b'kahala*—perhaps to recite the Bar'khu, and perhaps additionally to recite the Kaddish.[8] Whatever the case may be, the community does forgive the dead man (as it seems God does as well), and so we learn that children can atone for the sins of their parents (*m'khap'rin avon avoteihem*).

This story is recorded in a longer and more descriptive way in the *Mahzor Vitry*, an eleventh-century compendium of Jewish law and lore composed by Rabbi Simhah ben Samuel of Vitry (d. 1105).[9] In the version of the story found in the *Mahzor Vitry*, the shift from Bar'khu to the Kaddish is explicit. In this version, the dead man is referred to as afflicted (*oni*) and his son grows up to lead the evening service and recite Kaddish for him afterwards. It is also interesting to note that in this version, the name of the son is Akiva—adding to the mystical, introspective element (*heshbon ha-nefesh*) of the story. It is not clear that Akiva had actually encountered anyone other than himself—or, better, his soul—throughout the narrative, and this perspective complements our exploration of the roles of those present during the recitation of the Kaddish.

The *Mahzor Vitry* uses this story for etiological purposes, concluding "and on account of this it is customary that a person who has neither father nor mother should pass before the Ark on Saturday night and lead services or Kaddish [or both]."[10] The Kaddish is for the benefit for the deceased. The child of the deceased recites the Mourner's Kaddish, compelling the community to faithfully respond—and, in doing so, absolves the deceased of his or her sins.

Rabbi Moses Isserles (1520–1572) further explains some of our customs surrounding mourning and the recitation of the Kaddish, referring to the above-cited text from tractate Kallah to explain why one recites Kaddish for one's mother or father.[11] The hope for forgiveness for transgression, the tearing up or nullification of an evil decree, atonement for sins—all these are important motivations for reciting Kaddish, but Rabbi Isserles offers a deeper look into the realm of the afterlife and the power that Kaddish has there. For twelve months following the death of a parent, the mourning child[12] recites what Rabbi Isserles calls the *kaddish batra*;[13] he also chants the *haftarah* and he leads the evening service on Saturday night. The reasoning behind the Saturday evening service is the most interesting. Rabbi Isserles teaches that it is at that moment that souls return to Gehenna.[14] When a child prays and sanctifies God in public (*m'kaddeish ba-rabbim*, here used to reference the recitation of Kaddish in the *minyan*), he releases his parent from hell.[15]

To be certain, this is obviously not everyone's opinion. A century after *Maḥzor Vitry* (and much later than tractate Kallah), we read the rebuke of Rabbi Avraham bar Ḥiyya Ha-nasi (1070–c.1140) in his *Sefer Higgayon Ha-nefesh*.[16] There, Rabbi Avraham ben Ḥiyya goes as far as to say that that such wayward thinking is considered "made-up thoughts" (*maḥashavot b'duyot*) and "vain expectation" (*toḥelet shav*) in the eyes of the sages.[17] In effect, based on this teaching, the only way one might find posthumous comfort and freedom from punishment is through the undoing of sin. For example, if the decedent had stolen something in his or her lifetime, then that item needs to be returned—and this responsibility pertains even posthumously to the deceased. Further, Rabbi Avraham writes, the primary path to salvation in the hereafter is to teach Torah while alive. In so doing, a teacher's merit grows with each generation taught, hopefully leading an ever greater number of souls onto the path of righteousness. Interestingly enough, this approach of Rabbi Avraham is complementary, not really antithetical, to the aggadic justification: the child of the deceased reciting the Mourner's Kaddish suggests to God that the deceased has left a legacy of faith and virtue behind and that this store of merit should really suffice for expiation. In most cases, deceased parents are not criminals, but decent and good people who no doubt sinned...but only because all human beings who live occasionally do. Hence, the necessity to recite Kaddish is a function of the obligation to honor (and thus also to redeem, even posthumously) one's parents. The recitation of the Kaddish, according to this understanding, is both for the community and for the deceased for whom it is recited—but not really for the mourner reciting it "for" one's parents.

Rabbi Yeḥiel Mikhel Epstein (1829–1908) further supports this notion, explaining that by reciting "*amen y'hei sh'meih rabba m'varakh*" in a loud voice and with clear and present *kavvanah*,[18] we too can have the gates of heaven opened for *us* ourselves, thus eliminating any need for our offspring to recite Kaddish on our behalf.[19] This makes the Mourner's Kaddish one of, if not *the*, most powerful prayers in our liturgical canon. And though efficacy of prayer itself is something with which many struggle theologically, Jewish tradition implies that the efficacy of Kaddish is absolute and mighty.

But if that is the case—if the Kaddish is as mighty as we now understand it to be—then it follows logically that worshippers should be allowed to briefly interrupt central prayers like the Amidah to respond cooperatively to commune with the Divine.[20] The Talmud shares that when Rav Dimi came from the Land of Israel to Babylonia, he reported that Rabbi Judah and Rabbi Simon the student of Rabbi Yoḥanan had taught that one could only interrupt one's Amidah in order to respond with *y'hei sh'meih*.[21] Although Rabbis Judah and Simon thought that one should interrupt *even* the Amidah to recite *y'hei sh'meih*, it is not clear whether this ruling was because of the communal responsibility to respond or because of the personal outcome of, and reward for, the response.

Another passage in the Talmud seems to suggest that we recite the Kaddish in part for God's benefit—or, perhaps even to influence God in some sort of inverted theurgy. Following a description of Rabbi Yosi's encounter with Elijah in a destroyed ruin (perhaps of the Temple), we find buried a significant teaching about the Kaddish: "Whenever the Jews go into their synagogues and study halls and respond *y'hei sh'meih gadol m'varakh*, the blessed Holy One shakes the divine head and says: 'Happy is the Sovereign who is thus praised in this house! Woe to the One who had to banish His children, and woe to the children who had to be banished from the table of their Parent!'"[22] We may ask: are we responding communally (by reciting *y'hei sh'meih*) in order to remind God of the fallen Temple, and express our longing for God to return to finite dwelling on this earth? Or is this passage bringing shame to the Kaddish, suggesting that it is spiteful to recite it—in a way praising God, but still effecting remorse and regret as opposed to divine ecstasy and contentment?

Rabbi Epstein is conflicted and teaches that the Kaddish is a great and awesome laudatory prayer set up by the members of the Great Assembly following the destruction of the First Temple.[23] We recite this prayer, ever praising God while still longing for a remorseful God who will provide a path back into the Temple and the rebuilding of God's Holy Place.[24] But then, the Kaddish is about making God feel sorrowful and full of regret. There seems to be some tension in play here. Reflecting again on the content of the Kaddish, the recitation of the Kaddish should imply that God is worthy of our praises, even in the bleakest of moments, and the *y'hei sh'meih* response is merely a rousing affirmation of this. On the one hand, the Kaddish must be recited to praise God; but on the other, the Kaddish is recited to incite God to action.

Perhaps distressingly, the Kaddish reciter—the mourner—is the only one for whom the act of reciting Kaddish does not have any intrinsic benefit. However, this does not take into account the fundamental routine of immersing oneself in a prayerful community and participating in the pattern of regular communal prayer. The simple, sublime act of getting lost in a sea of "responders" as one of the few "reciters" yields comfort. In fact, a text from the Shulḥan Arukh suggests that even the person who began the *minyan* with the group but who falls asleep or is otherwise occupied during the Kaddish can still count in the *minyan*.[25] This suggests that such a person's *y'hei sh'meih* is not as necessary as the recitation of the Mourner's Kaddish in the group by the mourner! But even earlier sources teach that if the *minyan* had begun as a *minyan* but then some people departed, the group could continue to function as a *minyan* through the conclusion of the service, as long as the majority remained.[26] Further, in synagogues in which everyone stands for the Kaddish, the mourner physically blends into the crowd.

Those who suggest that the Kaddish was composed in Aramaic, as a prayer for the masses that could easily be understood by all, seem to have missed a step along the way—because the Kaddish cannot be understood from its words alone at all! Those who recite the Kaddish are *meant* to get lost in the words. They are *meant* to focus and to cry with their hearts on their tongues. They are *meant* to pour out their soul, to cleanse the soul of those they have loved and lost.

The Kaddish is mysterious. It makes sense that its true meaning has been lost through the years. Is the Mourner's Kaddish recited for the mourner, for the comforter, for the deceased—and/or for God? It holds power within it for the deceased, but only through the recitation by the mourner. It holds power within it for the community, but only if they respond in turn. It holds power within it even for the one who recites it, and that is the strongest power of all: because it is likely their neighbors' presence during the recitation, more than the recitation itself, that brings serenity and comfort to the bereaved.

The Mourner's Kaddish opens the mysterious portal to the World to Come for all who would approach. And not surprisingly, this prayer, which is recited as a contemplative medium between this world and the next, is precisely the key to the world to come. And how appropriate: it is almost tragic that people do not realize it. By understanding the ever-shifting vantage point of the Kaddish, it becomes our life-goal to bring people closer to this holy prayer, so that they might in turn become closer to one another, closer to their inner selves, and closer to God. Then maybe we will each find the courage to proclaim once and for all: May God's great name truly be blessed forever and ever, by way of the Kaddish.

NOTES

[1] The word *shalom* is most commonly translated as "peace." However, sharing a triliteral root with *shaleim* (whole), the better translation for *shalom* may be "completeness," the shared idea being that it is when one feels whole and complete that one is truly at peace.

[2] S.A. Oraḥ Ḥayyim 55:1. A *minyan* is religious quorum of ten Jewish adults, traditionally restricted to men, that provides the requisite context for those parts of the service deemed to be acts of the sanctification of God's name, as is the Kaddish, Of course, requiring a *minyan* for Kaddish recitation ensures the presence of a physical community for the mourner to mourn *in*.

[3] B. Shabbat 119b.

[4] Ibid.

[5] *Muvtaḥ lo she-hu ben olam ha-ba*; B. Berakhot 57a.

[6] After wrongdoing, one who engages in *t'shuvah* (repentance) and gains *m'ḥilah* (forgiveness) from the aggrieved party can be considered to have "wiped the slate clean"—that is, to have cleansed one's soul. When a person responds to the Kaddish, he or she gets "credit" for good-doing and it counterbalances wrongs committed in the past, thus leading to the decreed edict being "immediately torn up."

[7] See Kallah 2:9, ed. Michael Higger (New York: D'vei Rabbanan, 5696 [1935/1936]), pp. 202–203. Kallah is one of the so-called "minor tractates," ancient rabbinic works that are not formally part of the Mishnah or Talmud but that date back to the same era. See also the analysis of this story in the essay elsewhere in this volume by Martin S. Cohen.

[8] It is difficult to accurately translate this Aramaic phrase. It could mean a person reciting a blessing in the context of a congregation, someone blessing "with" the congregation, or even someone formally blessing the congregation.

[9] *Maḥzor Vitry*, ed. S. Hurwitz (Nuremberg, 1923), pp. 112–113.

[10] The Hebrew reads: *v'al kein nahagu la-avor lifnei ha-teivah b'motza·ei shabbat adam she-ein lo av o eim lomar bar'khu o kaddish*.

[11] See his gloss to S.A. Yoreh Dei·ah 376:4.

[12] The mourning child is known in Hebrew as a *yatom*; hence the Hebrew name "Kaddish Yatom" (literally, "Orphan's Kaddish") for the Mourner's Kaddish.

[13] The term, no longer in current use, literally means "the last Kaddish" and probably denotes what we know as the Kaddish Shaleim, the "Full Kaddish." This version of the Kaddish often serves as a liturgical coda.

[14] Gehenna is the anglicization of the Hebrew *geihinnom*, a regular designation for hell in rabbinic literature.

[15] Hell in Jewish lore is a place of torment for the soul. It is a place not reserved solely for the wicked, but for all souls on their purgatorial path to paradise.

[16] In this treatise, as a philosopher and scientist, Rabbi Avraham bar Ḥiyya Ha-nasi explored the origin and development of the universe, coupled with ethics and psychology.

[17] *Sefer Higayyon Ha-nefesh* (ed. Leipzig, 1860), p. 58.

[18] The Hebrew word *kavvanah* denotes prayerful intentionality.

[19] *Arukh Ha-shulḥan*, Oraḥ Ḥayyim 55:2.

[20] Cf., e.g., S.A. Oraḥ Ḥayyim 104:7.

[21] B. Berakhot 21b.

[22] B. Berakhot 3a.

[23] The term "Great Assembly" references the assembly of sages that the rabbis of classical antiquity believed to have functioned from the beginning of the Second Temple period through the time of Simeon the Just.

[24] *Arukh Ha-shulḥan*, Oraḥ Ḥayyim 55:1 and 56:1.

[25] S.A. Oraḥ Ḥayyim 55:6.

[26] Y. Megillah 4:4, 75a, and cf. Y. Berakhot 7:4, 11c.

Mysteries of the Kaddish

Orna Triguboff

The Kaddish, in at least several of its versions, is recited at all Jewish prayer services, yet it is one of the least understood prayers in Jewish liturgy. In this essay, I will explore mystical and kabbalistic perspectives on the Kaddish by asking a few simple questions: What is the function of the Kaddish? Why do we need a *minyan* (a group of ten or more) to say it? And how are the kabbalistic explanations of the role of Kaddish in Jewish liturgy relevant to non-mystics?

The most influential work of Jewish mysticism, the Zohar, describes the Kaddish as one of the holiest and most powerful prayers.[1] Indeed, the name "Kaddish" derives from a root common to Hebrew and Aramaic, which generates words related to separateness or holiness. Building on teachings from the Zohar, the sixteenth-century kabbalist Ḥayyim Vital, in the name of his teacher Isaac Luria, described the Kaddish as a portal through which different worlds and planes can be accessed.[2] And Rabbi Zalman Schachter-Shalomi, founder of the Jewish Renewal movement, stated that "the Kaddish acts as a divine elevator."[3]

Kaddish, a Portal for Spiritual Travel

When we participate in a prayer service, there is a certain journey of the psyche that we undertake. We usually begin praying in a certain state of mind and hopefully, by the end of the service, we have been inspired or received something of benefit.

The order of the prayer service, developed over two thousand years, is designed to help take us on that journey. There is wisdom and craftsmanship in the way the order of prayer has been set, and this can be explained on many levels.

The placement of a given prayer within the larger service often provides a key to understanding its function. The Kaddish appears at transition points between different sections of the prayer service, so it may therefore be seen as a series of spiritual gateways through which we pass during the service.

Ḥayyim Vital describes the journey of the service as an ascent and descent of our consciousness.[4] We begin with our consciousness connected to the physical world, then our consciousness ascends into spiritual worlds, and by the end of the prayer service our consciousness has descended back to an awareness of the physical.

We begin the prayer service in the first world, the material world called *olam ha-asiyyah*, the World of Action. The next three worlds are spiritual planes to which our consciousness can rise at different times, such as when we are sleeping, relaxing, praying, or entering a very inspired state. The second world is called *olam ha-y'tzirah*, the World of Formation; the third, *olam ha-b'ri·ah*, the World of Creation; and the fourth and highest world, *olam ha-atzilut*, the World of Emanation.

The Zohar explains that the Kaddish acts as a gateway, allowing our soul to move between worlds: "Come and see...[the Kaddish] rises on all sides, above and below and to all sides of faith...so as to raise the glory of the blessed Holy One."[5] The movement through the worlds is both general and particular. When we recite the Kaddish, there is a rising of light in the world in general, a raising of the "glory of the blessed Holy One," and, inextricably linked to that process, there is an ascent and descent of our own consciousness in particular.

Ḥayyim Vital explains that during the weekday morning service, our soul ascends from the lowest world to the highest world, and the Kaddish acts as the gateway by means of which our soul or our consciousness moves.[6] We reach the highest world when we say the Amidah prayer, and from the end of the Amidah onward, our soul begins to gradually descend through the worlds until the end of the service, when we find ourselves back in the World of Action and ready to interact with the material world.

How does the soul ascend and descend? What is the engine that enables this movement? To understand this better, let's look in detail at how Ḥayyim Vital explains the function of the Kaddish and the soul's journey during the morning prayer service. We will relate to the various forms of Kaddish (the Full Kaddish, the Half Kaddish, the Rabbis' Kaddish, and the Mourner's Kaddish) in the same manner, for the purpose of explaining the journey into the different worlds. The Kaddish prayer was placed at slightly different points of the prayer service, depending on the century and the culture of the community. For our purposes we will use the Lurianic prayer structure from sixteenth-century Safed, as described in the writings of Ḥayyim Vital.[7]

At the beginning of the morning prayers, our consciousness is where it usually is, in *olam ha-asiyyah*, the World of Action. This is the ordinary state of mental consciousness. The beginning of the prayer service "warms us up" as we recite prayers with themes such as gratitude for being alive and for our bodily functions. After this we say the Kaddish, which acts as a portal that allows us to enter the next spiritual world, *olam ha-y'tzirah*, the World of Formation. In terms of the order of prayers, we begin a new section called Pesukei D'zimra, literally, "Verses of Praise," which includes prayers such as "Blessed Is the One Who Spoke and the World Came into Being" and various prayers of thanksgiving, as well as various psalms and collections of biblical verses.

Once we have completed Pesukei D'zimra, a Kaddish marks the transition to the next section, "The Shema and its Blessings." Ḥayyim Vital explains that when saying the Kaddish, our consciousness is drawn from *olam ha-y'tzirah*, the World of Formation, into the world above it, *olam ha-b'ri·ah*, the World of Creation. In this section of prayer, we acknowledge that we are praying in community and that we pray not only for ourselves, but also for those who are part of our community, and for the world as a whole. We also say blessings regarding light and love, and turn our awareness to the power of Oneness in the Shema prayer.

We are now ready to leave the World of Creation, and due to the extraordinary nature of the World of Creation, Vital explains, there is no need to say Kaddish.[8] Through our concentration and intention, we seamlessly enter the next and highest world, *olam ha-atzilut*, the World of Emanation. We do this by saying the blessing for redemption and then, without any diversion, proceed directly to the Amidah, which is said silently while standing. It is considered the highest spiritual point of the prayer service.

We complete the Amidah with a prayer for peace, and an intention to speak words that promote peace. When this section is completed, we begin our descent through the worlds, with the Kaddish again acting as a gateway, helping our consciousness descend from world to world.

Upon re-entering the lowest world, we say the Kaddish and then recite the Aleinu prayer, whose key words ("to repair the world...") direct our intention toward action in the world by directing our soul back into the World of Action. We end the prayer service in the same place as we started; however, since we have risen and descended, we are hopefully in a better and more inspired state of mind to function throughout the day.

A View of the Worlds and Moving
Within Them in Higher Resolution

To understand the process of moving from one world to another via the Kaddish, we need to explore the architecture of the worlds in higher resolution.

Ḥayyim Vital, in the name of Isaac Luria, developed an understanding of creation being made up of four worlds, which was in turn based on the writings of *Tikkunei Ha-zohar*.[10] Vital conflates the four worlds of creation with the Zoharic description of the *heikhalot*, seven heavenly "palaces." The names of the heavenly palaces are as follows:

1. The Palace of Sapphire Stone, *heikhal livnat ha-sappir*
2. The Palace of the Very Essence of the Heavens, *heikhal etzem ha-shamayim*
3. The Palace of Brilliance, *heikhal nogah*
4. The Palace of Merit, *heikhal z'khut*
5. The Palace of Love, *heikhal ahavah*
6. The Palace of Desire, *heikhal ratzon*
7. The Palace of the Holy of Holies, the highest place, *heikhal kodesh kodashim*

Vital described each of the four worlds as being made up of seven palaces, thus implying clearly that there are twenty-eight palaces.[11] Through our prayers—and in particular through the power of the Kaddish—all seven palaces of each of the four worlds ascend from below to above, entering into each other so they are nested one palace within the one above it, and one world becoming nested within the world above it. By the end of this ascent process, each of the palaces within the worlds are nested in each other, and a state of unity prevails.

Within each world, this nesting takes place in two steps. The first step entails a nesting of the six lower palaces, one into the next. The second step entails all six nested lower palaces then entering, as one unit, into the seventh and highest palace, the Holy of Holies of that particular world.

Once all the palaces of one world are nested within the highest palace, this highest palace then enters into the world above it. This transformation can take place only because the seventh palace of one world contains light from the world above it.

When the seventh palace of a lower world ascends and enters the lowest palace of the world above it, it is metaphorically described as "entering the cosmic womb of the Supernal Mother":

> Light that garbs the throne of the highest palace comes from [the lowest palace]…of the world above. She [the lowest palace of the world above] is the Supernal Mother of the world below her and She shines into the highest palace of the world below Her.[12]

> The seventh and highest palace [of one world], called the Holy of Holies, becomes integrated into the world above it, and is transformed to become part of the reality of the world above it.[13]

A Cosmic Pillar that Connects All the Palaces in Creation

As we will see in the Zohar excerpt below, the nesting of the palaces takes place by means of a central vertical pillar, which traverses all the levels. We might envision the palaces as horizontal planes with a vertical pillar or tube extending through all of them, connecting them.[14]

The concept of a cosmic pillar that connects all the planes, dimensions, or palaces within the creation is found in many cultures. For example, the Hindu Vedas describe a *skambha*, a vertical column connecting heaven and earth,[15] and early Christianity describes a pillar of light, as does Sufism, where it is called *amud al nur*, "the luminous column."[16] The Zohar describes it in this way:

> In the middle of this palace, a pillar is thrust, ascending to the middle of another palace. It [the pillar] is hollow and is set from below to above, so that spirit might connect with spirit, and so on to the highest of all, so that they will all be one spirit, as is said: "There is one spirit for all" (Kohelet 3:19).[17]

To give this excerpt some context, the Zohar gives the description of this pillar when it is describing the "architecture" of the palaces and specifically, in the description above, the Zohar is describing the pillar as the structure through which a person's soul ascends and descends during prayer.

In the following passage, we learn about the possibility of varied experiences while travelling through this pillar:

> In the middle of this palace stands a single pillar of many colors—green, white, red, and black. When souls ascend they enter into this palace. Whoever befits this color ascends within, and whoever befits that color ascends within—every single one as is fitting.[18]

This text seems to suggest that there are different colors within the pillar. Different people ascend in different colors, possibly suggesting different experiences during the ascent.

The Kaddish Is the Pillar That Connects Worlds and Palaces

The image of a central cosmic pillar is a kind of midrashic development of the Genesis account of the ladder that Jacob sees in his dream that led from earth to heaven (Genesis 28:12).[19] The mystical understanding of a vertical column that links earth with the heavenly realms ties in to the idea that our consciousness, or soul, can move up and down this column and, in this way, be connected to different palaces or levels of spiritual reality.

Integrating and expanding on these teachings from the Zohar, Ḥayyim Vital explains that this pillar functions as a connector between the seven palaces in each of the four worlds. Explaining the process of ascent within this pillar, from the lowest world, the World of Action, into the world above it, Vital writes:

> After the six lower palaces of the World of Action have been included one within the other through the order of the prayers...we have to raise them [the six lower palaces] by means of the mystery of one pillar that exists between each and every world and in the midpoint of every palace. By way of this pillar, each palace ascends into the palace above it and is included within it...And behold, the mystery of this Kaddish *is* this pillar. It [the Kaddish] is the aspect of this aforementioned pillar, which is in the midpoint of the World of Action.[20]

Here, Vital states that the Kaddish prayer becomes unified with the central pillar—that is, the divine elevator. This structure runs through the central point within each palace of each world. As the person praying says the Kaddish at the specific point in the prayer service, the palaces ascend. As the palaces ascend into each other, so too does the consciousness of the person praying ascend.

Interestingly, the cosmic column has a corresponding location within each person. Just as the palaces have a pillar at their core, so too each person has a middle pillar, through which soul-forces rise and descend. It is not a physical location, but rather a structure within the soul of a person. In Aramaic it is called the *amuda d'emtza·ita*, the "middle pillar." During prayer, the consciousness of a person becomes internalized and collected into this middle pillar, and from there it can move between worlds and states of consciousness.[21]

Ascent of the Worlds and Ascent of the Soul

There are a few ways of looking at the process of ascent and descent during prayer. Sometimes it is described as the soul moving and receiving light from different levels of consciousness. Yet, from another perspective, the worlds ascend into each other as they move up to be included within the world above them, so as to achieve a singularity. Upon descent, a process of differentiation or unpacking of the worlds ensues, so that they change from a state of singularity to being four distinct worlds again. Ḥayyim Vital writes: "The light from the highest world, the World of Emanation, shines and spreads into the lower three worlds."[22] Yet, he goes on to explain, this is not the essence of that world. To receive the abundance of the highest world, the lower worlds actually need to ascend and enter that highest world. They regularly need to connect with their source and be replenished.

From the perspective of individual human experience, when the soul connects with higher worlds, it comes into contact with the source and is nourished by it—on the level of vitality, on the level of comfort and compassion, and on the level of knowledge.[23]

The founding master of the Hasidic movement, the Baal Shem Tov (1699–1760), described his experience of ascent in a letter written to his brother-in-law.[24] During his spiritual journey during a time of prayer, he wrote that he saw visions of various spiritual worlds. The Baal Shem Tov is said to have had specifically powerful experiences on Rosh Hashanah, the Jewish New Year, on more than one occasion, and to have received inspiration about healing of the body and soul.[25]

Kaddish and Community

Tying into the powerful function of the Kaddish as a gateway to various dimensions of consciousness, the Kabbalah also gives a perspective on why the Kaddish is only said if there is a *minyan* of ten or more people present. The Zohar states that human consciousness comprises ten aspects (*s'firot*). While some prayers only engage specific parts of our being, the Kaddish engages all of our being, all ten aspects of ourselves.[26]

These *s'firot* are divine qualities that are found, in potential, within each person. Part of a person's life work, from a kabbalistic perspective, is to develop these qualities. Some of these *s'firot* are: Ḥokhmah (wisdom), Binah (understanding), Ḥesed (compassion), and Gevurah (strength).

Because of the power of the Kaddish and because of the symbolic power of having a group of ten, the Zohar states, we must recite this prayer in the presence of a *minyan*. The ten members of the *minyan* symbolically correspond to the ten *s'firot* of human consciousness.[27]

This idea speaks to the communal aspect of saying the Kaddish. The Kaddish is an engine for the ascent and descent of the soul, helping to raise divine palaces to their source so they can connect with their essential light. Bringing that source down to the "lower worlds," including the physical world, it also has a comforting effect on the soul of the deceased—as we will see below. These functions are understood as being so powerful that they require group energy to achieve them, and the group energy also protects the individuals. This points to an interesting phenomenon within Jewish spiritual practice. Whereas many traditions emphasize solitary practices as the best way to develop spiritual connection, kabbalistic teachers have often emphasized the balance between solitary practice and the spiritual power that can be found in community[28] From a social perspective, the *minyan* also helps build community, and this can be seen in particular with regard to reciting the Mourner's Kaddish, which is said with a *minyan* so as to bring solace to the mourners and to remind the members of the community of those in need of support.

Kaddish Yatom, the Mourner's Kaddish

The Mourner's Kaddish is said each day for eleven months after the death of a parent and on the *yahrtzeit*, the anniversary, of his or her passing. Recitation of the Mourner's Kaddish is different from the regular Kaddish in that it is said by the mourners themselves rather than by the prayer leader. This enhances the element of community-building and raises the community's sensitivity to the needs of the mourner. From a mystical perspective, there is significant power in the connection between the soul of the mourner and the soul of the deceased, so that when the mourner recites this specific Kaddish it can have an effect on the soul of the deceased.

What happens to the soul after death? In the Talmud, Rabbi Akiva explains that after death the soul is directed to Gehenna and resides there for a maximum of twelve months.[29] In Jewish tradition, Gehenna is a space where the soul undergoes a process of cleansing and purification from its actions during its life on earth. The image of a "river of fire" from the Book of Daniel (7:10) is often associated with Gehenna to denote the burning of the non-essential features it accumulated during its life on earth.[30]

The Gehenna-phase is understood to last anywhere between a few days to a full twelve months. Since one of the main factors determining the length of stay in Gehenna is directly correlated to the amount of cleansing the soul needs, it has become customary to say the Mourner's Kaddish for only eleven months, out of respect for the soul of a parent (i.e., so as not to suggest that the soul of the deceased required the maximum twelve-month period). Once this phase of cleansing in Gehenna is complete, the soul ascends to a light-filled level of the celestial Garden of Eden.[31]

The Talmud explains that during the period in Gehenna, the soul of the departed constantly ascends and descends.[32] The soul ascends to the celestial Garden of Eden for a short reprieve and then descends to Gehenna to continue its process of purification.

Ḥayyim Vital explains that when the Mourner's Kaddish is recited on a weekday, the soul of the departed can ascend and attain a brief respite from its time in Gehenna.[33] On the Sabbath and on festivals, the souls of the departed are considered to ascend for entire holy day.[34] Even though the soul of the deceased automatically ascends to the Garden of Eden on Sabbath and festivals, there are different levels within the Garden of Eden, Ḥayyim Vital explains; by saying the Mourner's Kaddish on these days, assistance is given to the soul to rise from one level of the Garden of Eden to another.[35] In this way, a mourner's prayer is considered to have an active and healing role in the afterlife journey of a decesased parent, even on the Sabbath.

The recitation of the Mourner's Kaddish is understood as instrumental in assisting the soul to rise as high as it can in the Garden of Eden. Ḥayyim Vital documented Isaac Luria's teaching in this way:

And it seems to me, in my humble opinion, [which I learned] from my teacher [Isaac Luria], may his memory be a blessing, that it is good to say this Kaddish [Mourner's Kaddish] for the death of one's father and mother throughout the entire year, even on the Sabbath and festivals, because it is not as most people think, that its effect is only to save the soul of the dead from the judgment of Gehenna alone. There is another benefit, and it is to make entry into the Garden of Eden possible, from level to level. And because of this [the Mourner's Kaddish is said] also on Shabbat and festivals.[36]

Note that, once again, there is an emphasis on the elevator effect of the Kaddish: for Luria's followers, the Kaddish is the engine that facilitates the ascent of the soul. Also, a subtlety is introduced regarding the concept of the Garden of Eden, which is not presented as existing simply on one plane but rather as having many levels; the souls of the dead may thus be assisted in rising from one level to the next within the Garden of Eden. Reciting the Mourner's Kaddish is a way for the living to become active participants in the journey of the soul of a parent after the death of the body.

One of the challenges in reading kabbalistic texts, such as that of Ḥayyim Vital, is that they often do not explain spiritual models in a clear fashion, and we have an example of this here. When writing about the effect of the recitation of Mourner's Kaddish on the soul of the deceased, Vital uses the term *gan eden*, Garden of Eden, and explains that it is made up of many levels through which the soul travels. Yet, when describing the effect of saying Kaddish on the soul of the person praying, Vital describes the soul as travelling into planes called "palaces" and "worlds." What we know is that in both cases:

1. The discussion is about spiritual planes, consisting of many levels.
2. The soul of a person ascends and descends within these

spiritual planes, and movement occurs independent of which term is given to the spiritual plane or whether the different terms are referring to the same planes or not.

3. Recitation of the Kaddish is described as facilitating the movement of the soul between spiritual planes.

Thus, the Zohar and the writings of Ḥayyim Vital give us a picture of an ascent and descent of the soul of the deceased between Gehenna and levels of the Garden of Eden. And this movement of the soul is facilitated by the recitation of the Mourner's Kaddish. We also have a description of the movement of the soul of a living person who participates in a prayer service (as described earlier in this essay). When a person participates in a traditional morning prayer service, that person's soul has the potential to rise to and descend from the highest palace of the highest world. And this is facilitated by the recitation of the Kaddish in its various forms.

Kaddish: A Prayer of Transition

The Kaddish in all its forms is used to signify an ending. Half Kaddish and the Full Kaddish mark the completion of a subsection and a section in the prayer service, respectively. The Mourner's Kaddish marks the end of the prayer service itself. Kaddish D'rabbanan marks the end of a study session. The Burial Kaddish completes the burial.

An endpoint is also the beginning of something new, and in this sense Kaddish can be seen as a transition. The Kaddish is more than just a marker between sections of prayer—it is a portal into a new experience, a gateway through which one world enters the one above it, the means by which the soul of one who prays passes through worlds and palaces, and it is how the soul of the deceased can be "birthed" along its journey from one level in the Garden of Eden to the next.

How can the non-mystics among us find meaning in these deeply mystical ideas? First, I would like to point out that even people interested in mysticism might not be able to relate to all the details presented here. The teachings of the Kabbalah are a mystery and are not meant to be fully understood. We are invited to learn and re-learn them. Each time we do, a particular teaching might resonate with us, or ring true...and sometimes it will not. The Kabbalah is one aspect of the Jewish tradition and, by learning about it, we learn more about our multi-faceted tradition—each facet reflecting a slightly different light on the next, and each one shining light on the whole.

After reading these mystical reflections on the Kaddish, we might experience a prayer service in a different way. Each time the Kaddish is recited we might be reminded that one section has ended and another is beginning. We might straighten our spine, our central pillar, and feel a connection with a cosmic column of light. We might notice that with each Kaddish, we feel more uplifted. If the term "uplifted" does not feel resonant, we might notice feeling drawn further and further into a "quiet space" with each Kaddish—this "quiet space" reaching its pinnacle when we say the Amidah, the Standing Prayer. And toward the end of the service, with the recitation of the last Kaddish, we might feel that we are coming back to our regular state of mind, and we might also take note of what we have received during the prayer service and what we take with us as we go back into the world.

Interestingly, the sages of the Talmud described prayer as the "service of the heart."[37] As we have explored this kabbalistic explanation of prayer as an ascent and descent of our consciousness, we might also understand it as a journey into the depths of the heart.

NOTES

[1] Zohar II 105a and 129a–b.

[2] Ḥayyim Vital, *Sha·ar Ha-kavvanot* (Jerusalem: Yeshivat Ha-ḥayyim V'ha-shalom, 1983), pp. 14c–16d. Ḥayyim Vital was the main disciple of Isaac Luria in the city of Safed in the Galilee.

[3] Rabbi Zalman Schachter-Shalomi passed away in 2014. He spoke about the Kaddish as a divine elevator at a seminar titled "Meaningful Prayer," held at the Elat Chayyim Center, then located in the Catskill Mountains, on July 7–11, 2003.

[4] Ḥayyim Vital, *Sha·ar Ha-kavvanot*, pp. 14c–16d.

[5] Zohar II 129b.

[6] Ḥayyim Vital, *Sha·ar Ha-kavvanot*, pp. 14c–16d.

[7] Ibid., and see also the recent rendition of the Lurianic prayer book by Nissen Mangel entitled *Siddur T'hillat Hashem: Nusaḥ Ha-Ari z"l* (New York: Mercos L'inyonei Chinuch, 1995).

[8] Ḥayyim Vital, *Sha·ar Ha-kavvanot*, p. 15a.

[9] Ibid., pp. 14c–16d.

[10] *Tikkunei Ha-Zohar* is a later stratum and a distinct unit of the Zoharic corpus. The title can be translated as "New Adornments of *The Zohar.*" The text contains seventy explanations to the first verse of the Torah, and was most likely composed in the first half of the fourteenth century. It is written in a similar style to other later strata of the Zoharic corpus called the *Ra·aya Mehemna* and the *Tikkunim Hadashim*. In some communities, it is read during the forty-day period leading up to and including the High Holy Day, from the first day of the month of Elul until Yom Kippur. The text, which contains approximately 300 pages, is divided into 40 sections so that one section is read on each day during this period.

[11] Ḥayyim Vital, *Sha·ar Ha-kavvanot*, p. 14c. Here we have an example of the tendency in the Lurianic system of Kabbalah to exponentially increase the elements that comprise the structure of the Divinity. For more details see Lawrence Fine, *Physician of the Soul, Healer of the Cosmos* (Stanford: Stanford University Press, 2004), p. 139.

[12] Ḥayyim Vital, *Sha·ar Ha-kavvanot*, p. 15a.

[13] Ibid., p. 15b.

[14] Zohar I 42a.

[15] Raj Kumar, *Know the Vedas at a Glance* (New Delhi: Pustak Mahal, 2003), p. 89.

[16] Moshe Idel, *Ascensions on High in Jewish Mysticism: Pillars, Lines, Ladders* (Budapest: Central European Press, 2005), pp. 205–207. The Zohar (I 16b–17a) relates light of this cosmic pillar to the light of the first day of creation described in Genesis 1:3.

[17] Zohar I 42a. The translation is slightly modified from *The Zohar*, Volume 12 ed. Nathan Wolski (Stanford: Stanford University Press, 2016).

[18] Zohar I 39a–b; again, adapted from Wolski's translation (see note 17).

[19] For more about the symbolism of a ladder in different forms of mysticism and its connection to an ascent of the soul, see Moshe Idel, *Ascensions on High*, pp.187–192.

[20] Ḥayyim Vital, *Sha·ar Ha-kavvanot*, p. 15b.

[21] This corresponds to the Hindu concept of the middle pillar (called *sushumna*) that exists within a person's energy body, through which vital energy (*kundalini*) ascends and descends.

[22] Ḥayyim Vital, *Sha·ar Ha-kavvanot*, p. 15d.

[23] For more about the ascent of the soul and the concept of a cosmic pillar (including the connection between the central pillar and the human being), see Moshe Idel, *Ascensions on High*, pp. 205–207.

[24] Moshe Idel, *Messianic Mystics* (New Haven: Yale University Press, 1998), pp. 213–220.

[25] Moshe Idel *Ascensions on High*, pp. 144–145.

[26] For more about the *s'firot* and their connection to aspects of the psyche, see Daniel Abrams, *Ten Psychoanalytic Aphorisms on the Kabbalah* (Los Angeles: Cherub Press, 2010).

[27] Zohar II 132b. The Zohar applies this teaching to all the prayers qualified as *d'varim she-bi-k'dushah* ("prayers suggestive of [divine] holiness"), of which the Kaddish is one.

[28] For more information on the communal aspect of Jewish spirituality, see Lawrence Fine, *Safed Spirituality* (New York: Paulist Press, 1984).

[29] B. Shabbat 33b. Gehenna is the anglicization of the Hebrew *geihinnom*, a regular designation for hell in rabbinic literature.

[30] B. Ḥagigah 13b.

[31] Simcha Paul Raphael, *Jewish Views of the Afterlife* (Northvale, NJ: Jason Aronson, 1994), pp. 149–156. There are many understandings of the term "Garden of Eden"; for our purposes, we will use it in a broad sense to refer to heavenly realms—as this is how Ḥayyim Vital used it in his mystical explanation of this topic. The Hebrew phrase for "Garden of Eden," *gan eden*, is rendered as "paradise" by other authors in this volume.

[32] B. Shabbat 152b–153a.

[33] Ḥayyim Vital, *Sha·ar Ha-kavvanot*, p. 16a.

[34] Simcha Paul Raphael, *Jewish Views of the Afterlife*, p. 184.

[35] Ḥayyim Vital, *Sha·ar Ha-kavvanot*, p. 16a.

[36] Ibid.

[37] Prayer is described as being a "service of the heart" (*avodah she-ba-leiv*) at B. Taanit 2a. For a further discussion on this topic see Evelyn Garfiel, *Service of the Heart: A Guide to the Jewish Prayer* (New York: T. Yoseloff, 1958).

Say the Kaddish, Create the World
(for the Very First Time)

Barbara Thiede

Mourner's Kaddish demands much of mourners: Bless God! Praise God! Hallow God! Worship God! Acclaim, honor, thank, exalt! Do so, the prayer insists, beyond all song and psalm, beyond any language available to mortals. Jewish tradition tells the mourner: you must praise the Holy One—in the extreme—while you yourself are *in extremis*. Bless God's name. Proclaim the Holy One's awesome power. Watch, as the casket is lowered. Shovel earth into the grave. Remember the dead.

On the face of it, Mourner's Kaddish is the *coup de grâce* to a series of prayerful impossibilities. When a death is announced, we are to respond *barukh dayyan emet*, "blessed is the true Judge." At funerals, we are to read: *Adonai natan, Adonai lakaḥ, y'hi sheim Adonai m'vorakh*, "the Eternal has given and the Eternal has taken away, [yet] blessed [nonetheless] be the name of the Eternal" (Job 1:21). And during Kaddish, we are told to respond with the words: *y'hei sh'meih rabba m'varakh*, "may God's great name be blessed."

Isn't expecting us to shovel dirt onto the dead and read texts proclaiming the awesome greatness of God akin to asking the victim of sexual abuse to flatter the tormentor? How many of us have looked into the earth where our dead are to lie and resisted (or not) the urge to accuse God of a perverse self-satisfaction in requiring the recital of Kaddish at all? In The Last of the Just, a young survivor of a horrific pogrom tells just such a story:

> I buried them all, you know, the whole village without exception—didn't miss a fingernail. And for each one of them, even for that dirty little liar Moshele... for each one of them, I swear it, I said all the prayers from A to Z, because in those days I was a famous praying man before the Eternal.... And when it was done, I felt queer all over, you know? It was in the cemetery. I woke up and I grabbed a handful of rocks and began to throw them at the sky. And at a certain moment, the sky *shattered*. You understand?[1]

The text may be fictional, but the experience behind it is surely historical. Survivors of pogroms did bury the dead, reciting Kaddish—again, and again. Did such Jews, enraged and alienated from the God they prayed to, ever attack the heavens, attempt to destroy faith itself?[2] It is hardly unimaginable.

Why, then, did the rabbis press a prayer of unbounded praise into the service of grieving? After all, they were the ones who canonized its literary opposite in the Book of Lamentations, a text that names horror and articulates rage. Clearly, they understood the importance of retaining—even sanctifying—the right to protest. When we are suffering grief and rage, denial and disbelief, when we are disconnected and disassociated, we are then permitted bitterness, even anger, at God.

The rabbis honored the anguish of Lamentations in canonizing it, but they understood it to embody individual, personal grief. All the behaviors of mourning are those, they say, of the Ninth of Av—a day of dismantling, of repeated and remorseless destruction in Jewish history.[3] The rabbinic legal tradition offers mourners a list of directed readings that include the "ominous" portions of Jeremiah, which predict the disasters the Book of Lamentations records.[4] The first devastation of Jewish existence—the loss of Jerusalem and the Temple—is thus tied to every other ruin, personal and communal. It is understood: those who mourn may read the rawest text of grief found in the Tanakh.

In the centuries that followed the First Crusade of 1096, medieval rabbis added the Kaddish as required liturgical practice.[5] Three times a day, if the mourner has buried a father or mother, for eleven long months. One can avoid the horror and grief to be found in Lamentations—no one will force a mourner to read a text depicting starvation, torment, even cannibalism—but there is no escaping Kaddish. It is, now, a vital organ in the body of Jewish liturgy.

The first step toward re-inscribing Kaddish as a prayer for mourners is to be found in a well-known talmudic story, introduced by a timely conversation over how the night hours are divided.[6] Rabbi Eliezer describes the Holy One marking each watch with a roar, citing the menacing Jeremiah 25:30 as his prooftext. God's rage is announced: the destruction of the First Temple is imminent. Another rabbi, Rabbi Isaac bar Samuel, speaks in the name of Rav, transmuting the roar to one of divine regret.

Enter Rabbi Yosi, standing in "a certain ruin" of Jerusalem, apparently praying in the wreckage of the Second Temple. Later, he encounters Elijah. The prophet tells the rabbi that he ought to have prayed instead on the open road. Elijah is adamant: "Avoid the ruin," he says. Rabbi Yosi, in turn, describes the cooing call, the lamenting, sorrowing voice of the *bat kol* rising from the midst of the destruction. Elijah retorts that God's voice is to be heard directly, but in a wholly different setting. God is a happy sovereign, the prophet says, sustained by the commitment of a people who continues to pray *y'hei sh'meih rabba m'varakh*, "may God's great name be blessed." But they do this, Elijah points out, where there is no outward sign of the misery that has befallen their people. They pray surrounded by the untouched, undamaged walls of their synagogues and study houses.

Rabbi Yosi worships in a ruin. He stands amidst the evidence of God's apparent abandonment,[7] and yet he *praises* God. Standing near or, who knows, perhaps in the very spot where the Holy of Holies once stood, just after Jews have been starved, enslaved, and slaughtered *en masse*, he utters *y'hei sh'meih rabba m'varakh*. Elijah responds to the rabbi's experience by asserting God's joy and acceptance—even pride— in a people that continues to affirm God's greatness, three times a day no less. The Holy One listens—in delight. Even when we mourn?

Though God, in the end, admits to exiling Israel and worries over the people's future, the Holy One's regret engenders no promises. There is no new covenant ensuring that such a disaster will never recur. The text encourages—even advocates—a kind of psycho-spiritual compartmentalization. Rabbi Yosi stands in a desolation. It is God's prophet who insists that the rabbi leave the ruins behind; it would be better for him to pray on the road. Worship in the space of wholeness: pray in new synagogues, unspoiled sanctuaries. Get out of the ruin, Elijah says; do not stand in the place of pain. If Elijah is acting as God's messenger, what is God saying to a decimated people? Are they to heal through denial of the ordeal they have suffered?

The talmudic text links the phrase most fundamental to Kaddish in all its forms to a time of utter destruction. Once again, the Temple is destroyed; once again, lamentations are in order. Yet, Elijah tells Rabbi Yosi to join his people in the synagogues to pray, to bless God's name. When in grief, when in mourning, amidst the ruin of your people's life—praise God.[8]

Reciting the entire Kaddish in the service of grief is a much later innovation. Kaddish becomes embedded as part of mourning rituals after the First Crusade ushered in the slaughter of as many as one out of three Jews of Northern France and of Germany. Over the next centuries, harrowed by more Crusades, by the introduction of the blood libel, and by yet more slaughter, post-talmudic rabbinic authorities responded with fasts, martyrologies, and a liturgically creative transformation of Kaddish.

One longs for medieval voices to rise from the ashes, to admonish and accuse God as Daughter Zion did. Some fifteen centuries prior, Lamentations had endowed her with a powerful, unforgettable, accusatory voice. And she had used it: she had called God to account, indicting the Deity for indulging in a demonic killing rage, wholly incommensurate to the crime. Lamentations does not mince words: Daughter Zion even compares God to a mass murderer.[9]

In the Middle Ages, Jews simply buried their dead. Instead of calling God to account, their spiritual leaders prescribed Kaddish. One effect of the genocidal attacks on Jews of central Europe was to introduce *y'hei sh'meih rabba* and the text surrounding it into the liturgy, for a wholly new function than its earlier doxological one: grieving. Over the next few generations, the Kaddish found its way into daily, Shabbat, and festival services as the Mourner's Kaddish, a telling translation of its actual name, *Kaddish Yatom* (literally "Orphan's Kaddish"). The Crusades made orphans of multitudes of Jews, whose communities were destroyed; Kaddish was re-visioned, in part, for them.

Over time, the custom of asking a mourner to lead the Kaddish became normative liturgical practice. Consider the task: the mourner stands out by standing up and before all others, exposed in sorrow and grief.[10] Regardless of any resistance the grieving person might feel, the challenge is this: in front of a *minyan*, at least, and perhaps as much as the entire community, the mourner will have to say words of praise while acknowledging loss.[11] At the very moment of loss, one says nothing about it. In the face of death, one praises the Source of life.

There's more. According to the Shulḥan Arukh, a mourner should function as the formal prayer leader, as the *ba·al t'fillah*.[12] Why? Because God prefers a broken vessel.[13] But must we be grieving, must we be in pain in order to utter our most powerful prayer?

Some prayers must be said. So claimed Isaiah of Trani, among the foremost rabbis of Italy, born just a few years after the Second Crusade and during the century that added the blood libel to Christianity's perverse list of alleged Jewish crimes. Which prayers must be uttered? Prayers that will, he writes delicately, "cause anguish." No lament is greater than Mourner's Kaddish, he adds, and the Kaddish is not meant to serve merely as acceptance of God's judgment.[14] Perhaps reciting this prayer was one more way to process the latest collective disaster, to sublimate rage at the oppressor (read Christian Europe, this time), to insist that while Jews might die, their covenant with God never would. Kaddish: an act of defiance in the face of negation and annihilation.

Contemporary liturgical practice continues to insist on the recitation of Kaddish. So do Jews, regardless of the ruin that surrounds them. Narratives and stories emerge from the Shoah describing survivors at the moment of liberation, reciting the words of Mourner's Kaddish. Surrounded by corpses yet to be bulldozed into the earth, they uttered praise of an awesome God. Today, there are rabbis who will invite congregants to stand and recite Kaddish— not for relatives or even friends, but for those who have no one to say it for them. The Shoah gave us (yet) another reason to say Kaddish.

The poet Edmond Jabès wrote: "I say that after Auschwitz we must write poetry, but with wounded words."[15] How can we simply repeat the words of the Kaddish, words that betray no sign of our wounds? How can we?

It is incumbent on all who ask the mourner to rise for Kaddish to question, especially after the Holocaust: should we require that mourners say this prayer? If Jabès is correct, it will not suffice to claim that the words of Kaddish are, as Rachel Adler says, "words of power," text that no other text can replace.[16] Not after the murder of a million children.

Present-day rabbis must be honest, though it may hurt. They cannot afford to alienate future generations by channeling Tevye the Dairyman: it will not do to insist on what is ritually expected simply because it is known. Tradition, through mere repetition, is not adequate justification for retaining a practice. Not if the practice is predicated on a theologically troubling perspective. Not if Kaddish puts us in the place of victims who praise our Punisher.

In "Yosl Rakover Talks to God,"[17] author Zvi Kolitz forces us to acknowledge what the Shoah destroyed. In fewer than twenty-five pages, we traverse a man's life and his death. The story is imagined, but there is no doubt: the cruelty is factual. The narrator, Yosl, describes the Nazi persecution and the inexorable, gradual loss of his family. First, his wife and infant child are mowed down by planes attacking refugees hiding in the forests. Then two additional children go missing. He and his surviving children make their way to Warsaw, where one child is shot by Nazi sentries for stealing food and the other dies of tuberculosis. His own death is certain. He writes to God in the last hours of the uprising, as the ghetto goes up in flames. His words echo Daughter Zion's. Yes, he says, his people have sinned; they deserve punishment. "But," he asks, "I want You to tell me if there is any sin in the world that deserves the punishment we have received?" In defiance, he proclaims: "You have done everything to make me cease to believe in You. But I die exactly as I have lived, an unshakeable believer in You. Praised be forever the God of the dead."[19]

Human beings—Jews among them—cling, even now, to a God who offers reward and punishment, who treats humanity like either erring or well-behaved children. Yet, as Emmanuel Levinas (1906–

1995) writes,[20] such is the narrative of an infantilizing religion. We must know better than to fall into this trap. When God hides, the righteous are abandoned. There is no protection to be had—not from humanity, and not from God. Our only triumph is that of our conscience, and for that we will suffer.

Confronting God's absence, Levinas suggests, inevitably offers us the knowledge of a divine power that is both awesome and intimate. The distant God, he says, becomes *my* God.[21] That God directs us to the challenge of being human. Once we know what we are charged with—complete accountability for the created world—only then can we can know God as our close companion. Richard Cohen writes:

> Regardless of God's silence or absence, indeed inspired by the responsibilities which devolve upon us through this silence and absence, we must be moved in our afflictions by the afflictions of our fellow humans. Perhaps only in this way, finally, without making any demands, without expecting any rewards, without reservation or reserve, without miracles, can each of us, for the first time as adults "walk humbly with your God."[22]

Humanity will have to walk a path to God that must be walked "in part without God."[23]

When we grieve, we face realities: Life is fragile; fate is unpredictable; horrors are everywhere. God will neither reward nor punish in this world. One must acknowledge this reality in order to become an adult who can pray as an adult.

The rabbis, too, lived through horrific ordeals. They witnessed carnage and catastrophe; they endured personal and communal loss. They knew that there was no true and lasting path to God that did not admit of God's hiddenness from humanity. So they prescribed the continual process of affirming—again and again—that God is, in fact, too magnificent for words. The text of Kaddish demands that we admit that the Holy One is so far and above all that is human that there is no earthly speech that can be adequate. No words suffice to describe God.

Judaism asks us to proclaim God's greatness in the moments of our deepest losses. We repeat words that seem alien, perhaps. But at some point, standing at the juncture of life and death, praising God, the knowledge of our precious smallness emerges through the awareness of the Creator's awesome, indescribable nature. "The knowledge of God comes to us like a commandment, like a *mitzvah*," Levinas writes. "To know God is to know what must be done."[24]

In Romain Gary's surreal novel *The Dance of Genghis Cohn*, a dybbuk haunts the SS soldier who murdered him. Humans attempt to bring God down to earth. They hope to make God halt the course of the destruction they continue to wreak. But they fail. The dybbuk realizes that if the world really wanted to exorcise him and the horror he represents, there would be just one sure way: "They've only got to do what they have never done: *create the world*. I'm not saying create a new world: I say: *create the world*. It will indeed be for the first time."[25]

The rabbis say that by repeating *y'hei sh'meih rabba m'varakh*, we Jews aid God in affixing and affirming the foundation of the world.[26] We co-create the world, itself spoken into existence, by the act of reciting Kaddish. We use all-powerful speech while simultaneously admitting its patent inadequacy. Beyond all psalm and song? We are only human. Our words—even those we use to praise the Holy One—are wounded ones. They must be, if we are to be adults.

To acknowledge God's greatness demands that we see ourselves for what we are: the heirs and the trustees of the human condition. So we learn that we must rise to our God-given task: the ethical and moral work of fashioning the world. Say the Kaddish. Then, create the world. It will indeed be for the first time.

NOTES

[1] André Schwarz-Bart, *The Last of the Just,* trans. Stephen Becker (New York: Atheneum, 1960), p. 92.

[2] In Elie Wiesel's *Night* (1958; new trans. Marion Wiesel [New York: Hill and Wang, 2006]), the author describes how prisoners began to recite Kaddish after arriving at Auschwitz: "I don't know, whether during the history of the Jewish people, men have ever before recited Kaddish for themselves" (p. 33). Later, when a prisoner asks others to say Kaddish for him after he dies, they promise and forget (p. 77). By the death march, he tells us, Jews fell and no one recited Kaddish over them (p. 92).

[3] The list of violent acts inflicted on this day on an already decimated people makes for painful reading: they range from the expulsion of England's Jews in 1290 to the Nazis' liquidation of the Warsaw Ghetto. Biblical descriptions of expressions of individual and communal grief, as well as those described by other ancient Near Eastern texts—such as refraining from anointing, fasting, and going barefoot—suggest that a set of specific mourning practices in response to personal and communal calamity became normative in later Jewish practice. See Xuan Huong Thi Pham, *Mourning in the Ancient Near East and the Hebrew Bible* in *Journal for the Study of the Old Testament* (Supplement Series 302; Sheffield, UK: Sheffield Academic Press, 1999), pp. 13–27.

[4] B. Taanit 30a. For a comprehensive study of rituals described in early rabbinical texts, see David Kraemer, *The Meanings of Death in Rabbinic Judaism* (New York: Routledge, 1999).

[5] The eleventh-century story in *Maḥzor Vitry*, featuring a tax collector whose son must recite the Kaddish to redeem him from punishment, is considered a later interpolation into an earlier story. Still, Leon Wieseltier suggests that the Kaddish, in Rashi's day, is playing a role "in and out of mourning." By the thirteenth century, Isaiah of Trani (c. 1180–c. 1250) wrote about the Kaddish as if its role in the process of mourning is self-evident. Cf. Leon Wieseltier, *Kaddish* (1998; rpt. New York: Vintage Books–Random House, 2000), pp. 54 and 67.

[6] See B. Berakhot 3a.

[7] Interestingly, this became the dominant Christian reading: the Gospels and the work of the early church fathers, in significant part, assume that the decimation of Jerusalem, the destruction of the Second Temple, and the horrors Jews experienced in the Judeo-Roman War are proof that the Jews have, in fact, forfeited their covenantal status. They interpret those events as evidence that God is rejecting and punishing the previously chosen people because of their stubborn rejection of Jesus as the messiah. Christians thus inherit the covenant.

[8] Or, perhaps, talk God out of God's rage. In Eikhah Rabbah 24, a number of ancestors, beginning with Abraham (the passage opens with him lamenting as he walks among the ruins of the First Temple), defend the people from God's

judgment: they have transgressed against the Torah. The Torah is called to testify but is reminded that the people are the ones who accepted her when all others refused. The *alef-bet* is called to testify, but similar arguments are invoked. Abraham alludes to his willingness to sacrifice his son for God; Isaac reminds the Holy One of his willingness to be sacrificed. Eventually, Moses comes to remind God that he was refused entrance into the Holy Land. But the Holy One is unmoved. In the end, it is Rachel who finds a way to negotiate for a broken people. She reminds the Holy One that she was not jealous of her sister, though she waited for Jacob for seven years. And she insists that if she, a mere mortal, can rise above jealousy, why should the Holy One be jealous of idols of no substance, and banish her children on that account? The Holy One is convinced and promises restoration of the people. Maurice Lamm claims the Kaddish was associated with consolation "as far back as ancient times" (Maurice Lamm, *The Jewish Way in Death and Mourning* [1969; rpt. New York: Jonathan David Publishers, 2000], p. 147).

[9] Adele Berlin writes, particularly of Lamentations 2:21, that Daughter Zion argues that the "God who slaughters his people is no less a cannibal than the mothers who eat their children" (Adele Berlin, *Lamentations: A Commentary* [Louisville: Westminster John Knox Press, 2004], p. 76). Carleen R. Mandolfo points out that in the following verse, Daughter Zion accuses God, her enemy, of consuming the children she loved and reared. See Carleen R. Mandolfo, *Daughter Zion Talks Back to the Prophets: A Dialogic Theology of the Book of Lamentations* (Atlanta: Society of Biblical Literature, 2007), p. 99. Admittedly, other voices in the five poems that constitute Lamentations assert an eventual return; God will be back: "The kindness of God has not ended; God's mercies are not spent" (Lamentations 3:22). The text as a whole, however, is not one of certainty.

[10] Perhaps this explains why it was once the custom of medieval Jews to wrap their heads and cover their faces while in mourning. When some of the congregation appeared so during services, the leader of the service announced, "Gentlemen, demand the reason!" Latecomers were asked the same question. Those in attendance would respond to the question by invoking and blessing the Judge of truth. Why this ritual? Wieseltier explains: "Since not every mourner has the ability to say what he feels, the early sages instituted the demanding of the reason to break the silence, so that the consoling may begin." Rightly, Wieseltier notes that had the mourners themselves been asked to explain their appearance, they, too, would have said, "because we are demanding the reason." See Wieseltier, *Kaddish*, pp. 88–89.

[11] And during those centuries, as Mourner's Kaddish became liturgically embedded in Jewish practice, we find a moving discussion going on amongst rabbinic authorities: is it best for one voice to recite the Kaddish? Should the "many" who represent so few survivors all say Kaddish? Whose grief will be honored the most by the obligation to recite for the congregation? See

Wieseltier, *Kaddish*, pp. 510–511.

[12] S.A. Yoreh Dei-ah 376:4.

[13] Wieseltier, *Kaddish*, p. 366. Wieseltier refers to a responsa from 1981 written by Rabbi Moses Feinstein that quotes Rabbi Joel Sirkes, a seventeenth-century Polish authority who, in turn, cites Rabbi Solomon Luria (1510–1573) as the author of the idea that a mourner leads prayer because God prefers "a broken vessel."

[14] Quoted in Wieseltier, *Kaddish*, p. 67.

[15] Jabès made this statement in a 1983 interview with Marc C. Taylor; his description of the interview can be found in his foreword to Edmond Jabès *The Book of Margins*, trans. Rosemarie Waldrop (Chicago: The University of Chicago Press, 1993), p. x.

[16] Rachel Adler, *Engendering Judaism: An Inclusive Theology and Ethics* (Boston: Beacon Press, 1998), p. 80. Leon Wieseltier writes about two men who appear at his synagogue to recite the Kaddish: "The sounds that they uttered made no sense to them. But there was so much fidelity, so much humility, in their gibberish" (*Kaddish*, pp. 18–19).

[17] Zvi Kolitz, *Yosl Rakover Talks to God*, trans. Carol Brown Janeway (New York: Vintage International, 1999).

[18] Ibid., p. 18.

[19] Ibid., p. 23.

[20] Emmanuel Levinas, *Difficult Freedom: Essays on Judaism*, trans. Sean Hand (Baltimore: The Johns Hopkins University Press, 1990), p. 144.

[21] Ibid., p. 145.

[22] Richard Cohen, *Ethics, Exegesis, and Philosophy: Interpretation after Levinas* (Cambridge, MA: Cambridge University Press, 2001), pp. 282–283. The biblical citation is from Micah 6:8.

[23] Levinas, *Difficult Freedom*, p. 143.

[24] Ibid., p. 17.

[25] Romain Gary, *The Dance of Genghis Cohn*, trans. Romain Gary and Camilla Sykes (New York: The World Publishing Company, 1968), p. 150. The dybbuk, Genghis Cohn, also forces his executioner to learn Yiddish, to cook Jewish foods, and, of course, to recite Mourner's Kaddish—the latter on the anniversary of the rising of the Warsaw Ghetto (p. 26).

[26] In B. Sotah 49a, we find the rabbis declaring that this phrase has sustained the world. In B. Shabbat 119b, Rabbi Joshua ben Levi and Rabbi Yoḥanan assert that reciting *y'hei sh'meih rabba* will influence heaven's decree, and Reish Lakish says that the gates of paradise will open for those who respond "amen" with all of their might.

Kaddish as a Vehicle for Rabbinic Political Revolution

Kerry M. Olitzky

The Mourner's Kaddish is among the most consoling of prayers that is found in Jewish liturgy, suggestive of a sustained liturgical effort to provide comfort to the bereaved through the medium of prayer. The reassurance that this prayer provides the mourner, particularly at a time when one as a human is contemplating one's own mortality and mourning the loss of a loved one, is probably more of a direct result of the Kaddish's cadences than of the specific words of the prayer. As a result, the rhythm of its verses have become familiar to many. Obviously, the solace that the prayer offers the mourner is bolstered by the community that supports the individual during the period in which the Kaddish is being said—whether during the initial stage of grief, the annual anniversary marking the death of one's loved one, or even during memorial prayers aligned with the major holidays. However, the real genius of the Kaddish prayer—and the subject of this brief essay—is how it can effectively help to soothe the mourner while simultaneously making a political statement that establishes (and then continuously reaffirms, even as the text evolves) the authority of the rabbis in the Jewish community.

It is remarkable that such a recognized prayer, seen by many as paradigmatic of Jewish prayer itself, can continue to reveal its secrets to those who utter its words—even after so many years of its repeated and recognized use as a memorial prayer. And for those who pray regularly, its familiarity is heightened by the various forms that the Kaddish takes beyond the prayer's use by mourners; those other forms are not the subject here[1]. Perhaps the intimacy that, over the centuries, Jews have experienced with the prayer is what prevented those who recited its words from grasping the profundity of its political dimension. Its recital became routine. Generations were so close to its recitation that they simply took the words and function of Kaddish for granted and continued to repeat it until it became a *kavvanah*, a sacred mantra of sorts that would soothe the soul in time of loss. This allowed for the words to transcend into the meta-rational realm of deep and profound prayer.

In order to understand the political claim of the rabbis who sought to wrest communal authority from the priests prior to the destruction of the Second Temple—a struggle that became moot with the Temple's destruction in 70 C.E. when the rabbis, as an indirect result of the Temple's devastation, achieved hegemony over the community—one has to understand the origins of the Kaddish prayer, how it originally functioned, and what was being communicated through its words.

While the specific details concerning the actual composition of the Kaddish prayer are unknown, the prayer and its variations seem to emerge from a one-line doxology—a "proto-Kaddish"—that served as the Aramaic equivalent of what was said in affirmation in the Temple precinct: *barukh sheim k'vod malkhuto l'olam va-ed*, "Praised be God's wonderful name (read: reputation), whose sovereignty is forever and ever."[2] This Kaddish, in its simplest form, was originally recited in the house of study, following the study of sacred literature.[3] One might naïvely assume that this was merely a transporting of the Temple prayer to other places, translated into the vernacular so that it might be readily understood. But by transferring the prayer, the rabbis also shifted the perceived efficacy deemed to be taking place elsewhere. Moreover, because these words were said at the end of the study of sacred rabbinic texts, in the language in which these texts were written and discussed, it cleverly linked the legitimacy of such study (of the Oral Tradition) with the authenticity of the Temple cult (and the Written Law). The so-called proto-Kaddish prayer also provided those who gathered together to study an opportunity to affirm God's presence in their lives in what seemed to be the most basic of terms outside of the Temple walls, away from the sacrificial system. Some will argue that the words of this proto-Kaddish were chosen to convey a specific message of divine grandeur. Certainly the words that eventually made up the Mourner's Kaddish were chosen by its author (or authors) for specific reasons, but I believe that they were chosen for their aural quality—that is, the actual sounds of the spoken words—more than to convey specific characteristics about the Divine. According to David Blumenthal, the Kaddish was already well-known in the talmudic period. Blumenthal argues that by then it already had contained within it the idea of salvation, which guaranteed the deceased a place in the World to Come and relief of punishment from any final judgment.[4]

Nevertheless, the words that were carefully selected were those that subtly distinguished rabbinic theology from the theology that was promulgated by the priestly cult. I am arguing that the words of the Kaddish as we know them were not later inventions or accretions. Rather, they probably had their origins in spontaneous additions to the early form of the one-line Kaddish, much like the prayers of the Amidah had their origins in the personal prayers of the early rabbis. Those charged with the recitation of Kaddish added their own lines—some of which eventually became the accepted form of the prayer. Even if this were not the case, the setting in which the proto-Kaddish was originally recited was a reflection of the rabbinic construction of the community, which rewarded those with competence in Jewish law rather than focusing solely on the hierarchical structure of the priesthood and thus precluding any preferential treatment for those outside the priestly class. We can assume this original context because of the nature of the Aramaic chosen for the text: more rabbinic academy or schoolhouse language than the colloquial Aramaic that might have been spoken in the streets.[5]

After a period of time, the practice of reciting the proto-Kaddish was probably transported to the home of a deceased scholar known for the teaching of such sacred texts.[6] In both cases, the recitation of the proto-Kaddish (and the lines that were added) served as a very poetic and prayerful response to the liminality of such study and as a way of paying homage to God—and to the teacher of God's words—following the teaching of a sacred text. The sacred texts being studied were part of the Oral Law, the teaching championed by the rabbis that complemented the (written) Torah, which itself was the sole focus of the priests. Jewish tradition, as taught by the rabbis, assigns divine origin to these sacred texts whose teachings were passed down orally through the generations.[7] This is perhaps why Mourner's Kaddish, the Kaddish D'rabbanan (recited at the conclusion of study), and the Kaddish said at the conclusion of the study of a tractate of Talmud all present variations on the same theme: it made sense to thank God and acknowledge the role of the Divine in the formation of these texts, our connection to them, and appreciation for them and the place of God in our lives. In so doing, the recitation of Kaddish elevates the authority of the teachers of these texts (namely, the rabbis) over the authority of the priests, and the message of the rabbis over the version of spiritual endeavor promoted by the priests. Eventually, the recitation of the Kaddish prayer alone replaced the study of the sacred text when a scholar died. Finally, the responsibility of affirming God's name was extended to all mourners, irrespective of whether or not the deceased was a scholar.[8]

When the practice of reciting Kaddish entered the synagogue, it was used to conclude the service and was often led by a minor, who was otherwise not permitted to lead worship—hence, the technical name for Mourner's Kaddish as "Orphan's Kaddish."[9] In the presence of numerous mourners, the rabbis devised multiple norms to determine who would be given priority to recite Kaddish. Apparently the Sephardim maintained the tradition of all mourners reciting the prayer, a practice that was not adopted by the Ashkenazim until the eighteenth century. Eventually the mourner recited the Kaddish at the conclusion of the service irrespective of whether or not he led the service.[10] The link between the recitation of Kaddish by a surviving child and the deceased parent's entrance to Paradise probably emerged in the twelfth century,[11] and it remains an underlying notion that prompts its recitation even among post-modern Jews. According to Abraham Idelsohn, Kaddish became a memorial prayer because of the hope it provided—that is, in the form of a World to Come, of Paradise.[12] This idea was always implicitly present in the text.

It is also important to note that the various forms that the Kaddish took probably reflected the fluidity of prayer texts during the rabbinic and medieval periods. By adding more specific phrases to the original line of the proto-Kaddish, liturgists were able to secure for the various forms of Kaddish a more specific place and function in the liturgy.

Moreover, the Kaddish serves as a vehicle to affirm the covenantal relationship between the Jewish people and God—and therefore between the individual and God—without saying so explicitly. Thus, the original recitation of the proto-Kaddish added the layer of prayer (which replaced the sacrificial cult as the ancient center of Israelite religion) to the context of study. This is important to note since its first recitation was not in the expected place of prayer (namely, the synagogue); it did, however, help to create a bridge from the proto-Kaddish to the Kaddish as we know it. In the period prior to the destruction of the Second Temple, prayer developed as a means of

communicating with the Divine (in the synagogue, led by the rabbis)—
even while sacrifices (in the Temple, led by the priests) similarly helped
the ancient Jewish people in their quest to get closer to God.[13]

It was not fully clear to those who originally recited Kaddish (or
even those who recite it today, particularly in the form the prayer
takes for mourners), that all are participating in an act with potential
political import, one that affirms the original formation of the
rabbinate and its structure. This prayer works much like the pithy
sayings of Pirkei Avot, which likewise camouflage its function as a
document of rabbinic authority and independence.[14] The argument
that the Kaddish served an implicit political function is strengthened
by a simple analysis of its evolved content. If the words of Kaddish
now speak to the existence of a World to Come and the resurrection
of the dead and such a world was an invention of rabbinic theology
(since it is not included in the Written Torah and therefore not
claimed by the priests), then reciting the original proto-Kaddish
served to subtly advance the theology of the rabbis (while effectively
undermining that of the priests).[15]

A remnant of the early function of the Kaddish is found in the
rabbinic directive that allows for the study of a sacred text—in honor
of the memory of the deceased—when a *minyan* (prayer quorum, a
traditional requirement for the recitation of Kaddish) is not available
for the Kaddish to be said.[16] If history is the best arbiter of the success
of ritual, then certainly the current form of the Kaddish speaks to the
masses, who seek a way both to honor the memory of the deceased
and to affirm their faith in God during the time when such faith may
be challenged.

While the Kaddish eventually transcended its political function, it
now serves primarily to comfort the mourner. It might be said that it
has become part of the folk-religion of the Jewish people. If it was a
powerful tool in the claim of rabbinic authority over the community,

one wonders whether the diminution of numbers of those who feel the responsibility to recite Kaddish at its appointed times, to mark the anniversary of a death, for example, will also help to undermine the role of the rabbinate which is currently being challenged. Only future historians will be able to make that determination retrospectively. Nevertheless, the Kaddish stands as a creative model of the wresting of authority of one generation's leadership over another, for others in future generations to follow.

NOTES

[1] Other uses of the Kaddish include versions used to mark a full or half stop between sections of the fixed prayer service.

[2] Some have suggested that the text of the Kaddish may well be based on Midrash Mishlei to Proverbs 14:28 and B. Sotah 49a. See also B. Berakhot 3a.

[3] David De Sola Pool, *The Kaddish* (1909; rpt. Jerusalem: Sivan Press, 1964), pp. 8–10: Ismar Elbogen, *Jewish Liturgy: A Comprehensive History*, trans. Raymond P. Scheindlin (Philadelphia and New York: Jewish Publication Society and the Jewish Theological Seminary, 1993), pp. 80–81.

[4] David Blumenthal, "Kaddish" in *The Jewish Spectator* (Fall 2011) and available online at http://www.js.emory.edu/BLUMENTHAL/Kaddish.html. A short form of the essay appeared in *Judaism* 197:50 (Winter 2001), pp. 35–51. Another shorter version of article appeared in *The Jewish Spectator* (Fall 2001), pp. 29–36.

[5] Hayim Halevy Donin, in *To Pray as a Jew* (New York: Basic Books, 1980), p. 218, argues that because the name of God is not mentioned in the doxology, it indicates that the Kaddish started in the house of study rather than in the synagogue.

[6] Abraham E. Millgram claims that it was originally recited after study at the conclusion of *shiva* for a scholar, and then, later, at the conclusion of *shiva* for anyone; see his *Jewish Worship* (Philadelphia: Jewish Publication Society, 1971), pp. 80–81.

[7] See, for example, Pirkei Avot 1:1.

[8] In tractate Sofrim (19:9), we are told about *ḥazzan* (prayer leader) in Jerusalem who attempted to console mourners after Shabbat worship using the words of a slightly abridged Kaddish.

[9] In the *Maḥzor Vitry*, we see that an orphan is directed to lead the service on Saturday night. This is probably because of the traditional belief that the deceased are judged and then either rewarded or punished at the conclusion of the Sabbath. See *Maḥzor Vitry*, ed. S. H. Hurwitz (Nuremberg: J. Bulka, 1923), p. 113.

[10] There is a remnant of this notion in the obligation of the mourner to serve as the prayer leader, whether during the period of mourning or at the anniversary of the death of one's loved one (*yahrzeit*).

[11] This transition may have occurred in the thirteenth century, when the Kaddish became a mourner's prayer in direct response to the Crusades. See Lawrence A. Hoffman, editor, *May God Remember: Memory and Memorializing in Judaism* (Woodstock, VT: Jewish Lights Publishing, 2013), p. 123.

[12] Abraham Idelsohn, *Jewish Liturgy and its Development* (1932; rpt. New York: Schocken, 1967), p. 86.

[13] It is important to note that the Hebrew word *korban* (sacrifice) shares a root (*kof-resh-bet*) with the Hebrew words that denote getting close or drawing near.

[14] See Leonard Kravitz and Kerry Olitzky, *Pirkei Avot* (New York: UAHC Press, 1993), pp. xi–xiv and *passim*.

[15] See Ellis Rivkin, *The Shaping of Jewish History: A Radical New Interpretation*. (New York: Scribner, 1971), chap. 4.

[16] This alternative option is noted by Maurice Lamm in his *The Jewish Way in Death and Mourning* (New York: J. David, 1969), p. 174, as cited by Judith Hauptman in her essay, "Death and Mourning: A Time for Weeping, A Time for Healing" in *Celebration and Renewal: Rites of Passage in Judaism*, ed. Rela M. Geffen (Philadelphia: Jewish Publication Society, 1993), p. 250, n. 18.

The Mourner's Kaddish:
An Enduring Inspiration and Challenge

Peter S. Knobel

Although the Kaddish in a certain sense is only a doxology (that is, a prayer that praises God) and does not even mention death, nonetheless it somehow possesses the ability to connect one generation to the next, as the mourner's expression of grief *par excellence*.

Primarily, the power of the Kaddish derives from its language. That too is a kind of a paradox, in that the Kaddish ultimately expresses the concept that God is beyond verbal description. Indeed, its core idea is precisely that language is inadequate for providing a vocabulary that conveys the praise of God in a manner befitting the grandeur and magnificence of the Deity. Lawrence Hoffman, writing in his *Canonization of the Synagogue Service*, suggests that its origins might be found in the literature of the so-called "Merkavah" mystics of early rabbinic times. "Worship's purpose," he writes, "was to praise God...and to escape the fetters of worldly habitation in order to break through the barriers of the various heavens and see God in his splendor."[1] Today's worshipper, while not necessarily seeking a mystical experience *per se*, may nevertheless experience the presence of the transcendent through the medium of prayer. As Hoffman further points out,

> words which have different meanings when translated into English ("praised," "adored," "sanctified," "lauded," etc.) [are]

> regularly strung together by mystics without, however, any
> necessary thought about their cognitive significance. They
> were all synonyms of the general picture of praising God,
> and were never meant to be analyzed into fine differences
> of meaning. Said together, one after another, perhaps even
> repeated time and again, one could reach beyond oneself
> to holy vision that beckoned....Mystical liturgy tends to
> have synonyms piled up together and...their meaning is
> insignificant, content being secondary to effect.[2]

Hoffman is surely correct that it is the rhythmic repetition of words chanted, sung, or recited, rather than their explicit definitions, that creates the powerful effect worshippers all seem to find in the Kaddish. In some sense, this is analogous to the experience of worshippers at the Kol Nidrei service on the eve of Yom Kippur. For many Jews, the words themselves are irrelevant—and not least of all because most would be repelled, or at least put off, by the concept of pre-emptively annulling vows. Instead, it is the melody and the setting that transform the dry, legalistic formulary into a powerful spiritual experience, one capable of setting the mood and tone for the rest of Yom Kippur. Similarly, it is the sense of obligation to recite Kaddish for deceased relatives—and thus to play a role of some sort in their posthumous repose—that makes the recitation of the Kaddish into such a powerful and transformative experience for so many. People customarily recite Kaddish for parents for a period of eleven months, but only for thirty days when mourning children, siblings, or spouses. Since Kaddish requires a *minyan* (a prayer quorum of ten), it is by definition a communal experience. And although the obligation to say Kaddish for a parent was largely restricted to sons in earlier times, there have always been, even in the pre-modern times, women who recited Kaddish for deceased parents. Today it has become increasingly common for women, even within Orthodox circles, to recite Kaddish.[3]

In a remarkable book, *Kaddish: Women's Voices*, readers can learn about the role that Kaddish can play in traditional circles when women accept the obligation to recite Kaddish and experience the profundity of prayer connecting one generation to another.[4] Kaddish is liturgy, but its performance is experience. One author in the aforementioned volume, Laila Goodman, reflects on the healing power of saying Kaddish for a father who committed suicide:

> Saying Kaddish for my father through the year was surprisingly healing. The daily davening was comforting. Feeling obligated to say Kaddish gave me *kavvanah*, purpose and intention. The words of Kaddish weren't particularly meaningful for me. I loved the rhythm and the familiarity of the sounds. The other prayers helped me to center, to keep my heart open, to ask for forgiveness for my harshness, cynicism, and loss of hope. I loved the English translation from Taḥanun in the Minḥah service: "We look to You, for alone we are helpless....Have pity, for we are sated with contempt." At the end of the Amidah, I felt Modim Anaḥnu Lakh was written for me: "May You continue to grant us life and sustenance." While mourning my father and hating the fact that he committed suicide, I was boosted up each day as I prayed for sustained life, as I chose life each day. Every morning or every afternoon or both, I would say Kaddish and at the end, after taking steps forward I would say, "I love you, Dad."[5]

These last words—"I love you, Dad"—precisely encapsulate the intensely personal meaning of the Kaddish for the individual mourner. Obviously, relationships are complex. And it surely also bears saying that Kaddish does not bring *everyone* closure or reconciliation. Still, for many, the daily recitation of Kaddish comes to symbolize the deep connection one generation can feel both to the future and to the past, to those for whom Kaddish is said and to those whom we hope will say Kaddish for us. Kaddish is thus the recognition of mortality *and* the hope for immortality.

As noted, the Mourner's Kaddish does not mention death. This unexpected feature, however, was addressed in 1940 by the editors of the old *Union Prayer Book*, the longtime *siddur* of the Reform Movement, when they revised the Mourner's Kaddish by adding an explicit reference to death in the Aramaic text of the Kaddish. That addition was not translated into English in the *siddur*, but would read as follows:

> For Israel and the righteous and all who have departed from this world according to the will of God, may they have great peace, grace and loving kindness from the Master of Heaven and Earth, and let us say: Amen.[6]

Instead of the translation, the editors chose to print the following English rendering on the page opposite the Aramaic text:

> The departed whom we now remember have entered into the peace of life eternal. They still live on earth in the acts of goodness they performed and in the hearts of those who cherish their memory. May the beauty of their life abide among us as a loving benediction.[7]

Classical Reform Judaism took a literalist approach to liturgy, and so the editors of the *Union Prayer Book* must clearly have believed that referencing death would enhance the experience of saying Kaddish for the bereaved worshipper. Yet, the line was removed in subsequent Reform *siddurim* because the connection between the recitation of Kaddish and the deceased was so well-ingrained that the addition of a special reference to death seemed superfluous—and, in some ways, even distracting. The removal of that line also mirrored a general trend, found in Conservative and even Orthodox prayerbooks in the post-World War II period in the United States, to take on a more traditional cast. While, at least in the Reform context, ideology was generally allowed to trump tradition, certain prayer texts simply resisted change and felt watered-down and less meaningful, a bit paradoxically, precisely because they had been updated. (In this way, popular religion withstood the innovations of the more elite editors of the prayerbooks in question.) Nor is Kaddish the only example of a prayer so entrenched in the popular psyche that it resisted all attempts to change or modify it: the same phenomenon can be seen in the many attempts of the rabbis over the centuries to eliminate Kol Nidrei from the Yom Kippur evening liturgy.

The essence of the Mourner's Kaddish is the praise of God and the reaffirmation of faith in response to the death of a close relative. But there is also the communal element to consider, and specifically in the many responses to the Shoah that incorporate the recitation of the Mourner's Kaddish on a much broader level. In the Reform Movement, for example, it was the custom for many years for the entire congregation (and not just the mourners in their midst) to rise and recite Kaddish together. This was justified with reference to the entire community needing to accept the responsibility for reciting Kaddish for those victims of the Shoah who had left behind no living relatives to mourn for them. In recent years, however, many Reform congregations have rejected this practice and moved back to a more traditional approach, wherein Mourner's Kaddish is recited only by those who are in mourning for a relative.

Yet, there were others for whom the recitation of Kaddish as a response to the Shoah felt almost like sacrilege. Those who felt this way often recalled the passage in Elie Wiesel's *Night* in which the author describes his discussion with his father upon arriving at Auschwitz:

"Father," I said. "If that is true, then I don't want to wait. I'll run into the electrified barbed wire. That would be easier than a slow death in the flames."
He didn't answer. He was weeping. His body was shaking. Everybody around us was weeping. Someone began to recite Kaddish, the prayer for the dead. I don't know whether, during the history of the Jewish people, men have ever before recited Kaddish for themselves.
"*Yisgadal, veyiskadash, shmey raba…*May His name be celebrated and sanctified…"whispered my father.
For the first time, I felt anger rising within me. Why should I sanctify His name? The Almighty, the eternal and terrible Master of the Universe, chose to be silent. What was there to thank Him for?[8]

Wiesel's point is well taken: the obligation to recite Kaddish is surely deeply ingrained in all Jews, but the Shoah raises disturbing theological questions about the appropriateness of praising a God who would permit the slaughter of Jewish people. Some of those caught up in the Nazis' web rejected traditional norms of expression. Others knew of no response *other* than to recite Kaddish. There are poignant photographs of lone Jews reciting Kaddish at the edge of a mass grave before they too were to be killed.

Still, years later, a special Kaddish with the names of the concentration camps interspersed was composed, and has subsequently appeared in many different settings:

V'yitkaddash, Lodz
Sh'meih rabba, Ponar
B'alma di–v'ra ki–re'uteih, Babi Yar
V'yamlikh malkhuteih, Maidanek
B'hayyeikhon u–v'yomeikhon, Birkenau
U–v'hayyei d'khol beit yisrael, Kovno

Ba-agala u-vi-z'man kariv, Janowska
V'imru amen.
Y'hei sh'meih rabba m'varakh l'alam u-l'almei almaya.
Yitbarakh v'yishtabbaḥ, Theresienstadt
V'yitpa·ar v'yitromam, Buchenwald
V'yitnassei v'yit·haddar, Treblinka
V'yitaleh v'yit·hallal, Vilna
Sh'meih d'kudsha, b'rikh hu, Bergen-Belsen
L'eilla, Matthausen
Mi-kol birkhata v'shirata, Dachau
Tushb'ḥata v'neḥemata, Minsk
Da-amiran b'alma, Warsaw
V'imru amen.
Y'hei sh'lama rabba min-sh'maya v'ḥayim aleinu v'al kol yisrael,
v'im'ru: amen.
Oseh shalom bimromav, hu ya·aseh shalom aleinu v'al kol yisrael,
v'imru amen.[9]

The recitation of this Kaddish has a harsh irony. The juxtaposition of the names of the concentration camps and the elaborate praise of God has a defiant almost heretical quality. It is a protest against the all-powerful God who theoretically could have intervened to prevent the Shoah. Yet, at the same time, it is an statement suggestive both of piety and of remembrance. To recite this Kaddish seriously is to keep faith with the victims of the Nazis and also with the greater history of the Jewish people. One is reminded of Rabbi Irving Greenberg's daring theological statement that God broke the covenant during the Shoah, leaving it as a voluntary relationship rather than a binding one. The use of traditional terms in this context is both comforting and challenging. Traditional forms and traditional words have the double function of conveying both continuity and rebellion. Continuity and discontinuity exist simultaneously both in the "Shoah" Kaddish and in contemporary Jewish life.

Leonard Bernstein's third symphony, called "The Kaddish," premiered just weeks after the assassination of President John F. Kennedy and is dedicated to his memory. It uses the text of the Mourner's Kaddish as a framework for theological reflection on God and humankind in the wake of loss. It is thus a protest against the failure of a God portrayed in traditional theological writing as just and powerful yet who allows injustice to exist in the world. Interestingly, Bernstein's original libretto was eventually replaced with a new text by the international lawyer and Shoah survivor, Samuel Pisar. The opening section sets the tone of magnificent and complex testimony regarding the themes at hand: death, rebirth, existential fear, hope, and gratitude:

> Eternal God, our Father in heaven, this is my personal Kaddish, an ode to life inspired by the ancient prayer for the dead. Written for the monumental symphony of Leonard Bernstein and dedicated to the memory of John F. Kennedy, both my beloved ministers and kindred souls.
>
> In our age of anxiety and turbulence, the Maestro wanted my living testimony drawn from the longest the depths of human suffering, and the miracle of my survival, to resonate in Your kingdom with his celestial music.
>
> Mine is a layman's Kaddish, Lord.
>
> Addressed to You and Your tormented children, Jews, Christians, Muslims and all others, believers and nonbelievers, yearning for peace, freedom, and justice in our genocidal, fratricidal, and suicidal world.
>
> I utter this lament with grief and anger welling up from my own traumatic past in the deluge of hatred, violence, and fear that is engulfing us today.

Everywhere, sworn enemies mired in bigotry and terror are again at each other's throats, even in Your Holy Land where they worship the same God and implore You to turn their swords into plowshares.

I weep for them all, the dead and the living. My first tears are for my family and my people, perpetual victims of religious and racial persecution that reached its historic climax in my childhood, destroying everyone and everything around me while You, supreme Ruler of the universe, stood idly by.

Equally indifferent were You when I agonized in Auschwitz, Maidanek, and Dachau where Eichman's and Mengele's gruesome reality eclipsed even Dante's vision of inferno.

To this day I am haunted by guilt for having survived, when so many of mine were murdered. Now I must atone for the ritual Kaddish I could never recite because I had no dates of their demise, no closure, no burials, no tombs for a stone, a flower, a prayer—a prayer for their redemption.

Magnified and sanctified be His great name. Amen.[10]

This is then followed by the chorus reciting the full Kaddish in Aramaic. As the text continues in anguish and sadness, the central theological question is one of theodicy, one of God's justice. It reflects the torment of the survivor and the survivor's continued commitment to the Jewish people and to maintaining a relationship with God; it is a plea for hope renewed by faith.

Further along in the libretto, Pisar returns to this central theme:

Yes I have never deserted Your fold. Nothing can ever shake my ancestral vow to worship You if only in my own unorthodox ways.

That emboldens me to say to You today: Behold a grave spiritual crisis is invading our minds and hearts. Many suspect that Your heavens are empty or, worse, that they breed superstition, discord and chaos on earth, that with or without You, we must count only on ourselves.

It's high time that You reaffirm our everlasting covenant, that You renew Your promise of a messianic age. Renew Your promise!!!

He then concludes with hope and pleas for a better and more peaceful world.

In the post-Shoah world, the Kaddish by its nature constitutes a theological challenge, functioning simultaneously as a statement of praise and as an accusation. Yet there can be comfort in facing such a challenge, and for many merely hearing the words of Kaddish recited aloud serve as an invitation to a rewarding, deeply personal spiritual journey. For many, it is the tie that binds the generations, by serving both as an expression of profound alienation from the promises of covenantal Judaism and as the context in which even the disaffected can experience moments of deeply satisfying comfort.

NOTES

[1] Lawrence A. Hoffman, *The Canonization of the Synagogue Service* (Notre Dame: University of Notre Dame Press, 1979), p. 60.

[2] Ibid.

[3] In this regard, see the essays elsewhere in this volume by Adena Berkowitz and Ruth Walfish.

[4] Kaddish: *Women's Voices*, eds. Michal Smart and Barbara Ashkenas (Jerusalem: Urim, 2014).

[5] Ibid., pp. 67–69.

[6] *Union PrayerBook*, revised ed. (New York: Central Conference of American Rabbis,1940), p.152. The Aramaic reads: *Al yisrael v'al tzadikayya v'al kol man di-f'tar min alma hadein ki-re'uteih d'elaha, y'hei l'hon sh'lama rabba ḥinna v'ḥisda min kodam marei sh'mayya v'ara, v'imru amein.* The English translation printed here is my own.

[7] Ibid., p. 153.

[8] Elie Wiesel, *Night*, trans. Marion Wiesel (New York: Hill and Wang, 2006), p. 33. Wiesel's memoir was first published in French in 1958; an earlier English translation by Stella Rodway appeared just two years later.

[9] Versions of the "Shoah Kaddish" appear in the Conservative Movement's *Maḥzor for Rosh Hashanah and Yom Kippur*, ed. Jules Harlow (New York: Rabbinical Assembly, 1972), pp. 566–569; Elie Wiesel and Albert H Friedlander's *Six Days of Destruction: Meditation toward Hope*(New Jersey: Paulist Press, 1988), pp.86–87; and in the Reform Movement's *Mishkan Tfilah: A Reform Siddur for Weekdays, Shabbat, Festivals, and Other Occasions of Public Worship*, ed. Elyse D. Frishman (New York: Central Conference of American Rabbis, 2007), p. 533. All are elaborations of the penultimate paragraph in André Schwarz-Bart's great novel, *The Last of the Just*, trans. Stephen Becker (New York: Atheneum Publishers, 1960), p. 374. For an attempt to set this kind of liturgical response to the Shoah in its larger context, see Tzvee Zahavy, "Judaisms and Memories: Systemic Representations of the Holocaust," the keynote address delivered at the Conference on the Effects of the Holocaust on the Humanities held at the University of Minnesota in March, 1989 and now available to readers on the author's website at www.tzvee.com/home/judaism-and-memories.

[10] This text is taken from the full text available at http://www.leonardbernstein.com/kaddish_pisar.htm.

Sound and Silence in Response to Grief

Martin S. Cohen and Dalia Marx

What is the ideal response to death? Should mourners be encouraged to remain silent as a way of signaling their understanding that the great questions of life and death are beyond human comprehension and thus best accepted without attempts at rationalization? Or should they be encouraged to proclaim their acceptance of the tragedy that has befallen them aloud in and in public, thus finding in speech—both of the formal and extemporaneous varieties—the path to healing in the wake of loss? In different contexts, Jewish tradition endorses both approaches...yet the latter became the hallmark of the traditional mourning experience, eclipsing the former and almost entirely obscuring it in all but the most traditional communities. In this essay, we will explore the interplay between these two ancient approaches to mourning and show how the tension between them has an unexpected latter-day echo in the secular kibbutz movement.

Silence in Lieu of Speech in the Bible

We begin by considering some biblical narrative passages about silence. In theory, of course, silence as a state of being doesn't exist at all and is merely the name for a state characterized by the absence of some other thing—in this case, of sound. Yet, when the Bible takes formal note of someone's silence, the point is never that the individual being described *merely* chose not to speak. Instead, the silence is always an important part of the story and hints at something more significant than simply the absence of sound or speech. Indeed, there are many passages that suggest that some emotions simply cannot adequately be encapsulated in language, particularly when an individual is overcome with awe vis-à-vis the Almighty or with grief in the face of death.

Abraham's servant, for example, is described at Genesis 24:21 as being struck speechless by the possibility that God had actually granted him success in his mission of finding a wife for Isaac. (The Hebrew term is *maharish*, an active verb that suggests doing something by remaining silent, not merely *not* doing something.) It seems that the narrative is not simply noting that he chose not to speak at this juncture in the story, but rather is inviting readers to consider that silence for what it might have been: a combination of awe-struck wonder, at the possibility of success; humility, rooted in the thought that God had watched over him and brought Rebecca to him almost immediately; and deep gratitude, of the variety that exists outside the sphere of spoken language.

There are many other examples of personalities who are depicted within the scriptural narrative as remaining silent at key moments in their own stories: Jacob remains silent about how to respond to the events concerning his daughter Dinah and Shekhem ben Ḥamor until his sons return from the fields (Genesis 34:5); Naomi decides not to respond verbally to Ruth's determination to remain by Naomi's side (Ruth 1:18); Saul, immediately following his identification by Samuel as Israel's future king, chooses to say nothing at all in the face of the taunting by the rabble who saw no hope of safety or security in a land over which Saul might reign (1 Samuel 10:27); Absalom grimly refuses to say a word to Amnon—his silence clearly suffused with rage and barely-controlled violence—in response to the latter's rape of Absalom's sister Tamar (2 Samuel 13:22); the people cower in silence in the face of Elijah's uncompromising challenge that they choose once and for all between the God of Israel and the Baal (1 Kings 18:21); and the nobles of Jerusalem could only find in silence a reasonable response to Nehemiah's enraged chastisement (Nehemiah 5:7). But the example of biblical silence that is the most crucial, at least for the purposes of this essay, is the one that the Bible sums up at Leviticus 10:3 in two words: *va-yiddom aharon* ("And Aaron was silent"), using an unusual verb that is specifically *not* used in any of the above-mentioned passages.

Aaron's Silence in the Bible

The story itself is told briefly, if powerfully. Moses' brother Aaron, patriarch of the priestly line, has four sons: Nadav, Avihu, Eleazar, and Itamar. As the narrative in Leviticus 10 begins, we see Nadav and Avihu filling censers with incense and setting them ablaze in the Tabernacle, thus offering the incense up in a way that did not conform to any specific instructions they had previously received; Scripture thus characterizes their offering as *eish zarah*, an "alien fire [offering]."[2] And for this indiscretion they both pay with their lives, as fire comes forth from "before the Eternal" and wholly immolates them, leaving behind only their charred remains. Moses notes that this rapid and decisive divine response to even the slightest ritual innovation in the newly inaugurated Tabernacle must be what God meant by "I shall sanctify Myself through those closest to Me and in so doing gain honor before the whole people."[3] And it is at that specific point in the narrative that Scripture adds the laconic comment, *va-yiddom aharon* ("and Aaron fell silent").

What exactly is the point here? The simplest explanation would be that Aaron was so breathtakingly stunned by his brother's callous insensitivity to the loss of his two sons that he simply could not think of any rational response, and so he said nothing at all. This would mirror the psalmist's use at Psalm 65:2 of a nominal form derived from the same three-letter root that also generates the verb used to reference Aaron's silence to remark that, when it comes to the praise of God, *l'kha dumiyyah t'hillah* ("to You silence is praise"). The psalmist seems to be suggesting that the notion that human language could ever reasonably suggest the fullness of the kind of praise due to the Almighty is patent absurd, and the only "real" way to praise God with anything approaching acceptable accuracy is to say nothing at all.[4] So here too would Scripture be asking us to understand that Moses' comment was so harsh and unsympathetic that Aaron could only respond to it reasonably by declining to respond at all.

Of course, there are other avenues of interpretation open to us as well: Aaron's silence could plausibly also denote defiance, or perhaps even anger so intense that it simply could not be expressed adequately—or perhaps even not at all—in words. But Scripture itself offers no clue at all regarding the reasons for Aaron's silence, and merely reports that such was Aaron's response to his brother's comment.

Rabbinic Responses to Aaron's Silence

However, that is not at all how Jewish tradition interprets Aaron's silence. Our ancient sources do take various stabs at interpreting Aaron's silence, but none is rooted in the notion that Aaron was stunned by Moses' insensitivity. Perhaps the least satisfying—or, at least, the least convincing—is the following midrash[5] that preserves a sermon once delivered by Rabbi Isaac (probably Rabbi Isaac Nappaḥa, late third century), who began his discourse by citing Jeremiah's slightly obscure remark that he "ate" God's words and found them a source of joy and lightheartedness (Jeremiah 15:16). Rabbi Isaac then cites a different sermon, one delivered on some earlier occasion by Rabbi Samuel bar Naḥmani, a slightly younger contemporary, that featured that rabbi's take on the very remark of Moses to which Aaron responded with silence.

In this earlier sermon/midrash, it is imagined that the words of God quoted by Moses to Aaron ("I shall sanctify Myself through those closest to Me and in so doing gain honor before the whole people") had been previously revealed by God to Moses at Sinai but not recorded at that time, precisely because Moses did not know what to make of them at the time. And so he now speaks to Aaron and says just that—that he had imagined that when God spoke of "sanctifying" the sanctuary, apparently with the death of a righteous soul, he (Moses) had imagined that God was referring either to himself or to Aaron—but now sees clearly that the intention was to do so with the deaths of Aaron's two sons, whom Moses characterizes as being *g'dolim mimmenni u-mim'kha* ("greater than me *or* you"). In this scenario, Aaron—delighted with this excellent, albeit posthumous, appraisal of his sons' worthiness but aware how vulgar it would be for him to express his pleasure openly even before his sons' bodies were properly buried—chooses simply to say nothing at all. And, the text continues, not only was this the correct decision, but one that God ultimately rewarded Aaron for making by elevating him personally to the rank of prophet and speaking, at least occasionally, to him directly. Thus, regardless of what moderns will make of the idea that the Tabernacle ultimately needed to be sanctified as a worship space with the death of at least one righteous soul, Aaron's silence here is specifically *not* understood as an expression of grief at all. Instead, the midrash understands his silence to reflect his pride in his sons and his joy that they died, as Moses specifically says in the text, *bi-sh'vil k'dushat sh'mo shel ha-kadosh barukh hu* ("for the sanctification of the name of the blessed Holy One").

This seems to have been a widely accepted interpretation of Aaron's silence in antiquity. This midrashic compilation, Vayikra Rabbah, is widely understood to have had its origins in Roman Palestine, but a passage preserved in the Babylonian Talmud suggests that the Jews of ancient Persia had a similar interpretation of Aaron's silence. There we read that Moses meant to imply something along the lines of: "My brother Aaron, your sons died only to sanctify the name of the blessed Holy One." Nor are we left in the dark about Aaron's response; the text relates that "once Aaron understood that [their deaths proved that] his sons were intimates of the Omnipresent (y'du·ei makom), he fell silent and for that eventually received a [divine] reward."[7] The reason for Aaron's silence, at any rate, feels the same in both of these midrashic traditions: delighted to learn of his sons' favor in God's eyes but also aware of how boorish it would for him to express that delight aloud before they were buried, he chose simply to say nothing at all in response to his brother's good news.

Another text on this same theme is preserved in the Avot D'rabbi Natan.[8] The setting is tragic: we are ushered into the presence of Rabbi Yoḥanan ben Zakkai immediately following the death of his son. The rabbi is inconsolable—as any bereaved father would be—and so rejects any attempt by his students to provide comfort with words in the wake of loss. Rabbi Eliezer ben Hyrcanus is the first to speak, and he encourages his master to accept words of condolence by reminding him that Adam too lost a son—Abel—yet allowed himself eventually to be comforted. (Rabbi Eliezer finds allusion to this at Genesis 4:25, which notes that Adam resumed marital relations with Eve some time after Abel's death.) Rabbi Yoḥanan, however, is not impressed and his response is trenchant: *lo dai li she-ani mitzta·eir b'atzmi, ella she-hizkarta li tza·aro shel adam ha-rishon.* ("Isn't it enough that I have to grapple with my own grief—do I really need to be reminded of Adam's grief as well?"). The next pupil,

Rabbi Joshua ben Ḥananiah, then steps forward to try his hand at comforting his master. Job, he notes, lost not one son like Adam, but *all* of his children—seven sons and three daughters—on the same day, yet he too found it in his heart to allow others to comfort him. This too, however, is rejected…and with exactly the same language that Rabbi Yoḥanan had used to rebuke Rabbi Eliezer, by observing that he already feels wretched enough and hardly needs to be burdened with other people's tragedies while he is still attempting to negotiate his own. Finally, another pupil, Rabbi Yosi Hakohen, steps forward to attempt to do what his two colleagues have so far failed utterly to manage. And so he brings up Aaron, noting that the latter lost two adult sons yet allowed himself to be comforted, to which Scripture alludes by specifically referencing Aaron's silence because, explains the midrash, *ein sh'tikah ella tanḥumin* ("silence [in this context] can only mean [that he agreed to accept] consolation")—and so should Rabbi Yoḥanan. For the midrash, the idea is clearly that Aaron's silence is deemed worthy of emulation because it was precisely by saying nothing that he was able to find comfort in the wake of horrific loss. Nor is the text's implication hard to seize: mourners seeking solace should be silent in the face of their loss. Saying more would be saying less. *Ein sh'tikah ella tanḥumin.*

Among the medieval biblical commentators, this notion that Aaron could only respond honestly to the loss of his sons by saying nothing at all took root in some interesting ways. Rashi's grandson, Rabbi Samuel ben Meir (c. 1085–c. 1158, called Rashbam), for example, suggests in his comment to Leviticus 10:3 that the Torah uses the words *va-yiddom aharon* to suggest that Aaron *wanted* to mourn and wail in the traditional mode because it was the expected thing, but could not bring himself to do so because he sought the kind of solace that only silence can bring.[9] Other commentators take a similar tack. Rabbi Baḥya ben Asher ibn Halawa (1255–1340, called Rabbeinu Baḥya), one of the first commentators to incorporate kabbalistic ideas into his biblical interpretations, says simply that "silence is one of the ideal modes (*mishpatim*) [of the mourning process]," and then goes on to justify his opinion with reference to the prophet Ezekiel (whom Rashbam also references in this regard). Ezekiel was instructed by God exactly how to behave after the death of "the delight of his eyes," usually presumed to be a respectful reference to the prophet's wife (24:15–27). And, indeed, among the instructions to the prophet is the unequivocal but oxymoronic *hei·aneik dom* (meaning something like "groan [or sigh or moan] silently")—and the word for "silently" here is from the same root that is used with respect to Aaron.[10] Rabbi Menaḥem ben Benjamin Recanati (1250–1310), whose commentary too is suffused with kabbalistic ideas, suggests a similar notion. Commenting directly on Leviticus 10:3, he writes: "The reason [that Aaron remained silent] is that it is simply inappropriate to second-guess the principle of rigorous divine judgment (*ein l'harheir aḥar middat ha-din*) and so must [pious individuals not merely accept God's judgment, but must by remaining silent indicate their willingness to] accept it with love."[11] And in this regard too must be mentioned the comment of Rabbi Hezekiah ben Manoaḥ (thirteenth century, called the Ḥizkuni after his sole surviving work, a commentary on the Torah), who also wrote that Aaron would naturally have wished to mourn in the traditional mode, but was simply dumbstruck by his grief and chose to give true voice to his unutterable sadness by saying nothing at all.[12]

At the heart of all these commentaries is the single notion that the ideal response to inexpressible grief is wordlessly to accept God's judgment and to signal as much by remaining silent. And, indeed, the Talmud seems to endorse such a view by preserving a comment of the Babylonian sage Rav Papa, who taught that the solace that a traditional house of mourning can offer the bereaved derives from the level of silence maintained.[13] Another talmudic tradition, this one preserved in the name of Rabbi Yoḥanan, says clearly that the mourner has the absolute right to insist that silence prevail in the house of mourning, and therefore none may say a word until the mourner formally and specifically permits it.[14] And, indeed, this lesson eventually entered the halakhic tradition as a legally requisite mode of behavior in houses of mourning.[15]

Silent Mourning in the Legal Tradition

Of course, Jewish tradition developed along other lines as well, eventually endorsing the notion that another way to deal with the great sadness that attends the loss of a loved one is not to remain silent at all but instead to come to synagogue for a specified period of time and to recite the Kaddish, a liturgical doxology that eventually became so inextricably tied to the process of mourning that it became known almost universally as the mourner's prayer par excellence.[16] In fact, the expression "saying Kaddish" eventually came to refer unambiguously to the mourner's effort to find solace in public speech. And so, as Judaism emerged from the medieval period, it somehow embraced both notions: that the ideal medium for coming to terms with grief is resigned silence to God's judgment in the face of personal loss, *and* that the therapeutic value of constant, day-in and day-out public speech as a mourner is the highway to coming through the mourning process emotionally and spiritually hale.

The basic rule about comforting the mourner eventually became that everything depends on the mourner him or herself—if the mourner feels the need to be silent, then the comforter should not speak. Moreover, the mourner is also empowered both to begin and to end the encounter and the conversation. Many sources link these rulings, but none as unequivocally as Rabbi Joseph Karo

(1488–1575) in the *Shulḥan Arukh*, later to become the foundational work of halakhic writing in the generations to follow, who writes unambiguously that "no [would-be] comforter is permitted to speak until the mourner speaks first. [Furthermore,] the mourner sits in the front of the room [and the comforters too may be seated], but once the mourner gives a signal—even one as subtle as a mere nod of the head—that clearly excuses the comforters, they are from that moment on *not* permitted to be seated in his or her presence."[17]

And so we are left with a complicated answer to what feels as though it should be a simple set of questions. Is silence the context in which people best find solace in the wake of loss? Or should the bereaved be encouraged to speak aloud, to express themselves verbally, to find in language—including the formalized language of public prayer—the path forward toward comfort? Jewish tradition clearly embraces both views, encouraging the public recitation of Kaddish *and* allowing the mourner to determine for him or herself whether speech or silence will prevail in the house of mourning. The latter notion, that silence is the only adequate response to devastating loss, has sound midrashic roots that go back to Aaron's famous silence and its plausible interpretations. But the former has its own place in Jewish tradition as well, one sanctioned by centuries of Jewish souls seeking comfort in the public recitation of Kaddish. Tradition thus offers not certainty but wise ambivalence, and supports the view that the road to restoration after loss will be paved with some combination of both silence *and* speech—the former born of principled resignation to God's decree and the latter suggestive of the need to affirm in public a dimension of reality that needs formally to be nurtured if it is to take root at all in a grieving soul attempting to come to terms with loss.

Modern Echoes[18]

How interesting to see this same quandary—regarding the best way to respond to loss—playing itself out in the wholly secular context of the emerging kibbutz movement, both before and after the establishment of the State of Israel! The common wisdom regarding the early days of the kibbutz movement was that the prevalent culture in those pioneering days was one based on the utter abandonment of the Jewish religion and its symbols. Accordingly the early pioneers are supposed to have made a conscious effort to create their own culture completely independent of ancient talmudic principles and the traditional practices of their ancestors. That image is widespread, but not entirely accurate: a more careful look yields a portrait of *kibbutznikim*, the kibbutz members, even in the very earliest days of the movement, possessed of a far more nuanced relationship to Jewish tradition than is generally supposed. Nor did the secular, even occasionally atheistic, formal pronouncements of the kibbutz movement leadership always match the actual decisions those leaders made, some of which evinced a distinct longing for rituals that they must have known and experienced as children. Indeed, the need to rely on traditional language and universally recognizable symbols was particularly evident at life-cycle moments and at turning points in the annual calendar. Significantly, some of the most genuine institutional re-interpretations of classical Jewish ritual and rite derive from the kibbutzim. Even those versions of the Passover Haggadah, some of which originated as parodies of the classical text, turned out, as time passed, to be possessed of unexpected staying power and abiding charm—and the same could be said of texts composed to mark the springtime harvest of the first fruits, the binding of the first sheaf of barley grain, and other festivals and ceremonies as well.

The members of the early kibbutzim were committed to be the masters of their own lives not only with respect to finances, education, and health-related issues but also with respect to culture and the life of the spirit. They sought to create a kind of new Hebrew-Israeli Judaism that would flourish in its new setting and that would specifically *not* be built on old models, no matter how tried and true they had been for previous generations. But that did not preclude borrowing from those same ancient models, sometimes in particularly daring ways. Berl Katznelson (1887–1944), one of the founders and leaders of the Labor Zionism movement, once made this explicit. "Our movement," he is quoted as having said, "is the heir to ancient Judaism in that [just as once was true of our ancient faith, so Labor Zionism too] requires strict adherence to its own commandments and demands of its followers that they serve with all their hearts, with all their soul, and with all their might."[19]

Facing Death with Silence and Restraint

Kibbutz funerals in the first decades of the twentieth century were characterized by an absence of formal, set ritual—either religious or secular. Instead, many kibbutz funerals consisted solely of spontaneously-conceived gestures of various sorts. Sociologist Nisan Rubin describes these various customs, noting that some of them, including the occasional recitation of Kaddish, were taken directly from ancient tradition, albeit divested from the religious framework in which they were originally conceived.[20] One kibbutz member related that, in the early days, "we would do what we could remember."[21] Also worth recalling is that the early kibbutzim were populated mostly by people who did not share familial bonds, and so it was often the case that even according to tradition there was no specific obligation for anyone present at the funeral of a deceased kibbutznik to recite the Kaddish. Nonetheless, the intimate nature of life on a kibbutz created bonds among members similar to familial bonds. It was for that reason as well that these questions of how to mourn for and memorialize members of the kibbutz became essential. And among the descriptions of early kibbutz funerals, there appear many descriptions of a kind of painful, deeply emotional silence—and these exist alongside descriptions of spontaneous behavior that include instances of unrestrained dancing and singing until late into the night.

Beginning in the 1920s, however, many kibbutz funerals took place in the kind of total silence that precluded both eulogies and prayers. Rubin describes two distinct periods as essentially separate stages of growth for the kibbutz movement: the first, during the first two decades of the twentieth century, featuring spontaneous ritualistic behavior and the second, in the decades that followed, featuring funerals carried out in total silence.[22] Nonetheless, it seems that there was no small overlap between these two modes of expression, partly due to the fact that the rituals reflected the style and ideology of each kibbutz and the responses to grief were different in each of the kibbutz movements. Occasionally, traditional Jewish content found its way into kibbutz funerals. Moti Zeira, a researcher of the kibbutz movement, certainly agrees that these funerals adopted parts of traditional funeral practice, but he labels such usage "eclectic, unsystematic, and fragmented, usually undertaken by a specific individual as a kind of spontaneous reaction to the dramatic death of a friend."[23]

A poem by Shalom Yosef Shapira (1904–1990, widely known as Shin Shalom) describes the "sanctuary of silence" that the early pioneers built to house their own grief in his poem "When Someone Dies":

When someone dies in the Jezreel Valley,
the ears of corn fall silent.
For the Jezreel Valley is the holy of holies
and crying is forbidden in the holy of holies.

When night falls on the Jezreel Valley
the stars become terrified;
they are the *yahrzeit* candles in the Jezreel Valley
that burn for those who have no one to say Kaddish....[24]

This intense poem offers an alternative religiosity, one at odds with the one rooted solely in ancient Jewish texts. Here the focus of the sacred, the holy of holies, is not in the Temple in Jerusalem, but in the Jezreel Valley itself, the hothouse of pioneering Zionism. Finding oneself in the presence of holiness, the appropriate response is self-restraint and control: none may cry at a funeral because it is inappropriate to weep in the Holy of Holies. And there is reward for such holding back as well: the heavens and the stars weep for those who have no one to say Kaddish for them. Nor is this silence "just" the absence of speech; it is not only the silence that represents reverence, but also absence of traditional language.

Perhaps the correct way to characterize the early pioneers' response to death, particularly given the high death rate among their numbers in the Promised Land, was not so much silence as muteness. Both the suicide rate, as well as death as result of diseases and conflict with the Arabs, were high. However the traditional prayers, and the Kaddish among them, were not acceptable to the pioneers as vehicles by with to express their grief—both because of their language and their content.

It seems that for the young pioneers, who wanted to take charge of every aspect of their life, it was impossible to give in to the tyranny of death. This severe self-discipline is reflected in the poem written by David Shimoni in memory of the writer Yosef Ḥayyim Brenner, who was killed in the course of the Arab riots in Jaffa in 1921:

> Mourn not.
> Weep not
> at a time such as this.
> Lower not your head!
>
> Work! Work!
> Harvester, harvest!
> Sower, sow!
> In a bad moment,
> work double-time,
> double-time create!
>
> And plant and hoe,
> clear rocks and build a fence.
> Clear a path and pave
> a path of freedom
> for the day now dawning.
> And plant and hoe,
> clear rocks and build a fence,
> a path of freedom
> for the day now dawning!
>
> The path of suffering
> leads to redemption. And the blood calls out
> to the soul of the people:
> Shake yourself off and act!
> Be redeemed and redeem![25]

Instead of giving himself over to feeling of grief and rage, the poet's charge is that the appropriate response to death unwarranted would be simply to go back to work. In his conception, work is the true revenge and also the remedy for misery. In a time as difficult as the one the members of the kibbutz community in pre-state Israel were negotiating, the poet's solution to their pain is plainly put: "Work double-time" and "Double-time create."

Silence also characterized funerals that were not directly connected to political tensions. The poet Yehuda Sharet (1901–1979), a member of Kibbutz Yagur, wrote in a letter to his mother about the funeral of a young man named Yehuda Schuster who was killed in a work accident that took place in Kibbutz Ein Ḥarod in 1923: "Not a groan. Not a moan. Not a scream. The sense of loss, overwhelming. Such should our funerals be! The mother's silence without her screams, and that was the whole thing…The mute funeral bears testimony to the detachment in our lives…and there is no other way, for we cannot choose our paths forward…and that itself is our path forward. The next day, everybody was back at work."[26] We will return later to Kibbutz Yagur and see how many far-reaching changes occurred in this particular kibbutz, as well as in the kibbutz movement with respect to this issue of liturgical silence.

Silence at funerals—the absence both of prayers and of wailing or expressions of emotional response to death—was an act of conscious abstention.[27] And Aaron David Gordon (1856–1922), a thinker, teacher, poet and the spiritual master of the pioneering movement, wrote the following in his will:

> And let me say some few words also about necrologies and eulogies, etc. It is natural for people to wish to honor those who have gone never to return, but they must also take into account the fact that the one who has thus left the world no longer exists. All that was that person has now become part of the great treasury, the great storehouse, of human deeds… and so, if they truly wish to honor that person, they must

understand that the only true expression of honor would be silence. Let each [mourner] find a secluded corner in which privately to ruminate, or secretly to weep, about the fate of the departed and of the fate of humankind in general. Would that not be enough?

That is how I conducted myself. I honored the departed with silence and so would I wish that others would behave with respect to me. Those who wish to honor me, let them do so in silence. For at least a year after my death, no one should speak or write about me at all.[28]

For Gordon, silence is largely understood as the appropriate response to the cruelty of death. It is possible to take this silence to represent a kind of defensiveness against the inevitability of death, or even as a kind of rebelliousness on the part of people devoted to building a society in which making personal, conscious choices was the basic right of all. But it also mirrors the ancient dictum *ein sh'tikah ella tanḥumin* (as discussed above), and has at its core the same idea: in the face of death, the only truly honest response is to say nothing at all.

Creativity and the Discovery of an Authentic Jewish Voice of the Kibbutz

The need to determine how best to deal with death and the formal structures of mourning became acute in the 1960s, as the founders of the kibbutzim began to pass away in ever-increasing numbers.[29] Moreover, many kibbutz members found the notion of silence in the faith of death inadequate and insufficient. In 1962, Yitzḥak Tabnakin (1888–1971), one of the leaders of the kibbutz movement, was quoted as saying in a private conversation that there was a clear need to turn to the "thinkers" and poets of the kibbutz movement and to ask that they create some expressive text for kibbutz funerals that would correspond to "our love of life." In effect, he was rejecting the *ein sh'tikah ella tanḥumin* model and asking for a new approach to mourning, one that would be deemed meaningful in the changing demographic reality of the kibbutzim.[30]

Shortly after that, Tzvi She'er (1904–1987), one of the Kibbutz Yagur educators who also worked in the fields, composed what eventually came to be recognized as the first version of the so-called "Kibbutz Kaddish," a formal text at least partially derived from the traditional Kaddish and intended specifically to be read at burial ceremonies on kibbutzim. This specific text came to be known as the Yagur Kaddish.[31] According to some witnesses, She'er composed his Kaddish specifically as a response to the absolute silence that had become a feature of kibbutz burials, but which was beginning to elicit negative responses from at least some kibbutz members. The text is as follows:

> Magnified (*yitgaddal*) be the man who retains his sense of hope from life's early morning until his final day, a man whose heart never retreats, whose deeds are upright, who never despairs regarding redemption, in whose heart the suffering of the world and its joy reside, and whose splendor he himself represents both openly and in secret.
> Nor shall his hopes end with him, for the way of the upright shall never lead astray.
> May the dignity of this man be ever blessed.
> Magnified (*yitgaddal*) be the Hebrew man on his land, and may the one who lives imbued with the memory of those once alive who have gone before him be sanctified.
> This life, sealed in the earth of Yagur, in its labor and in the heart of his comrades, has come to an end.
> May his memory be a blessing in our midst.[32]

She'er makes use of the traditional text of the Kaddish—the Hebrew for "magnified," *yitgaddal,* is the first word of the Kaddish—and elicits the strong emotional response that prayer is capable of producing in even secular communities, even though he has obviously changed the meaning of those borrowed words drastically. And so, instead of a hymn of praise to God and a supplicatory prayer about the establishment of the kingdom of heaven on earth, his praise is for human beings, and instead of the kingdom of heaven his idealized society is the kibbutz itself.

The use of the opening line of the Kaddish in secular contexts had actually began decades earlier, in the days of Yosef Ḥayyim Brenner (mentioned above in the context of David Shimon's poetic response to his death), who concluded an essay that he wrote as a response to the Russian Revolution of 1905 with the words, "May the Hebrew man be magnified and sanctified."[33] It is not at all clear how well known this line from Brenner was, so it is difficult to say if She'er was consciously mimicking Brenner or not. At any rate, the first to make use of the traditional liturgical text of Kaddish in a secular setting was Berl Katznelson (also mentioned above), who composed a version of the traditional Yizkor memorial prayer to honor those who were killed at the Battle of Tel Ḥai in 1920 that began "May the people Israel remember its sons and daughters who gave their lives…"—thus transforming the prayer from a supplication directed toward heaven ("May God remember…") into a call to Jewish humanity to honor its martyrs.

She'er's Kaddish was not universally accepted, yet the secular "Kibbutz Kaddish" inspired many to follow in its author's path. Consider, for example, this version of the prayer written by Yigal Talmi, a member of Kibbutz Mishmar Ha-emek:

May his great name be magnified and sanctified
and may the memory of ____ be preserved in our midst forever.
May your image be regularly before our eyes,
for you were the bone of our bones, the flesh of our flesh,
our comrade along the way, our sibling and friend in this house,
sharing sadness and joy, friendship and love,
on weekday and Sabbath, in life and in death.
May there be dew and the rain in this place,
and may the blessing of deeds be its inhabitants,
and may we all have happy lives, we and all Israel.
The one who makes peace shall make peace
for us and for all Israel.
May we know peace on our weekdays and our festivals,
tranquility in our courtyards and our homes.
May your name be inscribed in the Book of Life of this house,
and may your memory be blessed.

We can discern clearly three periods in the history of kibbutz funerals: a first period of funerals characterized by spontaneous outbursts of speech or song, or by complete silence at funerals; a second period characterized by tentative liturgical responses to death, and among them many texts that are clearly based on the traditional text of Kaddish; and a third period (which was not discussed here) characterized by the weakening of the earlier spirit of creative innovation, thus the adoption of some "ready-made" formulas presented by authoritative religious figures (almost invariably Orthodox or even ultra-Orthodox men, although not necessarily rabbis) that constitutes a retreat from the traditional kibbutz-style eagerness to determine independently the course kibbutz life takes.[34]

Conclusion

In its own way, these stages—or at least the first two of them—mirror the larger Jewish past, in which the message of the traditional texts adduced above that suggest that the ideal mode of expressing grief for the bereaved is total silence in the face of loss was eventually supplanted, or at least supplemented, by a kind of popular initiative to find a place in the synagogue service for mourners to proclaim their acceptance of God's decree aloud and repeatedly.[35] That the same set of ideas and practices characterized a Jewish movement as formally unbound to tradition as the secular kibbutz movement strikes us both as a fascinating turn of events. Apparently feeling unbound and unburdened by the need strictly to adhere to canonical tradition does not lead away from a traditional worldview...or from the obligation to grapple with the very same issues with which our forebears struggled as they sought to create a Jewish civilization that spoke to the deepest needs of its members and constituents.

NOTES

[1] The verb *maḥarish*, used of Abraham's servant, is also used regarding Jacob's silence and the young Saul's, but other passages express the same idea more elliptically. The term used regarding Aaron (see below) is unique, however.

[2] The word for fire, *eish*, is used repeatedly in Scripture metonymically to denote offerings to God burnt by fire (e.g., at Leviticus 2:3, 10 or at 4:35). By further extension, it is occasionally used even to denote grain offerings that are not burnt on the altar (e.g. at Leviticus 10:12). But the passage in question here is ultimately ambiguous, leaving unclear whether it was the offering burnt by fire or the fire itself that was so unacceptable so as to warrant the instant death of those responsible for its introduction.

[3] These words appear nowhere else in Scripture, yet are nonetheless presented by Moses in Leviticus 10:3 as an authentic—and presumably familiar—divine oracle.

[4] Cf. Rashi's comment *ad locum* to the effect that, because no one could find enough words fully to encapsulate the praise due God, to heap up more and more words in an attempt to say all there is to say is paradoxically to state God's praise less, not more, accurately. This mirrors the story preserved in the Talmud at B. Berakhot 33b regarding the sharp rebuke an anonymous prayer leader drew from Rabbi Ḥanina, presumably the *tanna* of third-century Roman Palestine, when he attempted to embroider upon the received liturgical text of the Amidah so as the better to suggest the full range of praise due to God. "Are you done fully listing God's praiseworthy attributes?" Rabbi Ḥanina asks acidulously, his question clearly rhetorical.

[5] Vayikra Rabbah 12:2.

[6] B. Zevaḥim 115b.

[7] The obvious question of why God would wish to sanctify the divine name on the occasion of the dedication of the Tabernacle by taking the lives of two righteous individuals is admirably, albeit not entirely convincingly, taken on by Baruch Halevi Epstein in his comment *ad locum* in his *Torah T'mimah* (1902; rpt. New York: Ziegelheim, 5743 [1982/1983]), p. 158.

[8] Avot D'rabbi Natan is a midrashic work organized as a kind of interpretive commentary on Pirkei Avot and usually grouped along with other shorter rabbinic works under the rubric of "minor tractates" that belong to the larger corpus of talmudic literature but are not actually part of either Talmud. The following translation is based on the Hebrew text published in Avot D'rabbi Natan, text A, chap. 14, ed. Solomon Schechter (5647 [1886/1887]; rpt. New York: Feldheim, 5727 [1966/1967]), pp. 58–59. Interested readers may also wish to consult Judah Goldin's fine translation of the text in his *The Fathers According to Rabbi Nathan* (New Haven: Yale University Press, 1955), pp. 76–77.

[9] Rashbam to Leviticus 10:3, ed. Martin Lockshin (Jerusalem: Chorev, 2009),

pp. 350–351, and cf. n. 29.

[10] *Midrash Rabbeinu Baḥya al Ḥamishah Ḥumshei Torah* (Oradea [Romania]: Binyomin Zev Rubenshtein, 5702 [1941/1942]), p. 36, s.v. *va-yiddom aharon*. The passage in Ezekiel is usually interpreted as a list of ways in which mourners usually express their grief, but which are being forbidden to the prophet. (That, indeed, is how the Talmud itself interprets the list of prohibited procedures at B. Mo·eid Katan 15a–b.) Elsewhere in Scripture, words formed from the same verbal root as *hei·aneik* reference the moaning of the poor (Psalm 12:6) or the incarcerated (Psalm 79:11, 102:21), and also the miserable sounds that accompany weeping (Malachi 2:13). At Ezekiel 26:15, a similar word is used to denote the groaning of the dying.

[11] Rabbi Menaḥem of Recanati, *Peirush al Ha-torah al Derekh Ha-emet* (Venice: Daniel Bomberg, 5283 [1522/1523]), *parashat Sh'mini*, s.v. *va-teitzei eish*.

[12] Rabbi Hezekiah ben Manoaḥ, *Sefer Ḥizkuni al Ḥamishah Ḥumshei Torah* (Vilna: Romm, 1859), p. 113.

[13] The question of who it is who is ideally supposed to remain silent in a house of mourning is debated by the commentators; see the comments of Rabbi Baruch Halevi Epstein in the passage cited in note 5 above, where the author determines convincingly that it is the mourner whose decision to remain silent is a sign of pious resignation to God's judgment. The phrase for "house of mourning" in the talmudic passage cited is *bei tamya*, literally "house of bones," and is open to interpretation. Our interpretation here follows Rashi's comment to B. Sanhedrin 112b, s.v. *k'lal b'aseih u-f'rat b'lo ta·aseh*.

[14] B. Mo·eid Katan 28b.

[15] Cf. S.A. Yoreh Dei·ah 376:1, citing verbatim the Arba·ah Turim of Rabbi Jacob ben Asher (c. 1269–c. 1343), Yoreh Dei·ah 376:1. Rambam, not referencing Rabbi Yoḥanan's lesson verbatim, nonetheless decrees that those who come to visit should sit "stricken" (*davin*), as though it were they themselves who had suffered the loss.

[16] In the case of the loss of a parent, the period is eleven months; following the loss of a spouse, sibling, or child, it is thirty days.

[17] S.A. Yoreh Dei·ah 376:1.

[18] What follows in this essay is a reworking and streamlining of material published in much greater detail by Dalia Marx, "From the Rhine Valley to Jezreel Valley: Innovative Versions of the Mourner's Kaddish in the Kibbutz Movement," in *Between Tradition and Modernity: Rethinking Old Opposition, Essays in Honor of David Ellenson*, eds. Michael A. Meyer and David N. Myers (Detroit: Wayne State University Press, 2014), pp. 123–141; and idem, "Secular[?] Versions of the Kaddish in the Kibbutz Movement," *CCAR Journal* (Summer 2015), pp. 74–91. A "kibbutz" (plural: kibbutzim) is a specific kind of Jewish communal settlement in pre-and post-state Israel, from which derives

the term "kibbutznik" (plural: kibbutznikim) for a resident of such a settlement.
[19] Abraham Zivyon, *Diyukno Ha-y'hudi shel Berl Katznelson* (Tel Aviv: Sifriyat Poalim, 1984), p. 272.
[20] Nissan Rubin, "Death Customs in a Non-Religious Kibbutz: The Use of Sacred Symbols in a Secular Society," *Journal for the Scientific Study of Religion* 25:3 (1986), pp. 292–303.
[21] Oral communication with Dalia Marx (winter 2013).
[22] Nisan Rubin, "Personal Bereavement in a Collective Environment: Mourning in the Kibbutz," published in his *New Rituals — Old Societies* (Boston: Academic Studies Press, 2009), pp. 92–109.
[23] Mordechai Zeira, *K'ru·im Anu: Zikkatah shel Ha-hityash'vut Ha-ovedet Bi-sh'not Ha-esrim el Ha-tarbut Ha-y'hudit* (Jerusalem: Yad Yitzchak Ben Tzvi, 5762 [2001/2002]), p. 277.
[24] Published in Tzvi Shua and Aryeh Ben-Gurion, *Yalkut Aveilut* (Beit Hashitah, Israel: Vaadat Ha-hevrah Ha-beinkibbutzit, 1990), p. 144, and set to music by Moshe Rappaport. The title of the poem derives from Numbers 19:14.
[25] Later, this poem was set to music by Yosef Milet, cf. *Sefer Shirim U-manginot L'ganei Y'ladim U-l'vatei Sefer II*, eds. Moshe Gorali and Daniel Sambursky (Jerusalem: Kiryat Sefer, 5760 [1999/2000], pp. 138–139.
[26] Shua and Ben-Gurion, *Yalkut Aveilut*, p. 128.
[27] It is interesting to note how Nurit Feinstein distinguishes in her doctoral dissertation between abstention from the recitation of liturgical texts at funerals and the abstention from actual crying or calling out in grief; see Nurit Feinstein, *Ha-sifrut Ha-ivrit B'mei·ah Ha-esrim*, doctoral dissertation submitted at Ben Gurion University of the Negev, 5771 [2011], pp. 376–377. It seems that both abstentions mirror the same phenomenon of restraint from the expected as a matter of choice, and also as an expression of opposition both to formalized and spontaneous reactions to death.
[28] *Darkah shel Degania: Sippur Hamishim Sh'not Ha-kibbutz* (Tel Aviv: Davar, 1962), p. 123. It is interesting to note that Gordon himself is described as having recited Kaddish for one Yosef Busel after the latter drowned in the Kineret in 1919.
[29] Rubin, "Death Customs" (see note 20), p. 298-300.
[30] Shua and Ben-Gurion, *Yalkut Aveilut*, p. 145.
[31] Ample testimony to the unique position of this "Kaddish" is provided by the fact that there have been whole books written regarding the circumstances of its composition. According to some, it was extant already in 1948 and was formally composed in response to the death of Yehoshua Glauberman, the Haganah commander, who is regarded as the first among the fallen in the War of Independence. Cf. *Yalkut Aveilut*, p. 147. There is evidence, however, in the Kibbutz Yagur archives—which is supported by the oral testimony of several kibbutz members—to the effect that the Yagur Kaddish was composed in the 1950s.

[32] Shua and Ben-Gurion, *Yalkut Aveilut*, p. 146. The Hebrew word *adam*, here translated as "man," can be used to reference women as well. Later, a specific version for women came into use.

[33] Yosef Ḥayyim Brenner, *Mikhtavim L'russiya*, originally published in the periodical *Ha-me'oreir* 1(5666 [1905/1906]) and now available in Brenner's collected words (Tel Aviv: Ha-kibbutz Ha-me'uḥad, 1985), p. 193.

[34] On the retreat to traditionalism in the kibbutz mourning customs, as well as new budding religiosity within the kibbutz movement, see Marx, "From the Rhine Valley to Jezreel Valley" (see note 18), pp. 136-137; and idem, "Secular[?] Versions of the Kaddish" (see note 18), pp. 85-88.

[35] For more about these three stages, see Dalia Marx's essays referenced above in note 18.

My Kaddish

Herbert Bronstein

One Sunday morning when I was nine years old, my father took me to his store. At that time, my father was accustomed to seeing friends or special customers. One of these, referring to me, asked, in a mock high-flown tone, "And who is this young gentleman?" My father answered, "This is my Kaddish." At that time I had only the vaguest inkling of what he meant, save that it betokened a special relationship with my father and that, since I had heard the word "Kaddish" before in the synagogue, it had something to do with what today I would call my relationship, as a Jew, with God.

It has taken me many years to realize the breadth of meanings in the Kaddish prayer, as an expression of a Jewish outlook and sensibility. For Jews (and even for many non-Jews), the Kaddish is one of the most familiar of Jewish prayers, and further, a kind of "marker" of Jewish identity. At the same time, within the wider scope of its origins and roles in Jewish religious thought and practice, we find a wellspring of meanings that can appeal to many people from a wide variety of backgrounds and beliefs. Perhaps this is one reason that so many works of art—whether musical, visual, poetic, dramatic or choreographic, and intended for very diverse audiences—are entitled, simply, "Kaddish."

In addition, though the sources and texts of the Kaddish prayer are rooted in the ancient world, its themes and motifs are relevant to our modern world. In this respect, the Kaddish is a prayer of hope and aspiration for a better world. In the ancient world, the Jewish people was repeatedly battered by great empires, one after another. In response, ancient prophets of Israel provided the consolation of hope for a time of peace and security. There would come a time when people would beat their swords into plowshares and their spears into pruning-hooks, when nation would not lift up sword against nation nor learn war anymore (Isaiah 2:4), when no one would hurt or destroy in all of God's holy mountain (Isaiah 11:9). We also find in ancient Israelite prophecy a repeated call for a higher standard of moral behavior within the nation of Israel itself. The leaders of the people were especially exhorted to be faithful to the sacred covenant, made with the people of Israel at Mount Sinai—to forsake the idolatries of greed and mere ritual, and to heed God's commandments by caring for the most vulnerable among the people: the poor, the widow, and the orphan.[1]

Along with passages of prophetic rebuke, we also find in the Bible prophetic visions of consolation (*nehamah*), and hope for a future time when justice and compassion will prevail not only between nations, but also within the nation of Israel.[2] The prophet Jeremiah went so far as to envision a renewed covenant with Israel in that future time, a covenant "written in the heart" (31:32)—that is, at that future time, people would not have to be taught to behave humanely, because it will have become a natural way of life. And the prophet Ezekiel spoke of God someday replacing the people's "heart of rock" with a "heart of flesh" (36:26).

The hoped-for and promised redemptive future is expressed by the rabbinic phrase "the sovereignty of God," pointing to a time when all people would live according to God's laws. This idea of the sovereignty of God is widely affirmed in Jewish liturgy and is voiced explicitly in the Kaddish:

May God establish His sovereignty in your lifetime, and
during your days,
and in the life of all of the House of Israel, in a near time;
and say: *Amen*...

May there be great peace from heaven, and life,
upon us and all of Israel;
and say: *Amen*.

May God, who makes peace in His high places,
bring peace upon us and all Israel;
and say: *Amen*.

Scholars of liturgy have argued that the text of the well-known
(Christian) "Lord's Prayer," presented in the New Testament as part
of the Sermon on the Mount, suggests that the aspirations voiced in
the ancient Jewish Kaddish were widespread throughout Jewry at
that early date:

Our Father who art in heaven,
hallowed be Thy Name;
Thy Kingdom come,
Thy will be done,
on earth as it is in heaven.[3]

In addition to hope for a better world, there is yet another important
motif in the Kaddish: the theme of praise of God, evident to anyone who
reads the prayer. In this way, the Kaddish is representative of a dominant
mode of Jewish prayer—namely, praise.

In order to better understand the emphasis in Jewish worship on
praise, we must first explore the meaning of "Messiah" in Judaism
(especially as opposed to its meaning in Christianity). "Messiah" is the
English transliteration of the Hebrew word *mashi·ah*, which literally
means "anointed one"—which pointed to the ancient tradition of

anointing individuals with oil. King David, for example, was installed as king over the people Israel when the prophet Samuel anointed David's head with oil (1 Samuel 16:13). For all time following that, a claimant to the throne of Israel had to be a descendant of David, "an anointed one." The term *mashi·ah* thus came to mean the legitimate heir to the kingship of Israel. During times of Roman oppression, the Jews yearned for independence under their own anointed king, their *mashi·ah*. Thus, from early rabbinic times, the prophetic vision of a better world was closely bound up with the belief in the coming of a descendant of King David—"an anointed one" (Ezekiel 20:34), an ensign and leader of the future age of redemption from all social evils.[4]

In Christian circles, this all played out quite differently, because Paul gave an entirely different meaning to the word "messiah" (translated into Greek as *christos*): he understood it to mean "savior of the individual soul" for other-worldly salvation (or, in popular parlance, "heaven"). Paul taught that salvation of the individual soul after death has already been assured for Christians who believe in the saving power of the Messiah—identified with Jesus, a descendant of King David and the "son of God" whose death on the cross has vicariously atoned for their innate sinfulness (or, in Christian terms, for original sin).[5]

Scholars of liturgy recognize that the dominant prayer motif of Christian liturgy is thanksgiving. (In fact, the name of the main element of Christian worship, the Eucharist, literally means "thanksgiving.") Christians can and should give thanks that the salvation of their souls has already been assured through the vicarious sacrifice of Jesus as atonement for their sins.

Not so, however, with Jewish worship. The goal of Judaism—the messianic future of deliverance from social evils—is still far from being achieved. The Messiah has not yet come; thanksgiving in this pre-redeemed world, therefore, cannot exist in the absolute sense. But we can give praise for everything good in present daily life. Praise of God is the religious expression of the affirmation of life, a way of saying "yes" to life against the nay-saying of perennial skepticism, cynicism, and nihilism, still so evident in various elements of the culture of our own time.

Praise of God—and thanksgiving for the delights, wonders, and satisfactions of everyday life—are ubiquitous in Jewish tradition.[6] Once, while driving high school students to school in the morning, a non-Jewish young woman said to me: "I have often been to your services. I even know words of your prayers in Hebrew: *barukh atah Adonai!*"—words that are usually translated as "Praised are You, O God." She had heard that phrase so many times in the course of Jewish worship, because the call to Jewish worship is a call to praise. Indeed, the opening and concluding words of many important Jewish prayers are *barukh atah Adonai*.

Unfortunately, many translators have rendered the Hebrew word for "praise" in this phrase as "Blessed are You, O God." Examination of the word *barukh* in the Bible yields the interesting discovery that, when applied to God, the term clearly means "praised"; indeed, it is only when applied to human beings that it means "blessed."[7] And it seems more than likely that the rabbis—and the liturgists of the rabbinic period—also understood this term in its biblical sense, as an expression of praise.

Ancient rabbinic texts emphasized the praise-motif in the Kaddish in yet another way. The Jewish worship service begins with a call to worship: "Praise God, to whom our praise due!" The congregation responds, "Praised be God, to whom our praise is due for ever and ever." And, in unmistakably parallel fashion, the leader of the Kaddish begins with the words "Magnified and sanctified be God's great name in the world..." and the congregation responds: "May God's great name be praised for ever and ever."[8] This response was considered by the ancient sages to be the essence and core of the Kaddish. The ancient sage Rava even said that these words were "one of the elements on which the world is sustained."[9] It was not casually that Elbogen, the great scholar of liturgy, referred to that same verse of praise as "a hymn of hymns."[10]

In contrast to its clear function as praise, there is only one word in the Kaddish that could be used to argue for its function as a prayer of comfort to mourners. The Aramaic word *neḥemata*, in the phrase *tushb'ḥata v'neḥemata* ("all the praises and consolations"), indeed does mean "expressions of comfort" or "expressions of consolation."[11] In the Kaddish, however, that word does not refer to personal comfort for mourners at a time of loss but rather to the aforementioned hope for the future messianic age. It is important to note that the Kaddish does not appear as a mourner's prayer in either of the two most important early liturgical works to have survived, *Seder Rav Amram Gaon* (the earliest extant Jewish prayer book, composed by Rabbi Amram bar Sheshna, the head of the talmudic academy of Sura in modern-day Iraq, d. 875 C.E.) and *Maḥzor Vitry* (an eleventh-century compendium of prayers, laws, and customs composed by Rabbi Simḥah ben Samuel of Vitry, France). In these two liturgies, the Kaddish—in a version known as the "Complete Kaddish" (called in Hebrew the Kaddish Shaleim or the Kaddish Titkabbeil)—serves as a summary closing prayer, in which a line is added asking God to accept all of the supplications voiced in the preceding service. Similarly, in these founding prayer books, a short or "Half Kaddish" (Ḥatzi Kaddish) marks the transition between the major sections of the regular service.

Only the slightest connection between Kaddish and mourners is found in tractate Sofrim, a so-called "extra-talmudic" treatise usually dated to the eighth century C.E. At Sofrim 10:19, we are told that members of the congregation would visit the home of mourners after the Sabbath Morning Service and there say together a blessing (but without any indication of what that blessing actually was), and a Kaddish. Since this tractate is concerned with matters having to do to with the Bible, we might surmise that some words of Scripture that had been read that morning during the synagogue service might also have been recited during the visit at the mourner's home, followed by the Kaddish.[12]

The actual origin of the Kaddish as a mourner's prayer is very unclear and shrouded in legend. We find in the Talmud a statement to the effect that sinners suffer in Gehenna, a kind of purgatorial hell, for twelve months.[13] And we also find a statement in the Talmud that the Kaddish has "power over the living and the dead."[14] These ideas could have led to the practice of reciting the Kaddish as a mourner's prayer in the centuries following the close of the Talmud. Nevertheless, some scholars believe that Mourner's Kaddish came into being due to the massacre of Jews in 1095 and 1096 during the First Crusade.[15] These possibilities remain conjectural, however; it is not until the thirteenth century that we find the "founding legend" of the Kaddish as a mourner's prayer, in a tale in which the second-century sage Rabbi Akiva is depicted teaching an orphan boy to recite the Kaddish for his father in order to redeem the latter from Gehenna and ease his entrance into Paradise.[16] This legend gave rise to the idea that sons are obligated to act on behalf of their parents' souls by reciting the Kaddish for a year following their death. This period was shortened to eleven months in actual practice, so as not to reflect badly on the moral character and reputation of the deceased—who was certainly not deemed to be so wicked as to be in purgatory for the maximum twelve months. Two centuries later, a German Jewish custom (still widely practiced today) spread widely among Jewry, of reciting the Mourner's Kaddish annually on the anniversary of the relative's death.[17]

Though none of the early medieval legal codes included these practices as binding statutory observances, these customs were gradually adopted by Jews around the world. And the force of popularly created widespread custom is such that reciting Kaddish as a mourner's prayer is today widely observed by otherwise "non-observant" Jews.

Despite the growing practice of reciting the Kaddish in medieval times as a mourner's prayer, some major Jewish authorities urged instead other ways to commemorate the spiritual legacy of the deceased—such as increased study of Torah or acts of charity or kinds of good deeds.[18] But as early as the twelfth century in Mainz, Rabbi Eliakim ben Joseph had already expressed his opposition to the use of Kaddish as a prayer for mourners:

> It is not generally accepted that through the recitation of the Kaddish the son brings his father and mother to Paradise and that he who frequently repeats the Kaddish atones by that action for the sins of his parents and helps them to enter into the future world. For there is no foundation for the view that the Kaddish is for mourners. There is no basis for it either in the Jerusalem or Babylonian Talmuds or in the Tosefta. The only source is the legend of Rabbi Akiva, and we do not base laws upon legends.[19]

And ever since the thirteenth century—and continuing even to this day—religious authorities have continued to argue against the recitation of Kaddish as a way to protect the soul of the deceased from punishment.[20]

Nonetheless, there is wisdom and value in the repeated practice of praise as an affirmation and acceptance, which can lead to equanimity in the face of loss. Adopting the view that whether God gives or takes away, whether bad or good things happen to us, still we should always praise God,[21] the rabbis designed a prayer of praise to be recited on learning of a death: "Praised are You, O God, the Judge of truth." To be sure, it must have been that many of the ancient rabbis understood such praise of God—even in the face of death—as part of their general inclination to justify God's actions, including those that are beyond our comprehension.

Praise also helps the mourner to avoid the emotional and spiritual trap of self-pity. Because the recitation of Kaddish requires a quorum of ten adults, this ritual practice necessarily brings a mourner out of solitary self-involvement and back into relationship and involvement with others. Following burial, relatives and friends gather at the mourner's home for seven days, a well-known practice called *shiva* ("seven"); during this period, the mourners recite Kaddish during the daily prayer services. Then, after the week of *shiva*, the mourner attends synagogue services daily in order to recite the Mourner's Kaddish, where it is more than likely that he or she will be with other mourners as well, and will find empathy and compassion in their midst.

The recitation of Kaddish as part of the synagogue service also contributes to the quality and continuity of Jewish community life. The mourner is brought into contact with the synagogue—which, more than any other of the many Jewish organizations that have emerged and disappeared throughout the ages, has most ensured Jewish survival, continuity, and strength. As a rabbi, I have seen many Jews deepen their own religious life through attendance at a synagogue as mourners to recite the Kaddish.

Knowing that using the Kaddish as a mourner's prayer was a relatively late development, we would certainly like to know more about its original function in Jewish religious life. In fact, even before its role as a closing prayer at the conclusion of worship or to designate transitions between the main components of study toward Jewish worship, the Kaddish had long been associated with that central pillar of Jewish spirituality: the teaching, interpretation, and learning of Torah, the greatest sacred texts of Judaism. Elbogen puts it this way:

> Among the amoraim, Rava designates [reciting the phrase] "May the great name" as one of the great themes on which the world stands (B. Sotah 49a). Now what we find in Rava's language as a unified concept points to the origin of the prayer [i.e., the Kaddish]; it was originally used at the end of sermons…The rule was that the sermon had to conclude with words of conciliation, [generally] with reference to the messianic age. Some preachers added, in the course of time, such prayers…as became established as the Kaddish…The connection with the Aggadah also explains the Aramaic language of the Kaddish, for this was the language spoken by the sages…Just as the Targum [i.e., the Aramaic translation of the Bible] was transported from Palestine to Babylonia, so the Kaddish, which originated in Palestine, was prescribed and developed thanks to Babylonia, where it also achieved recognition as one of the "Pillars of the World."[22]

But even prior to Elbogen, the Kaddish had been identified as the prayer originally recited following the exposition of a homily based on a prophetic text of hope in the great work of Leopold Zunz,[23] as well as by Joseph Heineman, an acknowledged scholar of early rabbinic liturgy who spoke of the Kaddish as originally said "after the public homily."[24]

The following facts support the conclusion of these scholars that the Kaddish began as the prayer spoken after the homily on prophetic scripture. First, the simple wording of the Kaddish, the lack of any allusion to the destruction of the Temple, and the similarity to the "Lord's Prayer" are signs of its antiquity.[25] Further, readings from Scripture in general were a central element of Jewish gathering for group worship even from the earliest rabbinic times, and such gatherings generally included readings from the Prophets.[26]

Elbogen states that whether or not readings from the Prophets are later than readings from the Torah, these prophetic readings must be earlier than the closing of the canon of the Prophets.[27] Furthermore, the Mishnah lists prophetic texts for festival worships in a way that suggest that this was a well-known earlier practice.[28] Sometimes separate sections of the same prophets were put together in the same prophetic reading, called a *haftarah*, but in other instances selections from two separate prophets were brought together into one *haftarah* reading. Almost all of the prophetic readings of rebuke had to conclude with some verses of hope or promised redemption. And it was the verses of hope on which the preacher was to base his homily.

There is a further connection between the Kaddish and Torah study or learning. To this day, the completion of any period of study and learning of a tractate of the Talmud, or after Torah taught by a prominent rabbinic authority, a Kaddish known as the Rabbis' Kaddish (that is, the Kaddish D'rabbanan) is recited, which includes the following paragraph:

> [We pray] for our teachers, and their disciples,
> and the disciples of their disciples,
> and for all who study the Torah, here and everywhere.
> May they have abundant peace, lovingkindness,
> ample sustenance, and salvation
> from their Father in heaven; and let us say: Amen.[29]

*****

The Kaddish, as ancient as it is, speaks to a contemporary situation in our day both for Jews and for all those who have come under the influence of modernity. The modern world has experienced the greatest spread of philosophic materialism in all of human history to date. This outlook comprises both the view that the only thing that exists is matter and that there is no such dimension in reality that can be called "spiritual." According to philosophic materialism, "spirit" is considered by many as a "figment" only. Vulgar materialism refers to preoccupation with money and material goods, and with the sense that physical sensation is the most important of life's experiences. Many people—perhaps even most people—find the highest value in the realm of materialism alone. Together with this loss of a sense of the spiritual dimension, we have also witnessed the disappearance of anything we could call "holy" or "sacred."

From birth, human beings live in three dimensions: space, time, and relationship. From time immemorial, humankind has preserved special times, places, and relationships as especially sacred. However, according to a modern materialistic outlook these, as it were, islands of holiness are all considered to have come into superficial, contingent, or imaginary existence as a result of real underlying material conditions, whether economic, social, or psychological.

In the field of aesthetics and religion, too, there has developed a parallel sense of a loss of "enchantment" or "wonder." However, even in modern time, not only Albert Einstein and Albert Schweitzer, but also many other thinkers, writers, poets, have said that religion begins with a sense of wonder, to which the only response is awe voiced in the framework of praise. Anyone who recites the Kaddish as a prayer of praise of God, a prayer of aspiration for a better world, as a prayer that helps us maintain the wonder of everyday life, as a prayer to be recited after the study of a sacred text—such a person preserves a sense of the holy, and personally becomes a "Kaddish."

NOTES

[1] See, for example, Isaiah 3:14–15; Jeremiah 2:30, 34; or Amos 2:6, 4:15.

[2] For example, Isaiah 2:4 and 5:5, and Jeremiah 1:5.

[3] Matthew 6:9–10, Luke 11:2–3. For the relationship between the Lord's Prayer and Kaddish, see Ismar Elbogen, *Jewish Liturgy. A Comprehensive History*, trans. Raymond P. Scheindlin (Philadelphia: Jewish Publication Society and Jewish Theological Seminary of America, 1993), p. 81.

[4] For the early rabbinic concept of a messianic age, see the Tanna D'vei Eliyahu, a freestanding homiletical midrash, chapter 5; available in English in the translation of William G. Braude and Paul Kapstein (Philadelphia: Jewish Publication Society of America, 1981), pp. 46–60.

[5] James Hastings, "The Gospel of Salvation," in *Dictionary of the Bible*, eds. Frederick C. Grant and H. Rowley (New York: Charles Scribner and Sons, 1963), pp. 735–740.

[6] See, for example, the long collection of rabbinic prayers of praise and teachings about them in Ḥayim Naḥman Bialik and Yehoshua Ḥana Ravnitzy's *The Book of Legends: Legends from the Talmud and Midrash*, trans. William G. Braude (New York: Schocken Books, 1992), pp. 523–533.

[7] Ludwig Kohler and Walter Baumgartner, *Lexicon in Veteris Testament Libros* (Leiden, Netherlands: Brill, 1954), pp. 153–154.

[8] Both usages have biblical roots, e.g., at Daniel 2:20 or Psalm 113:2.

[9] B. Sotah 49a.

[10] Elbogen, *Jewish Liturgy*, p. 86, and cf. David de Sola Pool, *The Kaddish* (1909; rpt. Jerusalem: Sinai Press, 1964), pp. 69ff. and 79ff.

[11] Elbogen, *Jewish Liturgy*, p. 86.

[12] Cf. Sofrim 19:12.

[13] B. Rosh Hashanah 16b–17a.

[14] B. Shabbat 119b.

[15] A. Z. Idelsohn, *Jewish Liturgy and Its Development* (1932; rpt. New York: Dover, 1995), p. 88; Elbogen, *Jewish Liturgy*, p. 82.

[16] Elbogen, *Jewish Liturgy*, p. 82; Idelsohn, *Jewish Liturgy*, p. 87; de Sola Pool, *Kaddish*, pp. 102 and 109. The most important medieval sources for the legend are the *Sefer Or Zarua* by Rabbi Isaac of Vienna, and the *Maḥzor Vitry*, a compendium of halakhic decisions by Rabbi Simḥah of Vitry (d. 1105).

[17] Elbogen, *Jewish Liturgy*, p. 82, Idelsohn, *Jewish Liturgy*, p. 88.

[18] Idelsohn, *Jewish Liturgy*, p. 87.

[19] Ibid.

[20] Ibid.

[21] B. Berakhot 60a.

[22] Elbogen, *Jewish Liturgy*, pp.80–81. Leopold Zuna, *Ha-d'rashot B'yisrael*,

trans. J. A. Jak (Jerusalem: Mosad Bialik, 1947), p. 483. Zunz's magisterial work was originally published in Berlin by A. Ascher in 1870 as *Die gottesdienstliche Vorträge der Juden historisch entwickelt.*

[24] Joseph Heineman, *Ha-t'fillah Bi-t'kufat Ha-tanna·im V'ha-amora·im* (Jerusalem: Magnes Press, 1964), p. 158ff.

[25] Elbogen, *Jewish Liturgy*, p. 81.

[26] Ibid., pp. 130-132; and cf. the evidence of Matthew 5:2, Mark 1:26, and Luke 13:10.

[27] Ibid., p. 143.

[28] M. Megillah 4:2.

[29] Ibid., pp. 82–83; Idelsohn, *Jewish Liturgy*, p. 45.

Kaddish as Prayer and Confession

Jeremy Rosen

The Kaddish has become popular to the point of cliché in Jewish culture and religious practice. Whether in the original Aramaic and Hebrew or translated into English and other languages, most Jews are to some degree or another familiar with its text. This has as much to do with its association with the rituals of mourning as it does with the fact that, in one variation or another, it is the most oft-recited Jewish liturgical text in a synagogue setting. How did this prayer, composed sometime in the centuries after the destruction of the Second Temple—which says nothing about death or mourning—come to play such a significant role in Jewish religious consciousness, as part of the rituals of mourning? Should it be regarded simply as a formulaic ritual, or can we find spiritual meaning from the content and context of its function within the liturgy? This essay is intended to be less an academic analysis of the evolution of a prayer than an attempt to uncover its spiritual significance and message: an affirmation of life and one's relationship with God.

The loss of dear ones is a difficult and often traumatic experience. It plays out in both the communal and personal realms. The Kaddish, as it has evolved to this day, is remarkable in its ability to speak to both of these concerns. In addition, whether by intent or usage, it has become a spiritual confession that incorporates a mystical dimension as well as an obligatory one. But first, some background.

Death and Mourning in the Torah

The Five Books of Moses are sparing in their references to the rituals of death and mourning. That death itself is, in the words of Samuel Butler, "the way of all flesh"[1] strikes one almost immediately when, in the second chapter of Genesis, God warns Adam that if he eats from the Tree of Knowledge he will die. After he disobeys God, however, he does not die—which raises a question about what God meant by "death." In any event, the first example of death mentioned in Scripture is not Adam's at all, but his son Abel's (at the hand of Abel's brother, Cain). In the early chapters of Genesis, death is not associated with any rituals of mourning.

The practices of mourning described in later scriptural texts are not so clear. When Sarah died, it is reported that Abraham "went to mourn Sarah and to cry over her" (Genesis 23:2). Is this distinction between "mourning" and "crying" a hint at the distinction between public and private grief (and their associated rituals)? Jacob wore sackcloth and mourned the presumed death of Joseph (Genesis 37:34), and here too there seems to be a distinction between the public rituals of mourning (namely, tearing one's clothes and putting on sackcloth) and the more private tears.

The response to Jacob's death combines Egyptian ritual with ancient Israelite mourning rituals. After Jacob's death, Joseph weeps over and kisses his father (Genesis 50:1, 3, and 10). Forty days of mummification follow.[2] There is a clear distinction between Joseph's private mourning and Egyptian state obsequies. According to the Bible's report, Egyptian custom was to observe a period of seventy days of public mourning following the successful completion of the mummification process (Genesis 50:3). But when the cortege of Jacob's family, travelling from Egypt, arrived at Goren Ha-atad in Transjordan, another seven-day period of public mourning is recorded (verse 10). Finally, the body is taken across the Jordan and buried in the family cave in obedience with Jacob's deathbed wishes (verse 13). The forty days that Joseph mourned his father in Egypt contrast interestingly with the Egyptian standard, but even more of a contrast are the seven days during which Joseph mourns his father a second time, in what appears to be a purely Israelite ritual—a kind of biblical precursor of the later Jewish custom of sitting *shiva* for the dead. Perhaps Joseph's shorter mourning period was a deliberate attempt to differentiate himself from the extended Egyptian ritual practice. As for Joseph himself, when he dies we are simply told that he was mummified and that his mummified remains were placed in a coffin, which was eventually taken along by Moses himself when the Israelites left Egypt (Exodus 13:19).

Aaron was publicly mourned for thirty days (Numbers 20:29) and so was Moses (Deuteronomy 34:8). In both cases, the text refers to the people crying over their deaths. This is the source of the thirty-day mourning period that is observed by siblings, children, and spouses in contemporary Jewish practice; only parents are mourned for a full twelve months.[3] Nevertheless, there are no specific laws in the Bible about the prescribed period of mourning—or, for that matter, about the specific rituals for mourning. (There are some hints given here and there, mostly notably in the passage regarding the comely prisoner of war at Deuteronomy 21:12–13, where the text specifically states, "And she shall weep [i.e., mourn] for her father and mother for a month.") We know from later biblical texts about rows of mourners and public wailers, dirges, and laments, but the details seem left to local usage and custom.[4]

In the ancient world there were different gods of death. Sheol in the Canaanite world was the refuge of the dead during the posthumous period in which souls were judged while the body decayed. Mot was the Ugaritic god of death. Yagon was a Philistine god of death-throes, and so is the Hebrew word *yagon* used allusively in the story of Jacob's agony over Joseph's apparent death (Genesis 42:38).[5] All of this explains some of the sequences in biblical death narratives, but still do not enable us to understand the emergence of specifically Jewish rituals of death.

Deah and Afterlife

The question of life after death is treated at best indirectly in the Torah. Leaving aside rabbinic attempts to find scriptural supports for their beliefs regarding posthumous existence in the Bible, there simply are no unequivocal passages in Scripture that speak directly to the matter. The nearest one gets is the phrase "and he was gathered to his people," used of Abraham, Ishmael, Jacob, Aaron, and Moses. Does "gathered to his people" mean literally that one's bones were collected after the body had decomposed and then placed in a family ossuary? Or does it mean that the spirit or soul of the dead person went to join the souls of its predeceased kinspeople in some subterranean Israelite version of Sheol, or in a celestial paradise[6]? Perhaps the phrase is nothing more than a poetic way to describe death. No clear answer emerges, but support for all these views can be found in traditional Jewish biblical commentaries.[7]

Why are the Five Books not, then, explicit about describing any sort of life after death? After all, both in Egypt and Mesopotamia belief in an afterlife was such an important cornerstone of religious belief that it seems odd to imagine that the Israelites were uninterested in a topic that was of such import to their neighbors. One can only speculate on why this may have been. Perhaps it was intentional, this formal lack of engagement with the issue. Or possibly the belief was so deeply entrenched that it was taken for granted, and no biblical author felt the need to discuss it in detail. Perhaps it was simply that the Torah is primarily concerned with life, with providing a framework and a system for living, rather than with death.

It is a cornerstone of traditional Jewish belief that humans are endowed with a soul, divine sparks or something akin that continue to exist after we die. Rationalists such as Maimonides (1135–1204) take the view that only those of us who cultivate our souls will enable them to return to God after our deaths; otherwise they will simply cease to exist.[8] Mystics—in this, somewhat oddly supported by contemporary popular sentiment—argue that souls are indestructible, that they are recycled (so to speak) until they have achieved their spiritual missions, and that there is an ongoing relationship between souls on earth and souls on high.[9] And it is specifically this idea, of a relationship between this-worldly souls and their celestial counterparts, that underlies the belief that reciting Kaddish for a lost relative is of help to the souls of those who have died.

Such a belief was not always taken for granted: The author of Kohelet himself asks, "And who knows if the spirit of humanity rises upwards, and the spirit of the animal descends into the earth?" (Kohelet 3:21). Clearly, the issue of what happens to the human spirit after death was a matter of interest in ancient times, even if there is no biblical passage that sets forth a clear, cogent, developed theory of posthumous existence. This should not surprise us, however, given that the Bible is overwhelmingly a pre-philosophical (or at any rate, a non-philosophical) text.

The rituals of death and mourning we are familiar with in contemporary Jewish practice are largely post-talmudic (although they have their roots in biblical texts). The very idea of praying for the soul of the departed itself is innovative rather than conservative. Indeed, although the Talmud, building on biblical precedent, certainly discusses communicating with souls of the dead and lists various things that might prevent the soul from rising to heaven,[10] the idea of relatives actually praying for the soul of the departed does not figure as a significant custom or law until much later on. And so, starting in the early medieval period, we begin to see two distinct functions of the laws of mourning. One is found in the personal sphere, and focuses on the emotional state of the bereaved and how they ought to respond to their loss and express their grief. But the other has to do with the communal sphere, and sets forth expectations of how mourners are to act with regard to communal norms, and this aspect describes the community's responsibilities toward the mourners, no less than the public obligations of the mourners themselves.

Nowadays, in traditional communities, these two sets of ideas are universally accepted. For example, consider the custom that dictates that one only recite Kaddish for eleven months out of the twelve mourning months for deceased parents. The most common explanation is that saying Kaddish for a full twelve months, until the very end of the period of mourning, might inadvertently suggest that the departed had no merit of his or her own.[11] The other reason is to signal to the mourner that the time has come to get on with life. Either way, though, the earliest references to such a way of thinking are clearly medieval rather than talmudic.

Two questions suggest themselves for consideration. How did the text of the Kaddish emerge? And how did that prayer come to be associated with mourners?

"May His Holy Name be Blessed Forever"

It is misleading to call the Kaddish a prayer, because, at least historically, prayer is generally seen as petitional (as well as serving as an expression of thanksgiving). However, the Hebrew word for prayer is *t'fillah*, deriving from the three-letter root *pei-lamed-lamed*. Other words generated from this root are used elsewhere in the Bible to express an idea or hope. But to denote the act of praying, we most regularly find the verb is *l'hitpalleil*, which is a reflexive form that literally means "to express oneself."[13] Thus, prayer in this early understanding is less a recitation of a set formula and more an unstructured expression of inner feelings. But by the time we get to established liturgical practice in the early rabbinic period, the word *t'fillah* is used primarily to reference the formal thrice-daily Amidah prayer, a set liturgical frame that allows little room for individuality or free expression. This is because communal prayer had come by then to replace the (by then destroyed) Temple as the main setting for public religious worship.

During the periods of the two Temples, Jewish worship in its public expression had essentially focused on passive attendance at Temple ceremonies and witnessing sacrificial rituals at which priests officiated. At some stage, however, and probably in Babylon sometime in the fourth century B.C.E., the idea developed of bringing the community together in local centers outside the framework and rubric of Temple worship, which was centralized in Jerusalem. Rabbinic tradition has it that this was primarily to study rather than to pray. However, passages like Daniel 6:11 suggest clearly that praying three times a day had already become the norm centuries earlier. Over the next five hundred years, public prayer became more common, but without being formalized and made requisite. Only after the Temple was destroyed and the main rabbinic court was removed from Jerusalem to Yavneh, in fact, did Shimon Ha-Pakuli formalize the so-called Eighteen Benedictions, at the liturgical core of Jewish public prayer.[14] This is the same prayer elsewhere referenced as Amidah (i.e., as the prayer recited while standing). At that time, the *beit midrash* ("house of study") and the *beit k'nesset* ("house of gathering") became central institutions in Jewish public life, and this is where the Kaddish makes its first appearance.

The Kaddish is an essential element of public worship services and as such comes under the rubric of public prayer—even though it is a devotional declaration and not a petition at all, and it consists mainly of praising God and asking for protection and peace on earth. In fact, a short version of the Kaddish regularly acts as a marker delineating the different stages and importance of parts of the service. Nor is this public feel to the Kaddish at all *sub rosa*: the very fact that the text of the Kaddish is primarily Aramaic, the lingua franca of the Jewish community, suggests as much. (Almost all of the rest of the formal liturgy, apart from a few specific prayers and poems, is in Hebrew. There are minor variations in the text of the Kaddish among various Ashkenazic and Sephardic communities, but the mix of Aramaic and Hebrew is universal.)

The text of the Kaddish itself is anchored by a central refrain: *y'hei sh'meih rabba m'varakh l'alam u-l'almei almaya* ("May His great name be blessed forever and for all worlds to come"). This phrase hearkens back to Job 1:2: "And he said, 'I came naked out of the womb of my mother and I shall return naked. God has given and God has taken; may the name of God be blessed.'" At some stage in the talmudic era, this phrase was adopted as a quintessential expression of devotion. Its significance became such that the Talmud says that "any evil decrees already pronounced against an individual will be forgotten if that person answers 'May His great name be blessed' with all of one's heart."[15]

There is no evidence, however, as to why and how this phrase was co-opted into public prayer services. Although Temple worship was largely sacrificial and replete with ceremonial ritual, there was a liturgical component to the service as well, as the Mishnah makes clear in passages like this one:

The appointee declares "Recite one blessing" and they recited one blessing [that is, one of blessings that introduce the Shema]. They recited the Ten Commandments, the first paragraph of the Shema, the second paragraph of the Shema and then the third paragraph of the Shema, and then they blessed the people with three blessings: Emet V'yatziv, the Avodah, and the blessing of the *kohanim*. On Shabbat they would add a blessing for the watch [of *kohanim*] that had completed its turn of duty.[16]

But there is no mention here of any part of the Kaddish. Sometime after the destruction of the Temple, the : *y'hei sh'meih rabba* expression acquired a uniquely significant place in the liturgy. This is illustrated by the following talmudic passage, in which Rabbi Yosi encounters Elijah:

[In the ruin] I heard a spiritual voice moaning like a dove saying, "Woe to children who, because of their sins, have made Me destroy My house and burn My sanctuary, and exile them amongst the nations." And he [i.e., Elijah] said to me, "By your life, it is not only once that [this voice] declaims this, but it repeats it every day, three times. [And] not only [that, but when] the community of Israel comes into their synagogues and study houses and answer, 'May His great name be blessed throughout the world and for all worlds to come,' [God] nods His head and says, 'Happy is the sovereign who is praised thus in his own palace. What of the father who is forced to exile his children? But it is worse for the children who have been exiled from their father.'"[17]

In other words, this refrain as part of the daily services is the most intimate, reconciliatory link to the Divine in the wake of the destruction of the Temple. The significance of this prayer is further evidenced by this passage:

Rabbi Huna said, "If someone comes into the synagogue and finds them praying [the Amidah], if one can begin and complete what has been missed before the leader has reached "Modim," one should proceed to do so. Otherwise, one should wait."….It was asked: "What about stopping in the middle of one's own praying, to join in with 'May His great name be blessed'?" When Rav Dimi came he said, "Rabbi Judah and Rabbi Simon, pupils of Rabbi Yoḥanan, say that one does not interrupt except to say 'May His great name be blessed,' for even if one is involved in esoteric study one must still break off"—and that is the law.[18]

According to tradition, the obligation to recite daily prayers—and the text of the Amidah itself—were formalized to compensate for, or to replace, the sacrificial system. But we have no obvious clue as to why a connection developed between the Kaddish and mourners. We also know from several sources in the Talmud that there was a rabbinic disagreement between those who considered prayer to be the highest expression of one's interaction with God and those who considered study the most important.[19] The latter argued that, in theory at least, study would lead to action. This disagreement continued to be reflected in the ongoing competition between the mystical schools (with their focus on religious experience) and the institutional and authoritarian leadership (with their emphasis on obedience to the law). Although in fact the two points of view were to a large extent elided into one common rabbinic position, this dichotomy remains an important feature of Jewish religious life to this day. The introduction of the Kaddish as a prayer for mourners illustrates how these two strains were merged.

The Kaddish

Among the earliest sources that talk about the Kaddish is the passage preserved in the Talmud that responds to a remark by Rabbi Joshua (cited by Rabban Shimon ben Gamliel) to the effect that a non-accursed day has not passed since the Temple was destroyed. This text also follows several references to the significance of studying Torah to compensate for the loss of the Temple:

> Rava said: The curse of each day is more severe than that of the preceding one, as it says, "In the morning you will say 'If only God would bring evening' and in the evening you will say 'If only God would bring morning' (Deuteronomy 28:67)…So how does the world survive? Through the Kaddish recited after studying Torah, and the response of 'May His great name be blessed' that is said in the Kaddish after studying *aggadah*, as it says, 'A land of thick darkness, complete, a land of the shadow of death, without any order' (Job 10:22). If there is the study of Torah, it illuminates the thick darkness."[20]

Another text, from a far later collection of *midrashim* on the Book of Proverbs, relates:

> Rabbi Ishmael says, "When Israel gathers in the houses of study to listen to words of *aggadah* from a sage and afterwards they say 'May His great name be blessed,' at that very moment God is elevated in the universe and says to His attendant angels, 'Come and see how this people that I have placed in My universe praise Me so much.' They then cover Him with honor. That is why it says, 'In the multitude of people is the honor of the king' (Proverbs 14:28)."[21]

In both of these texts, we have the association of Kaddish with the core phrase "May His great name be blessed." The destruction of the Temple is what God mourns. We humans also mourn those close to us whom we lose. To recite the response is to accept divine judgment, following Job's example. This is what makes the connection between the Kaddish recited after study and the Kaddish recited by mourners. And this too illustrates the attempt to bring together prayer and study. Originally, study in itself was how the community responded to death: one needed to strengthen the community, to compensate it for its loss, and this was done through study. If one could not study, then one could at least recite the Kaddish said after study. The earliest source we have that connects Kaddish to mourners in this way is chapter 19 of the extra-talmudic tractate Sofrim.

The rabbis originally instituted the Kaddish to follow study. Mourners, even those who had not studied for whatever reason, could join in the recitation of Kaddish at the end of the study session. The fact that it was in Aramaic made it more familiar to the masses, for whom Hebrew was no longer the everyday spoken language. The earliest rabbinic Kaddish, however, was a complex and scholarly composition, whose original form is reserved in contemporary practice for the burial service or the completion of studying a tractate of the Talmud. Taking its place in the daily service is the Rabbis' Kaddish, also called the Kaddish D'rabbanan or the Kaddish Al Yisrael.[22]

Another important feature of Kaddish, quite apart from its connection with study, was its use as a "marker" within public prayer between different sections of the service—and this has become normative practice today. Since Kaddish D'rabbanan was to be recited after study, various mishnaic passages were introduced into the service to ensure that some study took place daily—whereupon the recitation of Kaddish D'rabbanan would follow. Additionally, Ḥatzi Kaddish ("Half" or "Partial" Kaddish) was recited upon the conclusion of the early part of the service (P'sukei D'Zimra) before continuing with the obligatory recitation of the Shema and its blessings, or after reading the Torah and before proceeding with the *haftarah*, or before the conclusion of the service in the various alternative textual variations according to local rites. A longer version, called Kaddish Shalem ("Full" Kaddish, also called Kaddish Titkabbeil), is recited after the Amidah—which was in fact the only part of the service officially called "prayer"—and before Aleinu, thus marking the conclusion of the post-Amidah part of the service (which includes Taḥanun[23] and, on Mondays and Thursdays, Torah readings).

What developed as the Mourner's Kaddish (also called Kaddish Yatom and sometimes the Kaddish "Y'hei Sh'lama") falls somewhere between the Full Kaddish and the Half Kaddish. Its form is simpler than Full Kaddish (since it does not include the *titkabbeil* line), and this made it easier for the ordinary person to say—and thus able to join in with the community in a public way, in memory of the departed. And, over time, extra psalms were added to the service, which were followed by further opportunities for reciting the Mourner's Kaddish. There was much debate in rabbinic circles whether Mourner's Kaddish should be recited by one person, or whether many could join together in its recitation. Central European custom tended toward a more disciplined approach of a single reciter, whereas the Eastern European approach, now the universal custom, tolerated the din of many people speaking at once and not always staying together.

The result of all this was that Kaddish evolved, rather informally, as the way a mourner joined in with the community to strengthen it and compensate it for the loss of one of its members. It was indeed a response that required one to be part of the community, for its recitation required a *minyan* and, in a way, it incorporated the private into the public. (In other words, one had to participate in a community activity or prayer in order to participate as a mourner reciting Kaddish.) Ideally a mourner should lead the services, and this obligation is still a factor in many congregations in the determination of which worshipper should serve as prayer leader.[24] But such a public response could not compensate for the sense of private loss. And that, I suggest, is where the connection to the souls of the dead came in.

Kaddish for the Souls of the Departed

There are various talmudic narratives that discuss the fate of the soul after death. One of the most famous, presented in the Babylonian Talmud at Berakhot 18b, describes souls hanging around in the graveyard, at least partially to bring back reports of what goes on in the Upper World. But it is not until late geonic and medieval periods that one finds sources that discuss the connection between souls rising to heaven and prayers recited on earth to aid in their transition. Many of these sources rely on later adaptations of a legend about Rabbi Akiva to establish a connection between saying Kaddish and the soul of the departed.[25] The earliest occurrence the legend is found in the so-called "minor tractate" Kallah Rabbati 2:9, and then expanded in the medieval *Midrash Tanḥuma, the Maḥzor Vitry* of Rabbi Simḥah ben Samuel of Vitry (d. 1105), and the *Sefer Or Zarua* of Rabbi Isaac ben Moses of Vienna (1200–1270). In the latter source, we read:

> Rabbi Akiva once saw someone struggling with a heavy load of wood on his shoulders and complaining about his lot in life. Thinking he might be a slave who deserved freedom, Rabbi Akiva asked him tell him about his life. He explained that he was the soul of someone who had sinned on earth and his punishment was to go on carrying this load of wood. He was unable to stop to talk, or his burden would be increased.

Rabbi Akiva asked if there was any way to free his soul and the "dead" person replied that the only way was if he had a son who would be able to get up in front of the congregation and say *bar'khu* (i.e., lead the services), or *yitgaddal v'yitkaddash* (i.e., recite the Kaddish), after which the congregation would reply *barukh adonai ha-m'vorakh l'olam va·ed* or *y'hei sh'meih rabba*.[26]

This legend does not tell us how the text of the Kaddish developed. But it does show how the Mourner's Kaddish evolved from simply a communal ritual into one that carried significance for the soul and the memory of the dead person. Not only are the origins of the practice obscure, but moreover, somewhere in medieval times, the custom developed not to say the Kaddish for one's parents for the whole year of mourning, stopping instead at the end of the eleventh month.[27] This reinforces my contention that saying Kaddish came to be regarded as a means of helping the soul of a departed individual on its journey, even though in earlier sources there is no indication of this. Limiting the recitation to eleven months merely meant that the deceased did not need all the help he or she could get in his or her journey—a sign of respect on the part of the living with respect to a late parent.

Confession

The Tzidduk Ha-din prayer is a form of confession that is made between the individual and God.[28] In talmudic times, it was recited on one's deathbed. It is both a justification of one's being and an entreaty for divine forgiveness. By the sixteenth century, it was incorporated into the daily prayers, except on festive occasions. The initial opening phrase, "God is pure in His deeds, His ways are just," derives from Deuteronomy 32:4 but also provides a link to the talmudic lesson that one must bless God for the bad as well as for the good.[29] In an expanded form in our liturgy, it forms part of the burial service—speaking to an acceptance of divine will, and a recognition of the existence of another spiritual world and dimension.

This formal resignation to divine will ("We bless God for the bad as well as for the good") is the predominant expression in rabbinic theology of how to respond to tragedy and to the bad things that happen, and primary among them is death. And this brings us full circle back to Job, as the Kaddish actually implies the very point that Job makes. At the moment of our greatest pain, we can say how great the Almighty is: "May His great name be blessed." We accept our fate because we realize our impotence and our subservience to greater forces. Religion does not answer all of life's questions. It simply gives the framework for coping with the challenges of life.

It is unknown whether the development of this dimension of Kaddish was formally introduced by a specific individual or is simply a folk custom that took root. No matter its origin, it adds to the mourning experience an element of guilt assuaged, responsibility, and personal grieving. It helps to pull us away from the dead person, away from the kind of self-referential solipsism that loosens an individual's ties to the community and into the recognition of our own mortality. It is law and custom that reinforce community ties, but it is personal *kavvanah* that links us to God.

The practice of reciting Kaddish after the loss of a loved one is remarkably effective. Indeed, many Jews who are otherwise unobservant appear to find solace and meaning in saying Kaddish daily during the year of mourning for parents. Some even continue their involvement in daily worship after the eleven months is up, although the majority admittedly do not.

It does seem to my more rational mind that the more utilitarian and functional use of Kaddish is to reinforce the community and our role in it. And this ought to be a sufficient public and private response to loss. But, human nature being what it is, the primordial desire to believe that we will see our loved ones again simply overpowers any rational response to loss.

Perhaps the significance, the hold, that the Kaddish has on us speaks to the persistence of superstition or the natural feelings of human guilt. It could therefore be seen as a concession to human frailty—in a similar vein to the way that k'ri·ah, the ritual tearing of one's clothing upon hearing of the death of a loved one, channels a need for a violent reaction into a harmless one. Maybe one could explain it in a way similar to Maimonides' effort in *The Guide for the Perplexed* to explain the function of sacrifices, as a way to wean the Israelites away from animal sacrifices in stages.[30] Perhaps our preoccupation with life after death, with doing our best to help the souls of the departed to rise to heaven, is simply such a profound emotional reaction to death that it had to be given a place and a role in our religious lives. But in my opinion, that is not the essential message and function of the Kaddish.

Such a dual approach, both rational and a mystical, can be detected in the development of the Kaddish. Rabbi Nachman Cohen develops the idea of these two coexisting strains in rabbinic exegesis in his *Mirrors of Eternity: Understanding the Disputes of Rabbi Yehuda and Rabbi Nechemia*.[31] He argues that there has always been a mystical strain that sees reciting the Kaddish, regardless of the meaning of the words, as a way of transcending our material world. In this view, it is a way of accepting our fate, of expressing devotion to God. It gives one an opportunity to participate in the religious community without raising awkward questions of belief or its absence. It is a rote verse, rather like a mantra, that requires focus without intellectual engagement, an expression of self that amounts to a combination of pain and loss as well as belonging and loyalty both to one's late relations and one's community. It might rise to a howl of pain or to a quiet expression of acceptance of the divine order. The words are less important than the effect. They amount simply to the equivalent of: "Here I am, here I stand as a Jew in the face of loss and the support of tradition, and this is the formula I have received, to give public and private expression to the significance of my loss."

In conclusion, one may simply say that the rabbis offered three alternative responses to death, all incorporated by the Kaddish: reinforcing the community in response to the loss of a member, praying for the soul of the departed to return to its divine source, and bringing comfort and solace to the bereaved. It is up to us embrace all of these responses or to choose the one that resonates with us most powerfully in our time of loss and pain. But, whichever one we choose, it places us firmly within community, while still allowing our individuality to deal with the pain of loss and to decide what resonates and how, what reinforces, and what comforts.

NOTES

[1] Butler's turn of phrase is in turn based on 1 Kings 2:2, where David begins his deathbed charge to Solomon with the words "I go [now] in the way of all the earth."

[2] The language "for thus they completed the days of…" at 50:3 incidentally mirrors the period of time that Esther underwent cosmetic preparation for her night with the king (Esther 2:12). This might have been intended as humorous comparison of cosmetic procedures for the living and the dead…or a less humorous comparison of a woman being sentenced to a kind of living death in a harem and actual physical death.

[3] In this regard, cf. Maimonides' codification of the laws of mourning in the Mishneh Torah, Hilkhot Eivel, chapters 2 and 6.

[4] Cf., among other sources, Jeremiah 9:16.

[5] Cf. S. Wagner, "Yagah [yod-gimel-heih]," in G. Johannes Botterwerk and Helmer Ringgren, *Theological Dictionary of the Old Testament*, trans. John T. Willis (Grand Rapids: Eerdmans, 1974), vol. 5, pp. 380–384.

[6] See, for example, Genesis 37:35 or Deuteronomy 32:32.

[7] For example, see the comments of Rashi or Ibn Ezra Genesis 37:35.

[8] M.T. Hilkhot Teshuvah 8:3.

[9] See, e.g. Zohar 1 93b or Zohar II 127a.

[10] See, for example, the material collected at B. Berakhot 18b.

[11] See, e.g., the comments of Rabbi Moses Isserles (called the Rema, 1520–1572) to S.A. Yoreh Dei·ah 376:4.

[12] Cf., e.g., Genesis 48:11.

[13] Cf. the way the verb is used at Psalm 106:30.

[14] B. Berakhot 28b.

[15] B. Shabbat 119b.

[16] M. Tamid 5:1. The "appointee" (in Hebrew, the *m'munneh*) was the priest appointed to supervise that day's ritual worship. The Avodah is the prayer preserved as the ante-penultimate blessing of the Amidah, the one beginning with the word *r'tzeih*. Emet V'yatziv is the blessing moderns know as the first blessing following the Shema in the morning service.

[17] B. Berakhot 3a.

[18] B. Berakhot 21b. The expression "When Rav Dimi came," which appears almost twelve dozen times in the Talmud, references the arrival in Babylonia of Rav Dimi, a sage of the Land of Israel; cf. Rashi's comment to B. Mo·eid Katan 3b, s.v. *ki ata rav dimi*.

[19] E.g., B. Berakhot 30b.

[20] B. Sotah 49a.

[21] Midrash Mishlei 14:3.

[22] This latter name derives from the fact that its opening section begin with the words *al yisrael*. But it is also called "Kaddish Al Yisrael because referring to *yisrael* includes the wider community and not just the community of scholars. This in itself illustrates one of the stages in the developmental process of the liturgy.

[23] An atonement prayer, introduced in medieval times.

[24] Cf. the comments of the Rabbi Moses Isserles, called the Rema (1520–1572) to S.A. Oraḥ Ḥayyim 53:20.

[25] See, e.g., the discussion of this in Daniel Sperber's book *Minhagei Yisrael* (Jerusalem: Mossad Harav Kook, 2007), vol. 6, pp. 83 and 117. I am tempted to suggest that the Christian predilection for lighting candles for the departed—a practice later adopted by Judaism—might be an example of a loaned ritual.

[26] *Sefer Or Zarua* (ed. Zhitomir, 1862), part 2, p. 11b.

[27] See above, note 10.

[28] Cf. Macy Nulman, *The Encyclopedia of Jewish Prayer: The Ashkenazic and Sephardic Rites* (Northvale [NJ]: Jason Aronson, 1993), *s.v.* Tzidduk Hadin, pp. 326–327.

[29] B. Berakhot 33b.

[30] Maimonides, *Guide to the Perplexed* III 32.

[31] Published in Yonkers, New York, by the Torah Lishmah Institute in 1996.

The Recitation of Kaddish: A Personal Odyssey

Ruth Walfish

In this essay I would like to describe how and why I adopted the practice of saying Kaddish for my mother. I will present the thoughts and conflicts that accompanied this personal decision, as well as some of the insights I have gained regarding the Kaddish text itself.

In Orthodox synagogues, the service is run exclusively by men. A quorum of ten adult men is necessary in order to recite key passages of the prayer service, among them the reading of the Torah, the Kedushah, and Kaddish. Having grown up in a traditional modern Orthodox home, I took it for granted that Kaddish was to be recited by adult males on various occasions, but particularly during the first eleven months after the death of a parent.[1] As a child, I did not experience the deaths of loved ones other than grandparents, and so I thought little about the Kaddish, consigning it to "older men" for whom it was relevant.

I do remember that, years ago, my mother spoke to me about the power of the Kaddish, that many Jews found their way back to Judaism through its recitation. The desire to express their grief over their loss brought some of the unaffiliated to the local synagogue, where their mourning could be affirmed by others. And many such people continued to connect to Jewish ritual and faith even after the period of mourning was up.

What is the Kaddish prayer? Originally Kaddish had nothing to do with mourning. It is first mentioned in an eighth-century work, tractate Sofrim,[2] as one of several prayers to be recited in a particular setting. According to Sofrim 10:7, one may recite Kaddish and Bar'khu only in the presence of ten adult males. The leader recites a particular text, and the congregation responds at designated intervals with a specific set of phrases. The word *kaddish* is Aramaic for the Hebrew *kadosh*, "holy," and the Kaddish text is a doxology—that is, a hymn or set of words praising God. At first the Kaddish was intoned at the end of midrashic sermons, in order to conclude the sermon with words of consolation.[3] One version of Kaddish was recited at the *siyyum* (celebratory completion) of a tractate of the Talmud.[4] Over time, various versions of the Kaddish were adopted primarily as overtures or finales to a particular section of the service and yet another, the best-known version, was recited by mourners for eleven of the twelve months of mourning following the death of a parent. The Mourner's Kaddish is the latest of all versions of Kaddish.[5]

The nucleus of the Kaddish prayer is generally understood to be the central line recited by the congregation, *y'hei sh'meih rabba m'varakh l'alam u-l'almei almaya* ("may His great Name be blessed forever and ever"). This pronouncement echoes Daniel's words in Daniel 2:20, that God's great name be blessed for all time, or the psalmist's similar prayer in Psalm 113:2. It is common to find in Jewish liturgy quotations of or allusions to biblical texts.[6] The Kaddish was meant to sanctify God's name in the public sphere and to allude to the redemption of the Jewish people, echoing the words of the prophet Ezekiel: "Thus will I manifest My greatness and My holiness (*v'hitgaddilti v'hitkaddishti*) and make Myself known in the sight of many nations, and they shall know that I am the Eternal" (38:23).

The Mourner's Kaddish was apparently introduced into the liturgy in Germany in the early thirteenth century. The custom of reciting Kaddish during the year of mourning and on the *yahrzeit*,[7] the anniversary of the death, spread throughout the Jewish world, including Sephardic communities. The Shulḥan Arukh, composed by Rabbi Joseph Karo in Spain in the sixteenth century (and acknowledged by many as the authoritative code of Jewish halakhic practice), does not mention the Mourner's Kaddish—although the gloss of Rabbi Moses Isserles on the Shulḥan Arukh called the *Mappah*[8] (Poland, sixteenth century) does, and from the time of its inception, recitation of Kaddish by mourners quickly became an established practice. It is likely that reciting the Kaddish may have been originally introduced as a substitute for having the mourner lead the entire Saturday evening service at the end of Shabbat. According to the *Or Zarua* of Rabbi Isaac ben Moses of thirteenth-century Vienna, mourners were expected to lead the daily public prayers.[9] Since not everyone knew how to lead the full service, the recitation of Kaddish was accepted as a kind of compromise: surely the mourner would be able to handle the text of the Kaddish! In addition, only one mourner would recite the full text, while the others could fulfill their obligation by simply responding. The end of the Sabbath was singled out as an appropriate time for mourners to participate in this way, because it was viewed as a time when the souls of the departed returned to their purification process, having been released at the onset of the Sabbath. Ashkenazic Jews of the twelfth century believed that the soul rested on the Sabbath but returned to its suffering in purgatory at the end of the Sabbath; thus, the bereaved individual assisted his deceased parent by praying on his or her behalf as the soul of the deceased returned to its ordeal.[10]

What, indeed, is the connection between Kaddish and death? Several explanations have been suggested. The Kaddish can be viewed as a statement of *tzidduk ha-din*, theodicy—that is, an effort to affirm belief in God in the face of evil. By intoning a prayer that affirms the greatness and sanctity of God, the child of the deceased declares that he does not see the death of his parent as an unjust act of God. Taken a step further, the Kaddish may be seen as an affirmation of God's greatness in the face of all death, insofar as there is something eternal that endures throughout all ephemeral existence. Kaddish can also be understood to connect to the death of a loved one in a more mystical way: several sources recognize the power of the Kaddish to elevate the soul of the deceased to heaven, and so even a person who lived a sinful life can make it to heaven if his or her child recites a form of Kaddish for him or her.[11] One who answers "amen" to any version of Kaddish will cause the gates of Eden to open up,[12] even affording the release of a parent already consigned to Gehenna.[13] Kaddish, then, represents a "second chance" for the sinner to achieve atonement. Even if the parent failed to sanctify God's name in his or her lifetime, the Kaddish may be the means by which he or she is able to erase the legacy of a wayward past. Furthermore, the task of rehabilitating the soul of the deceased is assumed by the child, thus strengthening the bond between parent and offspring—even after death. On some level the child is recognizing his debt to his parent, regardless of the nature of their relationship, and accepts responsibility for the fate of his parent's soul.

All of the sources assume that reciting Kaddish (just like leading prayer services) is an obligation that pertains to males only; women are assumed to be exempt from this obligation. But *may* one perform a ritual practice that one is excused from? Regarding the recitation of Kaddish by women, rabbis engaged with this question as early as the seventeenth century, including Rabbi Yair Bacharach, in his collection of responsa *Havvot Ya·ir*,[14] and Rabbi Yaakov Reischer, in his *Sh'vut Yaakov* collection, both of Germany.[15] There are certainly rabbis who have permitted it under certain circumstances, including Rabbi Yosef Eliyahu Henkin[16] and Rabbi Moshe Feinstein,[17] two highly regarded halakhic decisors of the twentieth century who lived in the United States.[18] However, it is not a widespread practice in

Orthodox circles, whether because traditionally it simply has not been done, or whether because of perceived halahkic problems with the practice.[19] Some scholars maintain that a daughter may not recite Kaddish for her parents in a public forum.[20] In addition, the question arises whether reciting Kaddish draws unnecessary attention to the woman, thus undermining her "modesty."

As with many halakhic issues, there are differences of opinion regarding a woman saying Kaddish. But as pointed out in the Beit Hillel rabbinic organization's halakhic decision, there is a strong basis on which to argue that women *are* permitted to recite Kaddish.[21] Therefore, I had to make up my own mind whether or not to take this practice upon myself. I will now discuss how I reacted differently to the deaths of my father and my mother, reflected by my reciting the Kaddish only in the case of my mother's death. My story takes place in Israel where I live, and within the confines of the Orthodox synagogue to which I belong, and as such it may differ significantly from the experiences of other women in other places.[22]

My father died in 2002 at the age of ninety-one. My parents had been married for sixty-one years, a marriage of boundless love and devotion. In the last two years of his life my father was declining physically, and my mother dedicated herself to him with even more single-mindedness than she had demonstrated previously in their long married life. I dreaded my father's death, for I loved and admired him with all my heart—but also because I was profoundly concerned about how my mother would handle it. Indeed, after my father died my mother went into deep mourning, perhaps even depression; ironically, what saved her and invigorated her was her gradual loss of memory, a process that had already started in my father's lifetime but intensified after his death. During the eleven months following my father's death, my two brothers recited the Kaddish at the three communal daily prayer services, never missing a single day. I was emotionally involved in my mother's coping with her grief, and was grateful that my brothers assumed unstintingly the recitation of Kaddish for our father. I was very strict about the traditional prohibitions of mourning—such as not attending any public celebrations, like weddings or bar and bat mitzvahs, or buying new clothes—but those were the only formal expression of my mourning. I do not recall feeling a need to express my mourning in any other way.

When my mother died ten years later at the age of ninety-five, the Orthodox world in which I live had undergone a shift. At my father's funeral, I had wanted to eulogize him alongside my brothers. However, the head of the Burial Society refused to allow me to speak in the hall before the burial—because I am a woman. He even threatened not to bury my father if I insisted on speaking. My family and I were outraged by this threat, but I was not in an emotional state to challenge him on it (though, in retrospect, I doubt that he would have carried out his threat). I ended up speaking after the burial, under a hot summer sun at the gravesite. This experience galvanized me into resolving that I would not allow myself to be bullied in this way ever again.

At my mother's funeral a decade later, officials of the same Burial Society did not attempt to stop me from speaking in the hall. Even they had come to the realization that times had changed! Rabbi Seth Farber, the head of Itim (an organization that seeks halakhic solutions to modern problems), came to the funeral at the behest of my sister-in-law—prepared to intercede on our behalf with the Burial Society, if needed. Moreover, he asked me if I wanted to recite Kaddish, a question that I had not previously considered. I replied in the negative. I was still operating under ingrained assumptions that Kaddish was appropriate for men only.

At the *shiva*, however, I suddenly realized that I *did* want to say Kaddish. I understood that I wished to express my grief together with my two brothers, and I wanted the community to acknowledge my sorrow. I think that some of the participants in the *minyan*, both male and female, were a bit taken aback by my decision, but I felt good about my resolve. All of a sudden it struck me just how anomalous it is that only men express their mourning publicly, while women's expression of sorrow is expected to be more "underground." It simply made no sense to me. For the last ten years of her life, my mother and I lived in close proximity to each other. I had witnessed her mental and physical decline, sharing with her the joys and sorrows of her final years. Kaddish was a way for me to connect with my mother, as well as to acknowledge that she was gone.

After *shiva* I had to decide how I would proceed. Did I wish to continue saying Kaddish? Would I commit to a daily communal prayer? How would my *shul* react to my saying Kaddish? In the vast majority of Orthodox synagogues women do not recite Kaddish, and changing tradition or custom in Orthodox practice is notoriously controversial. There had been a single case of a woman in our congregation saying Kaddish several years before, when our membership was much smaller, but many of the present *daveners* were relative newcomers who were not accustomed to this practice. Should I simply be grateful that my brothers were shouldering this responsibility and leave it at that?

I did not immediately decide to recite Kaddish. But at one Kabbalat Shabbat service,[23] about two months into the year of mourning, I spontaneously stood up and joined the men in the recitation of Kaddish. It was not easy, for a variety of reasons. I do not like to draw attention to myself and I wasn't comfortable with the surprised looks that I received from the other women present. In addition, it is hard to follow the men as they mumble their way through the text. But as time went on I gained more confidence and chose formally to alert the male mourners to the fact that I was joining them, going so far as to ask them to adjust their pace to mine. I was fortunate that, by and large, the men were amenable to my request. When I was a guest in other synagogues, I continued to recite the Kaddish—albeit more softly, in the hope that it would pass without notice.

Once I had decided that I would continue reciting Kaddish for the remainder of the eleven months, I had to decide what kind of commitment I wanted to make regarding praying in a *minyan*. Here is where I determined that being a woman gave me the latitude to pick and choose how often I wanted to say Kaddish. I was aware of the all-or-nothing approach espoused by some: namely, that a woman who chooses to take upon herself obligations traditionally reserved for men should do it just like a man—that is, three times a day. I know of a few women who have adopted this approach, and I respect them tremendously for it. But if this approach is inappropriate or inapplicable for the vast majority of women, why should they be excluded from saying Kaddish? An all-or-nothing approach would preclude many male mourners from saying Kaddish. Clearly, no men are questioned as to whether they have fulfilled their thrice-daily prayer obligations, before they are allowed to intone the Kaddish. In addition, I (and many other women like me) have the kind of home and family responsibilities that make attending a daily *minyan* very difficult. On Shabbat and holidays, however, I could participate in communal prayer, for these were the services that I regularly attended. It made sense to me, both intellectually and emotionally, to say Kaddish when I could attend communal services.

I gained several important insights from the experience of saying Kaddish for my mother. In the midst of everyday living, with its demands and duties, the memory of my mother would slip away. Saying Kaddish was a way of restoring her to me, of conjuring up the person she was and what she meant to me. One young woman in our congregation said to me, "I envy you that you are saying Kaddish for your mother. I lost my mother when I was a teenager and wanted so much to say Kaddish for her, but it simply wasn't done. Because of who you are, you make it acceptable for other women." I hadn't purposely set out to blaze a trail, but this young woman made me realize that I was establishing a precedent for other women in my *shul* who someday might want to recite Kaddish. She strengthened me in my choice to continue saying Kaddish, both for my own sake as well as for the sake of other women.

I also became aware of the fact that saying Kaddish for my mother was also saying it for my father. As a product of my culture and background, I had not reached the "tipping point" where Kaddish was my prerogative at the time of my father's death. In addition, I had been so involved in my mother's anguish when she was widowed that I hadn't mourned my father properly for myself. When I started saying Kaddish for my mother, my father's image rose up in my mind, and I regretted not having honored him with Kaddish. Because my parents had been such a loving couple, the memory of one almost invariably reminded me of the other. I came to understand my decision to say Kaddish for my mother as a way of also grieving for my father and honoring him, at the same time that I did so for my mother.

The attention I received from saying Kaddish also brought home another truth. Suddenly, people who did not know me asked me why I was saying Kaddish. My loss was being acknowledged by the public. I was not mourning privately, but was part of a larger community that took an interest in me. By responding to my Kaddish in a public forum, the other members of the synagogue were in effect saying to me: you too are a mourner in Israel.

There were times that I was almost sorry that I had taken this task upon myself. The question arose of what would happen if I was the only mourner present. Should I expect the congregation to respond to my Kaddish? Would they even be aware of the fact that a woman was saying it? (One Shabbat my brother was visiting us in Israel, and he attended services at our Orthodox congregation where men and women sit separately, women behind a *meḥitzah*. I had forgotten to tell him that I recite Kaddish, and at the end of the service my brother said to my husband and me, "I think there was a woman saying Kaddish in *shul*.") There are different halakhic positions regarding this situation, so I enlisted my husband to recite with me should the need arise. I was not entirely comfortable with this arrangement, because my husband's parents are alive and it is not customary to intone the Mourner's Kaddish under those circumstances.

At times I could not keep up with the men, or even hear them. All this made me feel unequal. A good friend of mine would then turn to me sympathetically and murmur, "Not easy, huh?" But if at times I lost heart, I thought of all the benefits of saying Kaddish. Most of all, I think my parents would have approved of my choice, and been proud to be commemorated in this way. All my life they had encouraged me to develop, to seek the right path, and to take responsibility for my choices. Saying Kaddish reminded me of what my parents had given me, and this was my way of thanking them.

NOTES

[1] Technically speaking, the period of mourning lasts twelve months after the death of a parent, but Kaddish is only recited for the first eleven. Nevertheless, Jewish people often speak loosely about a "year" of Kaddish.

[2] For the Hebrew version, see: S. Wasserstein, *Massekhet Sofrim* (Jerusalem: Sifrei Ramot, 5761 [2000/2001]), p. 95. For an English translation, see A. Cohen, *The Minor Tractates of the Talmud* (London: Soncino Press, 1965), p. 258.

[3] Yitzchak Moshe Elbogen, *Ha-t'fillah B'yisrael*, trans. and ed. Yehoshua Amir (Tel-Aviv: Dvir, 1988), p. 72. Elbogen's work was originally published in German in Leipzig in 1913.

[4] Interestingly, the version of Kaddish recited at a *siyyum* is almost identical to the one recited at a burial.

[5] Stefan C. Reif, *Judaism and Hebrew Prayer: New Perspectives on Jewish Liturgical History* (Cambridge: Cambridge University Press 1993), p. 210. Reif notes that prayers relating specifically to death and resurrection are unknown in Rabbinic Judaism, and probably emerged in Jewish liturgy around the time of the Crusade massacres in the eleventh century (pp. 218–220). The adoption of Kaddish as a mourner's prayer might have been influenced by these additions to the liturgy.

[6] Ibid, p. 210.

[7] It is not clear when the custom of reciting Kaddish on the *yahrzeit* became prevalent. Rashi, commenting on B. Yevamot 122a, s.v. *t'lata riglei*, notes that there was a custom during geonic times to mark the anniversary of the death of a great scholar by gathering at his grave. For a discussion of the customs surrounding the *yahrzeit*, see: J. D. Eisenstein, *Otzar Dinim U-minhagim* (New York: Hebrew Publishing Co., 1922), pp.154–155.

[8] The name "Shulḥan Arukh" literally means "set table," and the *Mappah*, which means "tablecloth," is thus a play on the name.

[9] Isaac ben Moses (called Isaac of Vienna), *Sefer Or Zarua* (ed. Zhitomir, 1863), part 2, *siman* 50, p. 22.

[10] See Israel Ta-Shma, *Minhag Ashkenaz Ha-kadmon* (Jerusalem: Magnes Press, 1994), p. 307.

[11] Seder Eliyahu Zuta §17, ed. Meir Ish-Shalom (1902; rpt.Jerusalem:Wahrman, 5729 [1968/1969], pp. 22–23.

[12] B. Shabbat 112b.

[13] Seder Eliyahu Zuta §20, ed. cit., p. 33. Gehenna is the anglicization of the Hebrew *geihinnom*, a regular designation for hell in rabbinic literature.

[14] *Sefer She'eilot U-t'shuvot Ḥavvot Ya·ir* (Lvov: Yaakov Meshulam Nik, 5656 [1895/1896]), responsum 222, p. 116a.

[15] *She'eilot U-t'shuvot Sh'vut Yaakov* (Offenbach: Bonaventura de Launoy, 5479

[1718/1719]), part II, §93, pp 26b-27a.

[16] Rabbi Yosef Eliyahu Henkin, *T'shuvot Ivra* (New York: Ezras Torah, 5749 [1988/1989]), chap. 1 §4, pp. 5–6.

[17] *Ig'rot* Moshe, Oraḥ Ḥayyim (New York: D. Feinstein, 1996), part 5 §12 p. 20.

[18] Rabbi Henkin permits a woman to recite Kaddish if she stands behind the *meḥitzah*, is dressed modestly, and is an observant Jew. (The term *meḥitzah* denotes the physical barrier that divides the men's and women's sections of a place designated for prayer in the Orthodox world.) Rabbi Feinstein does not respond directly to the question, but writes that in Europe a woman on occasion would enter the synagogue and recite Kaddish, implying that this was permissible. It is unclear from this statement what his position would be regarding a woman reciting Kaddish on a daily basis.

[19] There is a concern that one might construe the daughter's Kaddish as a *ḥiyyuv*—namely, that she is obligated to recite Kaddish.

[20] For example, Rabbi Yaakov Reischer allowed an underage girl (i.e., younger than 12) to recite Kaddish for her father in a *minyan* in her home but he forbade her from reciting Kaddish in the synagogue; see note 14.

[21] Beit Hillel is a rabbinic organization in Israel that includes men and women, rabbis, teachers, and community leaders, all of whom adhere to *halakhah*, believe in the centrality of both Zionism and modernity in Jewish life, and wish to make Judaism meaningful to all Jews. The source is available online in Hebrew at www. beithillel.org.il. For a synopsis of the Beit Hillel discussion in English, see Joel B. Wolowelsky's review of *Kaddish: Women's Voices* [see n. 21] in *Hakirah* 17 (Summer 2014), p. 173.

[22] For other women's experiences with and reflections about reciting Kaddish, see *Kaddish: Women's Voices*, ed. Michal Smart (Jerusalem: Urim Publications, 2013).

[23] Kabbalat Shabbat is the preparatory service that opens worship on Friday evenings and precedes the recitation of the formal evening service (Maariv).

An Enigma Wrapped in A Mystery[1]

Adena K. Berkowitz

The call came on a Sunday afternoon in February. I had just returned from a family fun day with my then five-year-old. I was looking forward to sitting down with a cup of coffee, happy to enjoy a few moments to myself and recover after a morning of activities for kids, including face-painting, balloons, and lots of accompanying tumult. My brother was on the phone and shared the news that my father had died. My dad had been active until the moment he passed away so, while he had been growing physically more frail as he aged, his death still somehow came as a surprise. Before I could even begin to come to terms with the fact that my father had passed to the World of Truth, my mind began to race. I had to check on my mother. I had to find a way to tell my children that their beloved grandfather had passed away. I had to inform family and friends about the sad news of my father's death and about details about the funeral. I needed to gather my thoughts for a eulogy. And then something else hit me: Kaddish. I had always wondered about what I would do regarding Kaddish. Would I be able to take upon myself the daily obligation of reciting Kaddish in a public prayer service? Would I find such a service, colloquially called a *minyan* (because of its requirement that there be a quorum, a specific number of worshippers present), nearby that was accommodating to women saying Kaddish?

The origin of saying Kaddish is attributed to Rabbi Akiva, among the greatest sages of ancient times.[2] Some of the early medieval authorities, like Rabbi Isaac ben Moses of Vienna (c.1200–c.1270, called the Or Zarua after his great halakhic compendium) and Rabbi Simḥah ben Samuel of Vitry (d. 1105), point to a legend that recounts how Rabbi Akiva saved a deceased person from the judgment of Gehenna[3] by teaching the deceased's son to sanctify God's name.[4] The tale concludes by saying that if a person's son "stands among the congregation and leads the congregation in praising God by intoning the Bar'khu call to prayer and the congregation responds appropriately, or if he says the Kaddish and they respond *y'hei sh'meih rabba m'varakh l'alam u-l'alamei almaya* ("may God's great name be blessed forever and for all time"), that person is immediately released from punishment."[5] The Or Zarua also observes that "our custom…and also that of the people of the Rhine is that after the congregation recites Ein Keloheinu, the orphan stands and recites Kaddish…following the lesson taught by Rabbi Akiva."[6]

The debate over women saying Kaddish extends back to a seventeenth-century responsum by Rabbi Yair Ḥayyim Bacharach (1639–1702; called the Ḥavvot Yair, after his collection of responsa), where he writes:

A strange matter took place in Amsterdam and is well known there. A person who had no son died. He left instructions that in the event of his death, ten people should be paid to learn [Torah] every day throughout the year of mourning, in his home. And subsequent to the learning session, his daughter should recite Kaddish. The rabbinic sages and leaders of the community did not protest her recitation….It may be that a woman is also required to observe the *mitzvah* of *kiddush ha-sheim* [i.e., the commandment to sanctify God's name]. This occurs by the fact that there are ten men present. Though the original source for the recitation of Kaddish is the story of Rabbi Akiva informing a youngster to recite Kaddish and that case deals with a male, not a female, logic would dictate that [a woman's recitation of Kaddish] would be beneficial and bring satisfaction to the soul [of the departed] in that she is the seed [of the departed]. Yet, one should be concerned that this would weaken the customs of the people of Israel, which are also deemed [an integral aspect of] Torah. [One must prevent] people from attempting to build a personal altar according to their own specific reasons and thus make a mockery of rabbinic laws....[In conclusion,] since the matter relates to a public gathering, one should protest it.[7]

The concerns of the Ḥavvot Yair seem to revolve around his concern with the public policy issue of a woman saying Kaddish, rather than a halakhic concern with her saying Kaddish. Similarly, in the modern era we have seen decisors weigh in with concern that, although they can permit women to say Kaddish in a synagogue, issues of gender propriety cannot be sidestepped in a less formal setting.[8]

Rabbi Moshe Feinstein (1895–1986) noted that "throughout the generations it was customary that, from time to time, a female mourner would enter the synagogue to say Kaddish." His concludes that "in practice, further study of this matter is required," and this seems based more on the concern of whether there is *meḥitzah* in placc in a study hall setting when a woman would come in to say Kaddish, rather than the issue of saying Kaddish specifically.[9]

Rabbi Yosef Eliyahu Henkin (1881–1973) wrote, "I recall that in my childhood, a young woman said Kaddish in the presence of the men in a pious, God-fearing congregation…"—which remark he concludes by saying "that if she also wishes to say Kaddish before women while Kaddish is being recited by the men in the synagogue, we are not particular."[10] His grandson, Rabbi Yehudah Henkin (b. 1945), also permitted women to say Kaddish, arguing that since we are now accustomed to saying Kaddish in unison,[11] there is no problem if a woman joins in and recites the Kaddish from the women's section of the synagogue. In his opinion, similar to the stance of the Ḥavvot Yair, this is preferable to her saying Kaddish by herself in a private *minyan* in her home. However, he felt that if no others were saying Kaddish in the synagogue, it would be appropriate for one of the men to say Kaddish so that the woman not recite it alone.[12]

In contemporary times, Rabbi Joseph B. Soloveitchik and Rabbi Aharon Soloveitchik have also ruled that a woman is permitted to recite the mourner's Kaddish, even alone, from the women's section.[13]

*****

Shiva for me was a blur of hundreds of visitors, as well as *minyanim* that met in my home in the morning, afternoon, and evening. Saying Kaddish within this environment did not prove a challenge, but finding the right synagogue environment would.[14] While the recitation of Kaddish by women has become more commonplace in recent years in the Orthodox Jewish community, in many ways it is still uncharted territory. As a member of the Orthodox Jewish community, I knew that as a woman saying Kaddish there would be times that I would encounter a host of difficult—and, at times, even uncomfortable—situations that women in the non-Orthodox community would never face.[15]

My allegiance to *halakhah* (Jewish law) and loyalty to being a part of the Orthodox Jewish world precluded my choosing an egalitarian synagogue. And yet relying on halakhic rulings permitting a woman to say Kaddish would not be enough if the synagogue environment did not support it. The net result was that it would take hard work and patience to find an Orthodox synagogue—even in a city as filled with synagogues as New York—that would be welcoming and a safe harbor for me.[16] As soon as my week of mourning was over, it was time to find a daily *minyan*. I still remember the first prayer service I attended at a local synagogue. I found myself relegated to the back of the room, behind a *meḥitzah* where it was hard to hear the prayer leader, and the physical distance created an even greater spiritual distance. Nor were the issues I was facing only theoretical; some were practical as well. If no women were present and the men were all too far away, who would be able to answer "amen" to my Kaddish? Would the men permit a woman to say Kaddish alone if no male mourners were present? I quickly realized that this particular synagogue was not going to be the right setting for me and so I soon decamped to another synagogue. I still remember the first day arriving there, unsure what the women's section was going to be like. I walked in and, while at first I only saw where the men were praying, I soon realized that there was an area for the women alongside the men, from whom the women were separated by a reasonable *meḥitzah*.[17] As the service began, I found myself thinking all the way back to high school, the last stretch of time in my life during which I worshipped routinely in a weekday *minyan*. Although I had continued over the intervening years to recite the weekday prayers at home, the pressure I now felt to get to a *minyan* on time in the morning weighed on me and took me back to my high school years. At the time, my Orthodox yeshiva did not require any of its students to attend daily services in school but we were on the honor system to recite our prayers at home (although the school would eventually change its policy and indeed require students to attend morning *minyan*). Nonetheless, throughout that first year of high school I took it upon myself to arrive an hour before the official start of school to attend the public service. I loved the davening (praying) and the camaraderie, but it was disconcerting to hear the male prayer leader publicly praise God for "not having made [him] a woman." Those words continued to bother me as I began my year of mourning,[18] but soon gave way to more pressing questions, such as: If there were no male mourners also saying Kaddish, would I be able to say Kaddish alone?

Within a few minutes of the start of the service, I soon realized that not only were there male mourners present but there were also other women in attendance—there were, in fact, two other women about half my age—whom I soon discovered had also lost their fathers, and thus was a bond immediately created between us, sisters in mourning and in Kaddish.

At the conclusion of the service, the *gabbai*, a kind of sexton, came over and introduced himself to me. It would take me a few weeks, but one day I delicately asked the *gabbai* if the prayer leader could drop his voice when publicly thanking God for the blessing of not have been created a woman, as has become the custom in some Orthodox synagogues.[19] Soon that accommodation was introduced and this, together with the initial welcome by the *gabbai*, exemplify the extreme sensitivity displayed by that particular *minyan*, especially regarding the *gabbai*'s personal effort to make women feel at home. The desire to create a welcoming environment was borne out by what happened one morning when I arrived late, assuming I had missed the first Kaddish.[20] As I entered the synagogue, I saw the eager looks of anticipation on the faces of the men, all of whom had surely been hoping that I would be the tenth man, the last worshipper required to form a *minyan* and whose presence would enable the service to continue; but alas, I was only the tenth person. Sensing their mood, I apologized for disappointing them! The *gabbai* quickly came over and said, "I just want you to know you that while we can't count you *for* the *minyan*, we count you as an important part *of* our *minyan*."

In essence, his remarks summed up the enigma I faced and yet embraced. I was valued as a part of the *minyan* community but I was not counted toward the requisite number that made up a *minyan*.

And yet, I was not deterred from participating. I had taken on the commitment to pray three times a day in a *minyan*, whether at my usual locale or in different settings—despite the fact that I was neither obligated to do so nor counted as part of the quorum. For the next eleven months, the daily routine of attending worship service three times a day proved challenging: not only because of the logistics involved (such as making sure my older children got off to school on time and getting back in time to walk my youngest to her school), but also because of my gender. There were several instances of needing to find a place to attend services and say Kaddish that proved challenging and complicated. But there were pleasant surprises as well: for example, our local Judaica shop, run by fervently Orthodox Jews, hosted a daily afternoon *minyan* and was entirely welcoming to women saying Kaddish aloud. But it was, at times, necessary to leave my comfort zone, which inevitably meant encountering people and communities that responded very differently to women. One modern Orthodox synagogue outside of Manhattan, for example, featured a rabbi who ended the service with the words "Have a nice day, gentlemen"—presumably, because he was so used to the prevailing norm of a male-only *minyan* that he failed to take note when women actually were in attendance.

As winter turned to spring things became easier, as the window for reciting the afternoon service became longer. One day, anticipating that I would be in Brooklyn until late evening, I attended an early afternoon service on the Upper West Side before heading to Brooklyn, assuming that I would be able to find a synagogue there for the evening service. I asked one of the local shopkeepers about the best place for Maariv and he directed me to one of the "*minyan* factories" where, from dawn until one o'clock in the morning, *minyanim* are held regularly, like clockwork. I asked the friend with whom I was shopping to come with me. As we entered the building, we noticed a beggar outside; he approached every single man, but ignored us. I turned to my friend and said, "Do you think this is a sign of things to come?" Clearly, it wasn't only rabbis who failed to "see" the women in their midst! Yet, as we entered the building, a man noticed us and asked us in a welcoming manner if we were looking for the "ladies section" and he directed us upstairs to the women's gallery. As we prepared to enter, we were met at the doorway by a youngish man in hasidic garb who was tutoring a student. Startled by our presence, he immediately asked us what we were doing there. Instinctively, I said that I had come to say Kaddish—which I immediately realized was the wrong thing to say. He began to shout at me that I had no right to be here and continued to berate me. We eventually agreed that he would cede one side of the women's gallery to me, and could continue to teach his student elsewhere in the space, with a table serving as a separation between us. And that was actually one of the better-resolved situations that I encountered, in communities that did not expect women to attend daily services; once, I had to stand in a stairwell because the synagogue I had chosen didn't have a women's gallery at all!

Yet, across the months and in different locales, I also had many positive experiences within ultra-Orthodox synagogues. In one, for example, the rabbi himself undertook to clear the men out of the women's section where they had been congregating, in order to make room for me...and that was after I made it clear I had come specifically to say Kaddish.

Even when I experienced rudeness and was made to feel wholly unwelcome, there were occasionally positive developments after the fact: for example, after insulting me publicly for wanting to say Kaddish, a man telephoned me a few days later to apologize for his boorish comments with reference to his own background: "I am from Brooklyn," he said. "I never saw a woman say Kaddish before and just acted on instinct to stop you."

Soon, the last day of saying Kaddish arrived. Traditionally the honor of leading the prayer service is offered to someone saying Kaddish, which is especially significant for someone who has reached the end of their eleven months of daily recitation of Kaddish. In an Orthodox congregation such a prayer leader must be male. I had noticed, a few weeks earlier, how a fellow worshipper had cried his way through his prayers as he completed his recitation of Kaddish. I began to consider how I myself, excluded from leading the service, could mark the experience of a final Kaddish meaningfully. And so, I asked my husband to join me at that *minyan* that day and act as my agent of sorts—a symbol of my completing my last Kaddish (which would actually take place later in the afternoon at the Minḥah service). That day, however, there were two other mourners present who had priority in leading the service. It was also Ḥanukkah—and since mourners are traditionally excluded from leading the Hallel prayer recited on holidays and Rosh Ḥodesh (the New Moon), they were not going to be reciting the Hallel prayer. The *gabbai* turned to my husband and asked him to lead that part of the service. The irony was not lost on me: I had been on my own the whole year, but at the very end had brought in my husband to do that which I couldn't—and instead, he was recruited for the very portion of the service specifically not permitted to those in mourning! This moment encapsulated for me the paradox of Orthodox women reciting Kaddish. I saw myself as part of the halakhic world and hence I accepted not being counted toward the *minyan* or leading the service. Many men in the Orthodox synagogues I attended seemed confused why a woman would seek to fulfill an obligation that tradition did not assign to them, and many expressed that thought out loud and in my presence. Others seemed almost apologetic for the differences in ritual obligations for men and women. And there were times when the exclusion was painful to me, as on this very last day of my saying Kaddish.

This inherent tension I experienced might have led others to seek an outlet within egalitarian synagogues. That was not an option I sought or desired, even as I came to realize more and more that within Orthodox Judaism the tension between *halakhah* and egalitarian values was a real one. The enigma and the mystery of an Orthodox woman saying Kaddish, with all the logistical and emotional navigation involved, would remain a continuing theme. Yet, for me, the comfort of saying Kaddish within a daily community of mourners and ordinary worshippers outweighed the negative emotions. It has stayed with me for years, as I continue to attend a daily morning *minyan*. More women have joined our ranks, primarily those who have lost parents and husbands. Some have come with their babies in tow, including one woman who arrived with newborn twins. As the children got older and more rambunctious, the women formed an informal "babysitting service" to watch over the children during the service. The synagogue even contemplated hiring actual babysitters to help keep the children occupied, so as to allow the mother time to worship without being constantly interrupted.

The experience of saying Kaddish for my father provided me with months of comfort. The daily *minyan* I attended regularly became more sensitive to presence of women on the other side of the *meḥitzah*. At the end of my year of Kaddish, I discovered that as much as Kaddish is thought to bring comfort to the soul of the deceased, it was no less powerful in bringing comfort to the one saying Kaddish. The support of a praying community meant that one was never alone. And the presence of women on the women's side of the synagogue also helped to confirm that.

NOTES

[1] I dedicate this essay to the memory of my father, Rabbi William Berkowitz ז"ל .

[2] Rabbi Akiva's dates are usually given as c. 40–c. 135 C.E.

[3] Gehenna is the anglicization of the Hebrew *geihinnom*, a regular designation for hell in rabbinic literature.

[4] See the responsum issued by Beit Hillel, an Orthodox organization comprised of 170 Israeli spiritual leaders, on November 18, 2014 and available on-line at http://eng.beithillel.org.il/responsa/may-a-woman-say-kaddish-for-her-parents/.

[5] Rabbi Isaac of Vienna, *Sefer Or Zarua*, *Part Two*, Hilkhot Shabbat §50 (ed. Zhitomir, 1862), p. 22, and Rabbi Simḥah of Vitry, *Maḥzor Vitry* 1:144 (ed. S. Hurwitz [Nuremberg, 1923]), pp. 112–113.

[6] *Sefer Or Zarua*, p. 22.

[7] Rabbi Yair Ḥayyim Bacharach, *She'eilot U–t'shuvot Ḥavvot Yair* (Lvov: Yaakov Meshulam Nik, 5656 [1895/1896]), responsum no. 222, p. 116a. For the same scenario of setting up a separate *minyan* but the opposite conclusion permitting a woman to say Kaddish at a separate *minyan* formed for her, see Rabbi Yehudah Ashkenazi, author of the *Be'er Heitiv* (commentary to S.A. Oraḥ Ḥayyim) sec. 132, n. 5, p. 27, in vol, 2 of the *Mishneh B'rurah*. The logic of setting up a separate *minyan* is based on the custom of that time when only one person said the Mourner's Kaddish and they would not permit a woman to displace a man in a synagogue-based service. See note 11 below and Wolowelsky, p. 87.

[8] For example, in the *Gesher Ha-ḥayyim* (Jerusalem: D'fus Salomon, 5707 [1946/1947]), chap. 30:8:5, pp. 277–278, Rabbi Yeḥiel Mikhel Tukachinsky (1872–1955) attests that "there are many places that permit her to say Kaddish in the synagogue." However, he concludes that "in any case, an adult daughter is not permitted to say Kaddish in the synagogue"—apparently, because it would be unseemly for a woman to do so. And cf. the unsigned responsum published online on the Beit Hillel website mentioned above in note 4.

[9] *Responsa Ig'rot Moshe, Oraḥ Ḥayyim, Ḥeilek Ḥamishi* (ed. Jerusalem, 5756 [1995/1996]), responsum 12, part 2, p. 20. Other authorities who have allowed women to say Kaddish include Rabbi Eliezer Zalman Grayevsky (1843–1899). In his book *Kaddish L'alam* (Jerusalem, 1891), p. 31, he writes that a daughter may say Kaddish and that it is of benefit for her parents, stating: "It makes no difference if the orphan is a son or a daughter…a woman may also say Kaddish to save the soul of the deceased and elevate it…and therefore women, too, can say Kaddish for their parents." It would appear that he preferred that the daughter say Kaddish herself, as opposed to hiring a man to say it, when there were no surviving male children.

[10] Rabbi Yosef Eliyahu Henkin, *T'shuvot Ivra* (New York: Ezras Torah, 5749

[1988/1989]), vol. 2, pp. 3–5. And cf. the author's comment there regarding women reciting the Mourner's Kaddish alone from the women's section: "The question as to whether a [bereaved] daughter may recite the Kaddish is bound up with her observance of the Sabbath, *kashrut*, and the laws of family purity. If she does keep these basic *mitzvot*, it is permissible for her to say Kaddish in the women's gallery while the men are doing so in the synagogue proper." The translation here comes from David Telsner's *The Kaddish: Its History and Significance* (Jerusalem: Tal Orot Institute, 1995]), p. 301.

[11] As explained in the Beit Hillel responsum: "It should be noted that according to the original custom, as opposed to our current practice, only one person recited Kaddish, while all the others would remain silent, and then respond to the call of the person saying Kaddish to praise God. The custom was that only one mourner said Kaddish so that the congregation would hear it clearly, inasmuch as 'two' and certainly 'three or four voices are not heard' (i.e., more than one voice is not heard clearly), and the congregation would then respond *amen, y'hei sh'meih rabba m'varakh l'alam u-l'almei almaya.*" Furthermore, the *Or Zarua* in accordance with this custom ruled that it is preferable that minors who cannot serve as prayer leaders say the Kaddishes recited at the end of the service, as the person reciting them need not be obligated to the performance of *mitzvot* or be a member of the congregation. (In this regard, see also the *Sefer Ha-agur* of Rabbi Jacob ben Judah Landau [d. 1493] §334 [New York: Menorah, 5719 [1958/1959], p. 35.) However, over the years, the custom developed by which all the mourners recite Kaddish in unison." See the Beit Hillel responsum cited earlier.

[12] See Beit Hillel responsum, citing *Responsa B'nei Banim* 2:7 (Jerusalem: Y. H. Henkin, 1992), pp. 23–30.

[13] See Rabbi Joel Wolowelsky, "In our Synagogues: Women and Kaddish," in *Women, Jewish Law, and Modernity* (Hoboken, NJ: KTAV, 1997), pp. 88 and 93, citing Rabbi Ezra Bick's correspondence with Rabbi Soloveitchik; and Rabbi Aaron Soloveitchik's comments in his *Od Yisrael Yosef B'ni Hai* 32 [Chicago: Yeshivat Brisk, 1993]). Rabbi Shaul Yisraeli (1909–1995) wrote, in his collection of responsa, *B'mareih Ha-bazak* 1:4 (Jerusalem: Ha-histadrut Ha-tziyonit Ha-olamit, 5760 [1999/2000]), p. 5: "If a women says Kaddish in a normal voice in the women's section, it can be permitted, and it does not constitute a weakening of custom."

[14] The issue of my saying Kaddish and the height and placement of the *mehitzah* did not pose any problem when I sat shiva. At Orthodox *minyanim* at a shiva home, one will see men and women praying separately, usually in side-by-side adjacent rooms or being in the same room but using a lightweight piece of furniture as a *mehitzah*; this is what occurred when I sat shiva.

[15] In non-Orthodox synagogues, services are almost always fully egalitarian: men and women sit together, women are counted along with men for the minimal quorum of ten required for a *minyan*, and women may lead the service. However, within Orthodox Judaism, while the role of women has also evolved,

ritual life has remained mostly male-centered. There are exceptions, such as in "partnership" *minyanim* (prayer groups), where men and women sit, equally, on either side of a *mehitzah* and in which women may lead certain introductory parts of the service and read from the Torah. However, women do not count toward a prayer quorum nor do they lead the main parts of the prayer services. For more about partnership *minyanim*, see www.jofa.org/Resources/ritual/synagogue/partnershipm.

[16] To understand the perspective of Orthodox Jewish women who choose to say Kaddish and remain Orthodox, see *Kaddish: Women's Voices*, ed. Michal Smart and Barbara Ashkenasi (Jerusalem: Urim, 2013).

[17] In Orthodox synagogues, men and women sit separately. The divider, called a *mehitzah*, may run from the front to the back of the synagogue, such that men's and women's sections are essentially side-by-side; or it may be placed so as to situate the women's section behind that of the men. It can be as low as four feet or as high as eight feet. The physical barrier may consist of a curtain, clear glass, or one-way mirrors (such that the women can see into the men's section, but not vice versa). In some synagogues, the women's section may be located in an upstairs gallery or balcony, which may afford those in the front rows visual access to the service; or in a separate room altogether, with more limited ability to see and hear the service being conducted from the men's section.

[18] This blessing is also said at the start of Shabbat morning services, but its placement at the start of prayers makes it easy to miss if one arrives even a few moments late to the prayer service.

[19] See Rabbi Yehuda Henkin, "The Blessing *Shelo Asani Isha*," in *Responsa on Contemporary Jewish Women's Issues* (Hoboken, NJ: KTAV, 2003) p. 20, where he writes that saying Birkhot Ha-shahar out loud in a synagogue is only a custom. Citing the *Sefer Me'orei Or* by Rabbi Aharon Ezra (ed. 1829, part 4, p. 20), he writes that "one should not publicly recite 'who did not make me a gentile' because of the danger of creating antipathy between gentile and Jew, nor 'who did not make me a woman' because of the likelihood of shaming women." Rabbi Henkin further notes (pp. 29–30) that while the Shulḥan Arukh (S.A. Oraḥ Ḥayyim 46:1–2) requires that the morning blessings should be said out loud, this specifically does *not* apply to the three introductory blessings. (Note this blessing has been changed in Reform and Conservative liturgy.)

[20] There is a Mourner's Kaddish that is recited just a few minutes into the morning service, which can only be recited by those who arrive on time.

Reflections on Saying Kaddish

Herbert A. Yoskowitz

These reflections on Kaddish are dedicated to the memory of Rabbi Harold Schulweis, of blessed memory, who echoed the Kaddish by praising God with his words and with his deeds.

What power does Kaddish hold over us? How can it be that one messianic piece, seventy-five words in Aramaic and Hebrew, has survived for centuries as a balm for the pain of loss? This short prayer is known to and recited by Jews from all denominations of Judaism—by both famous and unknown, young and old, men and women. It is unique and meaningful...and it connects the living to their beloved departed.

From time immemorial, people have grappled with the reality and the inevitability of death. Like all living creatures on land, in the sea, and in the air, the destiny of human beings is death. Everything that lives dies. All who have life will one day be grasped by death. We encounter death in our families. We suffer! We are perplexed! Rabbi Joseph B. Soloveitchik called this reaction to the "death of a near kin to whom [one] is emotionally bound...nihilistic pessimism."[1] We mourn, and, as mourners, we search for guidance as we walk the painful path of loss, mourning, and grief.

William Shakespeare eloquently expressed this painful journey after losing such a "near kin to whom [one] is emotionally bound" in Act I, scene 2 of *Hamlet*, where King Claudius is heard to say:

'Tis sweet and commendable in your nature, Hamlet,
To give these mourning duties to your father;
But you must know, your father lost a father;
That father lost, lost his, and the survivors bound
In filial obligation for some term
To do obsequious sorrow.

When bowed in sorrow, a perplexed and suffering person is treated with compassion by *halakhah*, Jewish law. The version of the Mishnah cited in the Talmud clearly addresses grief at the time of a final loss: "One whose dead relative lies before him is exempt from the recitation of the Shema and from 'the prayer' and from *t'fillin* and from all the precepts laid down in the Torah."[2] These obligations are voided in order to accommodate the highest need of a bereaved individual: to focus solely on the arranging for the appropriate funeral and burial of his or her loved one. And the rabbis were right to do so. I personally experienced the wisdom of this halakhic ruling after the sudden deaths of my parents and brother. I had intended to don my *t'fillin* and recite my morning prayers, as I had done everyday virtually uninterrupted since thirty days before my bar mitzvah. However, at that time—it was May 2, 2006, corresponding to 4 Iyar 5766—I found myself unable to do so, because my grief was simply too profound. What I experienced was best explained in the writings of a great teacher, Rabbi Joseph Soleveitchik, who wrote: "In spite of the fact that the *halakhah* has indomitable faith in eternal life, in immortality, and in a continued transcendental existence for all human beings, the *halakhah* did understand, like a loving sympathetic mother, man's fright and confusion when confronted with death."[3] In this painful time of immediate loss, one's only obligation is to prepare for the funeral and for the period of mourning that follows. And that, of course, is what I had to do...and what I did.

"If life is a pilgrimage," Rabbi Abraham Joshua Heschel wrote, "death is an arrival, a celebration. The last word should be neither craving nor bitterness, but peace, gratitude."[4] Rabbi Heschel taught us how to live life to its fullest—including accepting the reality of death as a homecoming, and that accepting that life is temporary need not be depressing. Indeed, for Heschel, the contemplation of death was enriching, not alienating, because he focused on living a meaningful life while at the same time teaching that the Jewish tradition had meaningful religious responses not only to life but to death as well. One such religious response after the death of a parent, spouse, sibling, or child—the relatives for whom one is obligated to say the Kaddish—occurs at the time of burial. With the recitation of Kaddish at the grave by the mourner, the stage of self-negation turns to self-affirmation. Mourning in total darkness ends. Sitting *shiva*— seven days spent at home mourning a death—is obligatory. Kaddish is recited in the midst of community.

When asked, "Why are you saying Kaddish for your parent daily, every single day for eleven months?" some mourners are very emotional in their response. (The question often masks the unspoken observation that the mourner has not attended religious services regularly as an adult.) To such a question, Leon Wieseltier, author of *Kaddish*, gave a straightforward and compelling response: "Because it is my duty to my father. Because it is my duty to religion....Because it would be harder for me not to say Kaddish. I would despise myself. Because the fulfillment of my duty leaves my thoughts about my father unimpeded by regret and undistorted by guilt."[5]

Wieseltier's passionate response is echoed by stories of people who are moved even by the mention of Kaddish. For example, Sylvia Cohodas of Ishpeming, Michigan, told the following story on July 5, 2002, on the occasion of the fiftieth anniversary of the founding of Ishpeming's Temple Beth Sholom. Her husband, Arnold Cohodas, had visited Jewish prisoners in the State Prison in Marquette (which in the 1950s had housed the infamous Jews of Detroit's notorious Purple Gang), and he had conducted religious services there. Sylvia recounted that Arnold told her that "the service didn't seem to have much effect on the prison group until the Kaddish. That brought tears."[6] Why did saying the Kaddish bring tears to Jewish prisoners, who were not otherwise devoted to the observance of Jewish rituals? That is a mystery, as is a column written in *The Wall Street Journal* by Michael S. Roth, president of Wesleyan University, who claims to be an atheist. Yet after the death of his father, Roth sought a synagogue where he could say the Kaddish in a quorum of ten adults. "I could say the prayer with them," he wrote, "and eventually I would stay on for the study sessions."[7] Why would a self-proclaimed atheist bother with a prayer that from start to finish only and fully unambiguously praises God?

Wieseltier, the Purple Gang members, and Roth—all from different backgrounds—would echo, I believe, the sentiments about Kaddish expressed by Rabbi Harold Schulweis, who died in 2014 at 89 years of age. Schulweis, who has been called "the most successful and influential synagogue leader of his generation,"[8] wrote and published both poetry and prose about the Kaddish. He wrote that it is a blessing to say Kaddish in a community of Jews:

> Envy the mourners
> Who with sweet bitter nostalgia
> Slowly recite the Kaddish.[9]

And in another poem, he wrote:

> Alone together
> But I mourn alone in the midst of my people
> In the Minyan
> Alone together,

An individual in community,
Present to each other,
We are each other's comfort....
A Kaddish must be answered
A Kaddish calls for response
Together we answer
Y'hei sh'mei rabba m'vorach.[10]

For Shulweis, being part of a community is indispensable for the well-being of both the mourner and the community. Being part of a community that shares in one's sanctification of life-events with religious ritual is indispensable. He noted: "What does not bring families closer together [are] riteless passages...a funeral without Kaddish."[11]

In a different poem, Schulweis looked to the future:

Once I wondered what to remember of them
Now I ask what my children will remember of me...
Will they come to the Synagogue,
Light a candle
Recite the Kaddish...
Once it was about a distant past
Now it is about tomorrow.[12]

And it is not just Schulweis; many Jews reflect on those who will say Kaddish for them after their earthly journeys are complete and express the hope that their children will abide by this tradition.

Rabbi Al Lewis is the subject of Mitch Albom's best-seller, *Have a Little Faith*. The author tells the story of his long-time family friend Rabbi Lewis, who spoke to his New Jersey congregation from the pulpit after the death of his four-year-old daughter, Rina. He told them "how the words of the Kaddish made him think. 'I am part of something here; one day my children will say this very prayer for me just as I am saying it for my daughter.'"[13] Rabbi Lewis knew that he was part of something—saying Kaddish—that continues from many generations before him and that will likely continue for many generations after.

In his powerful memoir *Living a Year of Kaddish*, Ari Goldman relates how he tried—most times successfully—to say Kaddish for eleven months for his deceased father. He relates: "The one thing my parents knew with reasonable certainty was that we, their sons, would be saying Kaddish for them. They would be physically gone someday but their Kaddish would live on." During his eleven months of saying Kaddish, Goldman—with a reporter's ear—heard many stories from the people who joined him for a daily Kaddish Minyan. One secular Israeli kibbutznik "claimed to have no religious life except for one thing: every year he would say Kaddish for his brother."[15] This kibbutznik asked one of the members of Goldman's Kaddish Minyan group to say Kaddish for his brother, who had died on Israel Independence Day (May 5, 1948), once he himself would be gone from the world...and that is exactly what the member of the *minyan* did: once a year on May 5, this member of the *minyan* would say Kaddish to honor this soldier he never knew. For eleven months, Ari Goldman discovered that "just about everyone [he] met had a Kaddish story."[16]

Ari Goldman's words are quite true: everybody has a Kaddish story. As a congregational rabbi, I have heard many such stories over the years and each one is personal, poignant, and unique. As a mourner, I realized that these Kaddish stories could help bring healing to new mourners who were just embarking on the path from pain to healing. To bring these personal Kaddish stories to the community, I scheduled an adult education program at our congregation. I invited to the program people whose stories would have universal appeal to mourners, regardless of their denominational affiliation. The three-session series on Kaddish attracted over one hundred participants. The attendance itself was impressive, but the response of the participants was even more so. Yes, there were the expected tears as the speakers' stories touched the heart, and an outpouring of sharing individual journeys through mourning and the eleven months of saying Kaddish. This unanticipated outpouring of emotion and sharing indicated to me the deep need for support and guidance for mourners, from those who have mourned their own losses and come through the experience whole and comforted.

As I reflected on this powerful three-session seminar, the idea for a book was born. I approached each speaker to solicit his or her participation and reached out to include others in the community, whose stories I thought would be particularly helpful. Each contributor had something unique to offer and I selected the stories for inclusion on that basis. Some had lost a spouse; others, a parent or a child. To my surprise, each person whom I contacted accepted my invitation. Not one person hesitated or refused to share in a way that could help others.

The Kaddish as a balm for the pain of bereavement is available to all, not just to the Heschels and Soleveitchiks among us. New mourners were helped by regular people—not rabbis or scholars— who had lived through eleven months of Kaddish and had emerged stronger and more whole after their suffering, and were then able to help other mourners wade through their own losses as they joined the Kaddish Minyan. During my own eleven months of saying Kaddish, one of the contributors to my book had helped me to understand the typhoon-like quality of suffering, and the way that saying Kaddish in a community helps a mourner to regain equilibrium. Here, a member of the Kaddish Minyan, a lay person, helped the rabbi. The wisdom of Jewish people floating up from the pews to the *bimah*, to the rabbi, was just as meaningful and powerful as it often is in the opposite direction.

As the editor of *The Kaddish Minyan: From Pain to Healing, Twenty Personal Stories*,[17] I, like Ari Goldman, heard many Kaddish stories and I included many of them in my book. In turn, the publication of the book in two editions generated other Kaddish stories, some of which were sent to me. Some congregations instituted their own Kaddish Minyan Projects. Ohr Kodesh Congregation in Chevy Chase, Maryland, is one example. On the first page of their July 2004 congregational bulletin, the headline story is titled "The Kaddish Minyan Project" and it begins with these words:

> Some of you may have read the book *The Kaddish Minyan* by Herbert Yoskowitz, which is available in the Ohr Kodesh Library. The book includes a number of essays by former *aveilim* (mourners) who participated in the daily *minyan* at a synagogue in suburban Detroit. The Religious Activities and Funeral Practices Committee would like to undertake a similar project for Ohr Kodesh…[and so] we are soliciting essays of two pages or less from our membership describing the role of the Ohr Kodesh daily *minyan* and Kaddish in your bereavement.

What was submitted remained the property of the synagogue and was not shared with me. But I was glad to learn that this and other such projects have been undertaken in other communities. Attending the Kaddish Minyan helped me when I was a mourner, as well as many other mourners—including those whose stories appeared in *The Kaddish Minyan*.

In a lengthy article for the Orangetown Jewish Center Congregation bulletin, Judy Umlas, a resident of Rockland County, New York, wrote that she read *The Kaddish Minyan* and "found stories about people like me, quite a few of whom had not been observant but were still drawn to the tradition. I felt greatly fortified by this slim tome and carried it around with me for strength for several weeks." She related that when she was scheduled to give a talk less than a month after her father's death "to an audience of 1,000 people in San Diego on the topic of the book I had written, *The Power of Acknowledgement*," she cried the day of her presentation and wanted to return home to her family and to her community. Should she cancel her talk, which had the potential to advance her career? She could not find a Kaddish Minyan in which she would be comfortable, but she wanted to say her daily Kaddish in a community. Perhaps, she thought, a community could be created "for the Kaddish with the 1,000 participants if they agreed." In the morning presentation, she explained to a room filled with 1,000 people "that I had chosen to take on the honor and the obligation of saying a prayer of mourning for my father every day in a community of at least ten people, normally in a synagogue...[and] it would be a very powerful way to honor my father if I said the Hebrew prayer with them. I asked if that would be okay with them and they all seemed to shout an enthusiastic 'Yes!' I then asked if I should do it then or at the end of my presentation and the overwhelming response was 'Now!'" Many voices joined with her in reciting Kaddish—"and at least fifty to one hundred people knew the words." Later that day, Judy laughed when she saw a sign on the company bulletin board put up by one of the attendees: "Jews needed tomorrow morning. Participate in a Kaddish Minyan for Judy's father and meet at the piano." Judy reports: "We had easily twice a *minyan* on that day."[18]

People like Howie Labow of Chicago, Illinois, who travels extensively for business needs, kept diaries of their eleven months of saying Kaddish. In the introduction to his diary, Howie wrote: "Through these past eleven months, through the disbelief and the anger and the numbness, I said Kaddish with one goal in mind: Say a beautiful prayer in the name of a beautiful woman...my mother, Jackie Labow."[19]

During the eleven months of saying Kaddish for a parent, nothing can fill the hole that our loved one's death has left in our world. For some people, keeping a journal or writing an article about experiences during the eleven months of Kaddish can help to lessen the pain of grief. For me, the Kaddish provided sacred time to be a mourner. Each time I stood to say the Kaddish during my year of mourning, I thought of different moments that I had shared with my parents and with my brother—all of whom died in separate locations within a single twenty-eight-hour period, and for whom I sat *shiva* all at the same time. Whether I was reciting Kaddish in a synagogue chapel or in my own sanctuary or in an office somewhere, I felt embraced by community. There is strength in community, I learned firsthand (after talking about it from the *bimah* for years), and there is the possibility of sanctity there too. During the *shiva* week I observed for my parents and for my brother, my daughter took a call for me from our weekly Jewish newspaper, *The Detroit Jewish News*. Please ask your father the reporter said, if he would write an article relating to the title of his book and explain how is he personally moving from pain to healing?

After *shiva*, while still feeling as though I was living a bad dream and still numb with pain, I did write that article, focusing on how comforted I was by our Jewish tradition. I wrote, in part:

> I found that pondering a text I had known for years, the debate in the Talmud between Rabbi Akiva and the sages about the reasonability of reciting a blessing that acknowledges God as our "just Judge" after hearing of someone's death, was not alienating (as I think I would have expected) but comforting, as I learned to know my own grieving soul. And, in general, I found that returning to Torah study after *shiva* was a welcome distraction from my grief. Saying Kaddish in what I came now to call a "Kaddish Minyan" provided

me with a framework that helped me to adjust to a world now absent of three essential people in my life. I was helped by my family, who surrounded me with love, and both by my Adat Shalom congregation and the larger community, all of whom together played some role in fulfilling the commandment that requires us both to honor the dead and to comfort the mourners in our midst in an exemplary way.[21]

Finally, I frequently reread my own book to return to the stories of people who inspired me by sharing the stories of their road from pain to healing during their year of saying Kaddish for a loved one. Those stories inspired me when I first heard them, helped me during my year of mourning, and continue even now to teach me about the importance of faith in God and the gift of being part of a caring community. I want to share some of the stories in *The Kaddish Minyan* so that we can absorb the gifts given to us by people who contributed their stories.

The Kaddish Minyan shares powerful personal reminiscences that are plainly spoken, even as they provide intellectual or psychological insight. Most moving are the reflections by four of the contributors who have lost children, but common to all of the pieces are reports of personal healing attributed to the saying of Kaddish in the company of others, and to the bond created among those who say Kaddish together.

George Cantor wrote that saying Kaddish for his daughter Courtney for eleven months, rather than the one month formally required when a parent loses a child, "was an unshakable personal obligation to [his] daughter's memory." And he adds: "What I never foresaw was that it would also restore my wife and me to life."[22]

Bill Graham wrote that his daughter Alex had died ten months before he wrote his reminiscence. For him, saying Kaddish was "a means of honoring our daughter and gaining comfort but, most of all, reaffirming my faith in God. It is my faith that has given me the strength these past two years. If it were not for my faith in God, I would never have been able to handle this tragedy. I have to admit that I'm beginning to have a panic attack. Kaddish will end in a month; I want it to last longer. However, eleven months is enough to say Kaddish. I have a lifetime to cherish the memories and will always have a special place in my heart for Alex."[23] And Bill's wife, Susie Graham, wrote: "Saying Kaddish is really about being with the community. It's...being with people basically in the same boat—with different losses—All going through the same kinds of things you are."[24]

Two contributors wrote of being with a parent when that parent was saying Kaddish for his or her own parent. David Schostak, for example, remembers how, as a twelve-year-old, he accompanied his father to morning services before being driven to school, during the period when his father was saying Kaddish for his own father. David remembers the "links that were forged with other members at the daily *minyan* who were also saying Kaddish," and he writes that all these many years later he still reflects fondly on the time they all spent together. Then, twenty-six years later David and his wife lost a child, and a very different experience of saying Kaddish ensued. During the first thirty days of mourning, called *sh'loshim* in Jewish tradition, he and his wife went to Israel to attend a previously planned bat mitzvah of a niece. He went from one synagogue to another during his travels in Israel, making a point of not noticing if the setting he was entering was Conservative or Orthodox, Ashkenazic or Sephardic. Regardless, he writes that he felt "immediate overwhelming warmth from all of the congregants," warmth that he understood to derive from the fact that "they knew that I, too, was there to say Kaddish."[25] The same bond that he had built with people who had become close friends when he accompanied his father to say Kaddish "immediately existed when we said Kaddish together...I am convinced that it is God's infinite wisdom that mourners spend time together. It not only helps their mourning and their healing, but builds lifelong relationships which enable everyone in mourning to gain something positive from their loss."[26]

Though Karen Hermelin felt passionate about her Jewish identity, she stated: "I hated *shul*. Every second of it. So I only went when I had to. Perhaps that's why though I've lived in Los Angeles for eleven years and am very involved with the Jewish community, I had never joined a *shul*."[27] Karen remembered that when she was eight years old, she went with her dad as he said Kaddish for his mother. Now, she went to *shul* twice each day to say Kaddish for her father. Her four siblings and Karen had witnessed their father say Kaddish three times in his life; now, they would do the same for him. Her young daughter accompanied Karen to services and loves being at services. It gives Karen "unbelievable joy that somehow my dad passed this love to my daughter."[28]

The world that God created is not perfect, and at times we experience profound sorrow and grief. Prayers like the Kaddish help us as we praise God and pray to see a world of peace, to accept the world's flaws, and to manage its disappointments. The Kaddish helps us to look forward to the day when we will repair the world in God's sovereignty, *l'takkein olam b'malkhut shaddai*.[29]

Anthropomorphically and without sidestepping their own absolute monotheism, the rabbis imagined God praying. They picture a compassionate, merciful God who prays, "May it be My will that My mercy conquer My anger, and that My mercy overcome My sterner attributes, and that I behave toward My children with the attribute of mercy, and that for their sake I go beyond the boundary of judgment."[30] When the Kaddish is said in a Kaddish Minyan, we praise God and we join with God in praying for a better world. Doing that gives us a greater sense of purpose and of serenity.

Just as I said Kaddish for my father, and he said Kaddish for his, I feel confident that future generations will continue to recite Kaddish in a *minyan*, drawing on the strongest spiritual tool there is to sustain them during their period of mourning. It will continue to connect the mourner both to the deceased and to the community that will support the mourner during the period of greatest grief.

NOTES

[1] Joseph B. Soloveitchik "Sitting Shiva Is Doing Teshuvah," in *Man of Faith in the Modern World*, vol. 2 (Hoboken, NJ: KTAV, 1989), p. 128.

[2] B. Berakhot 17b, to which may be compared the version that appears in the Mishnah itself at M. Berakhot 3:1. Cf. also the comments of Tosafot to B. Berakhot 17b, s.v. *patur mi-k'ri·at sh'ma*, and their comments at B. Berakhot 14b, s.v. *u-mi-kol mitzvot ha-amurot ba-torah*. In rabbinic texts, the expression "the prayer" (*ha-t'fillah*) invariably denotes the prayer known to moderns as the Amidah.

[3] Joseph Soleveitchik, "A Eulogy for the Talner Rebbe," cited in *Shi·urei Ha-rav*, ed. Joseph Epstein (Hoboken, NJ: KTAV, 1974), p. 67.

[4] Abraham Joshua Heschel, "Death as Homecoming," in *Jewish Reflections on Death*, ed. Jack Riemer (New York: Schocken, 1979), p. 72.

[5] Leon Wieseltier, *Kaddish* (New York: Knopf, 1998), pp. 25–26.

[6] Sylvia Cohodas, private correspondence received from her nephew, Rabbi Samuel Stahl, on March 22, 2015.

[7] Michael S. Roth, "A Place in the Classroom for Faith," *The Wall Street Journal* (February 21–22, 2015), p. C3.

[8] Tom Tugend, "A Rabbi of Rabbis," in *The Jewish Chronicle* (December 24, 2014); not paginated.

[9] Harold Schulweis, *Finding Each Other in Judaism: Death, Dying, and Immortality* (New York: UAHC Press, 2001), p. 104.

[10] Ibid., p.101.

[11] Ibid., pp. 2–3.

[12] Ibid., p. 102.

[13] Mitch Albom. *Have a Little Faith: A True Story* (New York: Hyperion, 2011), p. 182.

[14] Ari L. Goldman. *Living a Year of Kaddish. A Memoir* (New York: Schocken, 2003), p. 205.

[15] Ibid., p. 84.

[16] Ibid.

[17] *The Kaddish Minyan: From Pain to Healing. Twenty Personal Stories*, ed. Herbert A. Yoskowitz (Austin, TX: Eakin Press, 2003).

[18] Judith W. Umlas, "Honor Thy Father and Thy Mother," in *Orangetown Jewish Center Congregation Bulletin*, 2009.

[19] Howie Labow, "The Last Day of Kaddish For My Mother," online at https://travelingandkaddish.wordpress.com.

[20] B. Berakhot 46b.

[21] Herbert A. Yoskowitz, "28 Hours," in *The Detroit Jewish News* (May 25, 2006), p. 31.

[22] *The Kaddish Minyan*, p. 19.

[23] Ibid., pp. 30–32.

[24] Ibid., pp. 33–34.
[25] Ibid., pp. 49–50.
[26] Ibid.
[27] Ibid., p. 35.
[28] Ibid., p 37.
[29] The Hebrew words, familiar to every regular worshipper in synagogue, are from the Aleinu hymn that closes almost every worship service of the year.
[30] B. Berakhot 7a.

The Kaddish: How We Name the Blessed Holy One

Steven Kepnes

After the Shema, the Kaddish is perhaps the most famous of all Jewish prayers. The essential part of the prayer, *y'hei sh'meih rabba m'varakh l'alam u-l'almei almaya* ("May His great name be blessed forever"), goes back to the Book of Daniel (2:20). And some version of the Kaddish was used at the close of sermons beginning in the Second Temple period. The use of the prayer by mourners was a later, medieval, development. Yet, it was a development that clearly filled—and continues to fill—an important psychological need in the community. One could easily argue that the Amidah is a more important prayer liturgically. But since the Kaddish is said by mourners to remember the dead, it may be better known by the average Jew. The Kaddish is also said by the prayer leader at the end of every section and significant subsection of the liturgy, and its constant repetition ensures that it is well known. It is remarkable that the same prayer is used to both mark transitions in liturgy and to mark the most significant human transition, from life to death. Regular participants in Jewish prayer know the different meanings of the Kaddish not through a change in its words but merely by its placement in the liturgy and by the different melodies and tones that are used to say the words. Thus, when the Kaddish is said by mourners its tone is solemn and it is recited in a monotone. When the Kaddish is said to mark the end of the liturgy, it is often sung quickly and with a celebratory melody.

The prayer itself is unusual in the liturgy because unlike the language of most of the service, which is said in Hebrew, the Kaddish is uttered mostly in Aramaic. It therefore strikes a dissonant chord to the ear and that very dissonance calls for reflection, questioning, and interpretation. The obvious questions that the recitation of the Kaddish poses are several. Why should the central liturgy of the synagogue require that mourners mark the passing of loved ones by uttering the same prayer that the prayer leader uses to mark that service's major liturgical transitions? Why would Jewish law require that this prayer be said only if a quorum of ten Jews, a *minyan*, is present? Why does a prayer so closely associated with mourning not mention the dead at all? And, finally: What *is* this prayer supposed to mean?

Let us first look at the prayer itself. Although there are a variety of longer versions, we will present here its shortest form, called the Ḥatzi Kaddish (literally, "Half Kaddish"), for the sake of brevity:

Leader:
Magnified and sanctified
may His great name be,
in the world He created by His will.
May He establish His kingdom
in your lifetime and in your days
and in the lifetime of all the house of Israel,
swiftly and soon—
and say: Amen.

Congregation, then Leader:
May His great name be blessed for ever and all time.

Leader:
Blessed and praised, glorified and exalted,
praised and honored, uplifted and lauded
be the name of the Holy One,
blessed be He,

beyond any blessing,
song, praise, and consolation
uttered in the world—
and say: Amen.

The Name

Among all the names that Jewish liturgy uses to refer to God—
Sovereign, Holy One, Father, etc.—the Kaddish refers to God with
the term *sheim* or "name" itself. The naming of God in the Bible
is central to Moses' meeting of God at the burning bush (Exodus
3:13ff.), where he asks God to tell him the divine name.[1] God gives
the name as the Tetragrammaton, the four-letter name *yod-hei-vav-
hei* (YHVH; Exodus 3:15). This four-letter name is then treated
with special respect: the Decalogue prohibits Israel from misusing
it (Exodus 20:7) and the rabbis in the Talmud prohibited its direct
pronunciation.[2] Since the ancient pronunciation of the name is no
longer known, it has become traditional in Jewish liturgical usage
to pronounce YHVH as *Adonai* (literally, "my Lord")—even though
biblical scholars conjecture that the ancient pronunciation was
probably closer to "Yahweh."[3] In any case, YHVH seems to be the
special name that Israel is given by which to refer to God; the word
El or *Elohim* is a general term used in the Bible to refer to all deities.
In rabbinic Judaism the Tetragrammaton is seen as a conduit to
God at times of need and prayer, since it is taken to refer to God's
attribute of mercy.[4]

However, even as the name YHVH is the special name given to
Israel by which to refer to the deity, in its grammar and semantics
this name seems to declare the limits of the very act of naming God.
As an odd third-person future form of the verb "to be," *yod-hei-vav-
hei* might mean something like: "He will be."[5] In his discussion of
the Tetragrammaton, the German Jewish theologian Martin Buber

suggests that the word designates God, but without limiting God to something certain or nameable: "He will always be present, but at any given moment only as the one whom He is then."[6] The word *ha-sheim*, meaning "the name," only points to a reality that cannot be expressed or referenced.[7]

It may thus be the case that the Tetragrammaton has limited utility in naming or characterizing the essence of God; nevertheless, the theology embedded in the words of the Kaddish seems to suggest that this name is uniquely powerful—since the name itself (and not God) is to be "blessed and praised, glorified and exalted, raised and honored, uplifted and lauded...beyond any blessing, song, praise, and consolation uttered in the world." Here, the list of synonyms for praising is so long, and the semantic differences between the terms so slight, that we are also confronted with the limitations of language. The Kaddish seems to be saying that the very act of praising the name is *also* beyond language, and so the name of God seems to stand in the place of the unnameable God. The name thus serves to conceal God—like a cover over a sacred object, a cloud over the sun, or a garment over a body. In this vein we can see how the name of God takes on certain mystic powers, particularly in the Jewish mystical tradition, and most prominently in the Kabbalah, as the most famous iteration of that tradition is known. The name, then, is a kind of outer garment, a protective covering over God as the One who is unknowable, without end, no-thing (*Ein Sof*). We praise and glorify the name of God because doing so brings us close to the blessed Holy One without exposing God's awesome, omnipotent holy light to our mortal being. If praising the name of God brings us closer to God's *Ein Sof*, then the Kaddish effectively brings a glimpse of the mystical into every liturgical service.

The entire morning liturgy seems to use the strategy of multiplying synonyms for naming and blessing God. For an illustration of this literary device, I would direct the reader to the blessing after the Bar'khu and before the formal recitation of the Shema, but there are many other examples as well. The multiplication of epithets for God and for praise of God not only seems to confuse the process of giving designations for God, but also to whip this process into a kind of linguistic frenzy. And through this linguistic frenzy, perhaps, the Kaddish wants to move us beyond the attempt to communicate information, and toward a process of building emotional and spiritual energy.

The Hitpa·eil Form

One of the distinctive linguistic aspects of the Kaddish is its use of the future *hitpae·il* form, a grammatical paradigm that most often imbues verbs with a reflexive sense in Hebrew. (The corresponding form in Aramaic, however, often carries a sense of the passive.) This grammatical construction is used to great literary effect in the Kaddish. First, the assonance of the repeated verbal forms— *yitgaddal, yitkaddash, yitbarakh, yishtabbah,* etc.—gives the prayer its characteristic sound, meter, and rhythm. Also, the reflexive form brings us into a strange verbal and temporal dimension. It is not clear if we are being commanded in the imperative to praise God's name, or if worshippers are praising the name now, or if the name will be praised in the future at the time of the establishment of God's sovereignty on earth. Is it humans that praise God, or (given the reflexive construction of the verbs being used) is the Kaddish saying that the name will praise itself—or perhaps even that God will praise the divine name? Is the Kaddish about some future period of divine sovereignty that will come, or is it speaking about our ability to experience such a thing right now, in the liturgical moment?

The Temporality of the Kingdom

The Kaddish provides a theology of creation by declaring that God created the world "according to His will." But it also seems to assume that, despite this creation, the divine kingdom is not yet here. It thus implores God to establish the divine "kingdom" in the very lifetime of those who say the Kaddish, "speedily and soon." That the Kaddish moves from the third person into the second person—"in your lifetime and in your days"—suggests that those in the synagogue at the very moment of uttering the Kaddish are being addressed. So the Kaddish is meant to address the suffering of individual Jews and of the community Israel, and it seeks to bring healing and repair speedily and soon—that is, right now! The reference to suffering in the here-and-now, combined with the pointing to the future time of redemption in the kingdom to come, may provide a hint as to why the Kaddish is said by mourners: although the loved one is now dead and the mourner is suffering a loss, at the time of the future redemption—which will hopefully come speedily and soon—the mourner will again join his or her loved one, and endless praising and blessing of God will ensue. This is hinted at in the following line in the Kaddish, which is the high point of the prayer, where all the assembled join the leader of the prayer and cry out in unison: "Let His great name be blessed for ever and ever and to all eternity." Here, the collective does now what it will do in the eternal time of the coming of the kingdom—bless God!

One could say that our central task as Jews is to praise God. But only the living can do this; as the psalmist says, "The dead cannot praise God" (Psalm 115:18). Death is the great silence.[8] Death is the interruption of praise, the hiatus in the naming of God that can only be resumed by the dead in the time of the kingdom yet to come. Thus, for the community of the living to say that "we will bless God forever and ever for all eternity" is to forge a link between the abyss of death, on the one hand, and eternal life, on the other. Here, then, the praising of God in the Kaddish functions to mediate between this-worldly life and eternal life. The praising and hallowing of God in the Kaddish then becomes a sign of the eternality of the Jewish people.

The Kaddish and Death

The fact that mourners rise at the end of every service to praise God suggests that mourners, and even death, are meant to be a part of all Jewish liturgy. That the liturgy requires the presence of a quorum of ten in order to recite the Kaddish suggests that a mourner should not be left alone, but needs the support of the community. However, a remarkable aspect of the Kaddish is that the mourner is not a passive recipient of the community's love and support; instead, the mourner is thrust into role of leading the Kaddish prayer. Thus it is the mourner who will address the community and say, "May He establish His kingdom during your life and during your days." By making the mourner the leader, the liturgy expresses confidence in the spiritual resources of the mourner who now, even at this trying time—which may bring some to doubt—is still able to praise God. This act of spiritual triumph allows us to understand why the Kaddish, which makes no mention of the dead, is so appropriate as the mourner's prayer. The Kaddish is said by mourners because, in the face of death, it is a statement of faith in God. In the face of the challenge of mortality, the Kaddish is an assertion of the eternity of God and the eternity of the Jewish people. In the face of the challenge that death brings to God's creation and to the hope of living in God's kingdom, the Kaddish asserts a faith in the goodness of creation and in the ultimate coming of the messianic kingdom.

By giving the mourner the responsibility of saying the Kaddish, the liturgy appears to be intentionally blurring the issue of whether the community, through the *minyan*, is present to serve the needs of the mourner or if the mourner is present to serve the community.

The fact that mourners are required to come to the synagogue to remember their parents, children, or any close relative highlights the sense of family and peoplehood that is an integral part of Judaism. In some synagogues the rabbi reads the names of loved ones whose memories are being recalled, and these names are often inscribed on a special plaque in the sanctuary. Throughout the course of the liturgy, in prayers like the Amidah, our ancestors—Abraham, Isaac, and Jacob (and, in some synagogues, Sarah, Rebecca, Rachel, and Leah as well)—are recalled. One could therefore say that in recognizing the names of loved ones who have died and in giving mourners a central place in the liturgy of the synagogue, the dead find a place in the chain of generations that goes back to Abraham and Sarah.

As we have already noted, the Kaddish is used to mark central transitions in all Jewish prayer services. Given that the whole life of the Jew is to be lived under the canopy of Jewish law and *mitzvot* (commandments), it is not stretching the metaphor too far to suggest that all of life for the Jew is a series of liturgical acts. If this is true, then the Kaddish is an extremely appropriate prayer to be said to mark the passing of a life from here to the next world. Yet, because the dead cannot praise God, a relative says this prayer for the deceased. This act, then, must be seen as part of the series of *mitzvot* called *ḥesed shel emet* (that is, "acts of [unrequited] lovingkindness") that we perform for the dead without expectation of reward or recognition.

Conclusion

The Kaddish is one of the wonders of Jewish liturgy that makes a series of important theological statements. It explores the nature of naming and exalts the name of God, by simultaneously using language to designate God even while the ability of language to fulfill this task is questioned. The Kaddish manages beautifully to refer to God even while protecting God's essence from being seen or even imagined. In this sense there is a bit of what Maimonides called "negative theology"—that is, referring to God by referencing what God is not (such as: God is not nameable), rather than a positive designation (such as: God is omnipotent). Since the way in which the name of God is exalted and praised and blessed has within it a touch of mysticism, the Kaddish thus brings to the liturgy a mystical element. And since the Kaddish is said both at moments of liturgical transition (from one part of the service to the next) and by mourners at the end of the service, the Kaddish makes a powerful connection between liturgy and life—suggesting that just as liturgy continues from day to day and from generation to generation, so too will our loved ones find a kind of continuity in their transition to death. Death then is not to be understood as an end, but rather as a passage to another form of life. Finally, in saying the Kaddish, mourners receive multiple resources to cope with their loss. Firstly, the community is there with them. Secondly, the mourners are called on to lead, and the community thereby reaffirms its confidence in the spiritual and physical strength of the mourners at the time of loss. Finally, the Kaddish paves a way for the mourners to connect with God, the ultimate source of all strength, renewal, and eternal life.

NOTES

[1] That words have power in the Torah is seen right in the beginning, when God creates with the words "Let there be light" (Genesis 1:3). The power of words for humans is seen in human oaths, prayers, and blessings. There is also a connection between words and names, as many of the leading figures in the Torah have names that tell us something about the essence of the figure. Thus for example Abram means "father of many," Sarai means "princess," Israel means "he who struggles with God," and Moses (or rather, Moshe) means "drawn from water." Given this phenomenon of names signifying an essential characteristic of the person, the desire to know God's name may signify Moses' (and the general human) desire to know the essence of God. When God replies in Exodus 3:14 *ehyeh asher ehyeh*, "I am that I am" or "I will be present as I will be present," perhaps the sense is: "You cannot know My essence; I will be what I will be."
[2] Cf. B. Sotah 38a.
[3] G.H. Parke-Taylor, *Yahweh: The Divine Name in the Bible* (Waterloo, Ont.: Wilfrid Laurier University Press, 1975), p. 79.
[4] See, for example, the statement in Shemot Rabbah (to Exodus 3:6): "When I am merciful toward My world I am called YHVH/Adonai—for 'Adonai' refers to the attribute of mercy."
[5] The regular third-person future form of the verb "to be" would be spelled *yod-hei-yod-hei*. The claim that *yod-hei-vav-hei* may be a variant of that form is conjectural, as such a form is unattested in the Bible (although there are other words where *yod* and *vav* do interchange).
[6] Martin Buber, "The Burning Bush," in *On the Bible*, ed. Nahum Glazer (New York: Schocken, 1982), p. 59.
[7] It is also worth noting that *ha-sheim* is used as a pious circumlocution for "Adonai" by religious Jews, when reading or saying the name YHVH in non-liturgical settings.
[8] In the Bible, Sheol, the land of the dead, is also called *dumah* (literally "silence"), cf., e.g., Psalm 115:17.

The Kaddish, the Allegory of the Cave, and the Golden Calf: Meditations on Education and the Encounter with God

Geoffrey Claussen

May [God's] great name be magnified and sanctified...
May [God's] great name be blessed forever and for all eternity.
May the name of the Holy One be blessed and praised and
glorified and exalted and extolled and honored and lifted up and
lauded—beyond all of the blessings and hymns and praises and
consolations that are spoken in the world.

–The Kaddish

I think of the process of learning as always having the potential to be a process of encountering God, and I see this potential highlighted by the Jewish practice of reciting the doxology known as "the Kaddish" to conclude an experience of study.[1] While the Kaddish is popularly associated with prayer services and with mourning, it has a long history of being used to conclude an experience of study. The core words of the Kaddish, "May [God's] great name be blessed forever and for all eternity," and the subsequent words of the Kaddish that speak of the transcendence of "the name of the Holy One," can play an especially important role in connecting experiences of learning to the moral ideal that God's name represents.

One of the oldest sources to invoke these words of the Kaddish is a passage in the Babylonian Talmud[2] that reflects on the darkness of the centuries following the destruction of the Temple in Jerusalem. The fourth-century sage Rava is said to have claimed that, even amidst the chaos of destruction, "the world is sustained…by the [words of] sanctification (*k'dushah*) after study and by [the words] 'May [God's] great name…' after the study of *aggadah*"—the study of sacred narratives or other non-legal discourse. Rava's prooftext is Job 10:22, in which Job envisions "a land whose light is like darkness, the deepest gloom and disorder." Rava goes on to affirm that proper study—described with the word "order" (*sidra* in Aramaic, *seder* in Hebrew)—can provide light and reverse such disorder and darkness. But it appears from this passage that it is not just study itself, but rather the doxologies of sanctification (Kedushah or Kaddish) and the key words invoking God's "great name" following study that provided Rava with an experience of light that seemed to sustain the world. The expression of hope for God's great name to be blessed for eternity appears to have connected the experience of learning with the light provided by the "great name" of the Eternal.

God's Name and the Idea of the Good

What is God's "great name"? A long-standing Jewish tradition suggests that God's name cannot be fully articulated, but that human beings can use names that point toward the transcendent. Among the names invoked by traditional Jewish liturgy, I will focus on one that is of particular significance for reflections on learning: "the Good" (*ha-tov*). This name is given particular prominence in the Amidah, the silent prayer traditionally recited three times daily, which includes the declaration that "your name is the Good" (*ha-tov shimkha*). "It is fitting to give praise," the liturgy goes on to say, to God as known by this name.

Some Jews view the declaration that God's name is "the Good" as a declaration that God is a person, being, or force characterized by goodness. I do not, as I do not think that any person, being, or force deserves the ultimate devotion that Jewish law and liturgy see as appropriate to give to God. The particular Jewish philosophical tradition within which I locate myself suggests that God is not a person or being or force at all. Rather, God should be identified with "the Idea of the Good"—an infinite goodness that goes beyond the limited goodness that human beings can describe but that constitutes a moral ideal toward which all human beings should strive. "We can conceive of [God] only as we conceive of the Idea of the Good," as Hermann Cohen put it. "This is the simple, profound, true meaning of God's transcendence. God is in truth 'beyond me,' for [God] is the Holy One, the archetype of all human morality."[3]

God's goodness is "holy," separate from and transcending all human goodness but representing a moral ideal or archetype toward which human beings must continually aspire. What the Kaddish calls "the name of the Holy One" is "the Good," "the Idea of the Good" or, as Cohen puts it at one point, "the infinitely Good."[4] These are names that I think are appropriate to identify with "the great name of God" invoked by the Kaddish, for they are names that help us to understand that ultimate praise should be offered not to any "being" (whether tending toward omnipotence or impotence) or any "force" (whether a consciousness found in the world or a power found in our own inclinations), but only to an ideal of perfection that invites our continual reflection and moral growth.

We humans tend too often, I think, to worship gods that are easy to relate to because they are made in the image of our own ideals and identities. I honor the value of such worship and of God-language that is calibrated to human needs, desires, and cultures, as all language must be—for in using God-language, we must "speak in the language of human beings," to use the rabbinic phrase favored by Maimonides.[5] But the Jewish tradition of worshipping God by the name of "the Good"—as the "Idea of the Good," as an ideal of absolute goodness—

offers a helpful challenge to these honorable tendencies. The continual reminders within Jewish tradition to "turn toward God" have greater moral power when that to which we are turning is not an entity that reflects our needs but an ideal that exceeds our needs. When studying traditions that stem from particular human perspectives, it is good to lift up our eyes toward an ideal that transcends those perspectives. It is fitting to remind ourselves of a moral archetype of ultimate goodness that continually challenges us to look beyond ourselves, our cultures, and the natural world and instead toward greater moral goodness. It is "fitting to give praise" to such an ideal, keeping it in our minds and hearts, turning toward its infinite light with love, reverence, and a longing for moral improvement.

Practices of study can, I think, point us toward this ideal. In considering God as "the Good," Hermann Cohen pointed to Maimonides' emphasis on study—not just of *halakhah* but also of *aggadah*, and not just of "Torah" in a narrow sense but also of "wisdom" in a broad sense.[6] Maimonides built on aggadic traditions, Cohen contends, in developing his vision of the Torah as directing Jews to seek the greatest moral wisdom, which culminates in seeing the archetypal "lovingkindness, justice, and righteousness" toward which human beings must aspire.[7] Moral wisdom that seeks such ideals is the ultimate goal of the Torah, and the Torah's truth claims must be justified by critical philosophical inquiry, as "it is wisdom which must verify the teachings of the Torah through true speculation."[8] Cohen also pointed to Maimonides' claim that turning toward a true vision of the Good requires scientific inquiry into the nature of the world, for a commitment to truth will also yield longing and praise for God's great name: "When a person contemplates [God's] works…he will immediately love and *praise and glorify and long with a great longing to know [God's] great name*.…When he thinks of these things themselves, he will immediately recoil with fear and be conscious that he is a small, lowly, obscure creature, with extremely little understanding, standing before Perfect Understanding."[9] Here, scientific learning reminds one of the extreme limits of one's vision; but it also leads to praise of God's great name and a longing to know that name—a desire for further understanding of God's perfection, what Maimonides calls "great longing to know [God's] great name."

This same longing can be found in the words of the Kaddish, the meditation that connects study to the hope that God's "great name be blessed forever and for all eternity." Crucially, the words of the Kaddish go on to emphasize that God's name transcends the limited descriptions that human beings can offer. Blessing God's name "forever and for all eternity" requires awareness that human language is inadequate for speaking of infinite goodness. Thus the Kaddish continues with a prayer: "May the name of the Holy One be blessed and praised and glorified and exalted and extolled and honored and lifted up and lauded—beyond all of the blessings and hymns and praises and consolations that are spoken in the world." The ultimate moral goodness of "God's name" that Cohen described as "beyond me" is, indeed, beyond all that human beings can articulate. It is like a shining light toward which we are called—but our own vision will always be limited and can never describe the fullness of that light. As much as we strive to make God's name known in the world, as much as we can strive to increase goodness in the world through our learning and through our deeds, there is always more goodness that is beyond our reach.

Study and the Philosophic Quest

Most human beings, Maimonides claims in his *Guide of the Perplexed*, "grope about in [the] night...'they know not, neither do they understand; they go about in darkness' (Psalm 82:5). The truth, in spite of the strength of its manifestation, is entirely hidden from them, as is said of them: 'And now men see not the light which is bright in the skies' (Job 38:21)."[10] Rare individuals may see glimpses of light as from a luminous stone, or even as from a lightning flash: "sometimes truth flashes out so that we think that it is day" before "we find ourselves again in an obscure night." For prophets, however, "lightning flashes time and time again," and the greatest of prophets, Moses, apparently could see sufficient light that "night appears to him as day." But even Moses was not able to fully apprehend God's perfect goodness.[11] As Maimonides describes it elsewhere, prophets are inevitably separated from God by "veils"—their moral vices—and even Moses is separated from God, despite his virtue.[12] No human being is able to see God directly: "You cannot see My face," God tells Moses after the sin of the golden calf, "for none may see Me and live" (Exodus 33:20). Israel has engaged in worship of a golden calf, perhaps attempting to worship God through bowing down to the form of the calf; God's response might serve to remind Moses and the people of Israel that God transcends any form.[13] Nonetheless, God affirms that Moses can perceive some glimpse of God's transcendent goodness, which is identified with God's great name. "I will pass My goodness before you, and I will proclaim before you the name of the Eternal" (Exodus 33:19),[14] God tells Moses. Moses does perceive the great name and the qualities of God's transcendent goodness; in Maimonides' explanation, what he sees are moral ideals of "lovingkindness, justice, and righteousness" that exceed human reach but that provide an archetype toward which humans should aspire.[15]

Maimonides' vision of how human beings may encounter God draws on Plato's allegorical description of "our nature in its education and want of education,"[16] an allegory regarding the Idea of the Good that is also central for later Jewish thinkers like Cohen. The allegory describes human beings as bound within a cave, with a fire behind them, and puppeteers using the light of the fire to project images onto the blank wall in front of the prisoners. Unaware of the puppeteers, the prisoners understand the shadows on the wall in front of them to be undeniably real and true. True reality lies outside of the cave, where the sun—the Idea of the Good—may be found. But nearly all human beings are trapped within our cultures, unaware even of how our own fundamental beliefs, values, and myths are constructed by those "puppeteers" who have the power to teach us, and whose teachings may simply reflect their own selfish desires for power.[17]

The philosopher Socrates, the character who offers this allegory in Plato's *Republic*, imagines that there are rare individuals skilled in the art of "turning around," who can go through the painful process of detaching themselves from their cultures, climbing out of the cave; these are people whom Socrates calls philosophers.[18] Philosophers may gain some glimpse of the Good beyond the cave. They might, then, be compelled to return to their caves and gain control over the kinds of ideas and myths that are projected onto the wall of the cave. A philosopher could translate his insights from the outside world into narratives that could help to improve ordinary human life.

Plato depicts Socrates as compelled to do this work; Maimonides, in turn, envisions Moses as compelled to do this work. Just as Socrates must exercise great care in bringing his insights to the people of Athens, Moses must exercise great care in bringing his insights to the people of Israel, translating the infinite Good (God) into myths and rituals that his people can understand. The Torah of Moses takes human weaknesses into account, Maimonides argues, helping them to grow toward God while recognizing that "man, according to his nature, is not capable of abandoning suddenly all to which he was accustomed."[19] Bringing the people toward God must happen gradually, making many concessions to the weaknesses of human nature and to the particularities of Israelite culture—the Torah must, in the language that Maimonides favors, "speak in the language of human beings." Thus, for example, Maimonides viewed many commandments regarding worship—such as the use of language in prayer and, all the more so, the establishment of a sacrificial cult at a central shrine (eventually located in Jerusalem)—as concessions that would help the Israelites to avoid idolatry and focus on God.[20] The commandments are not perfect in and of themselves, but they are a means to an end: studying and performing the Torah's imperfect commandments help to bring human beings toward the perfection that God's name represents. Using the language of the Kaddish, we might say that studying the Torah brings people into contact with hymns and consolations that are developed for this world; but the process of study can also direct people toward an ideal of goodness, the holy name that goes beyond all of the blessings, hymns, praises, and consolations that are molded to fit the world.

Plato's *Republic* makes it clear that those who expose how myths and norms are constructed by "puppeteer" mythmakers and legislators will be viewed as grave threats to those who live within the cave, whether as puppeteers or as prisoners. Directing those within a culture to the universal goodness that lies beyond the constructions of a culture's particular political life—trying to release prisoners from their shackles—would result in the murder of a philosopher who (like Socrates) sought to release the prisoners. "If they were somehow able to get their hands on and kill the man who attempts to release and lead up, wouldn't they kill him?"[21] The *Republic* indicates that if philosophers are to have any power within a city, they must not engage in this kind of effort to free prisoners, but must instead accommodate themselves to the city's cultural norms and practical needs. Though any effort to be involved in gaining the power necessary to influence a culture would be unappealing to a true philosopher and would in any case corrupt that philosopher, Socrates continues to raise the possibility that philosophers should bring their insights to the political realm—perhaps making some improvement in the life of the city, perhaps creating a climate that will be friendly to the quest for the Good that philosophers like Socrates seek to undertake. The society shaped by the philosopher will inevitably be far from perfect, though. And even the greatest philosophers will be far from the Good, just as Socrates himself is always aware of his own ignorance, never satisfied with himself but always striving for further knowledge and virtue. Socrates shows how the process of learning always reveals new questions and the longing for greater growth.[22]

Plato's discussion of the relationship between human beings and the Good is paralleled by Maimonides' discussion of the relationship between human beings and God. Just as the philosopher, like Socrates, can ascend out of the cave and strive toward the Good, Moses can ascend Mount Sinai and strive to see God as clearly as possible— even if, in the end, he cannot see God's face. Just as the philosopher might ideally create myths that might bring his community closer to the Good, Moses creates myths that might help his community to gradually turn toward the Good—that is, toward God. And just as a city would seek to reject and even murder a philosopher who tried too overtly to release prisoners from their shackles, the people of Israel repeatedly rebel against the threat that Moses represents.

When he brings the people to Mount Sinai and asks them to devote themselves to God, Moses might seem, at least at first, to be asking Israel to "abandon suddenly all to which they were accustomed." The Torah that he brings from Sinai threatens to disrupt the lives of the people of Israel and asks them to turn away from all that they know. And the people are "stiff-necked" (Exodus 32:9), as God will go on to observe. They will do what they can to resist the call to change. Perhaps the Torah is especially threatening to those who would otherwise want to have power, and who resist the idea that Moses can, like a philosopher, ascend and gain radical insights into the Good that will demand a total restructuring of power among the people of Israel.

Indeed, one midrashic tradition suggests that the people of Israel respond to the threat of the Torah of Moses just as the people of Athens respond to the threat of the philosophy of Socrates: seeking to kill those who challenge the establishment. According to the midrash, Moses' brother Aaron and his nephew Hur, both prophets themselves, are left in Moses' place when the latter is on Mount Sinai, and the people rise up and kill Hur. Hur was guilty of challenging and rebuking the people when they sought to build and worship a golden calf, turning away from God and toward an idol. According to this tradition, "Aaron feared" (Exodus 32:5, as understood by the midrash) that the people would seek to kill him as well, and he seeks to save his life by making a concession to the needs of the people, supporting their efforts to build and worship the golden calf. Aaron saves his own life, and perhaps Moses' life as well, by conceding to the mob and supporting their idolatry.[23]

This tradition makes use of the ambiguities in the Hebrew narrative regarding the golden calf, explains why the character of Hur seems to disappear from the narrative, and, above all, helps to exonerate Aaron, explaining why it might be that such an admirable figure would seem to take the lead in efforts to worship the calf. The midrash might also lead us to see Aaron as in fact doing what we might see Moses as learning to do: making concessions to the people of Israel, supporting the development of imperfect traditions amidst a climate where prophets might be killed for the challenges they pose.[24] Perhaps, in fact, Moses learned to make concessions based on the model of Aaron. According to one reading of Maimonides—found in the writings of Isaac Abravanel—it is precisely the episode of the golden calf and the resulting political climate that causes the Torah of Moses to be filled with the concessions that it contains. While Moses cannot tolerate Aaron's concessions in building a golden calf, he realizes that the people of Israel require more tangible forms of worship, and so he introduces concessions that include not only sacrificial worship but, in fact, nearly all of the rituals of the Torah.[25]

After his vision of God's transcendent moral ideals, and his discovery that God is willing to make concessions despite Israel's sinfulness, Moses returns from his encounter with the Good with a new vision for how to bring flashes of divine light into the reality in which Israel lives. He has encountered the light of the Good such that "the skin of his face sent forth beams" (Exodus 34:29)—as Maimonides explains, such that "night appears to him as day."[26] I imagine that Moses discovered a new vision of how the people might gradually be guided to the encounter with God through a Torah that will speak in the language of human beings. The traditions that the people of Israel will practice and study will, from this point on, be like shadows projected against a cave wall by a prophetic puppeteer. They offer great potential for teaching the people of Israel about a God who transcends all human descriptions; but their potential is magnified if they are studied with the reminder of the Kaddish that God transcends the Torah and reaches "beyond all of the blessings and hymns and praises and consolations that are spoken in the world."

The Potential for Growth After the Golden Calf

The study of Torah has the potential to inspire growth and to remind people of the Good in this way, magnifying God's great name. By way of example, I have suggested how studying the golden calf narrative can help to remind its readers that although the Torah is not in itself perfect, it can point to the transcendence of which the Kaddish speaks. Staying with this example, I would add that studying the narrative of the golden calf can also remind people of the obligation to continually grow and strive toward an overarching moral ideal, guiding them away from the shadows on the wall and toward a greater light.

Rabbi Simḥah Zissel Ziv, one of the leading figures in the nineteenth-century Musar movement—a movement characterized by its relentless focus on seeking continual growth of moral character—saw this as the core message of the golden calf narrative.[27] As Simḥah Zissel notes, God's language (in Exodus 32:9–10) threatening to destroy Israel after their worship of the golden calf does not mention idolatry or the calf, but only that Israel "is a stiff-necked people":

> We should contemplate with understanding that [God] did not mention the fact of this great sin [with the calf], but only mentioned that this was a stiff-necked people. The explanation of the matter is that [Israel] was not able to turn its neck to listen, meaning it was not able to turn from the habit to which it had been habituated. And, God forbid, on account of this it was far from turning [t'shuvah; repentance]… for the character trait of stiffening against changing one's nature was worse than the great sin of the calf; were it not for this character trait, they would not have been fit to be destroyed.[28]

Israel is, here, collectively fixed in their habits, refusing to grow, refusing to turn to God. "They did not continue to grow and learn," as Simḥah Zissel puts it elsewhere, "and the essence of what the blessed Holy One loves is that one continues to grow and learn."[29] Israel showed no willingness to listen to criticism and instead responded to the criticism of Hur with hatred and violence: as Simḥah Zissel notes, "being stiff-necked is not continuing to learn, and therefore hating in the depths of one's heart the one who criticizes him."[30]

But many among the people of Israel who responded to Hur's criticism with hatred come to heed Moses' criticism, and they discover what Simḥah Zissel describes as "love of reproof."[31] They escape destruction, as they find that accepting and loving the criticism offered by a prophet can help them to move forward in their process of personal growth. Above all, Simḥah Zissel suggests, prophets can help the people of Israel understand how and why God needs them to grow in key virtues such as lovingkindness, compassion, and justice.[32] The best of prophets, like Moses, can accommodate the needs of the people and gradually help them to turn their heads and listen to the voices that challenge them to grow. To use the language of Plato, the best of philosophers, like Socrates, can gradually help the people of the city to turn toward the Good.

Indeed, Simḥah Zissel himself was struck by the way in which the figure of Socrates seemed to resemble an ideal Jewish sage who does not claim firm knowledge but always seeks to learn and progress toward greater goodness:

> It is an amazing thing that the philosopher Socrates said: "There are people who need to [claim to] know everything that is asked of them, for without this one is not a wise man. But I do not say this; [rather] all of my wisdom is that I know that I do not know." These are the words of the sage, Socrates. Accordingly, we have said, this is the reason that the sages in the Talmud are always called "the disciples of the sages" [talmidei ḥakhamim]...for all of their days, they are like disciples who are learning.[33]

From this perspective, the challenge offered by rabbinic sages and philosophers—and by prophets—requires that human beings acknowledge the limitations of their knowledge and commit to continual learning and growth. Israel, at the time of the golden calf, responded to this challenge by retorting that they did not want to join any quest for the Good that would disrupt their entrenched habits. But Moses ultimately persuaded the people to join him on a path of becoming "disciples"—not sages but "disciples of sages"—in the style of Socrates, who would always be seeking greater and greater wisdom. The path of continual study that they agreed to embark upon is a path of magnifying and sanctifying God's name—not because it claims knowledge, but because it accepts that humans must always seek greater growth. The process of learning should always be connected with the experience at Sinai, through which the people of Israel acknowledged their limited perspective and learned to turn from the golden calf—and toward "the name of the Holy One" which called them higher and higher, "beyond all of the blessings and hymns and praises and consolations that are spoken in the world."

During the Days of Repentance and on Yom Kippur, the Day of Atonement, the days on the Jewish calendar that commemorate the culmination of Israel's repentance and forgiveness following the episode of the golden calf,[34] it is appropriate that the words of the Kaddish are traditionally modified to even further emphasize God's greatness, proclaiming that God's name points "beyond—*and further beyond*—all of the blessings" and other worldly creations. When we focus on the potential for growth after the golden calf episode, we should be reminded all the more of God's infinite goodness and the corollary that one must "continue to grow and learn," reaching beyond and even further beyond our ordinary inclinations. It is fitting to conclude one's study of the golden calf narrative with the words of the Kaddish, which can remind us to challenge our assumptions in light of the Good that is beyond being.

Historical-Critical Scholarship and Its Challenge to Pious Certainty

Simḥah Zissel Ziv and the Musar movement thus developed a model of education that would help to inspire continual moral growth. And Simḥah Zissel criticized those whom he saw as rejecting that model and instead credulously accepting unjustified assumptions that limited their vision. He criticized traditionalist Jewish scholars whom he saw as valorizing talmudic scholarship but as unwilling to engage in the continual work of developing moral virtue, and he also criticized more liberal Jewish scholars whom he saw as credulously accepting the assumptions of Western culture. Simḥah Zissel hoped that reflective meditation[35] on texts like the golden calf narrative could inspire Jews to be scholars of a different sort, who would—like the classical rabbinic sages, like Socrates, or like Moses or other great prophets—continually question their assumptions and continually seek to grow in virtue.

But traditionalists like Simḥah Zissel, of course, refused to question their own dogmatic assumptions about the Torah in general or the golden calf narrative in particular. Simḥah Zissel may have encouraged questioning assumptions, but he also asked his students to have certainty about core values and not simply to claim ignorance. Like other traditional readers of the Torah, he wanted his students to stand firmly on the right side of the battle that is described in the golden calf narrative, and not to be like the people of Israel who floundered in their ignorance and uncertainty, building a calf because they "[did] not know what happened" to Moses (Exodus 32:1).

Indeed, the golden calf narrative seems constructed to demand certainty, not endless questioning. Once Moses returns from the mountain, the people of Israel are expected to choose sides in the battle between Moses and those who support idolatry. Moses calls out, "Whoever is for the Eternal, come here!" (Exodus 32:26), and those who do not come over to his side are sentenced to death. One might imagine an Israelite in the likeness of Socrates who does not claim knowledge of whether Moses is in the right but, rather, would want to question him carefully. Such a philosophic soul would likely be marked for death. In the Torah's account, Moses immediately orders the Levites who rally to his side to go and slaughter the three thousand Israelites who do not show their loyalty to God and to him: "Each of you put sword on thigh, go back and forth from gate to gate throughout the camp, and slay brother, neighbor, and kin" (Exodus 32:27).[36]

Simḥah Zissel saw justice in these efforts to divide the righteous from the wicked. Yes, he would point out, one should continually question and seek greater learning—but proper learning demands that one accept certain self-evident truths. Questioning Moses, questioning God, or questioning the perfection of the Torah was obviously inappropriate from his traditionalist perspective. True "disciples of the sages" must be humble, and their humility should not lead them to question their dedication to God's will as expressed in the Torah but should instead lead them to submit to it. God's name is sanctified and magnified through the study of Torah, from this perspective, precisely because the reader submits to God's will as found in the Torah.[37]

But an alternative path of study that I think better helps us to turn toward the Good acknowledges that the Torah does not perfectly capture God's will. The sort of epistemic humility attributed to Socrates—and, here, to the rabbinic sages, and to Moses—should encourage us to question our assumptions, to learn with openness and honesty—and thus to turn our necks to hear critical analyses regarding the formation of texts and traditions. Critical study of this sort may help us to turn toward "the name of the Holy One," that name which is "beyond all of the blessings and hymns and praises and consolations that are spoken in the world."

When one studies the golden calf narrative from the perspective of historical-critical scholarship, rejecting traditionalist assumptions about biblical authorship and seeking to discover the original contexts in which the Bible was composed, the narrative is easily seen as reflecting a variety of political agendas of interest to the various authors who may have contributed to its formation. Indeed, for many religious studies scholars who teach in contemporary academic contexts, the golden calf episode can be a key text in helping students to question assumptions about the unity and perfection of Scripture and in seeing the likely political motivation of biblical authors.[38] It is not easy to disentangle layers of sources within the golden calf narrative, and historical-critical approaches to the narrative yield few certainties, but such approaches do suggest that it is possible to see within the narrative various voices that advocate for various political agendas.

Thus, for example, one polemical voice in the narrative appears to be condemning the forms of worship encouraged by King Jeroboam's Northern Kingdom of Israel—whose central shrines involved the worship of God enthroned on golden calves—by associating such calves with idolatry and orgiastic celebrations. Why would an author condemn the Northern Kingdom's temples in this way? An author might do so if the author came from the rival Southern Kingdom of Judah, which at its central Temple in Jerusalem imagined the God of Israel enthroned on golden cherubs rather than on golden calves, and was eager to ridicule and delegitimize the Israelite shrines in the north.

Or, for example, the narrative—with its emphasis that "*Aaron* had let [the people] get out of control" (Exodus 32:25)[39] —also appears to contain a polemical voice condemning the family of Aaron, the leaders of the religious establishment in the Southern Kingdom of Judah. While condemning that family, it praises other Levites, emphasizing the piety of the levitical priests whose violence is applauded and who emerge as the heroes of the narrative. Why would an author implicate Aaron's family but praise other Levites? An author might do so if the author was a Levite who was—as all (non-Aaronide) Levites were—excluded from the priesthood by the politically powerful priests who traced their ancestry to Aaron. As many historical-critical scholars have concluded, the golden calf narrative was likely written or edited by writers pointing to the supremacy of the Jerusalem Temple and, at the same time, the legitimacy of priests from beyond the family of Aaron.[40]

The scholars who suggest the political motivations behind the golden calf story may resemble the philosophers in Plato's allegory of the cave who expose how myths and norms are constructed by "puppeteer" mythmakers and legislators who may be seeking above all to assert their own power. Exposing how individuals with certain political interests gained the power to produce the texts that came to be included in the Bible, historical-critical scholarship can help to guard against the dangerous traditionalist assumption that these texts are perfect, divine creations. This mode of scholarship helps to remind us that images of God and claims of divine favor for particular priesthoods or particular temples—like the non-Aaronide priesthood, or the Temple in Jerusalem that featured cherubs rather than calves—have been shaped by human political ambitions and are not of ultimate value. Such scholarship reminds us not to bow down before and idolize such human creations, even if we—like prisoners in a cave—have been long accustomed to thinking of these creations as being inherently holy.

And such scholarship can help us to resist the call, attributed by the Torah to Moses and by Moses to God, to divide communities into believers and idolaters and to strike out with pious certainty against brothers, neighbors, and kin who seem to cast their lot with the idolaters.[41] When we are habituated to such a call, it is difficult to turn our necks and to raise up our eyes to see beyond the puppeteers who have crafted our sacred texts. But historical-critical scholarship, reminding us that the language attributed to God in sacred texts reflects the motivations of its authors, can help us to lift up our eyes toward an infinite ideal that exceeds their perspectives—toward the Good, "the name of the Holy One" that reaches "beyond all of the blessings and hymns and praises and consolations that are spoken in the world."

The Philosophical Task of Critiquing the Critics

Those who are engaged in scholarship of any sort often have an honorable hope that their study will illuminate the darkness—as did the ancient sage Rava, discussed in the introduction to this essay. Rava, citing Job, suggested that proper study (*sidra* or *seder*) would bring order (*seder*) and light to "a land whose light is like darkness, the deepest gloom and disorder." So too, those of us who teach the art of biblical criticism, exploring the possible motivations of the authors who stand behind scriptural texts, may often think that we are bringing light and order to an otherwise opaque and confusing text. We can shed light, for example, on the mystery of why a story regarding a golden calf is included at all in the Bible, and why Aaron is at least partially blamed for the episode, and why the Levites turn out to be such heroic holy warriors on the side of God and Moses.[42] Historical-critical scholars may also be dedicated to the task of growing in virtue, moving toward the Good by developing intellectual virtues of openness, honesty, and integrity, taking the intellectual virtues that Simḥah Zissel Ziv saw in Socrates more seriously than a traditionalist like Simḥah Zissel was himself willing to do.

Thus, for example, as the biblical scholar Robert Coote put it in a 2008 essay on teaching the historical-critical method, that method above all should "foster inquisitiveness" and seek "virtues, or qualities of character, that contribute to critical learning. These include openness, honesty, courage, patience, humility, and sense of humor." Those are, Coote explains, virtues that he prays for at the beginning of the courses on the Bible that he teaches.[43] Such virtues are essential for the task of resisting certainty, for critical learning requires making tentative judgments but always resisting certainty. As Coote affirms in the name of communication theorist David Zarefsky: "To be critical is to make provisional judgments before an audience about matters that are significant but uncertain, by use of evidence and reasoning, in the common pursuit of truth or good decision, with a willingness to run the risk of being wrong."[44] Individuals are limited "by enculturation, experience, and feeling" and, moreover, "because the Bible was written through a process unlike our own and which we do not well understand, and in different times, places, and languages, interpreting the Bible always involves significant uncertainty."[45] Thus, "criticism starts by doubting that I understand."[46]

Coote seems to echo the commitment to uncertainty and continual growth in learning that Simḥah Zissel saw as shared by Jewish "disciples of the sages" and by Socrates. But whereas Simḥah Zissel was unable to question his own assumptions regarding the perfection of the Torah (and this may well have constricted his ability to continually grow), Coote rejects theological dogmatism and appears to embrace a deeper epistemic humility, recognizing the limits of his knowledge.

Still, historical-critical scholars, like all of us, may have their own limiting and dogmatic assumptions. Coote, though he may be an exemplar of the scholar who resists certainty, has in fact been criticized for his own overconfident claims regarding the meaning of the Bible. In an essay on historical-critical Bible scholarship, Jon Levenson points to the 1990 book that Coote co-authored with his wife, Mary P. Coote, *Power, Politics, and the Making of the Bible*,[47] as illustrative of the dogmatic certitude to which historical-critical scholars may succumb. In that volume, Levenson points out, the Cootes seem to claim that, because they understand the original political contexts in which biblical texts were composed, they can identify political motivations of authors and therefore they can hold themselves up as ultimate authorities who, "unlike those they study, know what they are doing."[48] Levenson sees the Cootes succumbing to a common temptation for historical-critical scholars: the "temptation to interpret the text as *ideology*, that is, as only a justification for political arrangements."[49] From this sort of perspective, the work of learning from the golden calf narrative is accomplished once the political motivations of those who opposed Jeroboam in the Northern Kingdom, or opposed the Aaronide priesthood in the Southern Kingdom, have been exposed. The Bible can seemingly play no role in guiding readers toward the pursuit of the Good in any other way. Rather, Levenson argues, "*Power, Politics, and the Making of the Bible* slams shut many of the portals to transcendence that religiously committed historical critics have, in a variety of ways, been struggling to keep open since the Enlightenment." [50]

The Cootes, I imagine, could defend themselves against these charges; at least by the time he wrote his 2008 essay, Robert Coote would insist on uncertainty and disavow any mode of scholarship that too readily shuts any "portals to transcendence." Indeed, as he indicates there, he encourages the cultivation of virtues through exercises that include prayer before study;[51] perhaps he might encourage his Jewish students to recite the words of the Kaddish following a study session. Still, Levenson's general concerns about historical-critical scholarship are worth taking seriously. Scholars certainly can, at times, slam shut portals of transcendence if they insist that the meanings of sacred texts are *limited* to the political motivations of their authors, and if they disparage readers who study texts in pursuit of a vision of the Good that extends "beyond all of the blessings and hymns and praises and consolations that are spoken in the world."

Historical-critical scholars may sometimes see themselves as philosophers in the style of the "Enlightenment"—philosophers who bring light into the cave, helping to turn prisoners around so that prisoners can see the puppeteers who have created myths simply to legitimate their own power.[52] The former prisoners may feel that they have been fully freed from their bondage, but their "enlighteners" are not in fact teaching them to seek portals that would allow them to glance beyond the cave. Scholars may, in fact, be re-enslaving prisoners under new assumptions, positioning themselves as the new puppeteers—who may not be seeking to transmit the Good to the prisoners at all, but may rather be (unconsciously or consciously) asserting their own power. "Might it be the case that the interpretation of religion as only a mystification of power arrangements," Levenson asks, "is itself an item in a discourse of power in which a new group, supported by new social arrangements, asserts its hegemony?"[53]

Levenson's criticism of historical critics—as he puts it, "suspecting the hermeneuts of suspicion"[54] (or, in the language of Peter Berger, "relativizing the relativizers")[55]—offers an important corrective for those historical critics who overrate the enlightening powers of their criticism. Historical criticism can help cultivate the many virtues that Coote has named, and it can help to inspire the pursuit of the Good for all the reasons that I have suggested above. But it is limited in the way that all human traditions are limited, and it emphasizes intellectual virtues while generally doing little to aid in the development of moral virtues. Simḥah Zissel Ziv would surely have developed a greater intellectual openness if he were to have studied the golden calf narrative with historical-critical scholars in a contemporary academic setting; but, so too, we could imagine historical-critical scholars benefitting from meditating on the golden calf narrative as was done in Simḥah Zissel's yeshivas, where the ideal of continual moral growth was above all linked with virtues of lovingkindness and compassion that are often overlooked in contemporary academic settings.[56] Many critical scholars would surely find Simḥah Zissel to be stiff-necked, "not able to turn his neck to listen," "not able to turn from the habit to which he had been habituated";[57] but many critical scholars would also have their own resistances to turning their own necks to the moral horizons toward which a thinker like Simḥah Zissel would point.[58] All of us, wherever we stand, would do well to realize the limitations of our own visions of learning and seek to grow further. Those of us seeking to contribute to the Jewish tradition might benefit from turning to the words of the Kaddish after study, reminding ourselves of how far we are from the infinite goodness represented by "the name of the Holy One" and how we are obligated to continue to grow and learn.

Conclusions: Revisiting Rava and His Legacy

The human obligation to magnify and sanctify God's name in the world—to increase goodness in the world—is an obligation that can be fulfilled through many paths. There are many ways that goodness can be increased in the world, so that "God's great name" is "magnified and sanctified." But study can play a key role in the process; for Jews, it is appropriate that engagement with Torah is linked with the Kaddish and the hope for the sanctification of God's name in the world. The study of Torah can provide a vision of striving in pursuit of the moral ideal that God's name represents, as Simḥah Zissel Ziv found in the golden calf story. The study of Torah can also point to the limits of humanly shaped Torah and the way in which God's infinite name points us beyond those limitations. The words of the Kaddish can remind us of how distant we are from this infinite goodness, but can also remind us that we are obligated to continue to reach toward its light, even though we know that we will never reach it.

As we have seen, Rava first pointed to the illuminating power of the words of the Kaddish amidst the darkness that followed the destruction of the Temple in Jerusalem. We might join him in hoping that the study of sacred texts and the words of the Kaddish can provide light and hope, and we might join him in thinking about how these words function for Jews who today continue to have no central Jerusalem Temple.

By directing his students' attention to ways in which study could sustain the world, Rava may have been turning their attention away from the Temple—perhaps responding, in part, to Jews who thought that the Temple marked the one spot on earth that could serve as a true portal to God's infinite goodness. As I have suggested in this essay, one might learn through study to doubt that narrative regarding the significance of the Jerusalem Temple. Through study, one might come to see the Temple as a concession following the golden calf episode and not as an ideal form—but one might also join Maimonides in appreciating the need for concessions when dealing with stiff-necked human beings, and affirm that the Temple could indeed provide a path to God. Or, through study, one might come to see the Jerusalem Temple as the project of kings and priests seeking political power, buttressed by narratives like the golden calf narrative that ridiculed and sought to delegitimize alternative temples—but one might also join Jon Levenson in understanding that texts and traditions outlive the political motivations that may have led to their creation. The words of the Kaddish may remind us that the texts and traditions that we study reflect limited perspectives and that God transcends them; but they may also remind us that these texts and traditions have the potential to guide us toward that transcendent horizon.

The recitation of the Kaddish is itself a tradition that has outlived the motivations that may have led to its creation. Rava himself may well have thought that the darkness of the world would ultimately be dispelled if "God's kingdom" (a phrase also used in the Kaddish) were established through the rebuilding of the Temple in Jerusalem and the reinstitution of its sacrificial system. But his effort to highlight the power of study can inspire new hopes for how the darkness of the world can, instead, be slowly challenged through study itself—if study is carried out with all the virtues that it requires and opens up new portals for moral goodness in the world, making the world more like a world that we could call "God's kingdom."[59]

For those of us today who see God's great name as a moral archetype toward which we are called, we need all the reminders that we can get to always be more thoughtful, more loving, and more just, and reminding ourselves of God's great name can be a source of inspiration. The Kaddish offers us no promises of enlightenment or redemption, but its words may guide us to look for insight and for glimpses of the Good—encounters with God—in all of our studies.

NOTES

[1] A doxology is a statement of praise. On the Kaddish as a "closing doxology" after study, see David De Sola Pool, *The Old Jewish-Aramaic Prayer: The Kaddish* (Leipzig: Rudolf Haupt, 1909), pp. 8–9. This volume has been reprinted as *The Kaddish* (Jerusalem: Sivan Press, 1964).

[2] B. Sotah 49a.

[3] *Reason and Hope: Selections from the Jewish Writings of Hermann Cohen*, ed. and trans. Eva Jospe (New York: Norton, 1971), p. 58. I have added capitalizations to the words "Idea" and "Good." For another example of the identification of God, morality, and Plato's ideal of the Good, from a later philosopher building on Cohen's work, see *The Pursuit of the Ideal: Jewish Writings of Steven Schwarzschild*, ed. Menachem Marc Kellner (Albany: State University of New York Press, 1990), pp. 150 and 251.

[4] Cohen, *Reason and Hope*, p. 85.

[5] See, for example, Moses Maimonides, *The Guide of the Perplexed* I 26, trans. Shlomo Pines, vol. 1 (Chicago: University of Chicago Press, 1963), p. 56. (Note that all subsequent citations of the *Guide* are to the Pines edition.) Some of the many rabbinic sources for the phrase (*dib'rah torah ki-l'shon b'nei adam*) include B. Yevamot 71a, B. Bava Metzia 31b, and Sifrei Bemidbar §112. The phrase is often attributed to the school of Rabbi Ishmael; on the linkage between this school and Maimonides, see Abraham Joshua Heschel, *Heavenly Torah: As Refracted through the Generations*, ed. and trans. by Gordon Tucker with Leonard Levin (New York: Continuum, 2005), pp. 45, 149–150, and 223–224.

[6] Hermann Cohen, *Ethics of Maimonides*, trans. Almut Sh. Bruckstein (Madison, WI: University of Wisconsin Press, 2004), pp. 80, 116, and 183.

[7] See ibid., p. 116; Moses Maimonides, *Guide* III 54 (vol. 2, pp. 637–638).

[8] Cohen, *Ethics of Maimonides*, p. 116, quoting Maimonides, *Guide*, III 54 (vol. 2, p. 634). On Cohen's efforts to reread Maimonides in ways that support Cohen's own approach, see Aaron Hughes, "Medieval Jewish Philosophers in Modern Jewish Philosophy," in *The Cambridge History of Jewish Philosophy: The Modern Era*, eds. Martin Kavka, Zachary Braiterman, and David Novak (Cambridge: Cambridge University Press, 2012), pp. 230–232.

[9] Maimonides, Mishneh Torah, Hilkhot Yesodei Hatorah 2:2, with my italics. This passage is quoted in Cohen, *Ethics of Maimonides*, p. 118. See also the discussion in Menachem Marc Kellner, "Philosophical Themes in Maimonides' Sefer Ahavah," in *Maimonides and His Heritage*, ed. Idit Dobbs-Weinstein, Lenn Evan Goodman, and James Allen Grady (Albany: State University of New York Press, 2009), pp. 15–16; David Hartman, *Maimonides: Torah and Philosophic Quest* (Philadelphia: Jewish Publication Society, 1976), pp. 206–209.

[10] Maimonides, *Guide* I 1 (vol. 1, pp. 7–8).

[11] Ibid., p. 7. On the limited vision even of great prophets, see Josef Stern, *The Matter and Form of Maimonides' Guide* (Cambridge, MA: Harvard University

Press, 2013), p. 43; and Howard T. Kreisel, *Prophecy: The History of an Idea in Medieval Jewish Philosophy* (Dordrecht, Holland, and Boston: Kluwer Academic Publishers, 2001), p. 213.

[12] Moses Maimonides, "Eight Chapters," in *Ethical Writings of Maimonides*, trans. Raymond L. Weiss and Charles E. Butterworth (New York: New York University Press, 1975), pp. 80–83 (chap. 7).

[13] See Ismar Schorsch, *Canon Without Closure: Torah Commentaries* (New York: Aviv Press, 2007), p. 310.

[14] Based on the NJPS translation, following modifications suggested by Martin S. Cohen.

[15] Maimonides, *Guide* III 54 (vol. 2, pp. 637–638). See also I 54 (vol. 1, pp. 123–128); Cohen, *Ethics of Maimonides*, pp. 69 and 71–72.

[16] Plato, *The Republic of Plato*, trans. Allan David Bloom, 2nd ed. (New York: Basic Books, 1991), book 7 (514a), p. 193.

[17] Ibid, book 7 (514a–520a), pp. 193–198.

[18] On the idea of "turning around," see ibid., book 7 (518c–d), p. 197.

[19] Maimonides, *Guide*, III 32 (vol. 2, p. 526). See also I 1 (vol. 1, p. 8), in discussing the transmission of insights: "Know that whenever one of the perfect wishes to mention, either orally or in writing, something that he understands of these secrets, according to the degree of his perfection, he is unable to explain with complete clarity and coherence even the portion that he has apprehended." On the link between this discussion and the Allegory of the Cave, see Kenneth Seeskin, *Searching for a Distant God: The Legacy of Maimonides* (New York: Oxford University Press, 2000), p. 36. Seeskin writes: "Like the prisoner in Plato's cave who sees the sun and returns to tell his fellow prisoners about it, those who are fortunate enough to receive these insights have trouble communicating them to others." See also Alan Mittleman, *Human Nature and Jewish Thought: Judaism's Case for Why Persons Matter* (Princeton: Princeton University Press, 2015), pp. 92–93.

[20] Maimonides, *Guide* III 32 (vol. 2, pp. 525–531). On Maimonides' attitude toward sacrificial worship, see Menachem Marc Kellner, *Maimonides' Confrontation with Mysticism* (Oxford: Littman Library of Jewish Civilization, 2006), pp. 140–148. On his attitude toward language, see ibid., pp. 155–178.

[21] Plato, *The Republic of Plato* (book 7, 517a), pp. 195–196.

[22] See Allan David Bloom, "Interpretive Essay," in *The Republic of Plato*, trans. Allan David Bloom, 2nd ed. (New York: Basic Books, 1991), pp. 391–412. On the openness and longing of the philosopher as *exemplified* by Socrates, which should be distinguished from the model of the philosopher-king as *described* in the *Republic*, see Laurence D. Cooper, *Eros in Plato, Rousseau, and Nietzsche: The Politics of Infinity* (University Park, PA: Pennsylvania State University Press, 2008), pp. 67–68, 109, and 312; Drew A. Hyland, *Finitude and Transcendence in the Platonic Dialogues* (Albany: State University of New York Press, 1995), pp. 78–82. I also draw inspiration from Iris Murdoch's reading of the Allegory of

the Cave and the importance of contemplation of the Good as discussed in Iris
Murdoch, *The Sovereignty of Good* (London: Routledge & Kegan Paul, 1970),
pp. 98–99.

[23] Leviticus Rabbah 10:3. The language of "rebuke" is used in the language of
Rashi on Exodus 32:5, s.v. *va-yomer*.

[24] See Avivah Gottlieb Zornberg, *The Particulars of Rapture: Reflections on Exodus*
(New York: Doubleday, 2001), pp. 425ff.; also Kenneth Seeskin, *No Other Gods:
The Modern Struggle Against Idolatry* (West Orange, NJ: Behrman House, 1995),
pp. 119–122.

[25] See Kellner, *Maimonides' Confrontation with Mysticism*, p. 146, n. 56 and p.
42, n. 26, citing Isaac Abravanel, *Perush Nevi·im Aharonim* [*Commentary on the
Latter Prophets*], (Jerusalem: Torah Va-Da·at, 1957), p. 328 (on Jeremiah 7).

[26] See Maimonides, *Guide*, I 1 (vol. 1, p. 7).

[27] See Geoffrey Claussen, *Sharing the Burden: Rabbi Simḥah Zissel Ziv and the
Path of Musar* (Albany: State University of New York Press, 2015), pp. 125–126.
On the broader theme of continually striving for growth in Simḥah Zissel's
writings, see pp. 113–124.

[28] Simḥah Zissel (Broida) Ziv, *Sefer Ḥokhmah U-musar* (Jerusalem, 1964), vol. 2,
p. 245. See Claussen, *Sharing the Burden*, pp. 125–126.

[29] Simḥah Zissel (Broida) Ziv, *Sefer Ḥokhmah U-musar* (New York, 1957), vol.
1, p. 33.

[30] Ibid., vol. 1, p. 34.

[31] See ibid., vol. 1, p. 137.

[32] Simḥah Zissel highlights these virtues in a section of text that culminates with
his discussion of the golden calf and the obligation to continue to grow and
learn; see ibid., vol. 1, p. 31.

[33] Ibid., vol. 1, p. 344. As Martin S. Cohen has pointed out to me, this idea is also
reflected in the Aramaic phrase *tzurba mei-rabbanan*.

[34] As Rashi explains (commenting on Exodus 34:11, s.v. *v'shav el ha-maḥaneh*),
the sin of the golden calf occurs on the seventeenth of Tammuz; after burning
the calf and punishing the sinners, Moses ascends the mountain and seeks
forgiveness amidst divine anger for forty days, until the first day of the month of
Elul. On the first of Elul, a new forty-day period begins, which are days of divine
favor. That period of divine favor culminates with God's complete forgiveness
of the sin of the golden calf on the tenth of Tishrei, the Day of Atonement. As
Rashi explains, "On the tenth of Tishrei the blessed Holy One was placated
toward Israel, joyfully and whole-heartedly, and [God] said to Moses, 'I have
forgiven in accordance with your words' (Numbers 14:20)." The language of
Numbers 14:20 is assumed to refer to the golden calf episode. Rashi, relying on
Seder Olam 6 and Tanḥuma *Ki Tissa* §31, explains the same basic timeline in
his comments on Deuteronomy 9:18, s.v. *va-etnappal*.

[35] For some of the models of meditation used for contemplating biblical and

rabbinic insights in Simḥah Zissel's yeshivas, see Claussen, *Sharing the Burden*, p. 17. Among the methods that I discuss there is one that involves meditation "on the descriptions of God's moral goodness so that [students] could meditate on these ideals and consider their own personal potential for improvement." The practice of meditating on the divine attributes of goodness that were revealed following the sin of the golden calf was emphasized during the period leading up to the Day of Atonement and especially on the High Holy Days themselves; see Dov Katz, *T'nu·at Ha-Musar*, 2nd ed., (Tel-Aviv: Beitan Ha-Sefer, 1952), vol. 2, pp. 176–177. I focus on Simḥah Zissel's understanding of divine attributes and striving to imitate them in *Sharing the Burden*, pp. 113–124.

[36] NJPS translation.

[37] Claussen, *Sharing the Burden*, pp. 89 and 194.

[38] See, for example, the presentation of the story in Richard Elliott Friedman, *Who Wrote the Bible?* (New York: Summit Books, 1987), pp. 70–74, or Michael David Coogan, *The Old Testament: A Historical and Literary Introduction to the Hebrew Scriptures*, 3rd ed. (New York: Oxford University Press, 2014), pp. 137–141.

[39] NJPS translation; my italics.

[40] See, for example, Martin Noth, *Exodus: A Commentary* (Philadelphia: Westminster Press, 1962), pp. 245–246; or Moses Aberbach and Leivy Smolar, "Aaron, Jeroboam, and the Golden Calves," in *Journal of Biblical Literature* 86:2 (1967), pp. 135–140. Alternatively, the author ridiculing Jeroboam's shrine and its calves might have been a northern priest excluded from Jeroboam's temple. See the discussion by William H. C. Propp in his *Exodus 19–40: A New Translation with Introduction and Commentary* (New York: Doubleday, 2006), pp. 567–578.

[41] On the rabbinic recognition of how authority is constructed through Moses' attribution of this call to God, see Abraham Joshua Heschel, *God in Search of Man: A Philosophy of Judaism* (New York: Farrar, Straus & Cudahy, 1955), p. 269.

[42] For a more extensive list of enigmas associated with this passage, see Friedman, *Who Wrote the Bible?*, p. 71.

[43] Robert Coote, "Critical Perspective in Biblical Studies," in *Spotlight on Theological Education (Religious Studies News)* 2, no. 1 (March 2008), p. viii. Coote teaches at the San Francisco Theological Seminary and the Graduate Theological Union in California. I would assume that the majority of his students are Christians, though he does not specify this; nor have I seen him specify his own religious commitments in his writing.

[44] Ibid.

[45] Ibid.

[46] Ibid., p. xii.

[47] Published in that year by Fortress Press in Minneapolis.

[48] Jon D. Levenson, *The Hebrew Bible, the Old Testament, and Historical Criticism:*

Jews and Christians in Biblical Studies (Louisville, KY: Westminster/John Knox Press, 1993), p. 115.

[49] Ibid., p. 111.

[50] Ibid., p. 113.

[51] As Coote specifies in "Critical Perspective in Biblical Studies," p. viii: "I begin my introductory class with a prayer for virtues, or qualities of character, that contribute to critical learning....I endeavor both to model these qualities and to encourage them in students."

[52] See Bloom, "Interpretive Essay," p. 403: "The Enlightenment, taken literally, believed that the light could be brought into the cave and the shadows dispelled; men, in that view, could live in perfect light. This Socrates denies; the philosopher does not bring light to the cave."

[53] Levenson, *The Hebrew Bible, the Old Testament, and Historical Criticism*, p. 116.

[54] Ibid. "Hermeneuts of suspicion" are, here, interpreters ("hermeneuts") who interpret biblical texts by distrusting their claims and suspecting biblical authors of only seeking their own power. As Levenson is pointing out, one might suspect that such interpreters are in fact themselves seeking their own power as they claim to offer their own authoritative understandings of reality; one might, of course, continue the chain of suspicion by suspecting Levenson's own suspicions, and so on. The concept of a "hermeneutic of suspicion" was first developed by Paul Ricoeur with reference to Marx, Freud, and Nietzsche; see Paul Ricoeur, *Freud and Philosophy: An Essay on Interpretation*, trans. Denis Savage (New Haven: Yale University Press, 1970), pp. 32–35.

[55] Levenson, *The Hebrew Bible, the Old Testament, and Historical Criticism*, p. 116. His reference is to Peter L. Berger, *A Rumor of Angels: Modern Society and the Rediscovery of the Supernatural* (Garden City, NY: Doubleday, 1969), pp. 31–53, esp. p. 45.

[56] I discuss these virtues in Claussen, *Sharing the Burden*, esp. pp. 141–168. I do think, however, that many aspects of these virtues were also overlooked in Simḥah Zissel's yeshivas; see ibid., pp. 176–181, 191–192, and 194–195.

[57] As quoted above, these are the vices that Simḥah Zissel himself emphasizes in *Sefer Ḥokhmah U-musar*, vol. 2, p. 245.

[58] See *Sharing the Burden*, p. 193.

[59] Hermann Cohen, *Religion of Reason Out of the Sources of Judaism*, trans. Simon Kaplan (Atlanta, GA: Scholars Press, 1995), p. 386, suggests in his brief treatment of the Kaddish that the recitation of the Kaddish helps to bring about God's kingdom: "One prays that the messianic kingdom of God might become present; through the prayer the messianic future is made alive in the present." See Daniel H. Weiss, *Paradox and the Prophets: Hermann Cohen and the Indirect Communication of Religion* (Oxford: Oxford University Press, 2012), pp. 197–199.

An Unlikely Prayer

Martin I. Lockshin

One of the best-known Jewish prayers today is Kaddish, perhaps only second to the Shema. Many Jews who do not pray regularly or even understand a Jewish language know Kaddish, or at least parts of it, by heart. Yet in many ways, Kaddish is an unlikely choice for this elevated status. It would be easy to formulate historical and halakhic arguments why Kaddish should *not* be a popular Jewish prayer. But the power of Jewish folk religion and the power of our feelings about deceased parents overcame many possible problems with Kaddish.

The Language of Kaddish

Relative to other prayers in the *siddur* (the Jewish prayerbook), Kaddish is not old. It is a linguistic mélange, mostly Aramaic with a smattering of Hebrew. (Aramaic and Hebrew are sister-languages with some shared vocabulary and grammar.) No Jews today speak the type of Aramaic found in Kaddish and very few read it with comprehension. Aramaic prayers in the *siddur* are few and far between and most of them were composed relatively late, probably towards the end of the first millennium C.E. or even later, after the heyday of Jewish liturgical creativity.[1]

Selections from the Hebrew Bible form the oldest core of our *siddur*, along with prayers that were composed, compiled, or edited by the classical rabbis in the Land of Israel around 2000 years ago. While the rabbis who created those prayers spoke Aramaic at least as well and as often as they spoke Hebrew, they avoided using Aramaic in prayers, preferring the "high" or holy language of Hebrew for liturgical purposes. The Kaddish prayer from a later period is an example of the opposite phenomenon. Indeed, the opening line of Kaddish, *yitgaddal v'yitkaddash sh'meih rabba* ("magnified and sanctified be His [= God's] great name"), is, in part, an Aramaized version of the first words of a Hebrew verse from the Bible, "I will manifest My greatness and My sanctity, *v'hitgaddilti v'hitkaddishti*" (Ezekiel 38:23).

In the eighteenth century, a few traditional Eastern European Jewish grammarians argued that Kaddish had a strong Hebrew core. They claimed that the two opening words ought to be pronounced *yitgaddeil v'yitkaddeish*, based on two dubious assumptions: (1) that the words were Hebrew, not Aramaic; and (2) that *yitgaddal* was not an acceptable form according to the rules of Hebrew grammar.[2] Nor is this just ancient history—the hyper-corrected pronunciation *yitgaddeil v'yitkaddeish* can still be heard today in synagogues that follow the rulings of Rabbi Yisrael Meir Kagan, author of the near-canonical twentieth-century halakhic compendium for Ashkenazic Jews, the *Mishnah B'rurah*.[3] However, scholars and the majority of rabbis today believe that the pronunciation *yitgaddal v'yitkaddash* is correct and original, and furthermore agree that the dominant language of Kaddish is Aramaic.[4]

The Origin of Kaddish

The central line of Kaddish, *y'hei sh'meih rabba m'varakh l'alam u-l'almei almaya* ("may His [=God's] great name be blessed forever and for all time"), is very old and the Talmud ascribes great power to its recitation: people who "respond" with this line are guaranteed a place in the World to Come[5] and any evil decree against them is annulled.[6] The use of the verb "respond" (*oneh*) suggests that the prayer alluded to in the Talmud may have been structurally similar to today's Kaddish in that one person leads the prayer, and this line was (part of) a communal response to the leader.

The earliest sources show that Kaddish originated in the study hall, not in the synagogue. At the end of a study session, a recitation took place that included the communal response, "May His great name be blessed forever and for all time."[7] Some scholars say that originally Kaddish was recited only after the study of *aggadah*, Jewish lore and legend, or perhaps after a sermon, and not after the pure study of Jewish law.[8] At the end of the study session or sermon, a communal recitation would remind the assembled that Torah is connected to God and that we Jews have an obligation to make God's name great. The fact that Kaddish is in Aramaic may be connected to its origin in the study house. Since study sessions in the first millennium were generally conducted in Aramaic, so was Kaddish, the closing prayer or ceremony. This reasonable explanation was first offered in the twelfth or thirteenth century: "They used to recite Kaddish after the sermon. Ignoramuses were present; not all of them understood Hebrew. So they established that Kaddish is said in Aramaic, so that everyone would understand it, for Aramaic was their [spoken] language."[9]

Today in many synagogues, a version of Kaddish called Kaddish D'rabbanan ("The Rabbis' Kaddish") is still recited after a Torah class attended by a quorum (*minyan*), even if no official prayer service has taken place and even if the study is not in a room that is used for prayer. Only later in history was Kaddish moved from the study hall to the synagogue service and detached from the study of Torah.

Who Is Addressing Whom in Kaddish?

In many Jewish prayers, human beings address God: "forgive us, our Father, for we have sinned"; "may our eyes witness Your return to Zion with compassion"; or "turn us back to You, O Eternal, and we will return; renew our days as of old."

Yet the first six Hebrew words of the Shema are addressed to human beings, not to God ("Hear, O Israel, the Eternal is our God, the Eternal alone"). In their original contexts in the Torah, the three paragraphs that follow this verse also represent communication between humans and God, but with God's words addressed to us. The first paragraph (Deuteronomy 6:4–9) is the part of Moses' long speech to the Israelites before his death in which he instructs them to "love the Eternal your God with all your heart…" The second paragraph of the Shema (Deuteronomy 11:13–21) alternates between God's voice (e.g., "I will give rain in your land in its season") and Moses' voice (e.g., "the Eternal's anger will flare against you"). In the third paragraph (Numbers 15:37–41), the omniscient biblical narrator says that God spoke to Moses, instructing him to address the people in God's voice: "Thus you will be reminded to keep all My commandments…I am the Eternal your God" (verse 40). In all three paragraphs, the person praying is not speaking to God, but is hearing God's words from the Torah spoken to him or her—either directly, or through the mouth of God's most trusted prophet, Moses.

Other Jewish prayers are two-way conversations between humans and God. For example, consider the prayer recited when the Torah is returned to the Ark after it is read in public, popularly called U-v'nuḥo Yomar after its first words. As the chart shows, this prayer begins with words addressed by humans to God and then shifts without warning to God's words to human beings. The last words of the prayer are again those of humans, requesting a reciprocal relationship with God: "Turn us back to You, O Eternal, and we will return; renew our days as of old."

Return, O Eternal, to the myriad thousands of Israel; advance, Eternal, to Your resting place...for the sake of Your servant, David, do not reject Your anointed one.	humans to God
I give you good instruction; do not forsake My Torah. It is a tree of life to those who grasp it...	God to humans
Turn us back to You, O Eternal, and we will return; renew our days as of old!	humans to God

In other words, the prayer creates a conversation between people and God.[10]

Kaddish is also a conversation, but between human beings. The leader of the prayer is speaking not to God but to the other congregants, expressing the hope that God's sovereignty will be established *b'ḥayyeikhon u-v'yomeikhon*, "in *your* lifetime and in *your* days." In Kaddish D'rabbanan, the form of Kaddish recited after public Torah study, the leader says: "May great peace, grace, kindness, and compassion...come to *them* [i.e., to people who are dedicated to Torah study] and to *you* [i.e., the fellow congregants or Torah students to whom the leader is speaking]." God is not spoken to nor even named in Kaddish, but merely alluded to. (The opening line simply mentions "His great name," without specifying who He is. The closing line refers to "the One who makes peace in heavens." In the middle the references are clearer: "the blessed Holy One," or "their Father in heaven.")

In sum, while Kaddish is *about* God, it fails to fulfill one of the most basic functions of prayer: communication between people and God. It serves the salutary purpose of having the congregants speak to each other. But if prayer involves speaking to God or reciting God's words, Kaddish does not seem to be a prayer.

Kaddish and the Dead

The lofty status of Kaddish in the Jewish community for the last few centuries came about because it served to commemorate and honor a deceased parent during the first eleven months after death and then annually on the *yahrzeit*, the anniversary of the death. (The expansion of the perceived "duty" that many Jews now feel to recite Kaddish in memory of people other than parents is a very recent development; the Hebrew name for the Mourner's Kaddish, *kaddish yatom* [literally, "Orphan's Kaddish"] reflects the original practice that only children of the deceased recited this prayer.[11]) This connection of the prayer with the dead came relatively late in Jewish history and for obscure, mystical reasons. Leon Wieseltier's monumental 1998 book *Kaddish* outlines how this prayer was understood in mystical and/or folk religion circles as a way to benefit the soul of a deceased parent who might be undergoing judgment from God during the first year after death.[12]

The Mourner's Kaddish makes no reference to death, dying, mortality, sadness, life after death, parents, bereavement, or the precariousness of the human condition. Occasionally people claim that Kaddish does address "consolation." And, indeed, the word *nehemata* in Kaddish does look like an Aramaic cognate of the Hebrew word, *n'hamah*, the word for the comfort or consolation extended to mourners. In the context of Kaddish, though, it is unlikely that it means that. Kaddish asserts that the blessed Holy One should be "blessed and praised...beyond any blessing (*birkhata*), song (*shirata*), praise (*tushb'hata*), or *nehemata* that is recited in the world." What would praising God beyond any "consolation" mean?

A leading Israeli scholar of Semitic languages, Moshe Bar-Asher, recently wrote an article about the Aramaic word *nehemata* in Kaddish.[13] Bar-Asher shows that the word is actually a cognate of the Hebrew word *ne'imot*, a regular term for "melodies." This Hebrew word often appears in the liturgy in contexts similar to that of Kaddish. For example, in the daily morning service we recite: *l'El barukh ne'imot yitteinu, l'melekh el ḥai v'kayyam z'mirot yomeiru v'tishbaḥot yashmi·u* ("to blessed God they [the angels] offer melodies [*ne'imot*]; to the Sovereign, the living and eternal God, they say psalms and proclaim praises"). In both prayers, the words *ne'imot* and *neḥemata* are parallel to terms denoting blessing, song, or praise. Bar-Asher's explanation makes perfect sense, but it removes the sole connection between the words of Kaddish and the concepts of bereavement and consolation.

Kaddish and Folk Religion

The status that the Mourner's Kaddish has attained in the last few centuries is strong proof of the enduring power of Jewish folk religion. The Talmud and other works of Jewish law from the first centuries of the Common Era outline many ways that children should honor the memory of their departed parents, but the Mourner's Kaddish is not even mentioned. Nor does it appear several centuries later in the basic legal codes of Rabbi Moses Maimonides and Rabbi Joseph Karo. It begins to be mentioned in codes of law only in the last five hundred years, although it presumably existed at the folk level for a number of centuries before that.

The dearth of classical sources on the subject was highlighted in the heated debate that arose in Orthodox circles in the late twentieth century about women saying the Mourner's Kaddish.[14] Generally an issue like this would be resolved by looking at talmudic sources or sources among the *ge'onim and rishonim*, the great rabbis of the seventh through fifteenth centuries. But the twentieth-century Kaddish debate could not do this since no such sources exist. Instead, the debate was more strategic than exegetical.[15] (In most modern Orthodox synagogues now, as in Conservative and Reform synagogues, women are allowed and generally encouraged to recite the Mourner's Kaddish. In *ḥareidi* [fervently Orthodox] synagogues, women are not.)

Another example of the power of folk religion is the now near-universal custom that many mourners recite Kaddish in unison. This is definitely not how any Kaddish was recited by Ashkenazic Jews before the last few centuries. In early modern times, some of the most detailed halakhic discussions of the Mourner's Kaddish involved the question of "priority" in reciting the prayer.[16] If two or more mourners were in synagogue, the halakhic literature tried to regulate which one of them received the honor of reciting the Mourner's Kaddish, based on the assumption that Kaddish recited in unison by more than one person was unthinkable. Writing in the middle of the nineteenth century, Rabbi Jacob Ettlinger, often considered one of the founders of neo-Orthodoxy, railed against the new custom of group recitation of Kaddish, labeling it a Reform innovation based solely on the need to keep mourners from fighting with each other and, at that, one contrary to the principles of Jewish law.[17] Even in the middle of the twentieth century, some rabbis still argued for the old custom of having only one mourner recite any given Kaddish.[18]

A relic of this halakhic issue can be found in the fact that some synagogues still carefully legislate who has priority to lead the prayers when two or more mourners are present.[19] Leading a prayer service involves reciting the Kaddish prayer solo more than once, in the form of the so-called "Half Kaddish" and "Full Kaddish" that serve as liturgical dividers between different parts of the service. But in virtually all synagogues today the Mourner's Kaddish is treated as an exception. In order not to deny any mourner who comes to synagogue the "right" to say Mourner's Kaddish, the rules were relaxed—despite the theoretically reasonable halakhic arguments of Rabbi Ettlinger and others.

The Enduring Attraction of Kaddish

It is no secret that many Jews today attend services solely because they feel an obligation to say Kaddish for a deceased parent. It is doubtful that any significant percentage of them really believes that their parent's soul is in limbo or purgatory for up to twelve months and the prayer that they are reciting is going to benefit that soul.[20] Yet many people, men and women, seriously inconvenience themselves, rearranging their work duties, their social life, and their obligations to living relatives, so as not to miss a Kaddish recitation. Why?

On the psychological level, many people feel guilt, or are possessed of a deep sense of lost opportunity, when a parent dies. Children worry that they might not have done everything for their parent that they should have, while she or he was alive. Even after arranging a respectful funeral, reciting Kaddish allows mourners to feel that they are doing something difficult, making a sacrifice, in order to honor a parent's memory.

So, functionally, Kaddish serves an important purpose. What of its content? The most moving explanation I have heard was in a short sermon delivered by Rabbi Irving (Yitz) Greenberg of New York, who says that Judaism teaches that our primary task here on earth is, as the Aleinu prayer puts it, *l'takkein olam b'malkhut shaddai*—to perfect the world and make it more godly, to bring God's sovereignty into effect here on earth. Whenever a Jew dies, in addition to all the personal sadness of the survivors, the community is also sad that the deceased did not succeed in that task. The world unfortunately is still unperfected and God's sovereignty has not yet been established. When a son or daughter of the deceased recites Kaddish and expresses the hope to the congregation that God will establish God's kingdom in our world "in your lifetime and in your days" (*v'yamlikh malkhuteih b'hayeikhon u-v'yomeikhon*), the community can feel some consolation. The deceased may not have established God's sovereignty here on earth, but he or she has left behind a child who still strives to achieve that goal.

Perhaps the Jewish folk religion displayed great wisdom when it promoted Kaddish into something much greater than we would expect when we study about it only from the perspectives of history and of *halakhah*.

NOTES

[1] See, e.g., Abraham Millgram, *Jewish Worship* (Philadelphia: Jewish Publication Society of America, 1971), p. 33: "The [classical] rabbis even opposed the use of Aramaic in prayer, notwithstanding the fact that Aramaic was considered a semiholy language." Other Aramaic prayers in the traditional prayer book include Y'kum purkan ("Since the prayer arose in Babylonia, it is in Aramaic" [Ismar Elbogen, *Jewish Liturgy: A Comprehensive History*, trans. Raymond Scheindlin (Philadelphia: Jewish Publication Society of America, 1993), p. 162]); B'rikh sh'meih (a section from the Zohar, a work dating from the thirteenth century); and Akdamut, commonly dated to the eleventh century (Elbogen, *Jewish Liturgy*, pp. 257–258).

[2] See, e.g., Isaiah 10:15 for a biblical example of the verb vocalized as *yitgaddeil*.

[3] See *Mishnah B'rurah* 56:2.

[4] Haim A. Cohen, "*Yitgaddeil veyitqaddeish*:A Study of the Growth of a New Pronunciation Tradition" (Hebrew), in *Masorot* 8 (1994), pp. 59–69.

[5] B. Berakhot 57a.

[6] B. Shabbat 119b.

[7] See, e.g., *Yalkut Shimoni*, Proverbs, §951: "Whenever they hear *haggadah* from the mouth of the sage and they answer *amen y'hei sh'meih rabba m'varakh*, the blessed Holy One is happy." See also B. Sotah 49a.

[8] Elbogen, *Jewish Liturgy*, p. 80: "...the origin of this prayer [Kaddish]; it was originally used at the end of sermons on Aggadah." Among halakhists, see for example the *Magein Avraham* commentary to the Shulḥan Arukh, Oraḥ Ḥayyim 54:3: "When one studies Mishnah, one should study *haggadah* afterwards in order to be able to recite Kaddish." In classical Hebrew, *haggadah* and *aggadah* are synonymous terms.

[9] Tosafot to B. Berakhot 3a, s.v. *v'onin y'hei sh'meih ha-gadol m'varakh*.

[10] I am grateful to Rabbi Ysoscher Katz who pointed out to me the structure of this prayer.

[11] See, e.g., Y. Y. Greenwald, *Kolbo Al Aveilut* (New York: Feldheim, 1947), p. 367: "This obligation [to recite Kaddish] was placed only on children"; and see the sources cited by Greenwald there. See also the language of the question sent by a rabbi to Rabbi Yeḥezkel Landau (1713–1793): "We have never seen [a source requiring that] a father recite Kaddish for a deceased child" (in *Responsa Noda Bihudah Tinyana, Oraḥ Ḥayyim* 8).

[12] Leon Wieseltier, *Kaddish* (New York: Knopf, 1998).

[13] "On the Noun *Neḥemata* in Kaddish" (Hebrew), in *Sefer Zikkaron L'Moriah Leibson: Meḥkarim B'mada·ei Ha-yahadut*, eds. Aharon Maman and Rivka Bliboim (Jerusalem: Hebrew University Press, 2011), pp. 75–97.

[14] In this regard, readers may wish to consult the essays by Ruth Walfish and Adena Berkowitz elsewhere in this volume.

[15] See the sources gathered by Rahel Berkovits, *A Daughter's Recitation of Mourner's Kaddish* (New York: Jewish Orthodox Feminist Alliance, 2011).

[16] One of the earliest such discussions is found in Rabbi Moses Isserles's glosses on the Shulḥan Arukh; see his comment at S.A. Yoreh Dei·ah 376:4.

[17] Jacob Etllinger, Responsa *Binyan Tziyyon* (ed. Altona 5628 [1867/1868]), responsum 122, pp. 35a–b.

[18] See sources cited by Greenwald in his *Kolbo Al Aveilut*, pp. 372–373.

[19] For an example of such a list of who has priority for leading services, see http://jecelmorashul.org/avodah/gabbai%20info.pdf.

[20] In this regard, see the essay by Martin S. Cohen elsewhere in this volume.

"Let the Power of the Eternal Be Great": Kaddish, Cosmos, and Covenant

Baruch Frydman-Kohl

A Personal Preface

As I reflected on the horrific evil of the Holocaust in the course of my rabbinic and philosophic training, I decided that the only way to salvage belief would be by reclaiming the Aristotelian God of Maimonides and his more radical interpreters. I thus removed God from history in order to preserve human freedom and dignity. But as a congregational rabbi, my pastoral training—particularly my experience in providing hospice care—and the relationships I formed with congregants as their lives ebbed away led me to realize that the purified God of medieval abstraction did not satisfy the desire for a caring and compassionate God for which many of us yearn, particularly at the end of life.

The influence of Rabbi Abraham Joshua Heschel, and my own study of Rabbi Isaac Arama (c. 1420–1494) and other thinkers who modified or rejected the Aristotelian theological model, brought me back to a more biblical relationship with God as the "most moved mover."[1] And a biblical quotation, recited as part of the Kaddish in Sephardic rituals (see below), helped me to develop and maintain a belief in a cosmic, transcendent Deity who is at the same time a compassionate God bound in covenant to the people of Israel.

Let the Power of the Eternal Be Great

The recitation of Kaddish, based on the adaptation of a biblical verse[2] and an Aramaic response[3] (each associated with pre-messianic hope), was often augmented or surrounded with additional prayers or the recitation of associated biblical verses.[4] Two additions, initially added prior to the opening words of the Kaddish,[5] are now rarely recited. Having associations with divine compassion and with an aspiration to influence or affect God, they read as follows: "And now, let the power of the Eternal be great, as You have spoken" (Numbers 14:17) and "Remember Your mercy, Eternal, and Your steadfast love, for they are from old" (Psalm 25:6). Why were these two verses inserted as a preface to the Kaddish and what might their meaning be for us?

Biblical Sources

According to the Book of Numbers, the people of Israel, while wandering in the wilderness following the failure of the scouting mission into the Land of Promise, call for a return to Egypt. In response, God declares a desire to do away with the people and to begin again with Moses. However, Moses intercedes with God on behalf of the people. And in calling for divine forgiveness, Moses says this:

> And now, let the power of the Eternal be great, as You have spoken, saying, "The Eternal is slow to anger and abounding in loyal love, forgiving iniquity and transgression, but by no means clearing the guilty, visiting the iniquity of the parents upon the children to the third and the fourth generation." Forgive the iniquity of this people according to the greatness of Your loyal love, just as You have pardoned this people,

from Egypt even until now." And the Eternal said, "I forgive, as you have asked." (Numbers 14:17–20)

These verses are a restatement of the words articulated in Exodus 34:6–7 (known liturgically as the thirteen attributes), when Moses is afforded a glimpse of the Divine Presence. The verse "And now, let the power of the Eternal be great (*yigdal-na*), as You have spoken" (Numbers 14:17) was introduced by an unknown liturgist as a phrase to be recited at the time when Kaddish was voiced in prayer. The word *yigdal*, which calls for the divine Power to be increased or made great, has the same verbal root as the opening word of the Kaddish (*yitgaddal*).

Along with this verse, a line from Psalms was also added. Similar to Moses' plea following the incident of the episode of the golden calf,[6] the author of Psalm 25 calls upon God to disclose the path of the Divine and to offer personal forgiveness:

Let me know Your ways, Eternal; teach me Your paths. Lead me in Your truth and teach me, for You are the God of my salvation; for You I wait all day long. Remember Your mercy, Eternal, and Your love, for they are from old. Do not remember the sins and transgressions of my youth; remember me with Your love, for Your goodness' sake, O Eternal! (Psalm 25:4–7)

Verse 6 of this psalm ("Remember Your mercy, Eternal, and Your love, for they are from old") strikes a similar tone to the passage cited above from Numbers. Recited in relation to Kaddish, these two verses represent a plea for divine compassion and a desire to find a path to God.[7]

Rabbinic Sources

In rabbinic literature, the verse from Numbers (14:7) is cited in different imagined encounters between God and Moses. In one scene, Moses ascends to heaven and sees God elaborately decorating the letters of the Torah with small decorative crowns:

> Rabbi Joshua ben Levi said: When Moses ascended on high, he found the blessed Holy One affixing crowns on the letters [of the Torah]. [God] said to him, "Moses, is there no *shalom* in your town?" [Moses] replied, "Can a servant offer his master *shalom*?" [God] responded, "You should have assisted Me [by encouraging My efforts]." [Subsequently, Moses] said to [God], "And now, let the power of the Eternal be great, as You have spoken."[8]

Moses doesn't offer a greeting of *shalom* to God because he views this gesture as overly familiar. In response, God indicates that a greeting of *shalom* can provide encouragement, even for the Holy One. At their next meeting (in the rabbinic timetable, when the shattered tablets were replaced), Moses states: "Let the power of the Eternal be great." As God had indicated, this greeting by Moses has the possibility of inspiring increased divine effort and success—this time, for the forgiveness of the people of Israel after the failure of the mission of the spies sent to scout out the land.

This idea, that humans have the ability to augment or deplete divine power, is usually associated with later mystical writing. However, its roots lie in rabbinic thought.[9] It is articulated, for example, when contrasting the verse "You weakened the Rock that birthed you" (Deuteronomy 32:18) with the verse from Numbers (14:17):

> Rabbi Azariah taught in the name of Rabbi Judah son of Rabbi Simon: When Israel does the will of the [One who is]

Present, they add strength to the Power above, as is written,
"We shall act valiantly for God" (Psalm 60:14). And when
Israel does not do the will of the [One who is] Present, it is as
if they weaken the strength of the Power above, as is written,
"You weakened the Rock that birthed you" (Deuteronomy
32:18). Rabbi Judah the son of Rabbi Simon taught in the
name of Rabbi Levi the son of Rabbi Tarfon: When Israel
does the will of the blessed Holy One, they add strength
to the Power above, as is written, "And now, let the power
of the Eternal be great" (Numbers 14:17). And when they
do not do the will of the blessed Holy One, it is as if they
weaken the strength of the Power above.[10]

According to Moshe Idel, this passage is an example of
"augmentation theurgy" found in rabbinic literature, which "assumes
a direct dependence of the power of the divine *Dynamis* upon
human activity."[11] Using the qualifier *ki-v'yakhol* ("as if to say"),
these midrashim indicate a belief that sin diminishes the strength of
the divine Power (what Idel calls the *Dynamis*), while fulfilling the
commandments contributes energy or strength to the divine Power.

In another biblical scene, this one described in Exodus 34:8,
Moses hurriedly bows his head and prostrates himself as he finds
himself in God's presence. The anonymous voice of the Talmud asks
what Moses saw that led him to bow down:

Rabbi Ḥanina ben Gamla said: [Moses] saw slow-to-anger
[as one of the aspects of Divinity]. The rabbis said: [Moses]
saw [the attribute of divine] truth. In support of the opinion
that claims that [Moses] noticed slow-to-anger: When he
ascended on high, he found the blessed Holy One sitting
and writing "slow-to-anger." [Moses] said, "Sovereign of
the universe! Slow-to-anger [should be reserved] for the
righteous." [God] replied, "Even for the wicked." [Moses]
said, "Let the wicked perish!" [God] said, "You will see what
you desire."

When Israel sinned [with the golden calf, God] said to [Moses], "Didn't you say to me that slow-to-anger should be [reserved] for the righteous?" [Moses] responded, "Sovereign of the universe! Didn't You say [this included even] the wicked? As it is written, 'And now, let the power of the Eternal be great, as You have spoken' (Numbers 14:17)."[12]

In this scenario, Moses is again in dialogue with God. The issue is not how to address or add support to God, but rather which aspect of the divine personality was particularly notable and how that characteristic would pertain to God's relationship to human beings.

Here, the question is whether the compassionate quality of God's patience, slow-to-anger, should be restricted to the righteous or extended to the wicked. While initially Moses thinks that slow-to-anger should apply only to good people, after the sin of the golden calf he comes to understand that it has merit and value for the entire Jewish people—including the wicked. In the Book of Numbers, as part of his plea to God, he says, "And now, let the power of the Eternal be great, as You have spoken." For Moses, as understood by this rabbinic source, divine power is expressed with anger restrained. Out of the dialogue, the divine personality is revealed.[13] The pathway to divine power is identified with patience.[14]

In the Pesikta D'rav Kahana, a linkage is developed between the theology of augmentation and the one that emphasizes divine patience:

Rabbi Jacob bar Aḥa, in the name of Rabbi Yoseh the son of Rabbi Ḥanina, and the rabbis in the name of Rabbi Yoḥanan taught: "May Your armies of compassion be strengthened. Let the attribute of compassion prevail over the attribute of justice. 'And now, let the power of the Eternal be great.'"[15]

Idel comments: "The augmentation of power is to be channeled to the attribute of mercy, in order for it to prevail over the attribute of judgment....The focus of interest is no longer upon the increase of power in the Godhead; human activity is now directed toward assuring the prevalence of one of the divine attributes over another."[16]

Based on a talmudic observation by Rabbi Joshua ben Levi, that when the words of Kaddish are recited "with all one's might, any [negative] decree against [them] will be ripped up,"[17] the emphasis on the intentioned passion of the individual became significant. At a later date, the recitation of Kaddish with intent was understood to invoke the power (ko·aḥ) of the divine Name; ko·aḥ and kavvanah (intent) were identified with one another.[18]

The theurgic power of ritual, prayer, and meditation on the divine Name became a major motif in kabbalistic literature. Medieval kabbalists understood God to have a tzorekh gavo·ah, a divine necessity, for human action, with the system of commandments as the means to respond to this divine need. Belief in the ability of humanity to alter the nature of the Divine and to repair the primary unity of the created world integrated conceptual and action-based theology.[19] For example, the Zohar speaks of adding to or detracting from the power and strength of God:

> For when the deeds of Israel are improper, they weaken, as it were, the power of the blessed Holy One; when deeds are proper, they provide power and might to the blessed Holy One. Of this is written, "Give strength to God" (Psalm 68:35). How? By proper actions.[20]

This comment reflects and reinforces the earlier midrashic discussion.

In the Idra Zutra section of the Zohar, there is a specific reference to the verse "And now, let the power [of the Eternal] be great." This section includes reports of the mystical visions related by Rabbi Simon bar Yoḥai to his circle in the gathering at a threshing floor (*idra* in Aramaic means "threshing floor"), many of which related to the anatomy of God:

> All the hairs of the beard of Ze·ir Anpin[21] are coarse and harsh; for they all subdue the aspects of judgment when the holy *mazal*[22] is revealed, and when [God] prepares to go to war. With this beard, [God] appeared as a warrior, a resolute man of war, regardless of whether [the beard] is pulled off or shaved, no matter who pulls off or shaves [the beard]. Those nine enhancements were said by Moses at the second time, when he should have transformed all of them to compassion. Even though the thirteen attributes were not articulated now, before beginning to mention the attributes he intended and mentioned them with *mazal*.[23] This is what is meant by "And now, give strength to God" (Psalm 68:35). Who is the *ko·aḥ ha-sheim* ("the strength of the Divine")? The One who is called the sacred *mazal*[24] is the most sealed of all that is sealed. For this *ko·aḥ* and enlightenment depend on *mazal*; he stated the nine enhancements that depend on Ze·ir Anpin, to illuminate them all, and not have any expression of judgment. Therefore, we say that everything depends on *mazal*.[25]

According to this extremely opaque text, the nine aspects of divine compassion articulated by Moses in the Book of Numbers (after the episode of the spies), as opposed to the thirteen attributes of mercy mentioned in Exodus (after the golden calf), needed the extra "strength of God" to augment the missing four elements of compassion. That strength—identified with *mazal* as an expression of the divine personality—is also associated with the beard of the Divine and adds the four forms of compassion already found in Arikh Anpin, the Patient One. Here, strength is associated with the compassionate identity of the Godhead.[26]

In Jewish Prayer

Prayer is a call from the individual to God and an affirmation of communal theology, as conveyed in regular repeated liturgy. While liturgy was more fluid in the early rabbinic period, it gradually became more defined and determined. At some point, the phrase "And now, let the power of the Eternal be great, as You have spoken" was added as a congregational preface or response to the words of the Kaddish.[27] The dating of this addition is uncertain, but it was clearly before the mid-eighth century C.E.

One of the earliest prayerbooks was edited by Rabbi Amram ben Sheshna (d. 875), the head of the Babylonian academy of Sura, in the middle of the ninth century. He indicates that there should be no interruptions between the conclusion of the early morning psalms (i.e., the section of the service today called P'sukei D'Zimra) and the blessings prior to the proclamation of the unity of God (the Shema). However, he notes that while some liturgies do insert a short Kaddish prior to the Bar'khu, the call to prayer, the *yigdal-na* verses (i.e., Numbers 14:17 followed by Psalm 25:6) should *not* be inserted preceding the Kaddish.[28] He viewed them as a clear interruption in the halakhically mandated liturgy. His opposition indicates that there already was an existing tradition that associated the *yigdal-na* verses with the short Kaddish.

That is confirmed by a comment in the prayerbook of Rashi (1040–1105), which records the instruction of Rav Amram to proceed immediately from the morning psalms to the Shema and its blessings, without interposing other prayers or verses. Rashi also notes a tradition, which he apparently opposes, that the congregation recites the *yigdal-na* verses as the leader begins Kaddish.[29]

The prayerbook of Rabbi David Abudarham (c. 1340), which represents the Spanish tradition, notes that the congregational response to the prayer leader's invocation of the divine Name, "May the great Name be praised forever and ever," contains twenty-eight letters. Hebrew uses the letters of the alphabet to express numerals; consequently, words may have numerical value and numerals may be understood as words. In this system of Hebrew numerology (known as *gematriya*), the number twenty-eight is the numerical equivalent of the word *ko·aḥ*, which means "strength." Thus, there appears to be a connection developed between the Kaddish and the notion of divine power.[30]

In his great halakhic code Arbaah Turim, Rabbi Jacob ben Asher (1270–c. 1340, popularly called the Tur, after the shortened title of his famous work) comments that the reason for including the word "consolation" (*neḥemata*) in the Kaddish is because of the hope for an end to exile. Moreover, for that reason, some people

> were accustomed to recite "Remember Your mercy, O Eternal" as the prayer leader begins Kaddish, to invoke the attribute of compassion at that moment. Similarly, one recites the verse "And now, let the power [of the Eternal] be great," which is related to the language of *yitgaddal* ["may God's Name be made great," at the beginning to Kaddish] recited by the prayer leader.[31]

It seems that Rabbi ben Asher was familiar with the additional phrases and their inclusion by the congregation. Rabbi Joseph Karo (1488–1575), the author of the extensive legal commentary called the *Beit Yosef*, does not take note of the custom to recite *yigdal-na* in his legal digest, the Shulḥan Arukh. However, Rabbi Moses Isserles (1520–1572), whose glosses on Karo's Shulḥan Arukh added the traditions and customs of Ashkenazic Jewry to the Sephardic work of Rabbi Karo, notes "And when [the prayer leader] begins *yitgaddal*, one should recite 'And now, let the power [of the Eternal] be great,' and 'Be mindful of Your mercy.'"[32] A glance at various prayerbooks indicates that the two-verse phrase was included in many prayerbooks during this period of time, going beyond any single community liturgy.

However, Rabbi Ḥayyim Joseph David Azulai (1724–1806, called the Ḥida), known for his exceptional erudition and extensive citation of earlier sources, reports an old tradition of opposition to the practice.

On page 5 of the book *Tz'ror Ḥayyim* (by Ḥayyim Yaakov ben Yaakov David of Tudela, 14th century), the author writes:

> There are people who recite "Let the power of the Eternal be great" when the *ḥazzan* begins Kaddish. I heard from my teacher the Rashba [Rabbi Shlomo ben Aderet, 1235–1310] who heard from his teacher Ramban [Rabbi Moses ben Naḥman, 1194–1270] that one should not say anything [at all at that moment in the prayer service]. However, people were accustomed [and allowed] to recite "Remember Your mercy," since it states in Berakhot that when one states "Amen, may the great Name be praised" that [God approvingly] nods His head. Our grandfather, the pious Rabbi Abraham ben Mordecai Azulai [1570–1643], author of the *Ḥesed L'avraham*, also ruled in this way in his glosses.[33]

The debate seems to have crystallized between those who saw a liturgical association between the verse from Numbers and the Kaddish prayer, and others who contended that there should be no interruption in the liturgy by non-mandated words.[34]

Surprising to me, given the Zoharic reading of the biblical verse *yidgal-na* and Rabbi Karo's acceptance of the custom, is the report that two great kabbalists, Rabbi Isaac Luria (1534–1572, called the Ari) and Rabbi Isaiah Horowitz (1565–1630, called the Shelah after his most important book, the *Sh'nei Luḥot Ha-b'rit*), also opposed the recitation of these verses in conjunction with Kaddish:

Rabbi Isaac Luria did not want people to say this [phrase]. He would become so excited that he would actually stutter, stating that it was not among the enhancements [i.e., acceptable meditations], so it should not be recited between [the prayers] Yishtabaḥ and [the first blessing before the recitation of the Shema, called] Yotzeir [in the morning service], between [the blessing after the Shema called] Ge'ulah and the Amidah [during the evening service], or any place when it would be prohibited to interrupt [the flow of the liturgy]. And see also the *Sh'nei Luḥot Ha-b'rit* of Rabbi Isaiah Horowitz and the *Bayit Ḥadash* of Rabbi Joel Sirkis [1561–1640], section 236, in the name of Rabbi Solomon Luria[35] [1510–1574]. [However,] in a responsum [that same] Rabbi Solomon Luria wrote that it may be recited between Yishtabaḥ and Yotzeir].[36]

These rulings apparently carried the day for later Ashkenazic authorities, although they do allow the phrase to be added to the Full Kaddish (also called Kaddish Titkabbeil), an expanded version of the Kaddish that is recited only at the conclusion of a major section of the prayer service.[37] Sephardic prayerbooks often include the phrase.[38]

We Need Each Other

In considering what including the phrase *yigdal-na* might mean for us, it is helpful to turn to the divine Name, which is the subject of the verse "And now, let the power of the Eternal be great." Hillel Ben-Sasson, a contemporary Jewish thinker, points to the difference between the rabbinic understanding of the disclosure of the divine Name at the burning bush and the philosophical conception of the Tetragrammaton, the biblical four-letter name of God. When the rabbis sought to explain what the four-letter Name means, they understood it as expressing a relationship, a familial affinity. The later declaration of the thirteen attributes of God (after the golden calf narrative) and the abbreviated re-articulation of those attributes (after the narrative of the spies and the statement *yigdal-na*) reinforce the idea of relationship. At the same time that the rabbis were speaking about relationship, though, Jews in the Hellenistic world were reconceptualizing what the Name of God meant. From an ineffable four-letter word, from the intimate name for a personal deity, came the idea that the four-letter Name represented an eternal being. The results of this encounter, initially developed by the third-century B.C.E. translators of the Septuagint[39] and the Hellenistic thinker and commentator Philo (25 B.C.E.–50 C.E.), were carried into the writings of the church fathers and eventually into medieval philosophers of all three monotheistic religions. God became a non-personal, eternal idea, uninvolved in this world, "the unmoved mover."[40]

The influence of Maimonides has been felt in every generation since his monumental works of *halakhah* and philosophy were first composed and disseminated.[41] This was certainly true in the last century when Hermann Cohen, Leo Strauss, Rabbi Joseph Soloveitchik, and Rabbi David Hartman, among others, each reacted to or built upon the Maimonidean philosophical worldview. But at the close of the twentieth century, due to the influence of Rabbi Abraham Joshua Heschel, mystical thought was beginning to reanimate Jewish theology.[42] Moving beyond the specific halakhic debate about whether Numbers 14:17 and Psalm 25:6 should be included in the Kaddish, what meaning might contemporary Jews find in the ideas of divine need (as exemplified by the verse "Let the power of the Eternal be great") and divine concern (as expressed in the verse "Be mindful of Your mercy")?

Heschel's doctoral thesis on the prophets of ancient Israel was published initially in Germany and, after the Holocaust and his resettlement in the United States, revised and reissued in English. In it, he introduced the idea of divine pathos to theological language. Forcefully rejecting the Aristotelianism of Maimonides, Heschel not only claimed that the biblical God was "moved and affected by what happens in the world, and reacts accordingly," but that this was the key idea of biblical religion and of Judaism.[43]

In a 1949 essay on Jewish mysticism, Heschel discussed rabbinic texts that imagine humanity having the "privilege, as it were, to augment the Divine in the world…[and suggest that] not only is God necessary to man but that man is also necessary to God." Heschel linked midrashic texts to later Zoharic sources which state that "man's relationship to God should not be that of passive reliance on His Omnipotence but that of active assistance…[human] actions are vital to all worlds, and affect the course of transcendent events….Now the act below stimulates a corresponding activity above….The significance of great works done on earth is valued by their cosmic effects."[44]

Reuven Kimelman notes, "Unlike Gershom Scholem and Martin Buber, who saw in Kabbalah a gnostic phenomenon that deviated from the biblical and rabbinic traditions, Heschel saw in this body of medieval mysticism a reformulation of the rabbis' concept of God's dependence on man."[45] In his later work on rabbinic theology, when discussing a statement by Rabbi Judah the Patriarch that we need each other, Heschel restates this continuity from biblical to rabbinic to mystical thought, as follows:

> In the phrase "we need each other" is embedded the concept of Israel's power to diminish or enhance God's might. This opinion, which served as a cornerstone of kabbalistic teaching, is already alluded to in a homily in Sifrei…[and] achieved its classic formulation in the mouth of R. Judah ben Simon, an

amora of the third to fourth generation of Eretz Israel: "As long as the righteous comply with the divine will they augment the Power above"….According to the Zohar, this idea is intimated in the verse "Give might to God" (Psalm 68:35).[46]

As Kimelman shows, these ideas are central to Heschel's works of constructive theology, *Man Is Not Alone* and *God in Search of Man*.[47]

Heschel made this clear in a presentation to Jewish educators on Jewish theology, when he stated:

> God is in need of man. The idea of God being in need of man is central to Judaism and pervades all the pages of the Bible and of *Chazal*,[48] of talmudic literature, and it is understandable in our own time….In the light of this idea, of God being in need of man, you have to entirely revise all the clichés that are used in religious language….Without the principle of God in search of man, the whole idea of *Shekinah* [sic] is not intelligible…. It permeates rabbinic literature and post-rabbinic thought in Judaism, and it is missing in our discussion and in Maimonides's list of dogmas. Actually the idea of pathos, which I consider to be the central idea in prophetic theology, contains the doctrine of the *Shekinah*….Without an understanding of the idea of *Shekinah* we fail completely to understand the field of Jewish theology or the theme of God in search of man, which I consider to be the summary of Jewish theology.[49]

Heschel has consolidated the diverse details of kabbalistic theurgy, conceptualizing the core idea of Judaism as the interactive relationship between the Divine and the human.[50] This could also be understood as a reformulation, writ large, of the theology implicit in *yigdal-na*.

While Heschel downplayed the details of Lurianic Kabbalah

in favor of a hasidic reading of the mystical tradition, Hans Jonas (1903–1993), another European transplant to North America, built upon the general scaffolding of the Lurianic myth to construct his own philosophical understanding of the interdependence of the Divine and the human. Like Heschel, Jonas had lost most of his family during the Holocaust; his early studies of gnosticism led him to a profound embrace of the unity of all life. His later writings on the philosophy of biology and environmental ethics argue for an integration of the material and moral aspects of nature.[51] The linkage of the physical and biological elements of our world entail human ethical responsibility for the continuity of life on earth.

Turning to philosophical theology, Jonas contends that the notion of a God who *voluntarily* limits divine power is insufficient in the wake of Auschwitz. Instead, he believes that the "existence and autonomy" of the world and full human responsibility for history and Holocaust *necessitate* divine self-denial and self-limitation in the very act of creation.[52] Using the Lurianic idea of *tzimtzum*, divine contraction, Jonas states:

> Without this retreat into himself, there could be no "other" outside God, and only his continued holding-himself-in preserves the finite things from losing their separate being again into the divine "all in all."[53]

As did Heschel, Jonas rejects the abstract, omnipotent God as conceptualized by Maimonidean-Aristotelian thought in favor of a suffering, becoming, and caring God, "emerging in time instead of possessing a completed being that remains identical with itself throughout eternity….[God's] continual relation to the creation, once this exists and moves in the flux of becoming, means that he experiences something with the world, that his own being is affected by what goes on in it."[54] Jonas explains that "by the events of Auschwitz, I was impelled to the view…that it is not God who can help us, but we who must help God."[55]

Discussing what he terms "the wager of creation,"[56] Jonas contends that "the Infinite ceded his power to the finite and thereby wholly delivered his cause into its hands.…God has no more to give: it is man's now to give to him."[57] He cites the diary of Etty Hillesum, a young Dutch Jew who was murdered in Auschwitz, who wrote, "If God does not continue to help me, then I must help God…as well as I can.…With almost every heartbeat it becomes clearer to me that you cannot help us, but that we must help you and defend up to the last your dwelling within us."[58]

Just as every living entity, from microbe to human life, shows concern for its own survival, Jonas claims for humanity full responsibility for the future of life. Through that imperative and our power, "the cause of God trembles in the balance."[59] While Jonas rejects the abstract and omnipotent Maimonidean God, he does accept—with all the caveats of philosophical thought after Hume and Kant—a type of Maimonidean natural theology that brings together biology, chemistry, physics, and metaphysics. In this contemporary conception of God, we see a turn toward science for the *yigdal-na* idea that humanity can somehow augment the power of the Divine.

The integration of scientific thought, a rejection of Maimonidean omnipotence, and the dependence of God on human action is also articulated in the recent work of Rabbi Bradley Artson. He imagines humanity and God "in continuous, dynamic change, of related interaction and becoming," transforming chaos into cosmos.[60] Artson carries this theological interdependence further than either Heschel or Jonas:

> The world, then, is self-created and self-creating. The cosmos is a partner with God in the becoming. We are partners with

the cosmos and with God in our own becoming....God is infinite in how God is in potential prior to creation. Having created, God enters into relationship with us, and in entering into relationship there are aspects of God that are finite.... God is separate from creation in some respects, and in some respects, part of the creation....God works with and through material reality. The universe is not merely passive stuff that God molds into shape; it is a co-creating universe.[61]

Artson points toward cosmological research that indicates a gradual development—over billions of years—from structures of a lower order, to the development of a higher order. He reviews the change from the chaotic explosion of a singular point of dark energy to progressive differentiation into atoms of hydrogen and carbon, to more specific elements, inorganic compounds, and crystals. Eventually, this leads to astronomical, atmospheric, and biological cycles that build their own continuity. He sees God in the emerging novelty and increasing complexity of the cosmos.

Through this evolving process, Artson contends that human beings have a responsibility to act—both ritually and ethically—to bring joy and justice, love and life into the totality of the cosmos. Our actions add moral value to the universe, which he identifies as God. Paradoxically, as Artson seeks to shift away from an abstract Maimonidean deity to a more relational God, he simultaneously situates humanity within a cosmic process that many would see as impersonal.

Both from a scientific and social perspective, as well as from what I term the *yigdal-na* viewpoint, humans are not simply passive in this cosmological process. We are part of the woof and warp of the universe. A *yigdal-na* model of human-divine interaction need not require the type of mythic elaboration that Rabbi Isaac Luria brought to his vision of the Godhead, although it draws from the extended tradition that Heschel described and articulated. The way that Heschel, Jonas, and Artson speak of God's need for human action is a softer expression than a full Lurianic articulation of human intervention through deeds, words, and thoughts in the life of God and the perfection of the cosmos.

In different iterations of what is termed the "anthropic principle"—the notion that the natural processes of the universe are "just right" for conscious and sapient life—the possibility of human consciousness is understood as being part of, or inherent in, the cosmic development.[62] Recent speculation also has looked to quantum entanglement—the idea that autonomous entities are somehow connected—as a way to provide a scientific grounding for this theological perspective. In quantum entanglement, two sub-atomic particles become twinned in such a way that the measurement of one always determines the properties of the other, no matter how far apart they may be in space or time. As explored by John Polkinghorne and others, this suggests that physical distance may not matter and that the universe is deeply relational in character. As humanity goes through the cognitive, agricultural, and scientific revolutions that have changed us, we also change the world around us.[64]

The way we think of God affects the way we understand our religious practices. If we conceptualize God as having a personality, emotions, and being directly accessible to us, this affects our thoughts during prayer, our belief in miracles, our acceptance of prophecy, and our ability to focus intently on ritual behavior, without being distracted by doubts concerning the reality of the God we are trying to serve. On the other hand, if we think of God as an eternal and unmoved Being, or as a dynamic natural Process, then God is properly discovered through science, mathematics, and cosmic order; personal intention is insignificant and prayer does not—indeed, cannot—affect God.

I have found myself shuttling back and forth between these two approaches. I believe that God works through the constancy of physics and chemistry, as well as through the evolutionary novelties of biological life, to create opportunities for human growth and development. But I also want to believe in a God who is more than a cosmic process. I yearn for a personal God of conscious concern and covenantal love who is affected by our intent, our words, and our actions. Can there be "togetherness in separation"?[65]

I look to the model of light, which can be understood and explained as a wave or as a series of individual particles (photons). It was Einstein who suggested, back in 1905, that light might best be understood as a wave/particle duality. Recently, an experiment captured the first photograph of light as both a particle and a wave.[66] Using this model, I have come to see God as both the cosmic ground of all existence operating through the stable systems of physics, chemistry, and biology, and also the intimate, compassionate God, a caring Companion whom we need and succor. "God will become as he will become, he will be what and however he wills, but even through change, the covenant remains."[67]

Yigdal-na, "And now, let the power of the Eternal be great, as You have spoken," might, in this way, apply both to the cosmic interconnection of humanity and God, and to the personal request for divine compassion. "Be mindful of Your mercy, O Eternal, and of Your steadfast love." The God of Being is simultaneously the God of Covenant.

NOTES

[1] See *Ḥazut Qashah: Faith, Felicity, and Fidelity in the Thought of Yiṣḥaq Arama* (DHL thesis, Jewish Theological Seminary [2004]), where I discuss the move away from Aristotelianism and the adoption of some non-technical kabbalistic ideas ("kabbalah light") by Spanish thinkers in the 1400s. The phrase "most moved mover" is Fritz Rothschild's; cf. his introduction to his *Between God and Man: An Interpretation of Judaism, From the Writings of Abraham Joshua Heschel* (New York: Harper, 1959), p. 25.

[2] Ezekiel 38:23:"So I shall magnify Myself (*v'hitgaddilti*) and sanctify Myself (*v'hitkaddishti*) and make Myself known in the eyes of many nations; then they shall know that I am the Eternal."This verse comes at the conclusion of a prophecy about the eschatological conflict of Gog and Magog.

[3] The response, "May [God's] great name be praised for ever, and to all eternity," is based on Daniel 2:20.

[4] See Stefan C. Reif, *Judaism and Hebrew Prayer* (Cambridge and New York: Cambridge University Press, 1993), p. 208. This "pattern of surrounding the statutory prayers with what are originally optional extras is not a novel one" and led to various versions of Kaddish, as well as the addition of biblical verses to the basic prayer.

[5] See, for example, *Siddur Sefat Emet*, 22nd edition, ed. Wolf Heidenheim (Rödelheim: S. Lehrberger & Co., 1906), p. 58.

[6] As found in Exodus 33:13–16, which reads as follows: "[Moses] said, 'Now, if I have found favor in Your sight, let me know Your ways, so that I may know You and find favor in your eyes. Also see that this nation is Your people.' [God] said, 'My presence will go with you, and I will give you rest.' And he said [to God], 'If Your presence will not go, do not bring us up from here. For how shall it be known that I have found favor in Your sight—I and Your people—unless You go with us? We shall be distinct—I and Your people—from every people on the face of the earth.'"

[7] B. Shabbat 119b states: "Those who hear the opening words of the Kaddish and respond with all their strength, *y'hei sh'meih rabba m'varakh* ("may the great name be praised forever"), have any [negative] decree [against them] ripped up." Apparently, the recitation of and response to Kaddish were linked to the idea of divine forgiveness and pardon.

[8] B. Shabbat 89a.

[9] In his essay on the history of the concept *tzorekh gavo·ah* ("divine necessity"), Yosef Avivi provides a short history of the talmudic sources that lie behind this mystical idea. Although initially this phrase refers to the needs of the Temple, it later comes to mean human actions to benefit the Divine. Avivi identifies the first use in this sense by Rabbi Moshe Ben Naḥman (1194–c.1270, called

Ramban), in the latter's commentary to Exodus 29:46. See Yosef Avivi, "History of Divine Need," in the *Festschrift in Honor of Rav Mordekhai Breur*, ed. M. Arend and M. Bar-Asher (Jerusalem: Akademon, 1992), pp. 1–48.

[10] Eikhah Rabbah 1:33.

[11] Moshe Idel, *Kabbalah: New Perspectives* (New Haven: Yale University Press, 1988), p. 158, uses the term *Dynamis* (from the Greek *dynamis*, Power) for *Gevurah* and contends that, in midrashic literature, the terms *gadol* ("great") or *gibbor* ("mighty"), otherwise standard *attributes* of God, transform into another *name* for the Divine: *Gevurah* (*Dynamis*).

[12] B. Sanhedrin 111b. Variations on this theme are found in Bemidbar Rabbah 16:22.

[13] See Jacob Neusner, *The Incarnation of God: The Character of Divinity in Formative Judaism* (Philadelphia: Fortress Press, 1988), p. 166 and *The Emergence of Judaism*, (Louisville, KY: Westminster John Knox Press, 2004), p. 82.

[14] Parallel sources are Midrash Tanḥuma (ed. S. Buber), *Sh'laḥ* §24; Midrash Tehillim (ed. Solomon Buber), §93; and Midrash Lekaḥ Tov, also known as Pesikta Zutrata (Jerusalem: Wagschal, 1986), *Sh'laḥ*, p. 214. See also Pirkei Avot 4:1, which identifies human power with self-control, and B. Megillah 31a, which links divine power to concern for the weak.

[15] Pesikta D'rav Kahana, ed. Bernard Mandelbaum (New York: Jewish Theological Seminary, 1985), § 25:1, s.v. *s'liḥot*; cf. *Pesikta de-Rab Kahana*. trans. William Braude and Israel Kapstein (Philadelphia: Jewish Publication Society, 1975), p. 513. The same group of rabbis associated with augmentation theology—Rabbi Simon, his son Rabbi Yudin, Rabbi Azariah, and Rabbi Levi—are cited in an adjacent midrash reprising the earlier statements about human actions and their ability to effect divine strength or weakness.

[16] Idel, *Kabbalah*, p. 164.

[17] B. Shabbat 119b.

[18] See the *Beit Yosef* commentary of Rabbi Joseph Karo (1488–1575) to A.T. Oraḥ Ḥayyim 56, who cites Rashi to this effect. See *Siddur Rashi*, ed. Solomon Buber (Berlin: Mekitzei Nirdamin, 1911), p.10. Yehuda Leibes examines three mystical usages of *ko·aḥ* in his Hebrew-language essay, "The Power of the Word as a Basis for Meaning in Kabbalistic Literature," in *Davar Davur al Ofanav* (*A Word Fitly Spoken: Studies in Medieval Exegesis of the Hebrew Bible and Qur'an in the Middle Ages Presented to Haggai Ben-Shammai*), eds. Meir Ben-Asher, Simon Hopkins, Sarah Strumsa, and Bruno Chiesa (Jerusalem: Ben Zvi Institute, 2007), pp. 163–177.

[19] Morris Faierstein, "'God's Need for the Commandments' in Medieval Kabbalah," *Conservative Judaism* 36:1 (Fall 1982), pp.45–59. See also Byron L. Sherwin, *Kabbalah* (Lanham: Rowman & Littlefield, 2006), pp. 105–117.

[20] Zohar II 32b, trans. Daniel Matt (Stanford: Stanford University Press),

vol. 4, p. 138. See also Zohar II 64a, p. 348. The Ze·ir Anpin references the "Lesser Countenance" of the Impatient One, the kabbalistic configuration of divine attributes cast in the heavenly pleroma as the embodiment of the short-tempered aspects of divine judgment.

[22] *Mazal* means star, planet, or constellation. In rabbinic literature, it refers to planetary influence, leading to the concept of *mazal* as luck or good fortune. There is a talmudic dispute in B. Shabbat 156a as to whether the people Israel is affected by such influence: "Rabbi Ḥanina said: Planetary influence gives wisdom and...wealth, and Israel stands under planetary influence. Rabbi Yoḥanan maintained: Israel is unaffected by planetary influence." In the Zohar, in addition to the notion of planetary influence, *mazal* refers to visage or *partzuf* of the divine personality. That is the intent in this sentence. Elsewhere in our text, the Zohar will present a wordplay using the same term in multiple ways.

[23] Here, *mazal* means "good fortune."

[24] Here, *mazal* means " aspect of the divine personality."

[25] Here, mazal means "good fortune"; Zohar III 295b (my translation).

[26] I am following the extended discussion by Leibes (in the essay cited above) about this difficult text.

[27] See Louis Jacobs, "The Kaddish Prayer," available online at www.myjewishlearning.com. Also see Hanoch Avnery and Rochelle L. Millen, "Kaddish," in *Encyclopaedia Judaica*, eds. Michael Berenbaum and Fred Skolnik (Detroit: Macmillan Reference USA, 2007), vol. 11, pp. 659–698.

[28] *Seder Rav Amram*, ed. Aryeh Frumkin (Jerusalem: Zukerman, 1912), chap.14, p. 184.

[29] *Siddur Rashi*, ed. Solomon Buber and Yaakov Freiman (Berlin: Mekitzei Nirdamim, 1912), p. 8.

[30] Later commentators will note that the seven words and twenty-eight letters of the central phrase of Kaddish, *y'hei sh'meih rabba m'varakh l'alam u-l'almei almaya*, "May God's great name be praised for all time," are parallel to the seven words and twenty-eight letters of Genesis 1:1 and Exodus 20:1. Thus, reciting Kaddish becomes an affirmation of creation and revelation. Cf. the material by Rabbi Dr. Dovid Fox presented at http://thoughtonparsha.blogspot.ca/2015/02/a-thought-on-parshas-yisro.html.

[31] A.T. Oraḥ Ḥayyim 56.

[32] Even though it was opposed by Rabbi Jacob ben Moses Levi Moelin (1365–1427, called the Maharil), who served a source of Ashkenazic law and tradition for Rabbi Isserles.

[33] *Birkei Yosef* to SA Oraḥ Ḥayyim 56:4 (ed. Livorno 5534 [1773–1774]), p. 18a. The talmudic reference is to B. Berakhot 3a.

[34] Dror Fixler, "D'rashot lifnei Musaf," Hamaayan 46:2 (5766 [2005/2006]), pp. 43–47, suggests that some authorities viewed the short Kaddish as beginning

a new section of prayer, while others saw it as concluding the previous section of prayers. If so, for the latter, adding the two additional verses prior to Kaddish would disrupt the order as it draws to a conclusion. For the former, adding the two additional verses while the leader has already begun the Kaddish would violate the framework of what had just begun.

[35] Unrelated to Rabbi Isaac Luria.

[36] *Magen Avraham* 56:7 and *Be'eir Heiteiv* ad loc.

[37] See, for example, *Siddur T'fillah* (Jerusalem: Koren, 1992), p. 61.

[38] See the *Orah Ha-shulhan* by Rabbi Yeḥiel Mikhel Epstein (1829–1908), Oraḥ Ḥayyim 56:9; the *Mishnah B'rurah* commentary by Rabbi Yisrael Meir Kagan (1838–1933), Oraḥ Ḥayyim 56:10–11; Elie Munk, *Olam Ha-t'fillot* (Jerusalem: Mossad Harav Kook, 1974), pp. 195–196 (now in English in the translation of G. Hirschler as *World of Prayer* [New York: Feldheim, 1961], vol. 1, p. 186); and Macy Nulman, *The Encyclopedia of Jewish Prayer* (Northvale, NJ: Jason Aronson, 1993), p. 187. And see also Avraham Landau, *Tz'lota D'Avraham* (Tel Aviv: Mintzer, 1958), p. 415, who elegantly summarizes the gamut of halakhic literature and notes that the phrase does remain within many Sephardic and Mizraḥi liturgies.

[39] The Greek translation of the Hebrew Scriptures.

[40] Hillel Ben-Sasson, "On the Subject of the Divine," in *Post-Subjectivity*, eds. Christoph Schmidt, with Merav Mack and Andy R. German (Newcastle upon Tyne: Cambridge Scholars Pub., 2014), pp. 221–241. Also see Hillel Ben-Sasson, "What Is God's Name?" available online on the website of the Shalom Hartman Institute at http://hartman.org.il.

[41] James A. Diamond, *Maimonides and the Shaping of the Jewish Canon* (New York: Cambridge University Press, 2014).

[42] Reuven Kimelman, "Abraham Joshua Heschel's Theology of Judaism and the Rewriting of Jewish Intellectual History," *Journal of Jewish Thought and Philosophy* 17:2 (2009), pp. 207–238. This trend can be seen in the recent works of Michael Fishbane, *Sacred Attunement: A Jewish Theology* (Chicago: University of Chicago Press, 2008); Byron L. Sherwin, *Faith Finding Meaning: A Theology of Judaism* (Oxford and New York: Oxford University Press, 2009); and Arthur Green, *Radical Judaism: Rethinking God and Tradition* (New Have: Yale University Press, 2010). Sherwin and Green were students of Heschel at the Jewish Theological Seminary, and Fishbane was deeply influenced by Heschel's thought.

[43] *The Prophets* (New York: Harper and Row, 1962), vol. 2, p. 4. See the quotation below from "Jewish Theology."

[44] Abraham Joshua Heschel, "The Mystical Element in Judaism," in Louis Finkelstein, *The Jews: Their Religion and Culture* (New York: Harper and Row, 1949), vol. 2, pp. 157–159.

[45] Reuven Kimelman, "The Theology of Abraham Joshua Heschel," *First Things*

198 (December 2009), pp. 35–39. And see also his "Abraham Joshua Heschel's Thesis on the Unity of Jewish Theology," *Tikkun* (November/December 2009), pp. 48–50 and 74.

[46] Abraham J. Heschel, *Torah Min Ha-shamayim B'ispiklaria shel Ha-dorot* (London and New York: Soncino, 1965), vol. 1, pp. 74–75, partially quoted in Heschel, *Heavenly Torah*, ed. and trans. Gordon Tucker (New York; Continuum, 2005), p. 113. The passage references Sifrei Bemidbar §319 and Zohar II 33a. See also Pesikta Rabbati 31:5 (144b).

[47] Kimelman notes that Heschel made the connection explicit when he wrote that the idea of pathos "is an explication of the idea of God in search of man." See Heschel, "Jewish Theology," in *Moral Grandeur and Spiritual Audacity*, ed. Susannah Heschel (New York: Farrar, Straus & Giroux, 1996), p. 160. See also Byron L. Sherwin, *Kabbalah*, p. 27.

[48] A Hebrew acronym for "our sages of blessed memory" (sometimes written in English as "Ḥazal").

[49] "Jewish Theology", pp. 159–160. See Kimelman, "Abraham Joshua Heschel's Theology of Judaism and the Rewriting of Jewish Intellectual History," *Journal of Jewish Thought and Philosophy* 17:2 (2009), pp. 207–238, who notes the relational quality of this concept.

[50] Moshe Idel, "Abraham Heschel on Mysticism and Hasidism," in *Old World, New Mirrors* (Philadelphia: University of Pennsylvania Press, 2010), pp. 217–233, also examines the different approaches of Scholem and Heschel. He sees Heschel's idea of mystical "exaltation" as combining the personal and experiential elements of mysticism with *mitzvah* observance that affects external reality. Rather than seeing Heschel as consolidating differing concepts of theurgy, he argues that Heschel marginalized the theurgic elements of medieval Kabbalah in favor of a hasidic reading that "consists of a more psychological understanding of the structure of the divine realm" (p. 220).

[51] Hans Jonas, *The Phenomenon of Life: Toward a Philosophical Biology* (New York: Harper & Row, 1966) and *The Imperative of Responsibility: In Search of Ethics for the Technological Age* (Chicago: University of Chicago Press, 1984).

[52] Although Jonas states that this is "stammering" and that his speculation borders on the heretical, this is because he identifies Maimonides' understanding of Judaism with the "oldest Judaic teaching." His usage of Lurianic Kabbalah, however, is indicative that he was aware of a counter-tradition, one more fully explored by Heschel. See Shoshanah Ronen, "Absolute Goodness or Omnipotence: God after Auschwitz in the Theology of Abraham J. Heschel and Hans Jonas," in *Abraham Joshua Heschel: Philosophy, Theology, and Interreligious Dialogue*, eds. Stanislaw Krajewski and Adam Lipszyc (Wiesbaden: Harrassowitz, 2009), pp. 137–144.

[53] Hans Jonas, "The Concept of God after Auschwitz: A Jewish Voice," in *Mortality and Morality: A Search for the Good after Auschwitz*, ed. Lawrence

Vogel (Evanston, IL: Northwestern University Press, 1996), pp. 131–143; the quoted passage appears on p. 142.

[54] Hans Jonas, "The Concept of God after Auschwitz," p. 137.

[55] Jonas, "Matter, Mind, and Creation: Cosmological Evidence and Cosmogonic Speculation," in *Mortality and Morality*, p. 191.

[56] "Matter, Mind, and Creation," p. 197.

[57] "The Concept of God after Auschwitz," p. 142.

[8] Etty Hillesum, *An Interrupted Life: The Diaries of Etty Hillesum 1941–43* (New York: Pantheon, 1984), cited in *Mortality and Morality*, pp. 142 and 192.

[59] "Matter, Mind, and Creation," p. 197.

[60] Bradley Shavit Artson, "*Ba-derekh*: On the Way—A Presentation of Process Theology," *Conservative Judaism* 62:1–2 (Fall–Winter 2010), pp. 3–35. See also his *God of Becoming and Relationship: The Dynamic Nature of Process Theology* (Woodstock, VT: Jewish Lights Publishing, 2013).

[61] Artson, *God of Becoming and Relationship*, p. 25.

[62] See William Craig, "The Teleological Argument and the Anthropic Principle," in *The Logic of Rational Theism: Exploratory Essays*, eds. William Lane Craig and Mark S. McLeod (Lewiston, NY: Edwin Mellen, 1990), pp. 127–153. For a discussion of some Jewish voices on this topic and its implications, see these three essays by Lawrence Troster: "The Love of God and the Anthropic Principle," *Conservative Judaism* 40:2 (Winter, 1987–1988), pp. 43–51; "From Big Bang to Omega Point: Jewish Responses to Recent Theories in Modern Cosmology," *Conservative Judaism* 49:4 (Summer 1997), pp. 17–33; and "Magic, Monotheism, and Natural Evil," in *Routledge Companion to Religion and Science*, eds. James W. Haag, Gregory R. Peterson, and Michael L. Spezio (New York: Routledge, 2012), pp. 259–269. See also Jonas, "Matter, Mind, and Creation," pp. 165–197.

[63] Zeeya Merali, "The Priest-Physicist Who Would Marry Science to Religion," *Discover* (March 2011), available online at www.discoverymagazine.com. Also see George Musser, *Spooky Action at a Distance* (New York: Scientific American/ Farrar Strauss, 2015).

[64] See Yuval Noah Harari, *Sapiens: A Brief History of Humankind* (New York: Harper, 2015).

[65] John Polkinghorne, "Mysterious Universe," *ReSource Magazine* (Summer 2012), available online at www.resource-arm.net/pdf/polkinghornemystery.pdf.

[66] "The First Ever Photograph of Light as Both a Particle and Wave," available online at http://phys.org/news/2015-03-particle.html.

[67] Ben-Sasson, "On the Subject of the Divine," p. 241.

L'eilla L'eilla (Higher and Higher): The Kaddish as Allusion to *Tikkun*

David A. Kunin

The Kaddish in all of its liturgical forms—Kaddish Yatom (the Mourner's Kaddish), Kaddish D'rabbanan (the Scholar's Kaddish), Ḥatzi Kaddish (the Half Kaddish), and Kaddish Shalem (the Complete Kaddish)—is at once one of the most recognized of Jewish prayers, and yet one of the most mysterious.[1] While the words sound familiar to us because they are so often repeated in the course of the synagogue service, actually reciting them correctly—and in Aramaic—is a challenge for many. Indeed, while Aramaic may have been familiar as the lingua franca of our ancestors, for us it only adds to the mystery of this prayer. The Kaddish's sonorous repetitive cadences cry out with forgotten hints from our people's past. It is almost a mystical incantation, where meaning is lost as its words draw us inward, or perhaps upward. Despite these mysteries, however, the Kaddish (in all its forms) helps to provide Jews with not only a sense of connection but also of common purpose, as we join together to create a world built on concepts of holiness (*k'dushah*). There is an underlying strength to the message of reciprocal obligation found within the Kaddish that is expressed both explicitly and implicitly in its words, rituals, and history. Each of these aspects of the Kaddish speak to the human mission stressed in its words, and each is a reminder that the fulfillment of its hopes is left to us rather than to God. Taken together they are a clarion call for human action.

At first glance, the prayer's purpose remains unclear. While originally a mere doxology intended to mark off sections of the prayer service (or the end of a teaching), today the most well-known version of the Kaddish (which dates only to the thirteenth century) addresses loss and memory, bereavement and the possibility of restoration. Despite this usage, as rabbis often tell their congregations, its words speak of the building of God's kingdom with no mention or even intimation of death. Perhaps it is this message of hope that provides comfort for mourners, or perhaps it is something even deeper than that. Perhaps it is the community of at least ten required for its recitation, which provides the Kaddish's true power. As the Kaddish is recited with its communal responses, the community speaks with one voice to the mourners, as if saying: "We are here with you in your time of pain. We are here to provide comfort, and to give you the strength to continue to stand with us and with God, as partners in the creation of God's kingdom."

These responses, in this way, are as important as the mourner's recitation of the prayer itself. They are a reminder that all Jews are part of a single people, and that when one suffers all suffer. They are a reminder that *kol yisrael areivim zeh ba-zeh*, that every Jew bears responsibility for every other Jew.[2] The responses are an affirmation to the mourners that life goes on, that the communal obligation for *tikkun olam* (that is, the "repair of the world"), expressed in the obligations of mutual responsibility, goes on.

Indeed, the Jewish concept of comfort is also rooted within the community. The recitation of the Kaddish and the observance of the laws governing the initial mourning week, colloquially called *shiva*, are times of communal support rather than isolation. This, perhaps, is hinted at in the prayer's very name. Kaddish, meaning "holy" or "sanctification" in Aramaic, is replete with meaning. Like the comfort provided by the prayer, holiness in the Jewish tradition is not found in isolation at some far-off ashram or hidden temple. Rather, it is most often found within the community. Bringing comfort, thus expressing and recognizing our interconnection with other humans, is one means of creating a holy community.

Hebrew, and other Semitic languages like Aramaic, are built on a system of verbal roots, which connect whole families of words and can thus hint at a whole spectrum of meaning. The root *kof-dalet-shin* (which generate the name Kaddish) is found throughout the Torah. One of its most striking usages is in *mikdash*, the word for the mobile sanctuary or tabernacle that, according to biblical tradition, was carried by the people Israel through the desert from Sinai to the Land of Israel, and its *aron* (ark), which was later enshrined in the Holy of Holies (*kodesh ha-kodashim*) in the First Temple in Jerusalem. God commands the people "Make me a *mikdash* so that I may dwell among them" (Exodus. 25:8). Does God really want a small box (such as the *aron*) as a dwelling-place, or is something else implied? Read more creatively, the text might be taken to mean, "Make Me a place defined by holiness, so that I may dwell among you." In other words: through your lives create a place of holiness, and I will then dwell within each of you. The creation of a place of holiness is, of course, a daunting lifelong task, far more difficult than the creation of a tabernacle—no matter how ornate. Yet, I suggest that the connections created by the communal interactive recitation of the Kaddish can play a central role in the creation of just such a sacred space.

Perhaps, on one level, the Kaddish is a reminder to the mourner (and to the community) that despite loss, the task of creating a world of holiness continues. And the Kaddish itself provides a hint to the means of fulfilling this task. In addition to the well known Mourner's Kaddish, there are several different versions of Kaddish, which fulfill different purposes in Jewish liturgy. Indeed, one of the most ancient (and still observed) usages of Kaddish was as a conclusion to a session of studying Torah. The recitation of Kaddish D'rabbanan emphasizes the holiness of the entire Torah, as a guide for human action. Ismar

Elbogan suggests that, as part of a complex development in usage, the Kaddish came to be recited at the time of a sage's death—perhaps signifying the end of his *torah*, but also recognizing that his teaching brought the (actual) Torah to life.[3] For many centuries, however, a somewhat shortened version of the Kaddish has been recited for the loss of close relatives.[4] The recitation of the Kaddish for every Jew may be a recognition that all Israel are part of a kingdom of priests, reminding us that all are equal in the sight of God, and it also acknowledges that Torah is only actualized when it is realized through the life of all the people. All Israel have the potential to be part of an *am kadosh*, a holy people.

Yet the word "Kaddish" also creates an intertextual link to a specific section of Torah, namely Leviticus 17–26, often called the Holiness Code. The Holiness Code contains a wide variety of laws, spanning both the ritual and the secular, which the biblical author states are necessary to create a holy society. The biblical text, however, does not actually define the concept of holiness (*k'dushah*).[5] Rather, it provides a hint of its meaning, stating: "You shall be holy (*k'doshim*) for I, the Eternal your God, am holy (*kadosh*)" (Leviticus 19:2). The verse suggests that holiness is not merely a state of being, but rather is actualized only through action. It suggests that we achieve holiness when we model our lives, to the best of our abilities, after our perception of God's actions in the world.

This understanding of holiness—that is, as a status that can be achieved from imitation of God's actions—is found throughout rabbinic literature. One talmudic text describes God's activities, as depicted in several biblical stories, as models for our behavior:

As God clothes the naked [Adam and Eve], you should clothe the naked. As the blessed Holy One visited the sick [Abraham, following his circumcision], you should visit the sick. As the blessed Holy One comforted mourners [Isaac, after the death of Abraham, and Aaron, after the death of his two sons], you too should comfort mourners. As the blessed Holy One buried the dead [Moses was buried by God], you should bury the dead.[6]

Each of the behaviors included in this text by which we imitate God are *mitzvot* (commandments) "between one human and another." They imply that we can most successfully imitate God only when we act together to build a strong and caring community. It is also not coincidental that comforting mourners and the burial of the dead come at the conclusion of this list, as these are communal obligations performed by the community at the time of a mourner's greatest vulnerability and need. They are also enacted as people join together to comfort and support each other by reciting and responding to the Kaddish.

This talmudic text also includes an implicit reminder to the Jew that the Torah is the Jewish guidebook, providing a roadmap to holiness. Each of the stories alluded to in the text was carefully selected, both to highlight a particular divine action that we are called upon to emulate (namely: clothing the naked, visiting the sick, comforting mourners, and burying the dead), but also to convey a more subtle message. The first story, concerning clothing Adam and Eve, comes at the very beginning of the Torah; and the final one, concerning Moses' burial, at its very end. This is a reminder that ultimately the entire Torah is a guide for emulating God and thus bringing holiness to the world.

The tradition teaches that the best way to achieve *k'dushah*, holiness, is through *imitatio Dei* (the imitation of God). This idea is found throughout Jewish liturgy. Jews read and chant the thirteen divine attributes (Exodus 34:6–7) on the holiest festivals not only to learn about God, but more importantly to learn what God expects of humanity. The ancient rabbis add this level of interpretation: "Just as God is gracious and compassionate, you too should be gracious and compassionate…"[7] Each day in the morning service Jews also read the following verse from Psalm 146, "The Eternal secures justice for the oppressed, provides food for the hungry, and sets free the captive…"—not only to remind us that God loves all created beings (and therefore takes care of all the disadvantaged of society), but also to remind us that humanity, as God's partners, shares in this responsibility. We can only experience God's presence in our midst if we allow God in, through living lives of holiness. We are partners with God in all that is done. The Kaddish calls on God to be sanctified, and for divine sovereignty to be established—yet the call-and-response recitation of the Kaddish is an implicit reminder that these can only occur through human action. Just as the Kaddish can only be recited in the presence of the community, so too the transformation of the world can only happen with the active participation of the entire human community.

The interconnection of one human to another, to the world, and even to the Divine in fostering *k'dushah*, calls to mind a hasidic mystical understanding of the world. Rabbi Israel ben Eliezer, called the Baal Shem Tov (1700–1760), is reputed to have taught that we should open our eyes—because everywhere we look, we would see that bushes were burning but not being consumed.[8]

At first glance, this teaching is a reminder that small and large miracles are happening all around us, yet we walk through the world and fail to see them. But within the context of hasidic theology, it is saying much more. We walk through the world and we see materiality. We see the objects we have constructed, as well as plants, animals, and other people, and each appears to be separate and discrete. Yet, with a mystical eye, we have the opportunity to see God's presence and being within everything, to see the presence of holiness wherever we look. To the mystic, everything is separate, on one level; but on another level, there is a unity to all existence—and that unity, and much beyond it, is the Divine.

To a mystic, God's all-encompassing presence is set forth in the Torah: "Know this day and set it upon your heart that the Eternal is God...there is none else" (Deuteronomy 4:39). The traditional reading of this text stresses the monotheistic idea that there is no god other than the God of Israel. The hasidic reading, however, takes the last two words—*ein od*, translated above as "there is nothing else"— to mean that everything is God, even though we don't always see it.[9] Hasidic mysticism teaches that the divine essence is constantly moving toward a state of *hitlab'shut* (clothing itself in materiality).[10] This garbing acts both as a means of hiding the Divine, but also—at the same time, ironically enough—revealing it.

The understanding that all is God and "there is nothing else" leads, perforce, to a sense of obligation toward all creation. If every human, and indeed everything on this earth, is interconnected and is an aspect of the Divine revealed in the world, then this creates a great responsibility for us. Humanity, unique among all that is part of this ongoing revelation, is both self-aware and powerful. No other creature on earth can shape the environment for the good or ill of all creation. No other creature has the power to drive whole species to extinction. This power gives us the obligation to care, as best we can, for the entirety of creation. This kabbalistic teaching naturally leads to the realization that when we destroy another human, another species, or indeed the environment itself, we are destroying an aspect of the revelation of the Divine.

This responsibility is reflected in Judaism by the concept that we are all partners with God in creation and the realization of revelation. God, according to tradition, did not finish the work of creation, but rather left it to be completed by humanity. This can be seen, for example, in the rite of circumcision: the male baby, intentionally created by God in an unfinished state, only enters the covenant after his parents complete the ritual. And this idea, that humanity has an obligation to work toward the completion of creation, can also be seen in the act of reciting the Kaddish as we comfort mourners: God leaves this act of comfort and healing to us, the mourner's human community. In these and many other examples, we are commanded not to wait for God to perfect the world—that is, in the words of Kaddish, to establish God's sovereignty (*yamlikh malkhuteih*)— but rather, we are obligated to at least begin the work ourselves.

Within the Jewish tradition, the establishment of "God's sovereignty" is explicitly tied to human action. A talmudic legend[11] recounts that Rabbi Joshua ben Levi once asked the Messiah (notably sitting at the gates of Rome with the most disadvantaged of society, the beggars and lepers) when he would come. The Messiah responded, "Today." When the messianic age failed to come, Rabbi Joshua asked Elijah the prophet what the Messiah had meant. Elijah explained that the Messiah was quoting Psalm 95:7, "Today—if you hearken to My voice." A hasidic rabbi, Mendel of Kosov (c. 1800), building on this text taught: "Why has the son of Jesse [the Messiah] not come either today or yesterday?....Because we are today just as we were yesterday."[12] Later, this sentiment was echoed by Martin Buber, who reported that an elderly Hasid (sometimes reported to be his grandfather), when asked why the Messiah had not yet come, told the young Buber that the Messiah was waiting for him personally (i.e., for each of us).[13]

This sense of human partnership with God is taken up in mystical sources. The Jewish mystical tradition (often called Kabbalah) presents a very different image of the Divine than the all-powerful, all-knowing God who is beyond all need of or connection to creation or to humanity. To the kabbalist, God needs us just as we need God. The Zohar (and other mystical texts, such as *Sefer Bahir*)[14] posits a process of emanation from an unknowable divine source denoted as the Ein Sof, which is beyond all human understanding or possible connection; this emanation leads to the revelation of more and more knowable aspects of the Divine, known as the ten *s'firot*. These are expressions of the attributes through which we perceive God's activities in our world. They are also models for our own interactions with other people and with the world. There are, for example, *s'firot* called Din or Gevurah (Justice) and Ḥesed (Righteousness). There are also male and female oriented *s'frot*: Binah (Understanding) and Malkhut (also called Shekhinah, the indwelling Presence of the Divine) are explicitly female, a reminder that all genders exist within the Divine, and that both male and female are created in the divine image. To the kabbalist these divine attributes are not static, but rather are part of a dynamic interaction which, when harmonious, facilitates the flow of energy from the Divine to the material world. It is here that human action plays a central role. Our observance of the commandments creates energy, which flows upwards, facilitating the harmony in the supernal realms that enables the energy to then flow down and vivify the world. This mutual reliance creates a sense of partnership between humanity and the Divine. This sense of partnership and interconnectivity is at the essence of the recitation of the Kaddish. Our mutual support of others, as we comfort mourners, is both an intimation of—and also a prime example of—the activity necessary to facilitate the flow of energy from the Divine.

This concept of partnership is expanded in the Lurianic recreation of the kabbalistic myth. Rabbi Isaac Luria (1534–1572), building on a focus on the theme of exile, suggests a catastrophic climax, due to a primordial sin or imbalance, to the process of emanation. He thus saw the *s'firot* emanated as vessels containing divine light or energy. The seven lower *s'firot*, referred to as the luminous vessels, shatter— leading to sparks of the Divine being spread across the universe. To

Luria, these sparks of the Divine were in exile from the supernal realms and their unknowable divine source. Within this new mystical myth, the human role—and the interdependence of the divine and the human—is expanded, as the divine sparks are lifted and returned to God only through human action, a process referred to as *tikkun*, "repair [of the world]." When we do *mitzvot* we actualize the inherent *k'dushah* that is found within everything and return it to its divine source, thus restoring creation to its original intended pattern.

The mythic language of *tikkun* creates a greater sense of connection, relationship, mutuality, and obligation. What we do matters, and not only to ourselves. It adds a level of even greater importance to the observance of commandments like the recitation of the Kaddish. It should shape what we do and how we look at the world. As partners with the Divine—indeed, as necessary partners—it is up to us to transform the world, to raise the sparks back to their source...and as we do so, to repair not only the earth but also the Divine itself. When we comfort mourners, and thus effect a repair of human relationships, we also raise sparks effecting a similar *tikkun* of the Divine.

This concept of raising sparks may be seen as a mystical commentary based on the word *l'eilla* ("higher") found in the third paragraph of the Kaddish. Interestingly, this word is inexplicably doubled during the High Holy Day season, between Rosh Hashanah and Yom Kippur. This is a period of intense introspection, but also rededication to *tikkun* (both of ourselves and the world). *L'eilla l'eilla* is a reminder that the interconnectivity enhanced through the communal recitation of the Kaddish is an extremely effective means of *tikkun*.

This process and partnership of human/divine repair is also hinted in the very last line (and the only Hebrew line) of the Kaddish: "May the One who brings peace (*shalom*) to the universe bring peace to us and to all Israel" (based on the language of Job 25:2). *Shalom*, at a very basic level, can only be created by us as partners with God working in the world. We are called on to "seek peace and pursue it" (Psalm 34:15) but we have the free will to act or to fail to act. Yet, the word *shalom* has a much deeper meaning than simply "peace." The Hebrew root *shin-lamed-mem* also hints at completeness and absolute unity. It points to a world where each human recognizes that he or she is connected with all other people, with the world, and with God. It therefore also leads us back to the hasidic realization that there is only God, a recognition realized as we open our eyes and see (and actualize) *k'dushah* in whatever we do and wherever we glance.

The Kaddish at first glance seems mysterious and its language unconnected with its use, either for mourners or for the completion of prayer or study. Yet, as we have seen, it has a message that creates interconnectivity and a sense of obligation—both of which are at the very essence of *k'dushah*. The reciprocal call and response reminds us of our interconnectivity with each human and also with the Divine. It provides both comfort and support, encouraging hope and reconnection with a mission to build a better world. Its language of holiness and vision of God's kingdom remind us that it is only through human action, as we serve as partners with God, that anything can change. The Kaddish calls on us to reconnect, and it also calls us to *tikkun olam*.

NOTES

[1] There is also a less familiar Burial Kaddish, recited at the graveside during a funeral.

[2] B. Shevuot 39a.

[3] Ismar Elbogen, *Jewish Liturgy: A Comprehensive History*, trans. Raymond P. Scheindlin (Philadelphia: Jewish Publication Society, 1993), pp. 80–84.

[4] Traditionally, Kaddish is recited for seven categories of close relatives: a mother, father, sister, brother, son, daughter, and spouse. Many, however, especially in more liberal synagogues, choose to recite it for a much broader list of loved ones.

[5] Readers interested in the concept of holiness may wish to peruse the essays in the first volume of the Mesorah Matrix series, *Kedushah: Sanctification* (2015), edited by Benjamin Blech and devoted to the concept of holiness in the Jewish tradition.

[6] B. Sotah 14a.

[7] Sifrei Devarim §49.

[8] This tradition is alluded to in Sidney Greenberg and Jonathan D. Levine, *Siddur Hadash* (New York and Bridgeport, CT: Prayer Book Press, 1992) p. 80.

[9] For a complete discussion of this idea see, Rachel Elior, *The Paradoxical Ascent to God* (Albany: State University of New York Press, 1993), chap. 11, especially p. 50.

[10] Ibid., p. 55.

[11] See B. Sanhedrin 98a.

[12] Quoted in Louis Newman, *Hasidic Anthology* (New York: Schocken Books, 1963) p. 247.

[13] Dan Avnon, *The Hidden Dialogue* (Lanham: Rowman and Littlefield, 1998) p. 26.

[14] The Zohar is one of the central texts of classical Jewish mysticism denoted as Kabbalah. Seen by the tradition as ancient in origin, most historians date it to the thirteenth entury. It is made up of a variety of books, largely presented as mystical commentaries on the Torah.

Kaddish as Expansiveness

James Moshe Jacobson-Maisels

Introduction

I write this essay in midst of the year of mourning for my mother and my daily recitation of the Mourner's Kaddish. Despite my many times saying Kaddish when leading a service, it is the experience of being a mourner,[1] more than anything else, that has acutely raised the question of the meaning of this prayer for me. Why do I, whether as a prayer leader or a mourner, recite these words to conclude a prayer service or a portion thereof? What is it that I, as a mourner, am meant to accomplish through the recitation of this prayer?[2]

The Kaddish is a prayer that appears in multiple forms. Here I will relate to the most essential of those forms: the Half Kaddish, whose core form also appears in every other form of Kaddish; and the Mourner's Kaddish, which includes two appeals for peace (one in Aramaic and another in Hebrew), which also appear in every form of the Kaddish other than the Half Kaddish. Here is the text of Mourner's Kaddish, which includes within it the full text of the Half Kaddish:

Enlarged and sanctified be His great name
in this world which He created according to His will.

May His majesty be made sovereign in your lifetime and your days and the days of all the House of Israel, quickly and soon, and say: Amen.
May His great name be blessed for ever and ever and ever.

Blessed and praised and extolled and exalted and elevated and glorified and uplifted and lauded be the Holy One's name, blessed be He,
beyond (and beyond) every blessing and song and praise and consolation that we say in this world, and say: Amen.

May there be great peace from heaven and life upon us and upon all Israel, and say: Amen.

May the One who makes peace in His high places make peace upon us and upon all Israel, and say: Amen.

Why do those in mourning recite this exaltation of the divine name? Why, when concluding a service, do we recite this acclamation of God? What could such a recitation accomplish and how might it actually enlarge and sanctify the great name of God?

The Nature of the Language of Prayer

To answer this question we must first briefly digress and explore the very nature of the language of Jewish prayer. While we most often think of language as a means of imparting information, that is not the case with the language of prayer. In prayer, even if prayer language were, in some sense, a normal bearer of information, surely it would have lost its efficacy in communicating its content after the thousandth recitation of the same prayer.[3] Intellectual information, once genuinely received and understood, does not benefit from repetition. It neither does me good nor deepens my understanding to be told endlessly that 2+2=4 or that the earth is round.

Rather, we can think about prayer language in two other ways. First, we can think about it as communication from the pray-er to the Divine. The person praying praises, thanks, and makes requests from God and in so doing communicates his or her awe, appreciation, and needs—and, in that process, cultivates a relationship with divinity itself. That is: the language of prayer is both a vessel for the pray-er to communicate feelings to God and also a means, as in human discourse, of creating intimacy and connection between interlocutors. Second, and more important for our purposes, we can see the language of prayer as performative. Prayer language is not meant to communicate something but rather to *do* something. Most importantly, it is meant to cultivate certain states and dispositions in the practitioner. When we say Barukh She-amar each morning, for example, we do not impart new information about God's creative powers, but rather cultivate a palpable sense of wonder and awe by reminding ourselves about, and affirming, divine creativity. As Abraham Joshua Heschel explained:

> Every evening we recite: "He creates light and makes dark."
> Twice a day we say: "He is One." What is the meaning of
> such repetition? A scientific theory, once it is announced
> and accepted, does not have to be repeated twice a day. The
> insights of wonder must be constantly kept alive. Since there
> is a need for daily wonder, there is a need for daily worship.[4]

Similarly, the imagery of prayer and its repetition—whether the prayer is about the natural world, or praising God, or about the extraordinary power of the Divine—cultivate in us various religious feelings even after many repetitions. So too, language that communicates God's love for us helps us to feel beloved and accepted, feelings that must be renewed each day. In this way the repetition is a way of fully actualizing or integrating the knowledge that is presented in the words of the repeated prayer. We do not know more, but we know it more deeply and fully.

Sometimes this performative element is expressed through modes of enaction and participation. When we recite the "Hallelujah" psalms, the recitation itself is a kind of enactment of joy, a performative exclamation that, when done truly, is itself an act of joy and wonder. When we express our thanks, we enact gratitude in that moment. When we not only mention the exodus from Egypt but when we ourselves *personally* recite the words sung by the Israelites after crossing the Sea of Reeds; and when we not only recall the angelic praise of God but ourselves *personally* become the heavenly choir in the Kedushah, we enact and participate in mythic moments—and in so doing become ourselves redeemed, angelic, and filled with awe. As Shefa Gold says of prayer more generally, "I'm not trying to understand the words. I'm trying to be the words."[5] The argument here is that this approach is part of the basic nature of Jewish prayer.

This performative element is further expressed in the linguistic structure of Jewish prayer itself. The repetition of the same words day after day, the use of strings of words (whether synonyms or complementary verbs and adjectives) and the mantra-like rhythmic nature of much of prayer language are all modes of enacting and ingraining the feeling and insights that the words offer. In all these ways, prayer is a practice of cultivation—and prayer language is a performative means of bringing into reality certain qualities, dispositions, emotions, and states of being. As Rabbi Kalonymus Kalmish Shapira, the Piaseczner rebbe, wrote, when a Jew recites the prayers for light,

> the Israelite does not tell that there is light, rather he reveals the light itself and the holiness of his God. He brings forth,

expands, and reveals the holy spark that sparkles in him.... One is not speaking of a deed which has light in it, but rather one is bringing forth the light itself in this speech itself. When one repeats [the word] more light, and even more light, and even more light is revealed each time.[6]

And in a similar vein, he also states: "One who simply describes God's greatness and His praise is like a person who reports that somewhere far away, there is a great light. But to actually sing God's praise is like bringing a candle back from the faraway light to this world."[7]

Kaddish and Expansiveness

What, then, is Kaddish meant to perform or enact? What is it that the words of Kaddish *do*? What is it that they bring into the world? My contention and experience, inspired by my friend and colleague Rabbi Jordan Bendat-Appell, is that the words of Kaddish are meant to expand us, to bring us into a state of mind and being that is wider, greater, enlarged, and beyond our normal experience.[8] Indeed this is the meaning of the opening word of the Kaddish: *yitgaddal*, may God's name be enlarged, greatened, increased, amplified, or expanded.[9] If we look once more at the core words of the Kaddish brought here again, we see this cultivation of expansiveness—of awe, greatness, sanctity, exaltation, elevation, glory, and ascension; of going and being beyond the normal and mundane; of growing, expanding, and ascending beyond this world, beyond time, beyond human reality and language.

Enlarged and sanctified be His great name
in this world which He created according to His will.

May His majesty be made sovereign in your lifetime and

your days and the days of all the House of Israel, quickly and soon, and say: *Amen.*
May His great name be blessed for ever and ever and ever.

Blessed and praised and extolled and exalted and elevated and glorified and uplifted and lauded be the Holy One's name, blessed be He,
beyond (and beyond) every blessing and song and praise and consolation that we say in this world, and say: *Amen.*

May there be great peace from heaven and life upon us and upon all Israel, and say: *Amen.*

May the One who makes peace in His high places make peace upon us and upon all Israel, and say: *Amen.*

In the Kaddish we call for the divine Name to be expanded, to be "enlarged and sanctified...blessed and praised and extolled and exalted and elevated and glorified and uplifted and lauded." In our very calling for this expansion, we actually enact the expansion of the Name and ourselves. We expand it, increase it, and amplify it to such an extent that we go beyond the ability of language to contain it, "beyond (and beyond) every blessing and song and praise and consolation that we say in this world." We go beyond the limitation of time and space, blessing the Name "for ever and ever and ever." We go beyond the ability of the human mind to contain it, beyond human comprehension—and in doing so, we take ourselves beyond our mundane sense of who we are.

Why? What is the connection between this expansiveness and the task of the Kaddish for mourners, prayer leaders, and community? The connection is the transformative power of that expansiveness, which we can see in multiple ways.

Expansiveness as *Mikveh*

In my experience, it is no coincidence that mourners are given this prayer of expansiveness to recite—for it is in the expansiveness itself, in the greatness of awe and sanctity, that the healing of loss takes place, that openness and stability are rediscovered. It is no coincidence that this prayer concludes prayer services and their subsections, for it is in this expansiveness that all that has arisen in these prayers, all the varied and conflicting emotions and insights, can be held in spaciousness and equanimity, and integrated into the practitioner. That is, what the Kaddish allows us and calls on us to do is to widen around our experience. *Yitgaddal*, it tells us: get bigger. Kaddish allows us to become a vessel, to create a vessel, that is wide enough to hold the truth of loss, the truth of helplessness to save a loved one, and the feelings of despair, anger, grief, denial, fear, and bitterness that arise. It does not tell us to "get over" our loss, yet nor does it allow us to get lost in it. Rather it helps us to become wide enough, expansive enough, to hold it all without having to reject any part of our experience and without getting trapped in any one aspect of our experience. Kaddish helps us hold the truth of our bereavement, and the truth of the majesty *and* horror of this world, with compassion and love. It lets us know—not in the sense of acquiring information, but in a felt sense of gaining the insight—that we are bigger than the bereavement, that the love is bigger than the horror. We may feel overwhelmed and helpless, having lost a loved one, being caught in the stress of life and work, or simply having poured out our heart in prayer and listed all the many unfulfilled desires and needs we have, but Kaddish allows us to hold the overwhelm and helplessness in something larger without having to deny our experience.

In this sense Kaddish is a kind of *mikveh*, a ritual purifying bath, but one with special powers and significance that can even, bit by bit, remove the impurity of death.[10] The *mikveh*, the Jewish ritual bath, is used as a means of cleansing oneself from ritual impurity. One accomplishes this by immersing oneself in the waters of the *mikveh*, which symbolically– ritually cleanses the one immersing, allowing him or her to be washed clean of the impurity by being held in the container of cleansing water. Kaddish, I want to claim, can achieve the same thing for the bereaved.

Day by day, as Kaddish is recited, the bitterness and anger of death is held in something larger and it is transformed. In the laws of *kashrut*, we speak of something being *bateil b'shishim* ("void in a mixture of sixty times its volume")—which means, practically, that if a piece of meat, for instance, falls into a pot of milk but constitutes less than one-sixtieth of the volume of milk in the pot, then it is considered as if it did not exist; but if it was not less than one-sixtieth, it colonizes the whole pot, turning it into a non-kosher state. We sometimes feel as if the pain of our loss, the bitterness, anger, helplessness, or depression, have colonized our being, turning us into something other than what we were and truly are. Kaddish allows us to keep expanding and expanding so that the acute pain and anger become held in something wider, until they eventually no longer define our being. They are still there. The meat doesn't actually go away. We never, in my experience, eliminate the sense of loss, nor should we wish to; but we no longer need to be dominated by it and defined by it. This is the process of mourning; this is the process of Kaddish.

Kaddish as *mikveh* allows this transformation because it allows us to see all of what is arising within us without being overwhelmed by it. In its breadth and width, it gives us the space, and so the equanimity and stability, to allow whatever is present to come to consciousness. No longer terrified of the demons that lurk beneath the surface but rather confident in our ability to be present with them despite the fear and discomfort, the demons sense the permission to arise and make themselves known. Expansive and open, we do not become trapped by the demons when they arise, but instead give them space to roam within our expansiveness of mind, heart, body, and soul, a spaciousness that defangs them. When we expand, when we cultivate the expansiveness of the Kaddish, we can see all of the things that arise—anger, fear, suspicion, jealousy, desire, fantasy, terror—as schools of fish swimming by in the immeasurable ocean, or as clouds moving through the vast sky. Sometimes the fish look like sharks, killer whales, or giant squids. Sometimes it seems to be not merely clouds but in fact lightning, storms, and gale-force winds. But when we are truly wide, when we are the sky and the ocean, then even *that* is acceptable. Even the most fearsome predator cannot hurt the ocean; the ocean *is* what holds it. Even the most terrible lightning bolt cannot damage the sky; the sky *is* its vast container and thus is untouched by the passage of the lightning bolt. If we do not become identified with any particular place, any particular emotion or moment, then we can hold them all in that expansiveness, and then we can hold *all* the terrifying monsters that arise, in compassion and love.

We can only hold them by growing larger. The contradictions, the feelings, the thoughts—whether of loss, prayer, or life—can only be held together in a large container. Sometimes we think about holding everything together as a kind of tense, desperate grasping onto the various out-of-control strings of our life. But we all know how that feels: tense, desperate, on the edge, and driven by constant struggle. We aren't really holding it all together; we are desperately resisting getting pulled apart.

Sometimes we hope to find resolution by seeking to harmonize the various components of our lives, our minds, and our hearts, so that the various disparate elements of our experience will no longer seem to be in tension with each other. This is the comfort of a grand unified theory, something that puts everything in the right place.

But, most often, such strategies fail as well. It doesn't all fit together smoothly. It isn't all resolved. There is no neat and tidy solution to the tensions of life.

But here, in the Kaddish, we hold the multiplicity contained in the many prayers we have recited, the many different feelings around mourning and loss—not grasping them or smoothing out the contradictions, but simply giving them a wider space in which to *be*. In this way, they are held together without being papered over. In this way, a deeper unity is found. Indeed, Dov Baer, the Maggid of Mezritch, tells us that this is precisely the expansive nature of the Divine: that which, because it creates this infinitely open space, the void of *ayin*, can hold together all opposites.[11] The expansiveness of Kaddish is then, in this sense, also the mystic place of the relinquishing of self. It is the way in which we get so wide, so beyond, that we exceed even our own ideas of who we are and so we rest in the infinite, in our ability to hold everything that arises in the limitless container of love. In this way Kaddish, in its place in the service, is like the pause of silence after a chant, the lying down at the end of a yoga session, the sitting in silence and wonder at the end of an extraordinary book or movie: it is the time to let it all in, to hold it in something larger, and to then allow it to be integrated into who we are.

Of course, this is exceptionally hard. First, because many of us harbor an unhealthy desire to identify with both the predator and the prey. Because of our natural human tendency to avoid pain and our natural reluctance to admit to our own shortcomings, we find it easy to rewrite our story, focusing on how we have fallen prey to something larger than ourselves (for example, an undeserved diagnosis or unwarranted suffering) and how nothing works out. Similarly, for those of us who fall easily into self-blame, we can become trapped in a story about what we did wrong. It makes us feel safe in some way. We want to get lost in our bitterness and anger at the loss, in our denial and blame—to a great extent, because doing so shields us from the enormity of the loss itself and the genuine sadness and grief that arise in its wake. Second, it is hard because it is simply scary to just be with the predator, to just look at those jaws filled with teeth and not run away, not flee, not do anything but compassionately be *with* that which arises. But if we do so, the lion might just put its head in our lap.

Kaddish is therefore a way for us to make friends with what arises, to expand around it. We hold it, we embrace it, we don't try to get rid of it...and in the embrace it just moves on by itself. In this way Kaddish, in its affirmation of divine expansiveness, majesty, and will in the face of loss, asks us to not fight our loss. It tells us that we change when we accept ourselves, that we are purified when we stop fighting what we need to be liberated from, that we are healed when we stop running away. In this way, it is the Divine itself which is the purifying bath; it is God who is, in Jeremiah's words "the *mikveh* of Israel."[12]

Expansiveness and Awe

The awe-inspiring nature of the Kaddish—the awesomeness expressed in words, posture, and solemnity—is an awesomeness of expansiveness. The hasidic masters speak about two types of fear, *yirah k'tanah* ("small fear") and *yirah g'dolah* ("great fear or awe"). One of the core practices of early Hasidism, particularly with regard to the hasidic revolution in the relationship to "alien thoughts" (*mahashavot zarot*), is the transformation of this small fear into awe. For example, the Baal Shem Tov, the founder of Hasidism, teaches:

> "And Isaac dwelt and dug anew" (Genesis 26:18)—a well, and the channel of awe (*yirah*), as is his quality...the aspect of Isaac, which is fear, has multiple aspects, external fear and dread (*yirah*)...God forbid, for external fear (*yirah*) due to

punishment, is called, God forbid, idolatry…
"And he dug yet another well" (Genesis 26:22)—internal awe
(*yirah*), it was called *r'hovot* (literally, "the wide place"), for "the
Eternal has granted us ample space," and the internality of awe
(*yirah*) is called *r'hovot*—understand![13]

Here the Baal Shem Tov distinguishes between external fear, the fear
of punishment, and internal fear, the awe of divinity. External fear, the
fear of punishment, is so degraded and so inappropriate a motivation
for serving God that it is labeled idolatry, a striking condemnation. It
is closed, fearful, and narrow. Awe, on the other hand, is called *r'hovot*
("the wide place)."

Thus, the very nature of genuine awe, of true service of the Divine,
is this nature of expansiveness. The transformation from idolatrous
fear to awe of the Divine is therefore the transition from constriction
to expansiveness. We make this transition, in my experience, by
making space, by expanding again and again around the place of
constriction—around the fear, anger, jealousy, bitterness, loneliness,
or a score of other feelings—and allowing the constriction to rest
in an ocean of space. We might bring our attention to the place of
constriction and then, with each breath, breathe in infinitely, filling
our lungs with the breath of the world and creating limitless space
for the constriction to rest in; and then breathe out infinitely, feeling
our breath filling the world and connecting ourselves to an even
vaster immeasurableness in which the constriction can be held. In
the Kaddish we might intend, with each word of enlargement and
ascension, that we expand bit by bit, creating just a little more space
for what is present to rest in infinity.

And then, on the Days of Awe, we get even wider. We are called
upon to expand, to see the awesomeness of divinity and this world,
again and again. To recognize the fleeting and uncertain nature of
our lives and the cosmic context in which we live, the finite nature

of our existence and the measurelessness of the divine. And so in the Kaddish, we push that expansiveness one step more. We say that the divine Name is "praised and extolled and exalted and elevated and glorified and uplifted and lauded…beyond and beyond every blessing and song and praise and consolation that we say in this world." Beyond and beyond, or above and above, or surpassingly surpassing, on the Days of Awe we expand that little bit more, we reach for a larger infinity, to recognize that however much we have expanded and seen the truth of this beyondness, we can yet expand a little bit more. We can go even farther and hold even that expansion in a wider, even more measureless, space.

Our Expansion and Reflexive Language

This expansion, as I have argued from the beginning of this essay, is an enlargement not only of the divine Name but of ourselves as well. Through our call to expand the divine Name beyond all limitations of language and thought, we ourselves are expanded. In part, this happens because the wishing, calling forth, or blessing of expansiveness naturally touches the sender as well as the recipient, just as our genuine well-wishing for others brings to our selves a sense of ease and well-being. Yet in another way, the language of the Kaddish itself points at this dual effect.

The verbs in the Kaddish are in the *hitpa·eil* form, which is generally taken to be reflexive.[14] We could then read the Kaddish as saying: "May His great name enlarge and sanctify itself." That is, Kaddish would be read as God's self-sanctification and self-expansion. Yet recited, as it is, in our mouths, who is performing this expansion and sanctification but us? We can make sense of this seeming tension by following the hasidic masters in their declaration that "there is no other," that everything is divine, including ourselves. In saying Kaddish, then, we—as the Great Name ourselves, as the Divine ourselves—are calling upon ourselves to expand and ascend. We are declaring our intention, hope, and task of magnifying the Name-which-is-us. We are exhorting ourselves to become real, sanctified, praised, and spacious enough to contain all that is present, to give it a place to rest in infinity.

At the end of the Aleinu prayer, we recite the verse from Zechariah that declares that "on that day, the Eternal will be one and His name one."[15] This is our task, the task of redemption, of *tikkun*. The Kaddish, in the sense we have been discussing, is the way in which we make the Name one by making ourselves one. We unify not by destroying any difference, but by creating a wider space in which all that is disparate can exist in a greater whole. This is perhaps why we conclude prayer services with the Kaddish. It is the seal, the unity, the unification, the holding all that is separated together, which allows the multiplicity of life and prayer to be held in one overarching space. It is perhaps why we say it as mourners—for the act of expanding we-who-are-the-Name allows us to truly mourn, to hold all the many feelings, memories, thoughts, and reactions to our loss in a loving container that allows everything that must emerge to arise and be held in love.

Self-Conscious Transcendence

We have discussed how the Kaddish expresses its expansive nature by using words to call for praise beyond all words: "Blessed and praised and extolled and exalted and elevated and glorified and uplifted and lauded be the Holy One's name, blessed be He, beyond (and beyond) every blessing and song and praise and consolation that we say in this world."[16] The expansiveness of Kaddish is thus emphasized even more when we recognize the prayer's own self-consciousness of its exceeding of the limitations of language. The Kaddish both exceeds

language and likewise calls on us to exceed language. Elliot Rabin, in
his discussion of the nature of Jewish prayer, argues:

> The strategy of Jewish prayer-poetry is to explode the
> mind with an overabundance of words to the point where
> the person senses what is beyond language. The davener is
> not meant to understand, visualize, internalize every word
> of *t'fillah*; that scenario is rendered impossible by the sheer
> verbosity in a Jewish service. (Davening Shaḥarit means
> reading a hundred-page anthology of Hebrew poems every
> morning!)[17]

In the Kaddish, the nature of the overabundance of words bears
witness to this claim; in addition, the Kaddish itself names its own
desire to go beyond language. Indeed, at times of greater awe and
heightened expansiveness, that self-conscious expansion beyond
language is even more prominent. Rabin's perceptive claim then
becomes even stronger in relationship to the Kaddish. It is further
bolstered by the fact that Kaddish is the only prayer of antiquity
that is recited with relative regularity that self-consciously refers
to itself in such a way.[18] The self-consciousness of the Kaddish in
this respect strengthens our previous claims about the Kaddish's
performative task as a prayer of expansion and transcendence, taking
the practitioner beyond human boundedness.

Kaddish, understood against the notion of expansiveness
presented here, thus presents a model that is both at odds with, yet
also deeply congruent with, the apophatic theology of Maimonides
and his successors.[19] Both stress the inadequacy of language to capture
the essence of the Divine. But whereas in Maimonidean thought
this results in an approach of silence and negation, the response in
Kaddish is instead an affirmation that consciously attempts to exceed
the mind's limitations through the excessiveness of language itself.[20]
This insight is essential to the work of the Kaddish and its radical

expansiveness. Its own words are not meant to be a boundary within which the prayer operates, but rather to point beyond themselves to an expansiveness that exceeds all borders and that in fact exceeds the very possibilities of language. Later forms of Jewish spiritual practice—such as the saying and unsaying of the Zohar (the Zohar continually uses a technique of saying and unsaying, such as claiming that the Divine is "known and not known") and even the stream of consciousness of Bratslaver *hitbod'dut*—may provide other examples of the use of language to self-consciously transcend its limitations.[21] In any case, like apophatic mysticism and theology, the Kaddish in this sense leads the practitioner to a state of aporia through its radical expansiveness, an insight into the unknowability and unbounded nature of divinity and ourselves. We thus conclude our prayers that are grounded in language with a prayer that takes us beyond language. We approach our loss and suffering not with words of comfort, but with words that take us beyond comfort—to a ministry of presence, an opening to the limitless transcendence of divinity.

The Truth of Things as They Are

Yet we do not only speak of expansiveness in the Kaddish. In addition, we say:

> Enlarged and sanctified be His great name
> In this world which He created according to His will.

We ask for the name to be enlarged "in this world which He created according to His will"—that is, we are asked to expand and open into this very world, a world created according to the divine will.

What does that mean, for the world to be created according to divine will? What does it mean for us to expand into that world? It means that we are asked to expand into things, to hold things, to accept things just as they are. To see that this is simply how things are and that it is larger than us. It doesn't mean "all is for the best in the best of all possible worlds."[22] That is nonsense. We don't accept things "as they are" in the sense that we say it is always good or right or justified that such and such happened. Rather, it means that we simply acknowledge deeply, without the internal resistance of denial, rejection, or aversion, that this is how things actually are in this moment.

This, I believe, is the meaning of the blessing we say when we learn that someone has died: "Blessed is the true Judge." We hear the news and then, instead of denying it, ignoring it, drowning it out, or using one of our many strategies for running away from discomfort, we stop and say, "I acknowledge this, I bless this truth, I accept that which is true, I bless the true Judge." This is how it is. It is not a justification, but a rather a profound seeing of the nature of things, the nature of life and death. This also is how we can understand God's response to Job's queries. God responds from the tempest, "Where were you when I laid the earth's foundations? Speak, if you have understanding!" (Job 38:4)—and then goes on to list, in an almost overwhelming manner, for four chapters, a series of questions and challenges that ask Job how he can presume to seek justification in the midst of the massiveness and majesty of this universe and God's power. God's response seems to be simply saying: This is bigger than you. It isn't right or wrong, it's just *bigger* than you. Can you recognize the hugeness?

And in this bigness, in this hugeness, there is a certain all-right-ness. In naming the truth and holding it in something larger, we are okay. Like the ocean is okay despite the storms, and the sky is all right despite the lightning. No matter how terrible the tempest, the ocean itself is fine. And when we are big enough, we are all right: we can recognize and accept things, even tragedy, just the way they are.

This is the truth, the true Judge. It isn't a justification of the judgment, for there can be no justification of tragedy. It is just saying, with great clarity and presence, this is what life is like. It is opening to the enormity of what is actually there without hiding.

At my mother's funeral, her rabbi, Rabbi Rachel Shere, said that she loved how honest my mother was. And she was. She didn't care that much about what was socially acceptable. She had her own ideas about what was right and she followed them. As her child, that wasn't always so comfortable. But, of course, the truth isn't. So when we say "this world which He created according to His will" and when we say "blessed is the true Judge," we are saying: "This is how it is." This is the truth, and I will bless it rather than run away from it. As our prayer tradition teaches us, "The Eternal, your God, is truth."[23] Or, as Rabbi Ḥanina taught: "Truth is the seal of the Holy One."[24] And, in the words of the prophet Jeremiah, "The Eternal is truth" (10:10)." If we want to be with God, we can't run away from the truth.

The Kaddish demands that we be with that truth. Expanding is not a means of running away; it is a means of being with. One of my teachers, Sylvia Boorstein, summarized mindfulness practice as: "Pay attention. Tell the truth. Don't duck."[25] If we want to wake up and be present, if we want to hold everything that arises, we have to acknowledge it and we can't duck. We have to meet it face-on and hold it in something larger. We have to meet it with a commitment to truth and clarity, and the strength to see that commitment through. The Kaddish, in this sense, is quite demanding. It makes us pull away all of the veils, all of the places we are hiding—or, at least, it has the potential to do so.

Yet the expansion, which precedes the "world according to His will," is also what makes the truth-telling possible. Only when we are wide enough is the painful truth not so overwhelming that we cannot tell it, cannot bear to be with it. For telling the truth is actually much harder than we realize. The hasidic master Rabbi Pinḥas of Koretz taught: "I have found nothing more difficult to overcome than lying. It took me fourteen years....I served twenty-one years. Seven years to find out what truth is, seven years to drive out falsehood, and seven to absorb truth."[26] How often do we prevaricate, lie, or mislead, in small or large ways? How easy is it for us to not tell the truth because it will be smoother, easier, less ruffling in some way? How does this turn into an inability to face the genuine pain, loss, difficulty, and confusion we have inside? Watch yourself. See if you can go one day without shading anything at all—a day of total honesty.

It isn't easy. But it helps if we recognize the pain of deception, the ways in which we hurt ourselves and others by not telling truth and not being willing to see the truth. Each time it happens, each time we hide something from ourselves or others, there is a small loss, a small pain, a small contraction, a small death. Kaddish demands from us that we face the truth. It reminds the mourner again and again: you are still mourning. It reminds the community again and again: your friend is still mourning, still in pain, still in loss. This is how we become wise. Indeed, these are two of the seven character traits of a sage: "Regarding something not previously heard, [a true sage] will [always] say 'I have not heard [anything in that regard],' and such [a scholar will always] acknowledge the truth" (Pirkei Avot 5:9).

The Truth of God

This truth of divine will, this commitment to seeing the truth, takes on an extra level in the thought of the hasidic masters. The Baal Shem Tov, the founder of Hasidism, tells a parable of a king who built a castle of many walls, partitions, and gates. At each gate, the king commanded money and treasures to be distributed, increasing in amount as the gates became more inward and closer to the king. Many who came to see the king took the money given to them at one of the gates and went on their way. A few, however, burning with desire to the see the king, ignored the proffered treasure and, after many travails, came to the king himself. Upon reaching the king, each one realized that in fact the walls and partitions had presented only an illusion of separation, for the walls themselves were the very substance and essence of the king, like a snail whose garment is part of its very self.[27]

For the Baal Shem Tov, the fundamental insight we strive to achieve and integrate is the divinity of all we encounter, the reality that there is ultimately nothing but God. Every day in the Aleinu prayer, we recite the verse from Deuteronomy (4:39): "The Eternal is God in the heavens above and on the earth below; there is no other." "There is no other" does not simply imply that there is no other *god*, but that there is no *other* of *any* sort.[28] We discover that everything we experience, everything we are, every being we encounter, every speck of sand, is in fact the Divine that is before us. This is what it means to see the truth. This is what it means for the world to be according to the divine will. It simply is divine will, for it is divinity.

Yet at the same time, this affirmation of presence, in its very nature as an affirmation and definition, limits the unlimited and bounds the boundless. Ultimately, therefore, this claim that there is no other is the claim of non-duality. In a combination of Maimonidean negative theology and hasidic panentheism, we realize that the fundamental insight is not the positive assertion of unity, which itself can be a kind of grasping, but rather the negative release of all concepts in non-duality.[29] This is Kaddish's claim that the divinity we recognize— the divine will we see in the world—is yet beyond all language and comprehension. The ultimate theological insight is to see the illusory nature of the walls we imagine separate ourselves from God, the world, and other people, to see the emptiness (*ayin*) of our sense of a separate self.[30]

This is the culmination of the expansiveness of Kaddish. This is where expansiveness leads us: to see that as we grow wider we see that in that infinite expansiveness, all is contained. That that expansiveness, the name of God, is the divinity that holds, within it and as part of it, the whole world. We feel there is something greater, something holding all this disparity together, the coincidence of opposites which is the Divine.³¹ As we get wider and hold this moment in more and more spaciousness, we feel the divine nature of everything we encounter—that nothing is excluded from the divine presence. We see the truth of things, just as they are, and that part of that truth is their divine nature.

Minyan: Opening with Others

Yet, as we have not yet noted, Kaddish is only said in a *minyan*, in a prayer quorum of ten. We only say these words and expand in this way in the presence of others. For if we do not acknowledge the truth and expand around it before others, if we do not expose to others our mind and heart, then in some way we remain hidden and closed. The solitary work is crucial, but opening before others is the next level of the challenge, the challenge embodied in Kaddish. It is allowing ourselves to be seen in our pain, confusion, and loss—a being seen that is profoundly healing.

Rabbi Abraham Kalisker (1741–1810), a third-generation hasidic master, saw this clearly in his teachings concerning *dibbuk haveirim*, the attachement of spiritual fellowship. In his instructions to his followers for a co-counseling practice in which people discuss their personal failings with a like-minded friend, he explains that, "when one has accustomed oneself to doing this, it will be found that when a person sees something wrong or objectionable in a friend and offers words of reproof, the latter will not feel ashamed before the former and will confess to the truth. Thus falsehood will fall and truth will begin to shine."[32] That is: part of what is crucial about this practice of sharing and reproof is that through the sharing and mutual acceptance, one can share one's failings precisely without feeling ashamed; and, moreover, it is the not feeling ashamed that allows the genuine confession of the truth. The healing, transformation, genuine self-critique, truth-telling, and genuine self-acceptance are made possible and powerful by the loving gaze of another who accepts you without condoning all of your actions. It is being held in the gaze of another and speaking the truth to them that creates the healing power of this practice.

Here we return to the deep importance of truth, but what is added is the power of telling that truth, of revealing, and embodying that truth, before others. Only when we are willing to name our truths, of every sort, before others can we be said to have fully embraced them. Only then "will falsehood fall and truth begin to shine." It can be a powerful practice to name things as they are in the presence of a loving community, expanding enough around the shame and embarrassment to admit to the fullness of one's feeling, struggles, and failures in the presence of others. Such a practice points to that truth not only in the expansiveness of the practitioner, and in that person's ability to touch the divine presence, but in the expansiveness of the community and the particularity of the loving faces all around.

Of course, to do this requires a certain kind of practice of the *minyan*. It requires spiritual fellows who are willing to hold that which each person expresses. It requires a community that is willing to be what the Torah (at Genesis 2:18) calls an *eizer k'negdo*, a helper-opposer—that is: a witness, challenger, and loving opponent who helps each person hold up a mirror to themselves in love. It requires people who will not run from displays of emotion, confusion, failure, and loss and who will not use shame or embarrassment to tamp down "unseemly" emotional outbursts, but who will rather see their task as allowing each individual to fully hold, express, and expand around their suffering and confusion. In this way, the love of the *minyan*, the love of spiritual companions, becomes the *mikveh* of expansiveness, the next layer of expansion and honesty that Kaddish leads us into.

Peace

Every form of the Kaddish other than the Half Kaddish (which is always followed, later in the service, by another Kaddish[33]) concludes, in Aramaic and Hebrew, with a prayer for peace. This, is, it seems to me, both a hope, an affirmation, and a consequence of what has gone before. That is: when we are truly open, when we are expansive, when we are willing to see things as they are, when we feel held and seen in community—then we find peace and equanimity, a fundamental all-right-ness in the world. The concluding benediction of peace is the capstone, in a way, of the expansiveness and acceptance of Kaddish. If we can expand around the loss and hold it in love, if we can have the courage and breadth to see things as they truly are, if we can be held in the love and acceptance of our fellows, then we can heal and move through the pain of loss. If we can expand around the chaotic diversity of the prayer service, the many places in us that have been touched and exposed (if we engage with our prayer practice seriously), then we can conclude with a sense of wholeness and completion, a bringing together that is not an erasure of difference but rather a holding of all this diversity in something wider.

Conclusion

Kaddish, as a practice, is the continuous expanding of our boundaries, the becoming wider around our places of tension, loss, confusion, despair, and pain, and our holding all that arises in the infinite expansiveness, beyond the ability of mind or language to grasp, that is divinity. It is the continual acknowledging of the truth of this moment, this loss, this uncertainty, and this pain. It is the being held in container of loving community and the peace that comes as a result of this practice. Each time we say the words, if we choose to practice in this way, we open a little bit more so that more can be held in the divine vastness. Whatever arises, whatever pain or fear, wherever we find ourselves hiding or running away, Kaddish asks us to turn toward the suffering and to hold it in something greater. It asks us to do so again and again until we become as wide as the universe, holding everything in divine love and discovering the peace, openness, and liberation that is the gift of such expansiveness.

NOTES

[1] Both currently for my mother and previously for my sister as well as for my great-aunt and great-uncle.

[2] I ask this question from a place devoid of metaphysics, seeking an answer that does not rely on some particularly metaphysical picture of the world we live in, such as certain ways of understanding the classical explanation of the elevation of the deceased loved one's soul. Rather I hope to ask the question and hear an answer that is directly relevant to my human experience as an emotional, psychological, embodied, spiritual being.

[3] Which, for one praying three times a day, would only require one year of prayer.

[4] Abraham Joshua Heschel, *God in Search of Man: A Philosophy of Judaism* (1955; rpt. New York: Farrar, Straus & Giroux, 1976), p. 46.

[5] Shefa Gold, as quoted in Mike Comins, *Making Prayer Real* (Woodstock, VT: Jewish Lights, 2010), p. 43.

[6] Rabbi Kalonymus Kalmish Shapira, *Derekh Ha-melekh* (Jerusalem: Va·ad Ḥasidei Piaseczno [Committee of Piaseczno Hasidim], 5755 [1994/1995]), sermon for the First Night of Rosh Hashanah 5691 (1930/1931), p. 250.

[7] Rabbi Kalonymus Kalmish Shapira, *Ḥovat Ha-talmidim* (ed. Warsaw, 5692 [1931/1932], "Torah, Prayer, and Singing to God," section 2, pp. 98–99. Non-Hebrew readers may profitably consult this text in Micha Odenheimer's translation, published as *A Student's Obligation* (Northvale, NJ: Jason Aronson, 1991), p. 166.

[8] Jordan shared this insight with me at a retreat where we taught together in December 2013, a few months before my mother passed away. He communicated that he thought he, in turn, had heard this insight from another friend and teacher, Rabbi Sheila Peltz Weinberg.

[9] The repetition here is a purposeful echoing of the Kaddish's linguistic structure and aims to help the reader feel the performative effect of such language.

[10] That is, this imaginative *mikveh* of the Kaddish is able to even exceed the power of an actual *mikveh* which cannot, according to the tradition, remove the impurity of death.

[11] *Sefer Maggid D'varav L'yaakov*, ed. Rivka Schatz Uffenheimer (Jerusalem: Magnes Press, 1976), §60, p. 91.

[12] Jeremiah 14:8, 17:13. In its original biblical context, the meaning is that God is the "hope" of Israel. However, since the same Hebrew word has both the meanings "hope" and "ritual bath," later readings took the verse to mean that God is a kind of purificatory bath, of sorts, to Israel.

[13] *Keter Shem Tov Ha-shalem*, ed. J. Immanuel Schochet (Brooklyn: Kehot, 2004), §93c.

[14] Most verbs that are conjugated in the *hitpa·eil* correspond to reflexive verbs in other languages. However, this is not invariably the case and there are many

verbs that are used in that grammatical pattern that do not appear to have any specific reflexive meaning at all.

[15] Zechariah 14:9.

[16] The extra "beyond" (*l'eila*) is added on the High Holy Days and throughout the Ten Days of Repentance.

[17] Elliot Rabin, "Tefillah: Poetry of the Sublime," in *HaYidion* 5 (Spring 2013), pp. 28–31, available online at https://ravsak.org/tefillah-poetry-sublime.

[18] As far as I can discern. The other prayers that come to mind in this regard are Nishmat Kol Ḥai, a perhaps similarly ancient prayer that tells us that "even were our mouths as filled with song as the sea...we could not sufficiently praise You...and bless Your name," and also the medieval hymn Anim Zemirot. Both of these, however, are only recited on the Sabbath and holidays.

[19] Apophatic theology is negative theology, a theology that seeks to describe the Divine only by negation, by what the divine is not. For example, one can not say that God is mighty, but rather that God is not weak.

[20] See Maimonides' *Guide for the Perplexed* I 57–59. There he explains that because language is inadequate to describe the Divine we must, as much as possible, be silent and, where that is not possible, speak of the Divine only negatively, through the negation of qualities (which are all qualities) that are not appropriate to ascribe to God.

[21] Bratslaver *hitbod'dut* is a stream-of-consciousness speaking-to-God meditation practice where the practitioner speaks non-stop to God. Michelle Kwitkin has suggested to me in a correspondence that this may also be true of the language of Ezekiel's vision, *ma·aseh merkavah*, where the word *k'ein* is used over and over to suggest that language is simply inadequate to convey the essence of the Divine. Yet the prophet does not respond to that thought by declining to speak about God, but rather uses this locution to indicate how language exceeds its limitations.

[22] As Voltaire's Pangloss repeats in *Candide*, mocking Liebniz's originally serious use of the term "the best of all possible worlds."

[23] The tradition is that the prayer leader combines the closing words of the last paragraph of the Shema with the opening words of the blessing following the Shema to render the sentence "The Eternal, your God, is truth" (*Adonai eloheikhem emet*).

[24] Rabbi Ḥanina was a first-century tannaitic sage; this teaching is found at B. Shabbat 55a.

[25] As cited in Jonathan Slater's *Mindful Jewish Living: Compassionate Practice* (New York: Aviv Press, 2007), p. 140.

[26] As told in Martin Buber, *Tales of the Hasidim*, trans. Olga Marx (1947; rpt. New York: Schocken, 1991), pp. 131–132.

[27] Rabbi Jacob Joseph of Polonne, *Sefer Ben Porat Yoseif* (ed. Lemberg, n. d.), p. 94a.

[28] See Rabbi Shneur Zalman of Liadi, *Sefer Ha-tanya* (ed. Brooklyn, 5716 [1955/1956]), *Sha·ar Ha-yiḥud V'ha-emunah*, chap. 1, pp. 152–153.

[29] Panentheism is the claim that, like pantheism, the world is God, but that, unlike pantheism, there is also a God beyond the world.

[30] For a fuller discussion of this claim, from which these paragraphs are excerpted, see my article, "Non-Dual Judaism," in *Jewish Theology in Our Time: A New Generation Explores the Foundations and Future of Jewish Belief*, ed. Elliot J. Cosgrove (Woodstock, VT: Jewish Lights Publishing, 2010), pp. 31–40.

[31] *Maggid D'varav L'Yaakov*, §60, p. 91.

[32] Rabbi Abraham Kalisker, *P'ri Ha-aretz*, Letters, Letter 6, as translated in Joseph Weiss, "R. Abraham Kalisker's Concept of Communion with God and Men," in *Studies in Eastern European Jewish Mysticism*, ed. David Goldstein (Oxford: Oxford University Press [The Littman Library of Jewish Civilization], 1985), p. 165. I have made minor adaptations in the translation in order to conform to the style of this volume.

[33] In other words: the Half Kaddish never itself functions as a conclusion.

Kaddish as *Neuzeit*:
Between the Nameless and the Named

Aubrey L. Glazer

To make each moment count, time must count. A recent outgoing voicemail message heard in Silicon Valley says it all: *"Hello, thanks for calling. You have thirty seconds to add value to my day—start now!"* Part of the tragedy of our accelerated lives in this "late capitalist" society is that humanity has never fully understood what we were in for with the onset of modernity.[1] When precisely was this moment that humanity was inalterably changed? Perhaps modern culture changed with the arrival of the printing press or the internet. Some may argue that the dawn of modernity started earlier, already affecting humanity after the Roman Empire finally vanished once and for all with the fall of Constantinople in 1453. But in our own generation, the sting of modernity has been felt most acutely since the day that Apple went public, because that is the moment when human beings really began to feel how alienated we have become from each other and how rapidly the "selfie" has become the new sovereign self.

To be precise about this feeling that life is on hyper-speed, it is helpful to consider that existence can be marked by the relationship between experience and expectation. The distance between the "space of experience" and the "horizon of expectation," according to Reinhart Koselleck, has become so eclipsed within the recent arc of historical time that modernity provides the human subject with a new experience of transition. By viewing the arc of historical time frame by frame, Koselleck points to *acceleration* as the means by which one's own time is distinguished from what went before.[2] The acceleration of modern or "new time" (*Neuzeit*), which emerges around the latter half of the eighteenth century, culminates at this "epochal threshold" at which history itself comes to be first perceived as "in motion."[3] Think of that indelible image of Charlie Chaplin in *Modern Times* (1936), as the Tramp finds himself stuck in the accelerated cogs of the time-clock he can no longer control. So in light of these accelerated times in which we find ourselves in post-modernity, in our hyper-accelerated world, what mind can be paid to rituals of an ancient past? Is there a prayer for accelerated times? I will argue in this essay that the Kaddish prayer can reasonably and profitably be read in just that light. Given our situatedness in a post-secular concept, this essay is a self-conscious journey through popular culture and song, rather than legalistic or exegetical discourse.[4] This approach to contextualizing Jewish liturgy within the post-secular will illustrate some specific ways in which Kaddish fits the bill.

Prayer demands contemplative time, not accelerated time (even though some *minyanim* today pride themselves for finishing before the arrival of the first commuter train to work!). To dwell on a word, even a letter, for more than a moment strikes us as absurd. The simple answer to the questioning spiritual seeker, caught like the Tramp in the clock of this vexing tension we navigate, is: "Never mind!" A few recent "never mind" moments, bordering on nihilism, seem apt to begin a reflection, in this hyper-accelerated world, on the timelessness of an ancient prayer, the Kaddish.

In his recent novel *This Is Where I Leave You* (2014), later adapted to film, American Jewish novelist Johnathan Tropper tells the story of a father who passes away, leaving four grown siblings to return to live together under the same roof, in their childhood home, as they sit *shiva* and recite Kaddish.[5] When two of the four siblings confront this request of their late father to mourn according to the tradition, the ensuing discussion is telling:

Judd Altman:
I don't understand the *shiva*. Mom's not even Jewish, and
Dad was an atheist.
Wendy Altman:
A Jewish atheist, and this is what he wanted.

This scene makes for good comedy, and in doing so it softens the
blow of an emergent and accelerated atheism that oftentimes seems
to typify the "never mind" generation of post-secular American
Judaism. There are some roots and cultural precedent here, whether
with the grunge of Nirvana's "Never Mind" (1991) or with the punk
rock of the Sex Pistols' "Never Mind the Bullocks" (1977).[6] Just
over a decade apart, each of these musical offerings captured that
urge not to feel anxiety or stress about the moment; that pervading,
nearly nihilistic sense of whateverness, nevermindity...and then
comes octogenarian Leonard Cohen with his audacious 2014 song,
"Nevermind." Like the descendant of the wicked child at the *seder*
symposium, Judd Altman in *This Is Where I Leave You* is trying to
understand what all these mourning rituals, like sitting *shiva* for
seven days and reciting Kaddish, could possibly mean to someone
from a highly assimilated, mixed Jewish background. And yet, this is
precisely what the self-proclaimed Jewish atheist father wanted—so
that when death would come knocking, he would not remain trapped
in a foxhole. The ability to pray beyond one's own circumscribed life
story is powerful indeed, as the Altman family finds out.

By contrast, consider the opening scene of the second season
of a recent noir television series written by Nic Pizzolatto, "True
Detective" (2015), which traces the disappearance of a city manager,
a man named Ben Casper. His disappearance disrupts a lucrative land
scheme and ignites an investigation involving three police officers and
a career criminal, Frank, who yearns to return to legitimate business.
As a voracious hustler and somnambulist, Frank is terrified that he

has no progeny to leave his fortune to, no land to bequeath, and no one to mourn for him. And as the mystery unfolds surrounding Ben Casper's death, the first and most brutal fact that emerges about this dead man is that he has no living family. He is discovered abandoned at the side of a road, comatose, with his eyes burnt out—and there is no one left to mourn for him.

The last place on earth one would expect to confront the mourner's prayer known as Kaddish, even so much as a trace of it, is in these opening vignettes for the second season of an award-winning noir television series. Aside from the montages that emit sparks of light amidst landscapes of deep darkness, it is the music of the intertwining lives of each character—apparently so vile and depraved, struggling with inner impulses impossible to vanquish or to imagine overcoming—that could only be the sounds of Cohen's "Nevermind." But Cohen, unlike Tropper, feels no need to soften the blow of atheism. Rather, this bard is content with expanding the space of agnosticism—so that any uncertainty within one's relationship to the Divine can be accommodated.

I will argue for a reconsideration of the Kaddish that invokes the Nameless Name in light of Cohen's seemingly alienated lyrics, always crossing that bridge between the nameless and the named. Cohen's song, "Nevermind," from his recent release *Popular Problems* (2014), evokes this dance:

> The story's told
> With facts and lies
> I had a name
> But nevermind

The refrain seeks to overcome the paradox of living "with facts and lies" and the consequent loss of a name once one straddles such a paradox of life.

...There's truth that lives
And truth that dies
I don't know which
So nevermind

The space separating the nameless from the named here is infinitesimal, yet it bridges existence, wherein blood is to life as death is to dust. As much as Cohen feigns protesting the need for prayer of any kind in a post-secular world, there remains an abiding appreciation for the power of the Name from which all other names emerge:

Names so deep
and Names so true
They're blood to me
They're dust to you

There is no need
That this survive
There's truth that lives
And truth that dies

The divine Name is that name of all names, the source from which all names emerge, holy and broken. This approach to tending to the broken, holy name through contemplative prayer predates Leonard Cohen's songbook and is found already in Jewish mysticism.

Let us consider the musicality of the mysticism, for example, in this extended passage from the Zohar:

Now that Israel are in exile, the entire structure, as it were, has collapsed. But in the time that is coming, when the Holy One shall redeem His children, Who [*mi*] and These [*eilleh*]— which were separated in exile—will join as one, the Name will be perfectly established, and the world will be fragrantly firm, as it is written: "Who are these [*mi eilleh*], that fly like a cloud, like doves to their cotes?" (Isaiah 60:8). Since this is one Name, it is not written "Who and these" [*mi va-eilleh*], but rather as "Who these" [*mi eilleh*]—one Name, indivisible. For in exile, "Who" [*mi*] has withdrawn above—Mother, as it were, away from children, and the children have fallen. And the Name that was complete—that supernal, primordial Name—has fallen. For this we pray and sanctify in synagogue, that this Name may be restored as it was: "May His great Name be enhanced and sanctified!" Who is "His Name"? That "great" one, first of all. For it has no structure without us: "Who" [*mi*] is never built up without "These" [*eilleh*]. So, at that time, "Who are these [*mi eilleh*], that fly like a cloud, like doves to their cotes?" (Isaiah 60:8). The whole world will see that the supernal Name has been restored to perfection. And if this great Name is perfected and rebuilt, then those who struggle with the Divine are responsible for all, and all other names recover their perfection, since they all depend upon "His great Name," first structure of all.[7]

Such a depiction of prayer in this classic text of Jewish mysticism is considered theurgic, meaning that the mystical shape of the godhead relies heavily on the permutations and reconfigurations of the mystic enmeshed in prayer and ritual. So strong is this co-dependent relationship between mystic and Deity that French scholar of Kabbalah Charles Mopsik (1956-2003) once described such theurgy as the very rituals that construct God.[8] As a theurgic moment embedded in standard liturgical ritual life, the Kaddish is what reconfigures the broken divine name precisely through those whose devotion is to the energy within every word, every letter of liturgy. This is less a fundamentalism and more an approach to prayer that demands a willingness to enter into a contemplative state with each word, in all its hyper-literality, as seen in the Zohar's reconfigured name of *Mi Eilleh* from Elohim. While refraining from entering too deeply into the garden of theosophical delights with this passage, it is important to notice why, according to this passage from the Zohar, existence is broken in prayer. Amidst this admission of the brokenness encountered each time the mourner, whose heart is torn, recites "May His great Name be enhanced and sanctified!" the question emerges from those very tears: "Who is 'His Name'?" It is this willingness to make space for questioning, uncertainty, and doubt that allows the Kaddish prayer to serve as an elixir to living in accelerated times.

It is no coincidence that such brokenness emerges early on in the mystical *imaginaire* of the Zohar, roughly the thirteenth and fourteenth centuries in Castille, most likely because of a clash between philosophy and mysticism. The strong influence of the ingenious philosopher-rabbi Maimonides and his search for the rational explanation behind every aspect of ritual life likely led to a dulling of the prayer experience for many seekers. By contrast, the contemplative circle of the Zohar, headed by Rabbi Moses ben Shem-Tov de Léon (1240-1305) envisioned a way of understanding his own displacement as a Jewish mystic from the Spanish Catholic milieu, amidst the endless disputations with his co-religionists as part of the arc of cosmic exile of the Divine Mother withdrawing from Her children.[9] A modicum of Solace thus began to emerge.

When a mother is separated from her children, everyone knows that even when the maternal caress is interrupted the bond still grows stronger. When the presently withdrawn Divine Mother[10] will be reunited with Her children, redemption will have arrived.[11] The same way that a mother communicates with her children, so too the Divine Mother communicates with Her children—namely, the mystics who are preoccupied with redeeming the nameless from the named so as to serve more effectively as the missing modality of intimate communication. Through the reunion of the Divine Mother with Her children, a finer frequency of contemplative communication emerges, as the broken names become restored. The finer frequency for Jewish mystics is broadcast in a manner something like an anagram, since *Mi Eilleh* and *Elohim* are really just anagrams of each other. This linguistic intimacy and oddity allows for a more cosmic drama to emerge: namely, that *Mi Eilleh* is the "broken" form of *Elohim*. This broken and divided name (*Mi Eilleh*), which reflects the brokenness of the manifest world, can be restored to its non-dual reality—as once "Who are these" of *Mi Eilleh* = *Elohim* as the divine totality. Those mystics in love with every word see how every waking moment in the layers of divisible time manifests the brokenness of eternal light that continually illumines limitless lacunae in the fabric of being, as the notion is rendered in the *Zohar Ḥai* commentary, which only now might be repaired by the salve of contemplative prayers.[12] And the more restoration the contemplative engages in with this broken, holy Name, the more that prayer must become a contemplative act, engaged in by those who sit and struggle with the divine—that is: Yisrael. While Leonard Cohen remains an intuitive kabbalist not beholden to any system, his rendering of this restoration of the broken, holy Name by way of contemplation still emerges brilliantly in his lyric, "Love Itself," in the following way:

> In streams of light I clearly saw
> The dust you seldom see,
> Out of which the Nameless makes
> A Name for one like me.
> …Then I came back from where I'd been.
> My room, it looked the same
> But there was nothing left between
> The Nameless and the Name.[13]

And this god-wrestler, Leonard Cohen, whose traces his lineage back to the priestly clan, cannot escape the pull of these prayers that reconstitute the broken, holy Name. His resignation to the task of contemplating—and so restoring—the holy, broken Name in a post-secular key comes through in this reprise of the song:

...Nevermind
Nevermind
I live the life
I left behind

I live it full
I live it wide
Through layers of time
You can't divide

I would argue that Leonard Cohen's post-secular songbook provides seekers today with the equivalent of a strong prayer experience, extending that erosion of spiritual authenticity caused by living solely in accelerated time.

When life is lived in a less accelerated manner—most pronounced as one traverses liminal moments like death, burial, and mourning—it allows for more expansiveness, through the indivisible layers of time hovering in a prayer like Kaddish D'ithad'ta. This is a liturgical variation and expansion of the regular Kaddish, which is recited during burial at a cemetery as well as upon the completion of studying a devotional book, when it is preceded by the Hadran prayer. (How remarkable, then, that the prayer known as Kaddish D'ithad'ta is indeed the same prayer recited at burial as upon the completion of a book of sacred literature! The ritual for the latter is known as a *siyyum* or completion of a cycle of learning that is forever returning. This is made apparent by titling the opening prayer that leads to Kaddish D'ithad'ta, as Hadran, which means literally "we shall return.") What is invoked at these liminal moments—an immanent transcendence over time-space—is what allows for the de-acceleration of distance between the "space of experience" and the "horizon of expectation." As the book is closed or the coffin is covered with earth, all of time-space remains open, a crossing-over the threshold into the web of eternal:

> In the future world, which the Holy One will create in
> unified consciousness, where the Holy One will revive the
> dead, construct the Temple, sustain life, rebuild the city of
> Jerusalem, uproot idolatrous worship from the Holy Land,
> and restore the holy devotion of the heavens to its place,
> along with its radiance, splendor, and Shekhinah, so may
> the Holy One blossom in redemption to hasten the onset of
> messianic consciousness.

In closing, contrary to the opening definition of acceleration as the eliding of distance between the "space of experience" and the "horizon of expectation," I would argue that strong prayer experiences like the Kaddish actually counteract that elision. Accelerated living leads to dysfunctional families, like the Altmans in *This is Where I Leave You*, and psychotic hustlers like Frank and Ben in *True Detective*. What normative Jewish liturgy (with its mystical undertones) provides is a way to live life in a less accelerated manner, thus allowing for more expansiveness through the indivisible layers of time hovering in a prayer like Kaddish. The ritual of reciting Kaddish, viewed through a Zoharic lens, sheds light on how much the divine name is in need of restoration. Every one of us is responsible for all names, in the process of recovering their lost unity. What Leonard Cohen dares to sing to us is how to sing "never mind to the *Neuzeit*," don't worry about those shrinking seconds left to say who shall I say calling. You are free, at least for this eternal moment, to allow yourself an elongation of that distance within but beyond those meaningful thirty seconds in the offing, a post-secular age between the "space of experience" and the "horizon of expectation," for its contemplative moment of restoring the Name to its lost wholeness, again and again.

NOTES

[1] Regarding the term "late capitalism," cf. the comments of Fredric Jameson in his *Postmodernism, Or the Cultural Logic of Late Capitalism* (Duke University Press: Durham, NC: 1991), p. xviii: "What marks the development of the new concept over the older one (which was still roughly consistent with Lenin's notion of a 'monopoly stage' of capitalism) is not merely an emphasis on the emergence of new forms of business organization (multinationals, transnationals) beyond the monopoly stage, but, above all, the vision of a world capitalist system fundamentally distinct from the older imperialism, which was little more than a rivalry between the various colonial powers."

[2] Reinhart Koselleck, "Is There an Acceleration of History?" in *High-Speed Society: Social Acceleration, Power, and Modernity*, eds. Hartmut Rosa and William E. Scheuerman (University Park, PA: Pennsylvania State University Press, 2009), pp. 113–134.

[3] David Cunningham, "Accelerationism and Its Discontents," *Radical Philosophy* 191 (May/June 2015), pp. 29–38.

[4] Undoubtedly, the magisterial study on Kaddish in English has already been written; see Leon Wieseltier, *Kaddish* (Knopf: New York, 1998). Wieseltier's reflections on the prayer emerge from his own experience of saying Kaddish, as a journal he kept fastidiously during the eleven-month period of mourning following his father's passing. Wieseltier based his reflections primarily upon dense legalistic and exegetical commentaries to the Kaddish prayer itself that are only available in Hebrew or Aramaic. The author is at times resistant and thus hyper-critical of the age that he sees characterized by Jewish illiteracy in America.

[5] Jonathan Tropper, *This Is Where I Leave You* (New York: Dutton, 2009).

[6] For more on the influence of punk ideology on cultural memes, see the prescient analysis in Dick Hebdige, *Subculture: The Meaning of Style* (London: Methuen, 1979).

[7] Zohar II 105a, trans. Daniel Matt (Stanford, CA: Stanford University Press, 2009), vol. 4 , p. 76 (slightly altered by myself).

[8] Charles Mopsik, *Les Grandes Textes de la Cabale: Les Rites qui Font Dieu: Pratiques religieuses et efficacité théurgique dans la Cabale, des origins au milieu du XVIIIe siècle* (Lagrasse Verdier: Paris, 1993).

[9] Hartley Lachter, *Kabbalistic Revolution: Reimagining Judaism in Medieval Spain* (Rutgers, NJ: Rutgers University Press, 2014).

[10] Known as sphere of divine consciousness called *Binah*.

[11] Zohar II 105a, ed.cit. vol. 5, pp. 76–77, n. 219.

[12] See Rabbi Yitzhak Itzik Yehudah Yehiel ben Alexander Sander of Kamorna, *Zohar Hai*, ad. loc. (R. Hayyim Aaron Zupnik & R. Hayyim Knalled: Premsyln, n.d.), p. 139a–b.

[13] Leonard Cohen, "Love Itself," *Ten New Songs* (Columbia, 2001).

Kaddish and God's "Great Name"

Mark B. Greenspan

I have recited the Kaddish thousands of times over the course of my life. I began as an eleven-year-old, following my father's death. As a daily participant in a synagogue *minyan*, I know that the Kaddish is a liturgical refrain as central to Jewish prayer as the Shema or the Amidah. When one considers the fact that the various forms of the Kaddish are recited at least twelve times a day as part of the traditional liturgy,[1] one realizes that the Kaddish is the most frequently said prayer in Jewish life. The Kaddish serves as healing words for the bereaved and as liturgical punctuation, separating the different sections of the daily service.

While we often think of the Kaddish as a prayer of praise or as an affirmation of faith for the bereaved, it is something more. God is not the focal point of the Kaddish. The Kaddish does not praise God but rather God's name. Yet the name of God is never explicitly mentioned in this Aramaic prayer. We speak of praising and hallowing the "great name;" of exalting and extolling the "name of holiness" even when it is beyond our ability to offer praise. The Kaddish, then, is an act of *kiddush ha-sheim*, of publicly sanctifying God's name, in the most literal sense of the word. Speaking of the importance of proclaiming and praising God's name in the presence of others is the locus of its theological outlook. While God and the expression the "great name" might be interchangeable, speaking of God as "the Name" serves as a powerful and mysterious way of relating to God. The words *sh'meih rabba*, "God's [literally, "His"] great name," are a bridge between heaven and earth—on the one hand, serving as an expression of God's distance, and on the other hand, serving as an expression of God's closeness in a world in which sorrow and suffering are a reality. Just as God is unseen, God's actual name is unstated. By speaking of "the Name" as a source of power and sovereignty, rather than actually pronouncing the name itself, we acknowledge both God's transcendence and immanence in the world. We also invoke God's presence in the world simply by speaking and praising the name. "The Name" is as intimate as language can allow us to be and yet as hidden from us as an unspoken appellation. The roots of this theology of the name can be found in the Bible, and the use of the expression *Hashem*, "the Name," continues to be a means of expressing popular piety today. (Observant Jews often speak of God as *Hashem*, literally, "The Name.") To speak of God's name as God's manifestation in the world has far-ranging implications for the ways in which we think about God's presence in our lives.

Sh'meih rabba is the central expression of the Kaddish. The Ḥatzi Kaddish, the Half Kaddish,[2] which contains the basic core of this prayer, is made up of three parts:

1. the reader's introduction: *yitgaddal v'yitkaddash sh'meih rabba*
("Hallowed and enhanced may His great name be throughout the world..."),

2. a congregational affirmation: *y'hei sh'meih rabba m'varakh l'alam u-l'almei almayya*
("May His great name be praised forever and ever"),[3] and

3. a response by the reader: *yitbarakh v'yishtabbaḥ v'yitpa·ar... sh'meih d'kudsha*
("Praised, glorified, and acclaimed...is His holy name...").

The central statement of the Kaddish is its communal affirmation. This passage is closely connected to two biblical passages: Psalms 113:2, "Let the name of YHVH be blessed now and forever," and Daniel 2:20, "Let the name of God (elo·ah) be blessed forever and ever." While the aforementioned verses contain the Tetragrammaton (YHVH) or a noun referring to God (elo·ah), any direct mention of God's name itself has been removed from the communal affirmation of the Kaddish, *y'hei sh'meih rabba*. What is the meaning of the expression? Why has the author of the Kaddish chosen to refer to God in this way? It is this expression that I wish to explore in this essay.

The Talmud emphasizes the importance of reciting this communal proclamation in praise of God's name:

Whenever the Israelites enter synagogues and houses of study and respond: "May His great name be blessed," the blessed Holy One shakes His head and says, "Happy is the sovereign who is thus praised in this house! Woe to the father who had to banish his children, and woe to the children who had to be banished from the table of their father!" [5]

Rava said, "[Ever since the Temple was destroyed,] the curse of each day is more severe than that of the preceding... In that case, how can the world endure? Through the praise recited after Kedushah D'Sidra, and the scriptural reading, and the response of 'great name' after studying *aggadah*..." [6]

Rabbi Joshua ben Levi said, "One who responds 'Amen, may His great name be blessed' with all his might [7]—that person's decreed sentence is torn up." [8]

It is no accident that two of these passages place the recitation of the words *y'hei sh'meih rabba* in the house of study rather than in the synagogue. Originally, this verse was a concluding supplication recited after a scriptural lesson or a sermon based on *aggadah*.

Nothing is said in these passages in the Talmud about the actual formula of the Kaddish, parts of which will both precede and follow the recitation of the central expression *y'hei sh'meih rabba*.[9] In his history of the liturgy, Ismar Elbogen suggests that "this prayer may at first have had no fixed formula but was freely worded by the preacher."[10] Thus, the preacher would conclude his lesson with a prayer of comfort and hope for the future, and the congregation would then respond by praising God's name. Elbogen's suggestion that the formula of the Kaddish was fluid is supported by Rabbi Joshua ben Levi's statement, above, which assumes that "Amen" is recited before the *y'hei sh'meih rabba*. This suggests that the line was a response to a prior statement uttered by the teacher or the prayer leader.

The essence of the Kaddish, then, is a single passage—*y'hei sh'meih rabba...*—which is framed by a call to prayer and followed by an extended meditation on what it means to praise God. In the opening passage, the leader calls on the congregation to sanctify the name so that God's sovereignty will be established during our lifetime and the life of the entire House of Israel. The congregation then responds: *amen, y'hei sh'meih rabba m'varakh l'alam u-l'almei almaya*. The opening passage, recited by the prayer leader (or the mourner) serves as a *kavvanah*, a meditation, in which the leader tells the congregation what they should be thinking about as they make the declaration *y'hei sh'meih rabba*. There are eschatological overtones in the leader's description of the praise of the name in this passage. Through our public declaration of praise, we establish God's sovereignty in the world. This is even more explicit in the Sephardic tradition, which includes the words *v'yatzmah purkaneih vi-kareiv m'shiheih*, "May He cause the blossoming of salvation and bring close His anointed one (i.e., the Messiah)," in the first paragraph of the Kaddish.

The passage following the communal affirmation speaks of the significance of praising God, but it also acknowledges our inability to fully praise God. One can praise God, but the holy name is "beyond all praise and song." As in the first half of the Kaddish, the name of God is referred to only obliquely in the second part of the Kaddish, as well. The words *b'rikh hu* in the second half of the Kaddish are often incorrectly adjoined to the previous words (*sh'meih d'kudsha*), creating the impression that one is saying *sh'meih d'kudsha brikh hu*, "the name of the Holy One, blessed be He." In fact, though, there should be a pause between *sh'meih d'kudsha* and *b'rikh hu*,[11] to yield the following meaning: "Glorified, praised, extolled, exalted, and lifted up... is His holy name. It is blessed (*b'rikh hu*) beyond all blessings and songs... spoken in the world." Thus, in addition to referring to God's "great name," the Kaddish speaks of the "holy name."

Together, these passages emphasize the importance of praising "great name," the "holy name," without ever explicitly stating God's name. By the time that recitation of Kaddish had emerged as normative liturgical practice, there was already a taboo against pronouncing the Tetragrammaton. But even if so, why not simply call God by one of the many names for the Divine found in biblical and rabbinic literature? While God's four-letter name could not be publicly pronounced, there are other names for God found in rabbinic literature and that are commonly used in Jewish prayer. The Tetragrammaton was pronounced as *Adonai* and God was commonly referred to by a variety of other names, either borrowed from Scripture or formulated by the rabbis. It seems strange that the Kaddish emphasized the name without ever stating it, or without using any of the other names for God.

The name of God has long been a source of reverence, adoration, and praise in the Jewish tradition. Reverence for the name of God dates back to the biblical period. We find references to the importance of revering God's name in, for example, Deuteronomy 28:58: "If you fail to observe faithfully all the terms of this Teaching that are written in this book, to revere the honored and awesome name, YHVH, your

God."[12] In Deuteronomy, the name of God appears to stand on its own as the subject of honor and reverence. God causes the divine Name to dwell in the place of God's choosing: "Then you must bring everything that I command you to the site where YHVH, your God, will choose to place His name..." (Deuteronomy 12:11). While the expression, "the name of God" and God's actual name (i.e., YHVH) are sometimes used interchangeably, the expression "His name" appears to be the embodiment of God's presence in the Temple, at least according to some. This idea contrasts with the passage in Exodus 25:8, where the people are commanded to build a sanctuary "so that I (i.e., God) may dwell among them." In Leviticus 24:11, the people are warned not to profane the name of God: "The son of the Israelite woman pronounced the name in blasphemy, and he was brought to Moses..."[13] In Numbers 6:27, the priests are commanded to "to place My name on the people of Israel, that I may bless them."

We find many references to the idea of loving and fearing the name throughout the Bible. For example:

• "Then David and all the troops that were with him set out from Baalim of Judah, to bring from there the Ark of God to which the name was attached—the name of the Eternal One of hosts enthroned on the cherubim" (2 Samuel 6:28).

• "Behold, the name of the Eternal comes from afar in blazing wrath, with a heavy burden..." (Isaiah 30:27).

• "Let those who love Your name exalt in You" (Psalm 5:12).

• "May the Eternal One answer you in the day of trouble; may the name of the God of Jacob protect you" (Psalm 20:2).

• "Eternal One, You have heard my vows; grant the bequest of those who fear Your name" (Psalm 61:6).

• "I will extol You, my God and sovereign, and bless Your name forever and ever. Every day I will bless You and praise Your name forever and ever" (Psalm 145:1–2).

Contemporary Bible scholars do not agree on the significance of the many references to God's name in Deuteronomy and in Deuteronomistic literature. While some see references to God's name as synonymous with God,[14] others argue that God's name became a type of hypostasis of God—that is, the name became the embodiment of God that replaced God's physical presence in the Temple.[15] This use of the name, it is argued, allowed early Israelite religion to move from the idea of a more mythologized embodiment of God, who was physically present in the Temple, to a more abstract and less mythological conception of God: "the name" was the embodiment of God's presence while God was present in heaven. Based on this understanding, Judaism was seen to be evolving from a more immanent conception of God to a more transcendent one. Later scholars have challenged this idea, however, and suggested that the expression *l'shakkein sh'mo sham*, "to cause God's name to dwell there," is not so much a theological statement as it is an idiomatic expression. The expression, in this understanding, was meant to imply ownership of the sanctuary and the land by God.[16]

Whatever its original significance may have been, the idea that the name of God was a source of power and reverence has its roots in the Bible. Commenting on God's declaration to Moses at the burning bush, "I am YHVH," (Exodus 6:2), Nahum Sarna writes:

> In the ancient Near Eastern world names in general, and the name of God in particular, possessed a dynamic quality and were expressive of character, or attributes and potency. The names of gods were immediately identified with their nature, status, and function so that to say "I did not make myself known to them by My name YHVH" is to state that the patriarchs did not experience the essential power associated with the name YHVH. The promise to them belonged to the distant future. The present reiteration…means their fulfillment is imminent.[17]

The Bible does not appear to be uncomfortable using God's name in all its different forms. The Tetragrammaton appears 6,828 times in the Bible. When Moses is commissioned to help redeem the Israelites, he expresses reluctance because he does not know God's name: "When I come to the Israelites and say to them, 'The God of your ancestors has sent me to you,' and they ask me, 'What is His name?'—what shall I say to them?" (Exodus 3:13). Moses' question presumes that the Israelite people must have been familiar with God's name; otherwise, of what use would it have been to tell them the name of God with which Moses had been sent to redeem them?[18] In the Book of Numbers, the priests are to bless the people, using God's name three times; they are commanded to "place My name on the people of Israel, that I may bless them" (6:27). The archaeological discovery at Ketef Hinnom of silver amulets containing the Priestly Benediction that date to the sixth or seventh century B.C.E. suggests that this expression was taken literally: people did, in fact, place the name of God on their bodies.[19]

By the rabbinic period, there had already developed a prohibition against pronouncing the Tetragrammaton.[20] The Talmud bases this prohibition on Exodus 3:15, "The Eternal, the God of your ancestors—the God of Abraham, Isaac, and Jacob—has sent me to you; this is My name forever (*l'olam*), and My appellation for all eternity." The word *l'olam* is written without a *vav*, leading the sages to the following interpretation:

> Rabbi Naḥman ben Ḥannah said in Rabbi Yoḥanan's name: As for the pronunciation of the Divine Name of four letters—the sages confide it to their disciples once in seven years; others state, twice in seven years. Said Rabbi Naḥman ben Isaac: Reason supports the view that it was once in seven years, for it is written, "This is My name forever (*l'olam*)," which is read as *l'alleim* ("to be kept secret"). Rava thought to lecture upon the divine name at a public session. Said a certain old man to him: "It is written *l'alleim* (to keep it secret)....The Holy One said: 'I am not called as I am written; I am written with *yod-hei* [i.e., *YHVH*] but I am read *alef-dalet* [i.e., *adonai*].'"[21]

We are also told that even when the priests pronounced the name in the Temple, they did so by "swallowing the name" so that it was not articulated.[22] In the Mishnah we learn that "one who pronounces the [four-letter] divine Name as it is spelled...does not have a portion in the World to Come."[23]

The use of the divine Name has a long and complicated history. Already in the fourth century B.C.E. the authors of the Septuagint (the Greek translation of the Bible) chose to replace the Tetragrammaton with the Greek word for "Lord" (*Kyrios*); in Hebrew, *Kyrios* is Adonai. Yet there are many sources that suggest that people did continue to use the Tetragrammaton into the next millennium. For example, the Mishnah makes a point of saying that the name of God could only be pronounced in the Temple, but could not be used, even in the Priestly Blessing, outside of the Temple:

> How was the Priestly Blessing pronounced? Outside the Temple it was said as three blessings, but in the Temple as

one blessing [with no interruption, because the response of "Amen" was not made in the Temple]. In the Temple the Tetragrammaton was uttered as written, but outside the Temple precincts, it was pronounced with a substitute name (*Adonai*).[24]

It would seem, then, that once the Temple in Jerusalem was destroyed, the Tetragrammaton fell out of use—due to either lack of knowledge, or fear of its use for improper purposes. But when did the divine Name (i.e., YHVH) become *ha-sheim*, the "name?" In rabbinic literature, the Tetragrammaton is referred to by a variety of other names: *sheim ha-m'forash* (the "explicit name"), *sheim ha-m'yuḥad* , (the "singular name" or the "name of God's unity"), and *sheim ben arba otiyyot* ("the four-letter name"). In the Avodah service of Yom Kippur afternoon, the Tetragrammaton is referred to as *ha-sheim ha-nikhbad v'ha-nora m'forash yotzei mi-pi kohein gadol*, the "glorious and awesome Name, stated explicitly from the mouth of the high priest." Only in the Kaddish do we find the name of God referred to as *sh'meih rabba*, the "great name." While it is logical to presume that the "great name" is the Tetragrammaton, the expression is generic enough to leave open the possibility that it might refer to some other divine name found in Scripture or in rabbinic literature. In the Book of Exodus, God is called *ehyeh* and *ehyeh asher ehyeh* (Exodus 3:12, 14). The sages also speak of a twelve-letter and a forty-two-letter name of God that was used by the Temple priests.[25]

But if the point was to refer to the Tetragrammaton in the Kaddish, why would the liturgist have used this more generic expression? The fact that the Kaddish originated in the house of study, and not the synagogue, might explain the use of this particular expression. The Kaddish was not, originally, part of the daily liturgy. It was a concluding prayer, recited in the vernacular, offered after a study session usually having to do with *aggadah*, non-legal material. Anyone might attend these sessions. Could it be that it was considered unseemly to refer to God by God's actual name in this non-liturgical setting? The use of Aramaic as the language of the Kaddish might suggest that the Kaddish was of lesser status than some of the other liturgical prayers.

Another reason for the use of the expression "His great name" might have to do with issues of modesty and dress. Both men and women could attend the sessions in the *beit midrash*. Since the house of study was open to the general public, the sages might have been more flexible about not imposing standards of modesty in this setting. This might have led the sages to temper the language of prayer by removing direct references to God's name. Although today we tend to associate the issue of modesty with women's dress, there certainly must have been similar norms for men as well in ancient times. It is plausible that there was in existence a code of appropriate dress in synagogues, as well as in houses of study. Could it be that the sages avoided praying in Hebrew for this very reason, and likewise used the expression *sh'meih rabba* rather than a more specific name for God (or even its rabbinic replacement, *Adonai*)?[26] The expression *sh'meih rabba* was a more generic way of referring to God.

Also, by offering a prayer in Aramaic at the end of a session of learning, the sages might have been addressing the needs of the uneducated public that did not understand Hebrew. Eventually, the Kaddish found its way into the liturgy, and its recitation was deemed to require the presence of a *minyan*, a quorum of ten worshippers. But it did not begin this way; it was originally simply a prayer of comfort together with a response that offered hope for the establishment of God's sovereignty on earth. It was also a means of publicly sanctifying God's name in the presence of the community. This was, ultimately, the purpose of the study of Torah.

The use of *sh'meih rabba* may also have universalized the prayer, rather than using a more particularistic expression of faith contained in a single name of God. God's "great name" was an expression with which anyone could identify. In the end, what can we know

about God other than the name by which we refer to the Divine?
While God's great name may have originally been a reference to the
Tetragrammaton, this expression offered an opportunity for each
person to speak of God in his or her own unique way. Whether
one refers to God as *Elohim, Shaddai, Ha-raḥaman,* or *Ribbon Ha-
olam,* God's name in all of its variety of forms is a great blessing to
the world.[27] The great name opened the door for some freedom of
expression in prayer. We might speak of God differently but we all
agree that all these expressions are God's "great name." In the context
of the house of learning, speaking of God's great name rather than
defining God's essence through a single name might have been one
of the earliest expressions of pluralism. Only in some future messianic
era would "the Eternal and His name become one," [28] as we say at the
end of the Aleinu. Until that time, God's name would be great but it
would not be singular in nature.

Certainly the sages and commentators must have been troubled
by the absence of God's name from the Kaddish, and this tension
is best captured in a comment by the Tosafot to B. Berakhot 3a.[29]
Commenting on the words *sh'meih rabba,* the Tosafot call our attention
to at least one interpretation of this passage that attempts to read
God into the Kaddish directly, rather than speaking generically of
the "Name":

> This passage contradicts the explanation in the *Maḥzor
> Vitry,* which claims that the prayer that we recite, *y'hei sh'meih
> rabba,* is a prayer that God's name should be complete. This
> is based on the scriptural passage, "Hand upon the throne of
> the Lord (*keis yah*)" (Exodus 17:16). God's name and throne
> cannot be complete until the seed of Amalek is wiped out.

According to *Maḥzor Vitry,* an eleventh century work by Rabbi
Simḥah ben Samuel of the French town of Vitry, the word *sh'meih*

should be spelled *shin-mem-yod-hei*—that is, including the letter *yod*—even though it is more regularly written without it. When we say *y'hei sh'meih rabba*, then, the word *sh'meih* can be read as *sheim yah*—that is, we pray that God's great name, Yah, shall become complete and blessed forever. The word *m'varakh* is a separate statement that God's name should be complete and it should be a blessing for the World to Come. But this does not seem right, since the passage should be read as one petition: "May God's great name be blessed" (which is what people do, in fact, say when they recite the Kaddish).

According to the *Maḥzor Vitry*, the word *sh'meih* is a combination then of two separate words: *sheim* and *yah*, meaning "the name of Yah." The name *yah* itself is made up of two of the four letters of the Tetragrammaton (*yod* and *hei*) and is a name of God in its own right. For example, it appears throughout the Book of Psalms in the word *halleluyah*, "praise Yah." It also appears in the story of the war against the Amalek : "Moses built an altar and named it YHVH-Nisi, meaning: 'hand upon the altar of Yah!' For the Eternal will be at war with Amalek throughout all ages" (Exodus 17:15–16). Yah is understood by the *Maḥzor Vitry* as an incomplete spelling of God four-letter Name. As long as Israel's mortal enemy Amalek was not defeated, God's name would remain incomplete. According to the *Maḥzor Vitry*,[31] when one recites the Kaddish, one says: "May the name *Yah* be great (that is, may it be whole). May it be blessed forever and ever." The Tosafot reject this interpretation, maintaining that *sh'meih rabba* should be read simply as "the great name"—a generic term for the Tetragrammaton—and that the passage should be read as a single thought: "May His great name be blessed forever and ever."[32]

The focus on God's name in the Kaddish is closely related to the notion of *kiddush ha-sheim*, "the sanctification of God's name." Maimonides includes *kiddush ha-sheim* among the 613 commandments in the Torah:

> The entire House of Israel is commanded regarding the sanctification of **the great name**, as is stated in Scripture: "And I shall be sanctified amidst the people Israel" (Leviticus 22:32). Also, they are warned against desecrating (God's holy name), as (the above verse) states: "And they shall not desecrate My holy name."[33]

While Maimonides discusses this concept in the context of martyrdom, *kiddush ha-sheim* can also be practiced through ethical actions through which one goes beyond the letter of the law,[34] as well as in public acts of prayer. That the Kaddish was considered an act of sanctification of God's name is also reflected in other scriptural sources for the opening words of this prayer: "Thus will I magnify Myself and sanctify Myself, and I will make Myself known in the eyes of many nations, and they shall know that I am the Eternal" (Ezekiel 38:23). Sanctifying God's name is defined in this verse as "making God known in the eyes of the nation," so that "people shall know God."[35]

Rabbi Norman Lamm explains the connection between *kiddush ha-sheim* and the Kaddish as follows:

> In the Kaddish, the key parts refer quite literally to the "sanctification" of the "Name." At a comparatively early period, the Kaddish was already ascribed to the biblical source of *kiddush ha-sheim*. The absence of any specific Divine Name in this prayer, and the emphasis on the "Name" as such, has been thought by some scholars to have been deliberate, in order to emphasize its idiomatic affinity to the biblical *kiddush ha-sheim*.[36]

Rabbi Lamm also suggests that originally the Kaddish might have been recited by people about to face martyrdom, in order to comfort the onlookers by speaking of the redemption and the Messiah "in your lifetime and in your days."[37] Whether or not this intriguing theory is correct, it is worth noting that Maimonides, in the passage from the Mishneh Torah cited above, speaks of *kiddush ha-sheim* as sanctifying "the great name," thereby connecting the Kaddish prayer, the idea of *kiddush ha-sheim*, and martyrdom. One sanctifies God's name through prayer and praise, through our actions (particularly vis-à-vis our fellow human beings), and ultimately through our willingness to sacrifice our lives in the name of our higher ideals.

The *sh'meih rabba*, the "great name," is a powerful metaphor for thinking about our relationship with God. It suggests that language is the means through which we experience God's presence in the world. To know God's name is to be in a relationship with God, and in some fashion, to change the world. To acknowledge that such a name exists implies that there is a unique relationship between human beings and the Eternal. The name embodies both immanence and transcendence. On the one hand, the name is hidden; on the other hand, we acknowledge that we have the ability to magnify and sanctify this unspoken name through words and deeds, as a way of bringing about God's sovereignty in the world.

The more Jews avoided pronouncing the Tetragrammaton over time, the more they began to speak about "the Name" as the embodiment of God's presence in the world. This was not so different from the Deuteronomist who spoke of God's name "dwelling" in the Temple. The name was the most real aspect of the Divine for people living in a world without prophecy or revelation. Jews came to treat "the Name" with reverence, when speaking of it in prayer, study, and in daily life. Yet they could not pronounce it, just as they could not give physical description to the Divine. "The Name" had a power

all its own that took on a semi-magical quality. It was so powerful
that one could not even pronounce it in prayer—one would simply
say *Adonai* instead. God's name became the subject of mystical
speculation as well as of midrashic creativity. The great name of
God was everywhere and nowhere, hidden in *gematria*, poetry, and
mystical speculation. Even the Torah was understood to be one long
name of God, which was ineffable as a name.[38] In his introduction to
his commentary on the Torah, Naḥmanides writes: "We possess an
authentic tradition showing that the entire Torah consists of names of
God, and the words we read can be divided in a very different way so
as to form an (esoteric) name…"[39] While this may not have been the
original meaning of "the great name" in the Kaddish, it is not difficult
to imagine that this is what others thought of in later generations,
as they praised God through the Kaddish. The great name was all
around them. God was present in the ways God's name was manifest
in the world. And we, in turn, have the power to sanctify that name
and thus repair the world.

The Name became a bridge between the realms of the divine and
the human. In an age when God could no longer be seen and God's
prophetic word could not be heard, the way humanity came to know
God was through the various manifestations of God's name. To
speak of the name was a way of speaking both of God's hiddenness
and God's presence in the world. God's name is ineffable, and yet we
have the power to bring God's name into the world. We can sanctify
the name of God through prayer and action, or we can distance and
desecrate God's name through transgression. We can testify to God's
reality by praising and declaring God's name in the presence of a
community. That is the importance of the Kaddish, and all the other
prayers that can only be recited in the presence of a *minyan*. But even
here we stop short of using the name—we speak of praising God's
great name without ever saying it.

In the end, God's name, like God's essence, is an ineffable mystery: we cannot see God and we cannot pronounce God's great name, yet we can make reference to God's name. The very idea that God has a name and that one time it was known to the Jewish people defines a unique relationship between the Eternal and the people Israel. God uses language to create the world and God comes to be known by the very existence of a name. God is as close to us as is human language. The knowledge that there is such a name serves as a bridge between heaven and earth. Even in sorrow and silence we have the ability to bring God's name into the world by proclaiming God's sovereignty and by living in a way that makes others aware that there is a God who calls us to service. Jews are the people of the unspoken Name.

NOTES

[1] The Kaddish is recited at least six times in the morning service, as well three times each in the afternoon and evening services. There are different formulas for the Kaddish: Ḥatzi Kaddish (the Half Kaddish), Kaddish Shaleim (the Full Kaddish), Kaddish D'rabbanan (the Rabbis' Kaddish), and Kaddish Yatom (the Orphan's Kaddish, often called the Mourner's Kaddish).

[2] It might be more helpful to refer to Ḥatzi Kaddish as the Partial Kaddish. The Full Kaddish concludes with three additional statements: *titkabbeil*, "May the prayers and supplications of the whole House of Israel be accepted by their Father who is in Heaven"; *y'hei sh'lama rabba*, "May there be abundant peace from heaven and life for us and for all Israel"; and *oseh shalom*, "May the One who creates peace in the heights create peace for us and for all of Israel." It is interesting to note that the last two statements are similar to one another; one is in Aramaic and the other in Hebrew.

[3] I use masculine pronouns for God when translating the Kaddish not to suggest any sense of gender, but in order to reflect the absence of God's name from the text. Hebrew is not gender neutral; pronouns and nouns are either masculine or feminine. That said, it should be noted that more often than not the metaphors and pronouns used in traditional Jewish literature to refer to God are masculine; God is "our Father, our King," "King of the universe," etc. Only in the Middle Ages with the rise of Kabbalah do we find the use of feminine metaphors such as Shekhinah as references to God.

[4] The four-letter name of God, the Tetragrammaton, is written as *yod-hei-vav-hei* and pronounced as "Adonai" in liturgical practice and, although translated elsewhere as "Lord," is generally translated as "the Eternal" in this volume.

[5] B. Berakhot 3a.

[6] B. Sotah 49a. Kedushah D'sidra refers to a passage recited toward the end of the morning service on weekdays, at the beginning of the afternoon service on Shabbat and festivals, at the end of the evening service on Shabbat, and at the beginning of the Neilah Service on Yom Kippur. It opens with a number of verses associated with the Kedushah (Isaiah 6:3, Ezekiel 3:12, and Exodus 15:18) and their Aramaic translations. According to Rashi it was designed to take the place of the daily study of the law. See "Kedusha D'sidra" in Marcy Nulman, *The Encyclopedia of Jewish Prayer* (Rowman and Littlefield Publishers United Kingdom, 1996). The word *aggadah* references the non-legal passages in the Talmud.

[7] What does it mean to recite *y'hei sh'meih rabba* "with all one's might"? Rashi, writing *ad locum*, comments that one must do so with *kavvanah*, deep concentration and directed prayer. In the *Mishnah B'rurah*, *Hilkhot Berakhot* 56:1: Rabbi Israel Meir Kagan explains:

"The early commentators (the *rishonim*) explained that by 'all one's might' the sages meant 'with all of one's mind and with one's entire body'—in other words, that one should say it with heart and soul, and should not only pronounce it with one's lips without having one's mind on what one is saying. One must also apply one's mind to hearing Kaddish uttered by the prayer leader, in order to be conscious of that to which one is responding *amen y'hei sh'meih rabba*; and so too for the *amen* after *da-amiran b'alma*. One must certainly be extremely careful to avoid talking in the middle of Kaddish or Kedushah. This is stated in the tractate *Derekh Eretz*, that Rabbi Ḥama found the prophet Elijah with several thousand camels laden with anger and wrath to repay those who talk then. The verse 'You have not called Me, Jacob' (Isaiah 43:22) may be applied to whoever speaks in these places."

A more novel explanation is that *b'khol koho*, "with all of one's strength," means that one has to recite the twenty-eight letters of *y'hei sh'meih rabba* with intensity. (The Hebrew word for strength, *ko·aḥ*, has the numerical value of twenty-eight.) See Seligman Baer's commentary to the traditional prayerbook, *Yakhin Lashon*, published in his *Seder Avodat Yisrael* (Rödelheim: M. Lehrberger & Co, 1901), p. 130.

[8] B. Shabbat 119b.

[9] While we cannot be certain what the formula before or after *y'hei sh'meih rabba* might have been, the inclusion of the word *amen* before the *y'hei sh'meih rabba* in B. Shabbat 119b suggests that the line was a response.

[10] Ismar Elbogen, *Jewish Liturgy, A Comprehensive History,* trans. Raymond P. Schendlin (Philadelphia: Jewish Publication Society, 1993), pp. 80–84.

[11] Cf. Baer, *Seder Avodat Yisrael*, p. 130.

[12] Only here, in this passage from Deuteronomy, and in Leviticus 24:11, is the name of God referred to with the direct article, "the name" (*ha-sheim*).

[13] The Hebrew for "pronounced the name in blasphemy" uses two verbs rather than one: *va-yikov...et ha-sheim va-y'kalleil.*

[14] Jeffrey H. Tigay, *Deuteronomy: The JPS Torah Commentary* (Philadelphia: Jewish Publication Society, 1996), p. 271.

[15] Martin Noth, among others. For a review and critique of the literature on "name theology," see Michael S. Heiser, "The Name Theology of Israelite Religion," available online at http://www.thedivinecouncil.com/ETSName.pdf.

[16] Sandra Richter, *The Deuteronomistic History and the Name Theology* (Berlin and New York: Walter de Gruyter, 2002), pp. 41–52.

[17] Nahum M. Sarna, *The JPS Torah Commentary: Exodus* (Philadelphia: Jewish Publications Society, 1986), p. 25.

[18] Ibid., p. 31.

[19] Jacob Milgrom, *Numbers: The JPS Torah Commentary* (Philadelphia: Jewish Publications Society, 1990), p. 52.

[20] Louis Isaac Rabinowitz, "The Prohibition of the Use of the Name of God" *Encyclopedia Judaica* (Detroit: MacMillan Reference, 2007), pp 676–678.

[21] B. Kiddushin 71a. Hebrew has a fluid orthography that allows for the use of internal letters to denote vowel sounds, but which does not consider such words to be incorrectly spelled when those vowel-letters are omitted. The *vav* in *olam* is an example of such a vowel-letter.

[22] Ibid.

[23] M. Sanhedrin 10:1.

[24] See M. Sotah 7:6 and M. Tamid 7:2.

[25] B. Kiddushin 71a.

[26] B. Berakhot 25b; Also see B. Yoma 35b, in which the other *kohanim* did not allow Eleazar bar Hasom to wear a sheer garment that allowed people to see his body. Also, in B. Shabbat 10 we learn that it was forbidden to enter a bath-house if one had a tattoo of the divine name on one's body without covering it. One could not even greet another person with the word *shalom* in such a place since it was considered one of the names of God, and the combination of nudity and the divine name was considered inappropriate.

[27] All these are names of God that appear in the Jewish liturgical tradition.

[28] Zechariah 14:9.

[29] The so-called "Tosafot" were the medieval scholars whose comments appear on the outside column of a page of Talmud, across from the commentary of Rashi. They are often referred to as the grandchildren of Rashi, as some of them actually were. They are more correctly called the *ba·alei ha-tosafot* ("Authors of the Annotations").

[30] Simḥah ben Sh'muel, *Maḥzor Vitry*, ed. Simon Hurwitz (Nuremberg: I. Bulka, 1923), p. 55.

[31] Ibid., pp. 9, 22, 25–26, and 55. *Maḥzor Vitry* consistently spells *sh'meih* with a *yod*. The comment of the Tosafot is mentioned by Hurwitz in his introduction, p. 169.

[32] See Daniel Sperber, *The Jewish Cycle: Custom, Lore, and Iconography* (Ramat Gan: Bar Ilan University Press, 2008), pp. 555–566. Sperber points out that the interpretation of *sh'meih* as "the name Yah" does not actually appear in *Maḥzor Vitry*—possibly because it was removed as a result of the Tosafot's criticism of this reading of the Kaddish. However, it was accepted by many other halakhists in the Middle Ages, including Rabbi David ben Joseph Abudarham (ibid., p. 558).

[33] M.T. Hilkhot Yesodei Ha-torah 5:1.

[34] Y. Bava Metzia 2:5, 8c, and Devarim Rabbah 3:3. When Shimon ben Shetaḥ returns valuables to a gentile vendor who inadvertently left them in a bag around

the neck of a donkey that he had just sold to the sage, the gentile vendor blesses the him by saying, "Blessed be the God of Shimon ben Shetaḥ."

[35] See the essay on "Kiddush Hashem and Hillul Hashem" on the website of the Jewish Virtual Library (www.jewishvirtuallibrary.org). For more on the idea of sanctifying God's name, and sanctification more generally, see the first volume in the Mesorah Matrix series, *Kedushah: Sanctification*, eds. David Birnbaum and Benjamin Blech (New York: New Paradigm Matrix, 2015).

[36] Norman Lamm, "Kiddush Ha-shem and Hillul Ha-shem," published on the Jewish Virtual Library website at https://www.jewishvirtuallibrary.org/jsource/judaica/ejud_0002_0012_0_11109.html.

[37] Yehudah Kaufman. *Midr'shei Ge'ullah* (Tel Aviv: Mosad Bialik/Mesorah, 1954), p. 58, n. 12, quoting Ḥayyim Naḥman Bialik. Kaufman also published under the name Yehudah Even Shemuel.

[38] Gershom G. Scholem, "The Meaning of the Torah in Jewish Mysticism," in *On the Kabbalah and Its Symbolism*, trans. Ralph Manheim (New York: Schocken, 1969), pp. 35–44.

[39] Ibid., p. 38.

Kaddish: The Practice of Praise

Avram Israel Reisner

When asked to contribute an essay to this volume on the Kaddish, I was eager to address the task, for I had long suspected that there was a story to tell that has not been told. Kaddish is that rarest of liturgical gems. It is not part of the statutory liturgical structure that makes up the heart of the private and public prayers (the twice-daily Shema and Its Blessings, the thrice-daily Amidah, and the Grace After Meals),[1] yet it has found itself liminal space to occupy around the liturgical units. It is highly regarded, even lionized, by the tradition (as we shall see)—but its origins have not, to my mind, been properly accounted for. In this essay I would like to challenge the received wisdom about the origin of the Kaddish and redirect our focus. I understand that the case I am making here is highly speculative; nevertheless, I hope that the new light I am proposing might better capture the meaning and intent of this extraordinary prayer.

No doubt much of the import ascribed to Kaddish is due in part to its role as the Mourner's Kaddish, recited by a mourner for his or her lost loved one—both to seek consolation and, almost magically, to assure the deceased of salvation. But Kaddish does not allude to the dead at all, and it is clear that the use of the Kaddish as a prayer for the soul of the dead is a late development, as has been amply demonstrated.[2] Long before that, Kaddish served, in several different versions,[3] as a repeating feature of the prayer service. And though, in that guise, it seems to play a subsidiary role—part of the wallpaper, as it were—it was reputed from the very first to be of unusual, even foundational importance.

Why?

I would like to propose that, true to its opening words (*yitgaddal v'yitkaddash sh'meih rabba*, "may His great name be magnified and sanctified"), the Kaddish is simply about praise by God's minions on earth and originates outside normative rabbinic structures in the early mysticism of Heikhalot literature, which describes a vision of the heavens and the parallel praise of the angels. It is, I think, in that context that Kaddish became beloved, and from there it worked its way into the traditional liturgy.

The Tale Told Heretofore

In his magisterial work on the origins of Jewish prayer, *Jewish Liturgy: A Comprehensive History*, Ismar Elbogen writes:

> Among the amoraim, Rava designates "'May the great name' [literally: His great name] of the Aggadah" as one of the things upon which the world stands (B. Sotah 49a). Now what we find in Rava's language as a unified concept points to the origin of this prayer; it was originally used at the end of sermons on Aggadah. The rule was that every sermon had to conclude with words of consolation—that is, with references to the messianic age—and some preachers added another short prayer to these eschatological conclusions.... One such prayer that became established in the course of time was the Kaddish. Its first sentence contains the two eschatological petitions for the sanctification of the name of God and for the coming of the kingdom of God. To these petitions belongs the blessing "May His great name be blessed,"[4] or, in its Hebrew formulation, *y'hei sh'meih rabba m'varakh* (B. Berakhot 3a)[5]....This is the core and the

original meaning of the Kaddish....It appears that besides these petitions and the blessing, the Aramaic clause *l'eilla min kol birkhata*, "above all blessings," also belongs to the first stratum, because it contains a clear reference to the aggadic sermon and its eschatological conclusion (*neḥamata*).[6]

It is noteworthy that the Kaddish is in Aramaic rather than Hebrew, as the latter is the language of the standard Jewish liturgy, and Elbogen ties that fact, as well, to this proposed context:

> The connection with the Aggadah also explains the Aramaic language of Kaddish, for this was the language spoken by the sages. Kaddish was not composed in the dialect of the common people but in the artificial dialect used in the house of study, and familiar from the officially recognized Targums.

This explanatory structure was used before Elbogen by David de Sola Pool in his monograph on the Kaddish and appears to date back at least to Leopold Zunz in the mid-nineteenth century.[7]

But the association of the origins of the Kaddish with the old aggadic sermon, or *d'rashah*, seems to me to be poorly established and weak in its explanatory power. Rethinking this matter is what has driven this essay.

What Do We Know of the Origins of the Kaddish

The earliest references that we have to the Kaddish focus on the power and import of the communal response that is at its heart. We have two tannaitic sources dating from the second century C.E., both of which are presented in the name of Rabbi Yosi.

One, found on B. Berakhot 3a, associates Kaddish equally with the synagogue and the study hall. Because this is part of a long passage, I shall cite only the relevant portions:

> It is taught: Says Rabbi Yosi: Once when I was traveling I entered one of the ruins of Jerusalem to pray. Elijah appeared and waited for me by the entrance until I finished my prayer. After I had finished my prayer, he said to me…"My son, what did you hear in the ruin?" And I said to him, "I heard a *bat kol* [that is, an ethereal voice] quavering like a dove, saying: 'Woe to the children on account of whose sins I have destroyed My own house…'" [Elijah] responded, "By your life! By the life of your head! It does not do so only now, but every day three times a day.[8] And not only that, but whenever Jews enter synagogues and study halls and respond 'May His great name be blessed,'[9] the blessed Holy One shakes His head and says: 'How fortunate is a king who is praised in his own domain. Imagine what it is like for a father who has exiled his children, and woe to the children exiled from their father's table.'"

In this text, Kaddish's central line is associated equally with the study hall and the synagogue, but the larger context is one of prayer, not study.[10] Rabbi Yosi's encounter with Elijah concerns his prayer, and Elijah's reference to the ethereal moaning "every day three times a day" is clearly envisioning the times of the daily prayers, and not less-regular study times. It is the synagogue, not the study hall, that is spoken of here as the extension of the Temple (God's house/domain), and it is the synagogue where prayers were regularly offered in lieu of the Temple's sacrifices. Thus this early source points to prayer, rather than study, as the context of the Kaddish's central communal praise.

The other tannaitic source about the Kaddish response seems also to be in the context of prayer, rather than study. In the ancient tannaitic midrash on Deuteronomy, Sifrei Devarim, there are several attempts to interpret the verse "When I call upon the name of the Eternal, speak[11] of the grandeur of our God" (32:3)—a verse that is peculiar because it begins in the first-person singular and ends in the second-person plural. The first interpretation[12] is presented in the name of the selfsame Rabbi Yosi, and applies that verse to the invitation to prayer at the start of public services, known as Bar'khu: "Rabbi Yosi said: Whence [do we learn] that when people congregate in the synagogue and say, 'Bless (bar'khu) the Eternal who is blessed (ha-m'vorakh),' that the people answer, 'Blessed (barukh) is the Eternal who is blessed (ha-m'vorakh) forever and ever?'[13] As it says…" The Sifrei next applies the verse to explain the requirement that a minimum of three people is necessary in order to say zimmun, the formal invitation to say Grace After Meals, in a group setting.[14] Next Sifrei applies the target verse to the response to the Shema, "Blessed is the name of His glorious kingdom forever and ever," after which we read:

> Whence [do we learn that] when [people] say "May His great name be blessed,"[15] that we answer after them "forever and forever and ever"? As it says: "Speak of the grandeur of our God."

The general midrashic context in which this verse is being interpreted up to this point is that of prayer.[16]

Moving from these tannaitic comments to the early amoraic period, which extends from the third to the fifth century in the Land of Israel and somewhat longer, until the sixth century, in Babylonia, we next encounter a talmudic text[17] that consists of a series of amoraic statements about the etiquette of praying the Amidah. In this context, a question is asked about the legitimacy of interrupting in order to respond "May His great name be blessed."[18] It is most likely that this, too, is referring specifically to interrupting one's Amidah. Rav

Dimi brings a response from the Palestinian amoraim Rabbis Judah and Simon, two students of Rabbi Yoḥanan, that one "may interrupt" (presumably, one's Amidah) for the response to Kaddish, for even one studying mystical lore would interrupt one's study in such a case.

Later, Rava seems to treat the Kaddish response in a context of prayer as well. In a different passage in the Babylonian Talmud,[19] what appear to be two dicta by Rava stand at the heart of a long, embellished passage. The first dictum concerns the way in which Hallel, the special collection of psalms that is added to the public service on holidays and the New Moon, is said in public: "Rava said: It is possible to learn many laws from the way in which Hallel is said." Several examples from Hallel follow, with appropriate talmudic embellishments. This dictum is directly followed by Rava's second dictum, again about the proper way to say certain prayers—this time focusing on one's personal behavior, beginning with another line of Hallel and then continuing directly with Kaddish:

> Rava said: Let one not say, "Welcome to the one who has arrived" (Psalm 118:26) and then afterward say "in God's name," but rather say it together....Let one not say: "May His great name" and then afterward say "be blessed,"[20] but rather say it together.

All these texts, then, have discussed the Kaddish solely within the context of prayer.

The confounding text is the one cited by Elbogen, which is found in the Babylonian Talmud at Sotah 49a. There Rava states that since the destruction of the Temple, every day is worse than the one before. The anonymous voice of the Talmud asks about that—"So, what keeps the world standing?"—and, again anonymously, comes the answer: "[What keeps the world standing are] *k'dushah d'sidra* and *y'hei sh'meih rabba d'aggadta*."[21] These references to *k'dushah d'sidra*, literally "*k'dushah* of the order," and the "Kaddish response of *aggadah*" are what set the tenor of the discussion of the Kaddish's origins, for "order" was taken to refer to a set body of study (as in an "order"/ *seder* of the Mishnah), and *aggadah* was taken to refer to the homily (*d'rashah*). But neither of those inferences are beyond question.[22] In any event, it is clear that this reference does not date to the fourth-century sage Rava, but to an anonymous hand in the sixth century C.E., or perhaps even later.[23]

All this suggests that in early rabbinic literature, the context in which Kaddish was considered was generally the synagogue prayer service. Indeed, nowhere does the text of the Kaddish itself allude to Torah or study, but simply to the praise of God.

That the Kaddish has become a feature of the prayer service is clearly attested by the next source that attests to the Kaddish, taken in chronological order. Tractate Sofrim,[24] generally assigned to the mid-eighth century and understood to be based primarily on Palestinian sources, refers not only to the Kaddish response that had appeared in earlier talmudic sources—it identifies the entire prayer by name. This tractate is divided in two parts, the first portion dealing with scribal practices in preparing a Torah scroll and the latter portion (chapters 10–21) dealing with the prayer service. It is in this latter half of the tractate that Kaddish is discussed. The Kaddish is named along with with the Bar'khu as an item whose recitation requires a quorum of ten adults,[25] but the context there suggests that the reference to "Kaddish" is not to our Kaddish at all, but to prayer known today as the Kedushah. However, elsewhere in Sofrim the references appear to be to our Kaddish prayer:

> [Regarding the prayer service on the Ninth of Av:] In the morning service, after the psalms and verses, one says Yotzer with Bar'khu in a low tone, and includes neither the Kedushah nor the Kaddish.[26]

After the *ḥazzan* completes the Musaf prayer, he goes behind the door of the synagogue or to the corner of the synagogue and there finds the mourners and their relatives. He says the blessing over them and afterward says Kaddish. But one does not say "in a world that stands to be renewed" except with regard to a student and with regard to the preacher.[27]

[Upon completing the Torah reading during the morning service on Purim,] one returns the Torah scroll to its place and says, "May the name of the Eternal be blessed from now and forever" (Psalm 113:2) and Kaddish, for there is no [Torah] reading that requires Kaddish before the return [of the Torah to the Ark], save on Shabbat due to the *maftir*. In that case, having read the *maftir*, one returns the Torah scroll to its place and [again] says Kaddish....At that time, when the people are standing, they respond "May His great name be blessed"[28] while [still] on their feet....One does not skip [a section] in the Torah, for if one were to skip even a single verse and return the Torah [to the Ark] and say Kaddish, one [would need to] reopen [the Ark], say the blessings, and read—himself and two others.[29]

By the date of the final editing of tractate Sofrim, then, Kaddish had attained a firm place in the prayer service, and few sources suggest that its origins were elsewhere.

Kaddish is referred to by name in tractate Sofrim, and its central response, "May His great name be blessed," is familiar from earlier sources. But it is only in *Seder Rav Amram Gaon* in the ninth century,[30] the earliest extant version of the Jewish prayerbook, that the text of the Kaddish is presented in full. Once more, it is presented in Rav Amram's prayerbook as a part of the daily prayer service.[31]

Recalibrating

A number of indications lead to the suggestion that the Kaddish arose in the practice of early mystics, tied to the study of *heikhalot*, the halls of the heavens, and *ma·aseih merkavah*, the details of the divine throne and its angelic retinue. As we have seen, the Kaddish was used both in the synagogue and the study hall, potentially suggesting that its origin was in neither, but somewhere else. Strengthening that impression is the fact that it came to reside not inside any of the statutory liturgical units, but in the spaces between them. That Kaddish is in Aramaic rather than Hebrew confirms its foreign nature. It must have been important, as the testimony of the sages confirms, to have penetrated in that way; but it must not have been of normative rabbinic origin to have remained outside rabbinic structures.[32]

A close analysis of the content of the Kaddish also attests to its single-minded focus on the praise of God, often described by Jewish mystics as the purpose of existence.

There are many forms of the Kaddish used within the prayer service. The shortest, known now in error as the Half Kaddish, is two paragraphs in length, whereas the others—the Full Kaddish (also known as the Reader's Kaddish), the Mourner's Kaddish, the Kaddish D'rabbanan, and the Burial Kaddish—are each embellished by several additional paragraphs. It is, however, clear from the content that that shortest Kaddish is the core, to which the other paragraphs were added.[33] The first paragraph asserts that God's name should be praised and God's sovereignty soon be established. This is followed by the response: "May His great name be blessed forever and forever and ever."[34] The second paragraph embellishes the theme of God's praises. All the remaining short paragraphs, however, deal not with God but with the people Israel. For example, the line "May the prayers of Israel be received" (*titkabbeil tz'lot'hon*) is added only at the end of a prayer service. The line "For Israel and their teachers" (*al yisrael v'al rabbanan*) is added only after study of rabbinic texts. And the last two paragraphs in all the embellished versions, essentially equivalent in idea but one Aramaic and one Hebrew, wish the people Israel peace and a good life (*y'hei sh'lama rabba* and *oseh shalom bi-m'romav*). In these additions and others we move far from that which Elbogen rightly called "the core and the original meaning of the Kaddish."[36]

But the two core paragraphs can be further reduced, to discover what was likely their original form. The current basic Kaddish is made up of only five discrete propositions:

> (1) *Yitgaddal v'yitkaddash sh'meih rabba b'alma di-v'ra ki-re'uteih,*
> May [God's] great name be magnified and sanctified in this world, as is His will,[37]
> (2a) *v'yamlikh malkhuteih b'hayyeikhon…*
> and may His sovereignty be evident in your day…
> (2b) *ba-agala u-vi-z'man kariv…*
> speedily and in a timely manner…

The congregation responds to this declaration, with the next clause:

> (3) *Y'hei sh'meih rabba m'varakh l'alam u-l'almei almaya.*
> May His great name be blessed forever and forever and ever.

The second paragraph repeats the primary theme of the first:

> (4) *Yitbarakh v'yishtabbah…sh'meih d'kudsha, b'rikh hu,*
> Praised, hallowed…be the name of the blessed Holy One,
>
> (5) *l'eilla min kol birkhata v'shirata…da-amiran b'alma*
> above all blessings and songs…that we say in the world.

As we noted, the prayer has grown longer over time through a series of accretions. Indeed, even the core prayer we have identified appears to have, in clause (2), a thematic insertion that is not of a piece with the theme of the prayer that is evident in clauses (1), (3), and (5). Thus Daniel Goldschmidt writes:

> It seems that the original context was (as follows): May God's name be praised in this world as He wills above all praises and songs...that we say in the world. And nested within this they added two responses: (a) May His great name...and (b) Praised, hallowed...be the name of the blessed Holy One.[38]

His fundamental insight is correct, though I'm inclined to disagree that clause (4) in the latter paragraph should be seen as an alternative response. The fact is that the tradition recognized clause (3) alone as a congregational response (*y'hei sh'meih rabba*), and has understood that the theme of clause (1) was being expanded and extended by clauses (4) and (5)—which reading seems to me to be preferable.

Thus we have here a prayer appropriate to the concerns of the literature of Heikhalot: the total absorption of all creation, of humans and angels, in the sanctification of God.

In tractate Sofrim we find a prayer, whose opening is quite similar to the Kaddish prayer, that is designated to be said during the Torah service.[39] Utilizing all the same verbs as are in the two paragraphs of the Kaddish, it reads: "May the name of the King of Kings, the blessed Holy One, the honored and awesome, be magnified and sanctified, praised and lauded...over all things, in the worlds that He has created, in this world and the next, as is His desire and that of His faithful ones and all His people Israel." Praise of God is here seen as the desire of both God and of all God's faithful. This text supports our understanding of the words of the Kaddish and reinforces its theme. In all of its original parts, the sole theme of the Kaddish was the praise of God—a praise that is so elemental and fundamental that, whichever of the many terms one may use to refer to it, it rises above all other praises that might be offered in the world.

But it is the style of the Kaddish that is the strongest link to its origins in Heikhalot literature, with its string of virtually synonymous terms for praise being the prime literary indicator that it has its provenance in the Heikhalot literature. When in the peroration of the text of the Haggadah we say *l'fikhakh anaḥnu ḥayyavim l'hodot, l'halleil, l'shabbei·aḥ, l'fa·eir* ("and therefore is it incumbent upon us to give thanks, to praise, to laud, to exalt...."), and continue with a long list of verbs that all mean praise, a similar line, but with an even longer list of synonyms, appears in the *Heikhalot Zutrati*,[40] followed by an alphabetic paean, akin to the Passover hymn Adir Hu, that describes God as Sovereign (*melekh*) with five to seven attributes for each letter of the alphabet. The alphabetic acrostic poem said on Yom Kippur, Ha-aderet V'ha-emunah, is found in a different Heikhalot text, the better-known *Heikhalot Rabbati*.[41]

It is instructive to specifically compare *yitgaddal v'yitkaddash* (followed by *yitbarakh v'yishtabbaḥ*, etc.) with the following paragraphs in the *Synopse*:[42]

§153 (HR): *tithaddeir titromeim titnassei melekh m'fo·ar*
§257 (HR): *titbareikh b'khol ha-b'rakhot tishtabbei·aḥ b'khol ha-tushbaḥot tithalleil b'khol ha-hillul, titkalleis b'khol ha-r'nanot*
§274 (HR): *titalleiz titkalleis titaddeir tit·haddeir titromeim titnassei titpa·eir titbareikh tishtabbei·aḥ titgaddeil titalleh titkaddeish*

The Kaddish simply reads like a prayer that emanates from Heikhalot literature.[43]

One of the overarching themes of the Heikhalot literature is the human search to become part of the angelic choir surrounding God's throne and join in the praise of God on high, exemplified by the great angelic doxology: "Holy, holy, holy is the Eternal One of Hosts; the world is filled with His glory."[44] But not enough attention is paid to the corollary in the literature of Heikhalot—namely, that there is a complementary praise of God occurring down below.

Consider this description in *Heikhalot Rabbati*, which finds its echoes elsewhere in more normative rabbinic literature:

> When the time comes for the angels to sing before God [at dusk], Shamiel, the angel, the great, honored and awesome dignitary, stands at the lower heaven's windows to hear, to listen to all the songs and praises that rise from the earth from every synagogue and study hall, in order to transmit this to them [the angels] before the heavens darken. Why does he stand at [the windows] of heaven? Because the angels who serve God do not have permission to sing first on high until Israel open their mouths in song below, as it says: "Extol the Eternal our God" (Psalm 99:9), and all the angels who serve [God], all the angels of heaven, who hear the sound of the songs and praises that Israel are saying below, open above with "Holy, holy, holy" (Isaiah 6:3).[45]

This story appears in two other places in the Heikhalot literature assembled by Peter Schäfer. In one of these, the verse is given a more complete explication; in the other, an additional dictum is attached. These texts read as follows:

> Why does he stand at the windows of heaven? Because the angels who serve God do not have permission to sing first on high until Israel open their mouths in song first below. As it says: "Extol the Eternal our God and bow to His holy mountain..." (Psalm 99:9)—these are Israel; "...because the Eternal our God is holy" (ibid.)—these are the angels of heaven.[46]

Samuel says: Israel is blessed to be more beloved to God than the angels who serve [God], for when the angels who serve [God] seek to sing first on high, they gather around the throne of glory….But God says to them, "Be silent, every angel, seraph, creature, and *ofan*[47] that I have created, until I hear the worship, the songs, praises, prayers, and beautiful paeans of Israel"…as it says: "When the morning stars sang together and all the divine beings shouted for joy" (Job 38:7). "The morning stars"—those are Israel, who are likened to stars…"and all the divine beings shouted for joy"—those are the angels who serve [God].[48]

This notion, that the very celestial praise which is fundamental to the universe is dependent upon Israel's praise, is recognized earliest in Sifrei Devarim §306, at the end of the section that we have already cited, which references *y'hei sh'meih rabba* as part of its focus on Israel's various responses of praise. That section concludes:

From what source do we know that the angels who serve [God] do not mention the name of the blessed Holy One on high until Israel mentions it below? For it says: "Hear O Israel, the Eternal is our God, the Eternal is one" (Deuteronomy 6:4). And it says [elsewhere]: "When the morning stars sang together and all the divine beings shouted for joy" (Job 38:7). "The morning stars"—those are Israel, who are likened to stars…."and all the divine beings shouted for joy"—those are the angels who serve [God].

That idea is likewise found in a tannaitic text cited in the Talmud that counts the ways in which Israel's praise is superior to that of the angels.[49]

Now it would make some amount of sense were we to identify the Israelite praise, that which is recited in the synagogues and study houses and which triggers the "Holy, holy, holy" of the angels, as the Kedushah that we recite in our prayer services. And that does appear to be the implication of yet another paragraph in *Heikhalot Rabbati*, which says that "the divine creatures open their mouths to say 'Holy' when Israel says 'holy' (*kadosh*)."[50] But the Kedushah is self-consciously not Israel's own praise, but a mimicry or resonance of the angelic praise above. Thus the Kedushah of the Amidah begins, "We shall sanctify Your name in the world, as they sanctify it on high, as is written by your prophet (Isaiah 6:3), '[the seraphim] call out one to another and say: 'Holy, holy, holy, is the Eternal One of Hosts....'" The Kedushah reports the angels' praise. What is the specifically Israelite praise below that triggers the daily praise above?

There are several calls to praise God in the daily formal public liturgy. The morning and evening services both begin with such a call by the prayer leader, *bar'khu et adonai ha-m'vorakh* ("Bless the Eternal, the One who is blessed"), upon which prompt the congregation responds with language of praise, *barukh adonai ha-m'vorakh l'olam va-ed* ("Blessed is the Eternal, the One who is blessed forever and ever"). Similarly, at the Grace After Meals, the invitation is *rabbotai n'vareikh* ("Colleagues, let us bless"), whereupon the diners respond, again with praise of God, *y'hi shem adonai m'vorakh l'olam va-ed*" ("May the name of the Eternal be blessed forever and ever").[51] Particularly the Bar'khu, morning and evening—or, more specifically, the direct praise of God that it elicits, "Blessed is the Eternal, the One who is blessed forever and ever"—seems to be precisely that human praise for which the angel Shamiel was daily on the lookout. And the Kaddish? The Kaddish, added at the end of the statutory service, added an additional nuance that seems crafted for this scene. For in the Kaddish, in fact, we do not offer praise, as in the prayers just mentioned. Rather, in the Kaddish we reflect on the need for God's name to be praised in the world, as it just was by us humans, and says, addressed now to the angels, *y'hei sh'meih rabba m'varakh* ("Let God's great name be blessed"). Now this can be understood as it was intended, as an action instruction to the angels above, a call to the angels to begin their own direct praise, "Holy, holy, holy."[52] We have done ours; it is now time for you, angels, to do yours.

In this telling, Kaddish is fully worthy of the accolade it receives in tractate Sotah,[53] that it is a pillar on which God's world stands. If the world was indeed created so that humans and angels should be able to praise God, humans first and angels only upon our lead, then Kaddish has a unique place in initiating and continuing that elemental cycle, and thus it assures the continuation of the world. That was, I believe, the mystics' understanding of the operation of the world, wherein by our praise we fulfill the purpose of human existence.

תם ותהילה לאל

This work is done.

Praise to the Holy One.[54]

NOTES

[1] These are each considered a liturgical unit, a series of associated prayers such that they open with a blessing for all and each subsequent section may open in reliance upon that opening blessing and needs only its own closing blessing; see B. Berakhot 46a. Kaddish stands outside these units and is not graced by the statutory blessing formula, "Praised are You, the Eternal, our God…"

[2] See Ismar Elbogen's classical study on the origins of Jewish prayer, originally published in German in 1913 and available now both in Hebrew (ed. Joseph Heinemann et al, *Ha-t'fillah B'yisrael B'hitpat·hutah Ha-historit* [Tel Aviv: Dvir, 1972]) and English (trans. Raymond P. Scheindlin as *Jewish Liturgy: A Comprehensive History* [Philadelphia: Jewish Publication Society and New York: Jewish Theological Seminary, 1993]). The relevant material may be found on pp. 73–74 of the Hebrew edition and on p. 82 of the English edition. Also, see Leon Wieseltier's idiosyncratic memoir of his study of Kaddish during his year of saying Kaddish for his father, *Kaddish* (New York: Knopf, 1998), which centers on this understanding of the import of the Kaddish and the medieval Ashkenazic community which developed that usage.

[3] The shortest form of Kaddish, known as the Half Kaddish, is two paragraphs in length, whereas others, the Full or Reader's Kaddish, the Mourner's Kaddish, the Kaddish D'rabbanan, and the Burial Kaddish are each embellished by several other paragraphs in addition.

[4] The Hebrew root *bet-resh-kaf*, from which derive forms such as *barukh* and *m'varakh*, has the connotation of receiving both blessing and praise. Thus, for example, Genesis 24:1, *vadonai beirakh et avraham ba-kol* ("the Eternal had blessed Abraham in all things"), is clearly establishing Abraham as the recipient of blessing, whereas the words of Abraham's servant in Genesis 24:27, *barukh adonai elohei adoni avraham asher lo azav ḥasdo va-amito mei-im adoni* ("blessed is the Eternal, God of my master Abraham, whose love and friendship He has not withheld from my master"), connote not that the servant is offering God some bounty, but rather that he is recognizing God's favor; the words might better be translated as "Praised is the Eternal…" Indeed, the words of Melchizedek the king of Shalem to Abraham (Genesis 14:19–20) illustrate three distinct meanings of this verb: "He greeted him (*va-y'var'kheihu*), saying: Blessed (*barukh*) is Abraham to the Highest God, Creator of heaven and earth, and praised (*barukh*) is the Highest God who has placed your enemies in your hand." Generally, as directed from humans to God, *barukh* is better understood as "praise," for in what sense can humans offer God blessings? However, it has become commonplace to translate the word as "bless" regardless of the specific connotation, and I do so throughout this essay in order to conform to the citations that I bring and in order not to have to justify the specific translation

of each use of the word. The reader is hereby forewarned.

⁵ Here the translator or his editor erred in dealing with this phrase. There is inconsistency in variants of the text of the Talmud on Berakhot 3a, as to whether the blessing as cited there is the Aramaic, *y'hei sh'meih rabba*, or a Hebrew version thereof, *y'hi sh'mo ha-gadol*. Referring to that, Elbogen (Hebrew version) reads: "To these petitions belongs the blessing *y'hei sh'meih rabba* or, in its Hebrew formulation, *y'hi sh'mo ha-gadol*."

⁶ Elbogen, English ed., pp. 80–81 (I have substituted transliteration where the original had presented Hebrew or Aramaic text); Hebrew ed., pp. 72–73.

⁷ Elbogen, English ed., p. 407, n. 2; Hebrew ed., p. 407, n. 2. De Sola Pool, *The Old Jewish-Aramaic Prayer: The Kaddish* (1909; rpt. as *The Kaddish* [Jerusalem: Sivan Press, 1964]), pp. 8–10, lists seven sources suggesting to him that Kaddish had its origin after the homiletic *d'rashah*. Only two, which I discuss below, are from sources that predate the end of the amoraic era (B. Berakhot 3a and B. Sotah 49a). All the rest might be influenced by the focus on the study hall of the geonic *yeshivot*. This consensus is repeated by Joseph Heinemann in his *Ha-t'fillah Bi-t'kufat Ha-tanna·im V'ha-amora·im* (Jerusalem: Magnes Press, 1964), pp. 23 and 163. But note, on p. 163, that he dates the origins of Kaddish to the tannaitic period and its association with the *d'rashah* only to the fourth century C.E.

⁸ Alluding to the thrice-daily prayer service. (See Psalms 55:18).

⁹ As noted above, versions differ as to whether the prayer cited here is in Hebrew or Aramaic.

¹⁰ Prayers were often recited at the study hall, and no doubt in many communities a single space served both functions. It is little wonder, then, that they are commonly referred to together.

¹¹ Literally, "give grandeur to our God." This verb is in the form of a command, addressed in plural to those listening to Moses.

¹² Sifrei Devarim §306 (end).

¹³ The designations of eternity differ in these formulae. I have translated *l'olam va-ed* as "forever and ever" and *l'olam u-l'olmei olamim* and its equivalent Aramaic *l'alam u-l'almei almaya* as "forever and forever and ever."

¹⁴ Midrashic logic can at times be opaque. The proof that a minimum of three is needed can be derived by recognizing that the singular speaker of the first half of the verse ("When I call"), plus the plural audience (minimally two) in the second half of the verse, yields a minimum of three people (1 + 2 =3).

At the top of this paragraph I attributed the comment that follows about *y'hei sh'meih rabba* to Rabbi Yosi. It is the apparent structure of the Sifrei text that all these examples were offered by Rabbi Yosi, for were there another speaker it would be expected that that new speaker would be named. However, the various examples are themselves anonymous and might not, in fact, be the continuation of the words of Rabbi Yosi.

¹⁵ In this instance, the response is presented in Hebrew.

[16] The Sifrei next moves farther afield, taking the verse into other contexts. Another use of the Hebrew form of "May His great name be blessed forever and forever and ever" is attributed to Rabbi Yosi the Galilean in Avot D'Rabbi Natan, version A, chap. 31 (p. 91 in the Schechter edition [New York: Feldheim, 1967]), but there it is formally unrelated to Kaddish but is rather being used as an extension of the reference to God as the blessed Holy One (*ha-kadosh barukh hu*).

[17] B. Berakhot 21b.

[18] In this instance, the response is presented in Hebrew.

[19] B. Sukkah 38a–39a.

[20] In this instance, the phrase is in Aramaic.

[21] In his discussion, Elbogen assumed that the response to the question was by Rava, in keeping with the talmudic scholarship of his day. Today, however, it has become clear that such side questions and answers that are not integral to an *amora*'s statement may be later additions—even quite a bit later. Thus this text too may have been composed under the influence of later practice.

[22] Might "the *k'dushah* of the order" refer instead to the order of prayer? The earliest prayerbook, that of Rav Amram Gaon, head of a Babylonian academy in the mid-ninth century C.E., was known as "the order" (*seder*) of Rav Amram Gaon. Indeed, the prayer that has come to be known as the Kedushah D'Sidra is actually at the end of the synagogue prayer service (where, Rashi [to B. Sotah 49a, s.v., *a-k'dushah d'sidra*] explains, it was established to mimic Torah study at the end of the prayer service). See Elbogen's discussion, pp. 70–71 (§10 [9]), Hebrew, p. 63. The reference of *aggadta* as regards the Kaddish response remains obscure.

[23] There are several other talmudic-era references to the response "May His great name be blessed." One, in the name of the Palestinian *amora* Rabbi Joshua ben Levi, on B. Shabbat 119b, testifies to the importance of this response ("whoever responds: 'Amen; may His great name be blessed' with all one's might, such a one's sentence will be overturned" [the response is here presented in Aramaic]), but adds no contextual information to help place when it may have been said. A second reference at B. Berakhot 57a that is difficult to assign—it may be tannaitic or amoraic, or possibly a later interpolation—likewise shows the import associated with the response ("whoever responds: 'Amen; may His great name be blessed' is guaranteed to enter the World to Come" [the response is here presented in Aramaic]), but does not hint at the context in which it was being said (although, suggestively, the immediately following item is about the importance of saying the blessings around the Shema—which suggests that this statement, too, should perhaps be understood in a context of prayer). Another reference to the response "May His great name be blessed" (presented in this case in Hebrew) appears in Kohelet Rabbah 9:15, and that text refers equally to a sage who is teaching and to a *hazzan*, a prayer leader, to either of whom the

people might be responding. One of De Sola Pool's stronger proposed proofs that the Kaddish response was tied to the *d'rashah* appears in Midrash Mishlei 14, citing Rabbi Ishmael (it is unclear if this is the known *tanna* or an unknown *amora*), to the effect that whenever people gather in the study hall, hear a homily, and respond "May His great name be blessed" (in different manuscripts this is alternatively given in Hebrew or in Aramaic), God is exalted. This, and the anonymous gloss to Rava in B. Sotah 49a, are the only texts that appear to refer specifically to Kaddish in regard to the homily. But immediately before Rabbi Ishmael is Rabbi Simon, an *amora*, who asserts that God is exalted whenever people gather in synagogues or study halls (naming both venues) and "praise and extol their Maker"—a similar statement set in the context of prayer. (See also Midrash Mishlei 10, which references "May His great name be blessed" in the name of Rabbi Ishmael and in close association with study, in an extended homily that goes on to refer to the study of viewing the divine throne.)

[24] *Massekhet Sofrim (V'nilvu Aleha Midrash Massekhet Sofrim Bet)*, ed. M. Higger (New York: Hotza·at D'vei Rabbanan, 1937).

[25] Sofrim 10:6–8 and 16:9.

[26] Sofrim 18:10. The psalms and verses referred to here are the preliminaries (known as Birkhot Ha-shaḥar and P'sukei D'zimra) before the statutory morning service. The statutory service, here called Yotzer (after its opening word), is introduced by the invitation Bar'khu. Unlike the instruction in tractate Sofrim, today a Kaddish separates the preliminary psalms from the statutory prayers, and the Yotzer does include a version of Kedushah.

[27] Sofrim 19:9. The Musaf prayer is the additional prayer for Sabbaths and holidays that is usually appended immediately after the morning service. The mourner's blessing, called Birkat Aveilim, is discussed in T. Berakhot 3:23–24 (and see the sources there in Tosefta, ed. Saul Lieberman *Tosefta* [New York: Jewish Theological Seminary, 1955], pp. 49–50). The language "in a world that stands to be renewed" refers to one of the variants of Kaddish that is used by Ashkenazic Jews today only at the time of burial. The idea of a Kaddish recited by the mourner that benefits the soul of the deceased does not appear until the Middle Ages. But the use of the Kaddish in the context of a prayer for mourners might well have been mother to that thought.

[28] In this instance, the response is presented in Aramaic.

[29] Sofrim 21:5–6. This passage is stating several laws that could use unpacking: (1) It is required to say Kaddish after the return of the Torah to the Ark, which is the practice suggested here for Purim. (2) Shabbat is different, due to the reading of an additional portion of Torah (the *maftir*) before the Torah is returned to the Ark; on Shabbat we says Kaddish before the *maftir* and, nevertheless—despite having just said Kaddish—we say it yet again after the return of the Torah to the Ark. (3) We say Kaddish after the return of the Torah to the Ark standing, since the people are already on their feet for the return. (4) Should a verse erroneously

be skipped, even though the return of the Torah had been completed and the Kaddish said (closing the chapter on the Torah service), it would nonetheless be necessary to again take out the Torah to read not just the skipped verse, but a full minimum reading, with three people called to the Torah.

[30] Rav Amram Gaon served as head of the academy at Sura, in Babylonia, from 858–870 C.E. The title "Gaon," literally "[our] pride," was used by the heads of the two most prominent academies in Babylonia, one at Sura (also identified as Mata Meḥasya) and the other at Pumbedita. On the first page of his book, the author refers to himself simply as Amram bar Sheshna.

[31] *Seder Rav Amram Gaon*, ed. Naḥman Natan Coronel (Warsaw, 1865), p. 3b; ed. Daniel Goldschmidt (Jerusalem: Mossad Harav Kook, 1971), Hebrew p. 11. One of the sources that David de Sola Pool used in his study of the Kaddish to confirm that Kaddish had its first and primary association with a rabbinic study session is from a later indication that Kaddish was associated with study, found in Coronel's edition on page 13b. It now appears, however, that that section was one of several addenda to Rav Amram Gaon's original text—see Goldschmidt, Heb. p. 39, line 62. The story reported there has God open the gates of heaven for those sinners of Israel who are in hell. The story appears as well in this form in Seder Eliyahu Zuta 20 (*Tanna Debe Eliyyahu*, ed. W. Braude and I. Kapstein [Philadelphia: Jewish Publication Society, 1981], p. 461). The story is based, in turn, on a dictum by Resh Lakish that appears in the Talmud at B. Shabbat 119b, where Resh Lakish says: "Whoever responds 'Amen. [May His great name be blessed]' with all his strength, they open the gates of heaven for him, as it says, 'Open the gates and let enter the righteous nation that keeps faith' (Isaiah 26:2)—do not read 'that keeps faith' (*shomeir emunim*), but [instead, read those words as if they were] 'that answers amen' (*she-omeir ameinim*)." (Note that the dictum by Resh Lakish does not appear to refer specifically to the Kaddish response, but simply to the response "Amen"— though I have inserted that text. I do so for the following reason: *In situ* on B. Shabbat 119b, Rabbi Joshua ben Levi, a close colleague of Resh Lakish who is regularly represented in head-to-head debate with him, begins this discussion specifically about the ramifications of the response "May His great name be blessed." After some intervening talmudic discussion about Rabbi Joshua ben Levi's prooftext, the Talmud resumes with Resh Lakish's alternative, which presumably sat directly next to Rabbi Joshua ben Levi's dictum in the original formulation of this debate. In that scenario, Resh Lakish's dictum here is simply abridged as part of the normal process of transmission.) This story, at any rate, seems to be the kernel from which medieval Ashkenazic Jewry crafted the concept of the Mourner's Kaddish redeeming the deceased from hell. Here, the deceased sinners themselves answer "Amen," whereas in the well-known later story of Rabbi Akiva and the porter, a son redeems his father from hell by reciting the Kaddish; this later version of the tale is best known from its

appearance with reference to Kaddish in *Maḥzor Vitry*, §144, ed. S. Hurwitz (Nuremberg, 1923), p.112, in a section that appears to be an addendum. That story in various forms—not always about Rabbi Akiva, and not referring to Kaddish at all but rather to Bar'khu, or more generally to serving as prayer leader—appears earlier in tractate Kallah Rabbati 2:9 (*M'sekhtot Kallah: V'hein Massekhet Kallah, Massekhet Kallah Rabbati*, ed. M. Higger [New York: Hotza·at D'vei Rabbanan, 1936)], and in Seder D'vei Eliyahu Zuta 17 [*Tanna Debe Eliyyahu*, ed. W. Braude and I. Kapstein, pp. 448–449], where it is told about Rabbi Yoḥanan ben Zakkai), and in a fragment published by Louis Ginzberg in *Ginzei Schechter* (New York: Jewish Theological Seminary, 1928), vol. I, p. 238. The story with reference to Kaddish also appears as one of three addenda to Rabbi Nissim bar Yaakov of Kairouan's *Ḥibbur Yafeh Mei-ha-y'shu·ah*, but appears not to be in the Arabic original.

[32] Another prayer, though added later, shares that trajectory from the Heikhalot literature into the fringes of the prayer service. Ein Keiloheinu, which is sung at the end of the Musaf service on Sabbaths and holidays, is first found in *Heikhalot Zutrati* (*Synopse* §383) and again in no identifiable collection (*Synopse* §946). There are many Heikhalot texts of different ages that have come into our hands in varying recensions and manuscripts, often in named works: *Heikhalot Rabbati* and *Heikhalot Zutrati, Ma·aseih Merkavah*, and others. These have been collected and their texts presented in synoptic fashion, in parallel columns, by Peter Schafer, Margarete Schluter, and Hans Georg von Mutius in *Synopse zur Hekhalot-Literatur* (Tubingen: J.C.B. Mohr, 1981). Since *Synopse* is a compilation of many independent works in the Heikhalot library, I will cite both the *Synopse* siglum and the work from which it derives, where that information is available.

[33] Elbogen: English p. 83, Hebrew pp. 74–75.

[34] Several variants of this first paragraph exist, but each is easily recognized as embellishing. Many Sephardic Jews add the words *v'yatzmaḥ purkaneih vikarev m'shiḥeih* ("may God cause His redemption to flourish and His Messiah to be near"), an additional entreaty for the coming of the Messiah, after the line expressing the hope that God's sovereignty be established. Among some Yemenites in general use, and among Ashkenazic Jews specifically at graveside, we have a text that replaces the reference to the created world with the words "the world that will be renewed, bringing the dead back to life and escorting them to eternal life, [a world] wherein Jerusalem will be rebuilt...." There is a similar expansion attested in fragments from the geonic era, wherein the wish that God's sovereignty be established "in your lifetime, in your days, and in the lifetime of all the House of Israel" is expanded to name the specific leaders of the community at the time. Compare the memoir of Natan Ha-Bavli (from 850 C.E.), published in A. Neubauer, *Medieval Jewish Chronicles* (Oxford: Clarendon Press, 1895), vol. 2, p. 84.

[35] The Full Kaddish is said twice on Shabbat morning, both at the end of the Shaḥarit (morning) service (before the Torah reading) and again at the end of the Musaf service. Both Shaḥarit and Musaf are considered in themselves complete services.

[36] Cf. n. 6 above.

[37] This text, slightly and very subtly altered from that said by most people praying in synagogue today, follows the suggestion of the Gaon Elijah of Vilna. As reported in Baer's Siddur Avodat Yisrael (Seligmann Baer, *Siddur Avodat Yisrael* [Roedelheim, 1868; rpt. Tel Aviv: Or Ha-torah, 1957], p. 129), the Gaon argued that the end of the first clause, *ki-re'uteih*, should be vocalized with a *kaf*, which vocalization understands there to be a pause (i.e., the equivalent of a comma in English) immediately prior to that word—rather than a *khaf* (the same letter in its softer pronunciation), which vocalization would suggest that the word grammatically followed directly after *b'alma di v'ra* (i.e., "in the world that He created"). This small grammatical change reflects a profound difference in the meaning of the text and yields a much better understanding of the prayer. The common pronunciation (with a *khaf*), reflecting no pause in the sentence, would be translated "May God's name be magnified and sanctified in the world that He created according to His will." Logically, it might then be asked, "According to whose other will might God have created the world, that this wants saying?" Rather, the words "according to His will" should be understood as attached not to the previous noun (viz., the world), but should instead, after a pause, be reflected back to the primary thought of the phrase—in other words, God's will refers to the divine desire that God be magnified. I have translated in accordance with this understanding.

[38] Ernst Daniel Goldschmidt, *Maḥzor L'yamim Nora·im* (Jerusalem: Koren, 1970), vol. 1, p. 25.

[39] Sofrim 14:6.

[40] *Synopse* §378. See note 32 above.

[41] *Synopse* §275.

[42] Note that the final *a*-vowel in the Aramaic forms in Kaddish is parallel to the final *ei*-vowel in the Hebrew-language Heikhalot texts.

[43] One more potential indicator bears mention, though it cannot stand on its own. In the various mentions of the Kaddish response that we have looked at, there have been four oblique references to the study of the ways of the heavens. B. Berakhot 3a spoke of an ethereal voice (*bat kol*), and in B. Berakhot 21b an *amora* noted that one should interrupt even when studying mystical lore about the divine throne. In the much later Midrash Mishlei is another reference to the study of the divine throne and the after-dinner scene in which David leads Grace After Meals in the halls of heaven. Given these other indicators, this does not appear coincidental.

[44] Alternatively, perhaps, "His aura suffuses the universe." This is Isaiah's vision of the heavenly hosts (Isaiah 6:3). It is recounted in our prayer service in the Kedushah, at the heart of the Amidah, as well as part of the morning service, and it is a central preoccupation of the Heikhalot literature.

[45] *Synopse* §178–179, *Heikhalot Rabbati.*

[46] *Synopse*, §788, *Seder Rabbah Di-v'reishit.*

[47] Like the more familiar seraph, an *ofan* is one among the various types of ministering angels.

[48] *Synopse* §529 and §789, *Seder Rabbah Di-v'reishit.*

[49] Found on B. Ḥullin 91b. The same idea is stated in the name of the *tanna* Rabbi Eliezer son of Rabbi Yosi the Galilean in Seder Eliyahu Zuta, chap. 25; see *Tanna Debe Eliyyahu,* ed. Braude and Kapstein, p. 483. Very close to the wording of the Sifrei is also reported in another tannaitic midrash, Midrash Tanna·im to Deuteronomy 32:3 (ed. D. Hoffman [ed. Tel Aviv, 1962]). This idea appears as well in Avot D'Rabbi Natan, version B, chap. 44, in the context of the Shema (ed. Schechter, p. 124). The text of Avot D'Rabbi Natan, however, lacks the angel's response to Israel's declaration of Shema. Presumably the text has in mind the standard response to Shema, "Blessed is the name of the glory of His kingdom forever and ever." That, in any event, is what is represented by the amora Samuel in Bereshit Rabbah 65:21. The prooftext from Job 38:7 appears in both.

[50] *Synopse* §101, *Heikhalot Rabbati.*

[51] Since the prayer leader has issued a call, but not personally offered praise, it is understood by the tradition that the leader should respond with the congregation to the call, so that they all together seize the opportunity to praise God. It is worth noting here that in his study of the Kaddish, David de Sola Pool, in discussing the response to Kaddish ("May His great name be blessed forever and forever and ever"), establishes that there was, from late biblical times in Israel, a simple doxology that served as a declaration of fealty *to* God and as praise *of* God, which the Kaddish response corresponds to. It consisted of three parts: a form of the verb *barukh*, to bless or praise; a name of God; and a reference to God's eternity. This form is found in Nehemiah 9:5, where the great pact undertaken by the people in Nehemiah's day begins with an exhortation by the Levites, "Bless the Eternal your God from eternity to eternity (*min ha-olam v'ad ha-olam*)," and again to begin Daniel's Aramaic prayer in Daniel 2:20. It is the peroration of David's prayer as reported in 1 Chronicles 16:36 and the beginning of his prayer as reported in 1 Chronicles 29:10. It appears numerous times in the Book of Psalms, including being reflected in the well-known first verse of Psalm 145 (Ashrei), *va-avar'kha shimkha l'olam va-ed* ("and I will bless Your name forever and ever"). This late biblical doxology, De Sola Pool notes, became a staple of rabbinic liturgy.

[52] My thanks to my wife, Rabbi Nina Beth Cardin, who made this connection

that I was failing to see.

[53] B. Sotah 49a.

[54] This language is a standard scribal colophon and is the one that appears in ms. Vat. Ebr. 228 at the Biblioteca Apostolica Vaticana in Rome, one of the manuscripts that contributed to Schafer's *Synopse zur Hekhalot-Literatur*. Listed in their catalogue as Mystical Miscellany, this colophon appears in the middle of the manuscript, at the end of a copy of *3 Enoch*, appearing in *Synopse* §80. The English translation is, perhaps, overly ornate for the simpler language of the colophon.

The Kaddish as a Speech Act

Michael Marmur

The Kaddish is prevalent yet obscure. Its liturgical versatility and the various layers of its historical development account for its ubiquity in traditional Judaism—it is recited many times in the course of daily worship. As a result of its association with death and mourning, a link first forged after the trauma of the Crusades, the Kaddish has also become an indicator of basic Jewish affiliation. Nevertheless, its content is enigmatic, its language impenetrable, its theology unclear.

Many have pointed to the fact that the meaning of the words of the Kaddish is both unknown and irrelevant to many less literate Jews. In a penetrating essay on the impact of the Kaddish in American Jewish culture, Hana Wirth-Nesher quotes a New York rabbi in the 1920s:

> The Kaddish, perhaps more than any other prayer, has become a soul-searching agency which brings back to the Jewish folds numerous erstwhile indifferent sons and daughters. Its mysterious charm cannot be rationalized. It perplexes the mind of the Theologian and fascinates the mind of the laymen. Practical business men, who otherwise remain unmoved by sentiment, melt wax-like when called upon, at the demise of a near or dear one, to "say" the Kaddish.[1]

What, then, gives the Kaddish its power? At the start of Allen Ginsberg's *Kaddish*, he has been up all night listening to the blues on the gramophone and reciting the Kaddish out loud. Perhaps in response, he exclaims: "the rhythm, the rhythm—and your memory in my head three years after."[2] Here it is the syncopation of the recited words that allows memory to come. For the words of the Kaddish to have this impact, it is not clear that a dictionary understanding of the text is necessary, or even desirable. The Kaddish is an extreme example of the impact of liturgy beyond understanding. In Leon Wieseltier's provocative formulation, "the liturgical function of the Kaddish has nothing to with its content."[3]

Despite this sweeping assertion, many have attempted over the centuries to suggest a link between the content of the Kaddish and its various liturgical functions. Even if the association of this prayer of praise with death and mourning cannot be traced back to ancient sources, and appears in the areas of Europe known as Ashkenaz in the wake of the Crusades, some readings of the text have been offered to connect it with bereavement. Hence, for example, Rabbi Joseph B. Soloveitchik offers a paraphrase to explain what a mourner is really saying when reciting the Kaddish. In his view it is a declaration that

> [no] matter how powerful death is, notwithstanding the ugly end of man, however terrifying the grave is, however nonsensical and absurd everything appears, no matter how black one's despair is and how nauseating an affair life is, we declare and profess publicly and solemnly that we are not giving up, that we are not surrendering, that we will carry on the work of our ancestors as though nothing has happened, that we will not be satisfied with less than the full realization of the ultimate goal—the establishment of God's kingdom, the resurrection of the dead, and eternal life for man.[4]

This is only one of a rich array of attempts to find meaning within the words of the Kaddish, and in this sense to counter Wieseltier's claim. However interesting and even uplifting such attempts may be, it is hard to deny that the power and ubiquity of the Kaddish cannot be ascribed or sufficiently explained simply by interpreting its words. Something else is at play. The purpose of this essay is to offer one possible reason for the resonance and significance of this prayer.

Is the Kaddish in fact a prayer? Is it a blessing, a hymn, a declaration, or what scholars of liturgy term a doxology? It has been felicitously described as "a speech-act wherein the whole of Jewish history is condensed."[5] The term "speech-act" entered philosophical and linguistic parlance following the publication of J. L. Austin's *How To Do Things With Words* in the early 1960s.[6] While Austin's book displayed no explicit interest in this field (although one or two of his examples are taken from the world of ritual), the ideas outlined in his groundbreaking work are of great significance in a discussion of the function of prayer.

Austin differentiated between performative and constative/ declarative acts of speech. In the latter category are descriptive words or statements that bear within them no call to action or response. Such utterances *say* something—such as describing a situation or naming an emotion. Performative utterances, by contrast, *do* something. They effect something in the world. The lines of demarcation between these two kinds of statement are never clear.[7] To take another example from the field of Jewish liturgy, the declaration that "the Eternal is our God, the Eternal is One" (Deuteronomy 6:4) may be seen as no more than a statement of fact, or at least a statement of faith. However, when it appears in the context of a call to the people Israel to take heed, and when it has been categorized by rabbinic tradition as "the acceptance of the yoke of the kingdom of heaven,"[8] the constative and performative are blurred.

Austin posits a distinction between locutionary, illocutionary, and perlocutionary performative speech-acts. The first of these refers to the act of "saying something" in a normal sense, and can be broken down further to three kinds of acts, the details of which are beyond the bounds of our current discussion.[9] In broad terms, these relate to the noises one makes when speaking, the use of comprehensible words and grammar, and the definite use and reference of these uttered words.

Austin explained that a locutionary act "is roughly equivalent to uttering a certain sentence with a certain sense and reference, which again is roughly equivalent to 'meaning' in the traditional sense." An illocutionary act is one that has a certain normative force—I inform, warn, promise, etc. And perlocutionary acts constitute "what we bring about or achieve *by* saying something, such as convincing, persuading, deterring, and even, say, surprising or misleading."[11]

"There is...no mention of God or of prayer in the writings of the major speech-act theorists J. L. Austin and J. R. Searle."[12] If we were to do something Austin never did, and to take the Kaddish as our example of a speech-act, we may suggest an analysis of this cornerstone of Jewish liturgy in Austinian terms.

The locutionary dimension of the Kaddish includes its recitation and the meaning (or possible meanings) of its words. To understand its illocutionary valence, we would need to inquire what the recitation of the Kaddish is intended to achieve by the person reciting it. We might presume that responses to this question would not only differ among individuals, but that the act of recitation would bear within it varied intentions. After all, setting aside the liturgical variations of the text, the same words are employed in quite different liturgical and ritual contexts. As to the third element—namely, the result achieved by using this particular formula of words—there are both transcendental and this-worldly social aspects to be considered. Wieseltier's *Kaddish* offers an exhaustive and fascinating discussion of the belief that the act of reciting Kaddish for one's parents impacts their journey *post mortem*. The more immediate impact of reciting the Kaddish can be more easily gauged: it calls for a communal response. Without the presence and participation of the community, the recitation of Kaddish cannot be said to have taken place. In Jewish law and traditional practice, an individual reciting the words of the prayer alone has not moved from the locutionary to the perlocutionary level. Without the engagement of a quorum of fellow worshippers, the Kaddish has not been recited. So whatever one believes about the cosmic impact of the Kaddish, it does serve definable ritual and social functions which have an impact beyond the inner life of the person reciting the words.

Is there a connection between the words of the text and the functions that the Kaddish is intended to fulfill? It is my contention that even for the individual unfamiliar with all the nuances of the prayer, there are aspects of its language that emphasize its role as a bridge between one state and another. In Austin's terminology, the locution of the Kaddish expresses some of its illocutionary and perlocutionary dimensions. Its language speaks to its essence.

From its earliest days, the Kaddish has lived on the edge, at the end, on the border. In study and in ritual settings, it has served as a line of demarcation between one state and another. It denotes both conclusion and transition. It may even be the case that this aspect of its function has as much to do with its acceptance as the great signifier of death and collective mourning than any intrinsic liturgical meaning to be adduced from its words. It is my contention that in its grammar and phrasing, the Kaddish reflects this role in liminal spaces.

Of the various extant versions, the text we will consider is the Kaddish D'rabbanan, traditionally recited after learning certain classical sources. This variation includes many (although by no means all) of the textual accretions to the Kaddish, a number of which support my assertion that the language of the Kaddish is an expression of its key function. Since the interest of this essay does not include an attempt to differentiate earlier and later stages of the development of the Kaddish, there is no problem in offering this somewhat expanded version of the prayer. Our text and its translation read as follows:[13]

1. **Leader**: *Yitgaddal v'yitkaddash sh'meih rabba. Amen.*
May His great Name be exalted and sanctified! Amen.
2. *B'alma di v'ra khiruteih v'yamlikh malkhuteih v'yatzmah purkaneih vikareiv m'shiheih. Amen.*
In the world which He created according to His will, and may He establish His kingdom, make His redemption spring forth, and bring the Messiah closer. *Amen.*
3. *B'hayyeikhon u-v'yomeikhon u-v'hayyei d'khol beit yisrael, ba-agala u-vizman kariv. V'imru: amen.*
In your lifetime and in your days, and in the lifetime of the entire House of Israel, speedily and soon, and respond: *Amen.*
4. **Congregation**: *Y'hei sh'meih rabba m'varakh l'alam u-l'almei almayya.*
May His great name be blessed forever and to all eternity.
5. **Leader**: *Yitbarakh v'yishtabbah v'yitpa·ar v'yitromam v'yitnassei, v'yit·haddar v'yitalleh v'yit·hallel sh'meih d'kudsha b'rikh hu.*
L'eilla min kol (l'eilla u-l'eilla mi-kol)   birkhata v'shirata tushb'hata v'nehemata da'amiran b'alma. V'imru: amen.
May He be blessed. Praised, glorified, exalted, extolled, revered, highly honored, and adored is the Name of the Holy One, blessed be He, beyond (during the Ten Days of Repentance: still further beyond) all the blessings, hymns, praises and consolations that are ever uttered in the world, and respond: *Amen.*
6. *Al yisrael v'al rabbanan v'al talmideihon v'al kol talmidei talmideihon, v'al kol man d'askin b'oraita, di v'atra (kaddisha) hadein v'di v'khol atar va-atar. Y'hei l'hon u-l'khon sh'lama rabba, hinna v'hisda v'rahamei v'hayyei arikhei u-m'zonei r'vihei u-furkana min kodam avuhon di vi-sh'mayya v'ara. V'imru: amen.*
For Israel and for our rabbis, their disciples, and their

successors, and all who engage in the study of Torah—in this (holy) place and in every single other place—may there be for them and for you great peace, grace, favor, mercy, long life, plentiful sustenance, relief from before their Father in heaven and earth, and respond: *Amen.*
7. *Y'hei sh'lama rabba min sh'mayya v'hayyim tovim aleinu v'al kol yisrael. V'imru: amen.*
May there be abundant peace from heaven, and a good life upon us and upon all Israel, and respond: *Amen.*
8. *Oseh shalom bimromav hu b'rahamav ya·asesh shalom aleinu v'al kol yisrael. V'imru: amen.*
He who makes peace in His celestial heights, may He in His mercy make peace for us and for all Israel, and respond: *Amen.*

Let us consider four such fault lines to which different aspects of the Kaddish alludes: voice, space, time, and language.

Voice, Space, and Time

The Kaddish is antiphonal. In its origin it involves a sole voice in conversation with the community as a whole. That sole voice, the prayer leader or mourner, speaks in the name of a collective ("our rabbis" in line 6, and "us" in line 7, for example), and then turns to the members of that collective with the instruction to respond. Even when the Mourner's Kaddish is recited by a number of mourners at the same time (which was most probably not the original practice), the same dynamic—between the single person (or singled-out people) and the entire praying community—is tangible.

In those liberal congregations in which the Kaddish is recited *in toto* by the entire worshipping congregation every time it is said, this interplay between the individual and the group is lost. There are a number of reasons why the practice of reciting Kaddish in unison developed—including the idea that in the wake of Shoah there were so many with none to say Kaddish for them, and so the responsibility fell to the entire community. It may also be that a democratic and egalitarian spirit has played its part in engendering this development. If this is indeed the case, there is certainly an irony to be observed here: all of us are likely to face the moment in our lives when we mourn a close relative. There is something democratic about that fact. By "leveling out" the experience of this recitation, we may deprive the mourner the experience of being singled out in the supportive presence of the community.

The Kaddish is meant to flow between singularity and plurality. This interplay is accentuated by the fact that in Jewish law a quorum (*minyan*) is required in order for the individual to recite the Kaddish. Hence the individual and the group are both needed in order for the prayer to be enacted. Even if the words are not understood, a dialogue between the one and many is effected as the Kaddish is recited.

Within the text of the Kaddish, another borderline is evoked: that which runs between this particular place and every other place (line 6). The worshipper is reminded that the act of demarcation taking place in this microcosm is repeated wherever worshipping Jews are creating their own universe, their own *alma* (line 2). And in the version under consideration, which is admittedly not that to be found in the most prevalent versions, both heaven and earth are mentioned (line 6).

Time is far more pronounced than space in the Kaddish. The first two lines alone move from a kind of subjunctive future tense ("may the divine name be exalted") to the past ("the world that God created"), and then on to a messianic future in which God's sovereignty will be established and the Messiah brought close. The hope is then expressed that all this will happen in our days—indeed, in some versions that have been preserved in the Genizah, great figures of the day are listed by name.[16] So the present is introduced alongside the past and the future. Terms relating to time—the immediate future, the primordial past—are employed in such a way that the great sweep of time is evoked throughout the prayer.

The expression *l'alam u-l'almei almayya* is of particular interest in the context of our discussion of space and time in the Kaddish. The word *alam* (cognate with the Hebrew *olam*), probably at its root denoting that which cannot be seen, bridges the two dimensions. The prayer evokes the blurring of the spatial and the temporal, world without end.

Language

The purpose of this essay is to argue that part of the mystique of the Kaddish is connected to its language. It is an example of the thing enacted in its own recitation: a demarcation, an acknowledgment of difference. A teacher at the end of a lesson, a worshipper at the conclusion of a section of the fixed prayer service, a service leader at the end of the reading from the Torah and before the reading from the prophets, a mourner situated at the border separating the living from the dead—all these individuals utter the Kaddish, and in so doing its illocutionary and perlocutionary purposes are mirrored or epitomized in the locutionary act. The Kaddish exemplifies what it intends to do.

Consider the language of the Kaddish. Overwhelmingly the Kaddish is in Aramaic,[17] although some Hebrew words and phrases, as well as line 8 in the version quoted above, are in Hebrew. Rabbi Solomon ibn Adret (1235–1310) addressed a responsum to the question: why does the Kaddish appear in two languages?[18] The example provided to substantiate the question appears in line 3, where the phrase "in your lifetime and in your days" (*b'hayyeikhon u–v'yomeikhon*) is in Aramaic but the phrase "House of Israel" (*beit yisrael*) is in Hebrew. Ibn Adret's responsum notes that the words uttered by the congregation in the version of the Kaddish to be found in the *siddur* of Rav Amram Gaon are all in Aramaic. Any Hebrew in the text, Ibn Adret proposes, is either to be uttered by the service leader, or simply represents a later accretion or translation of the Aramaic into Hebrew. The distinction between the sole voice of the prayer leader and the response of the community is accentuated by this linguistic contrast.

In the same responsum, Ibn Adret goes on to offer a further explanation for the existence of both languages in the phrase from line 3. He sees it as a case of bilingualism for the sake of emphasis, likening it to the verse in Job 16:19:

> *Gam attah hinneih va-shamayim eidi, v'sahadi ba-m'romim.*
> Even now my witness [in Hebrew] is in heaven, my advocate
> [in Aramaic] is on high.

The same idea in essence is rendered in two languages, and thus emphasized.

What are we to make of the fact that a prayer that has been described as "the irreducible minimum of Jewish religious allegiance"[19] is largely in Aramaic? It is not completely unique as an Aramaic text at the heart of the performative liturgical tradition, but its counterparts—certain parts of the Haggadah, and the Kol Nidrei declaration on the eve of the Day of Atonement—have a prescribed annual occurrence, while the Kaddish is a constant in daily devotion.

The most plausible explanation for the fact that the Kaddish has come down through the ages in Aramaic was offered by a tosafist:

The reason must surely be the one given in tractate Sotah, that "the world exists because of the Kedushah D'sidra and *y'hei sh'meih rabba* [recited] after an aggadic discourse," the custom having been to recite Kaddish after the sermon. There were unlearned people in the audience, not all of whom understood the Holy Tongue, so that the Kaddish was instituted in Aramaic, their vernacular, that everyone might understand it.[20]

In this reading, the fact that the Kaddish is in Aramaic is a historical accident, a reflection of its particular provenance. This commentator was aware, however, that there was another well-known explanation, which he considered so preposterous that he cited it only to ridicule it. According to this reading, one already to be found in the *Sefer Ha-pardeis* attributed to Rashi, the choice of Aramaic has something to do with the linguistic capacities of the ministering angels. Since they cannot understand Aramaic,[22] reciting the beautiful prayer will not provoke the angels' jealousy (the opinion ridiculed by the Tosafot)— or, in another version of this tradition, they will not conclude that the call to make the name of God great implies that the Divinity is incomplete (*Sefer Ha-pardeis*). In yet another medieval speculation, Rabbi Isaac Aboab I (fl. end of the fourteenth century)[23] offers a variant suggestion. The three archangels charged with the task of interceding for the Jewish people in the celestial realm do speak Aramaic, but the others do not. Consequently, we address them in a language unknown to those angels who might interfere with the work of our guardians. In all these cases, the failure of angels to understand Aramaic is cited as explanation of the use of that language in so prevalent and significant a prayer. In this way, the gulf dividing the human hordes and the celestial hosts is emphasized. The Kaddish is for mortals alone.

There is a tradition concerning the language of the Kaddish that in my view strengthens my assertion that the very words of the prayer, its locutionary content, reflect in some sense the intention of the act itself. In order to see how this tradition develops and to consider its bearing on our current discussion, we will dwell on two teachings, divided by centuries and by locales. It is perhaps not surprising that the Zohar, itself written in a peculiar version of Aramaic, considers the question of the Kaddish. Its mystical interpretation warrants citation here. The Zohar notes that the doxology known as Kedushah may only be recited with a quorum of ten men, but a particular version known as the Kedushah D'sidra may be recited by an individual. If a prayer offered in Aramaic may be said privately and does not require a quorum, the Kaddish appears to be an anomaly:

> Now, you might say, "What about the sanctification of the Kaddish, which is in Aramaic translation—why isn't that recited individually?" Come and see: This Kedushah is not like all other versions of that same prayer....Rather, this Kedushah ascends on all sides and below, in all aspects of faith, smashing locks and seals of iron and evil shells, so that the glory of the blessed Holy One will be exalted above all. We must recite it in the language of the Other Side, and respond with mighty power: "Amen! May His great Name be blessed," so that the power of the Other Side will be broken and the glory of the blessed Holy One be exalted above all. And when, by this Kedushah, the power of the Other Side is broken, the blessed Holy One ascends in glory and remembers His children and remembers His Name. Since the blessed Holy One is exalted in His glory by this Kedushah, it must be uttered only in the presence of ten.

The rare power of the Kaddish is unleashed precisely because it harnesses the power of the *Sitra Aḥra*, the Other Side. The act of reciting the Kaddish is described here as a smashing of locks and seals and evil shells, a penetration into the heart of darkness.

Rabbi Nathan Sternhartz of Nemirov (1780–1844), the premier disciple of Rabbi Naḥman of Bratslav, built on the Zoharic teaching in his discussion of the significance of the language of the Kaddish. In an extended reflection on this theme, he identified Aramaic as the language of the nations and the language that epitomizes the world of nature. Incidentally, he offers an ingenious explanation for the incapacity of the angels to understand this language. He links Aramaic, which he takes to be the quintessential language of translation, with the Tree of Knowledge of Good and Evil. Inherent in the act of translation, and perhaps also in the study of nature, is the concept of choice. It is precisely this concept which is incomprehensible to the angels, Rabbi Nathan argues. There is no choice for angels; their job is to fulfill their essence. In consequence, they cannot speak or understand the language of choice.

Rabbi Nathan offers an original reading of the significance of the language of the Kaddish in understanding its essence and purpose:

> This is the meaning of reciting the Kaddish in the language of translation, for now we read and uncover the divine will specifically in this language, for in so doing this Kedushah transfers anger into good will. This means that science and natural wisdom (*hokhmat ha-teva*), whose roots are in the language of translation, is transformed into a tool for uncovering the divine will. "The axe is taken from within the forest itself"[25]…and so *hokhmat ha-teva* will be finally defeated.[26]

For Nathan of Nemirov, the Kaddish is both a bridge between worlds and a missile sent against the dark forces, armed with material taken from "the Other Side." He builds upon the Zohar's image of the Kaddish as a metaphysical wrecking ball.

It is quite likely that in its earliest iterations the formula known as the Kaddish was rendered in Aramaic for the sake of maximum accessibility. Over time, as the linguistic landscape shifted, the language of the Kaddish became a symbol of profound otherness and difference. In some readings, as we have seen, this very otherness became part of its power and mystique.

In this essay I have tried to argue that there are aspects of the Kaddish—its use of terms denoting time and space, its language— that may go some way toward explaining its extraordinary resonance. Standing on the border between learning and the end of learning, between one liturgical unit and the next, between the words of the Pentateuch and the words of the prophets, between this world and the world of worlds, this speech-act acknowledges the borderline and seeks to reach out across it.

In reciting the Kaddish, a solo voice within a communal context, a praying Jew uses language to acknowledge the capacity of language. The "meaning" of the words may not be the most significant aspect of the act, neither for the Jew ignorant of the vocabulary and grammar, nor yet for the individual fully conversant with both. Rather, the Kaddish is a speech-act. To return to Austin's terminology, the illocutionary and perlocutionary aspects of the Kaddish can be debated. For some, the act in question is understood to have metaphysical implications: our relatives are released on their journey after death; the evil shells are smashed. Others will look to the psychological, communal, and cultural impacts of the act of recitation.

Here may lie something of the secret of the Mourner's Kaddish. It is of course possible to look to the meaning of the words in order to find comfort. Eugene Borowitz writes movingly of how the theological underpinnings of the prayer challenged his assumptions, even as they provided him with a degree of consolation: "Saying Kaddish meaningfully instructs us to let God be God and brings on the slow healing of God's covenanting nearness."[27] But the act of saying is itself an important part of this slow healing, particularly as experienced over many months during a period of mourning. As Borowitz himself notes, the grammar and the language of the text play their role, as well as the interpretation of the prayer's broad themes.

Faced with a void, our tradition offers language. Faced with the inexpressible, our tradition expresses demarcation, distinction, and connection. Faced with loss and the call of silence, our tradition insists we speak.

NOTES

[1] Rabbi Joseph Schick, first printed in *The Kaddish: Its Power for Good* (New York: Memorial Publishing Company, 1928), p. 13, quoted in Hana Wirth-Nesher, *Call It English: The Languages of Jewish American Literature* (Princeton [NJ] & Oxford [UK]: Princeton University Press, 2006), p. 163.

[2] Allen Ginsberg, "Kaddish," first published in *Kaddish and Other Poems 1958–1960* (San Francisco: City Lights Books: 1961), pp. 7–36.

[3] Leon Wieseltier, *Kaddish* (New York: Alfred A. Knopf, 1998), p. 32.

[4] Joseph B. Soloveitchik, *Out of the Whirlwind: Essays on Mourning, Suffering, and the Human Condition*, ed. David Shatz, Joel B. Wolowelsky, and Reuven Ziegler (Jersey City, NJ: KTAV, 2003), p. 5.

[5] Paul Ricoeur, *Living Up to Death*, trans. David Pellauer (Chicago: University of Chicago Press, 2009), p. 21. Ricoeur is referring here to the particular case of a dying person reciting the Kaddish about himself; I have quoted his expression here in a wider context.

[6] J. L. Austin, *How To Do Things With Words* (Oxford: Oxford University Press, 1962).

[7] See Richard van Oort, "Performative-Constative Revisited: The Genetics of Austin's Theory of Speech Acts," in *Anthropoetics* 2.2 (January 1997), pp. 1–14 and available online at www.anthropoetics.ucla.edu.

[8] M. Berakhot 2:2.

[9] J. L. Austin, *How To Do Things With Words*, pp. 94f.

[10] Ibid., p. 108.

[11] Ibid.

[12] W. Graham Monteith, "The Reality of Addressing God in Prayer," in *Theology in Scotland* 16:1 (2009), p. 67.

[13] The particular version and translation cited here is taken from the traditional Sephardic *nusaḥ* for the Torah blessings. As is the case with so much of Jewish liturgy, there are fascinating variant versions of the Kaddish, in both its different functions and the range of local traditions and variant readings that exist, a number of which are discussed in David Telsner, *The Kaddish: Its History and Significance* (Jerusalem: Tal Orot, 1995), pp. 42–67.

[14] The words in parentheses are substituted for the words that precede during the Ten Days of Repentance.

[15] The word "holy" is included in some versions of the prayer.

[16] See for example Telsner, *Kaddish*, pp. 110–111.

[17] Some have argued that it was originally in Hebrew. See Telsner, *Kaddish*, pp. 37–38.

[18] *She'eilot U-t'shuvot Ha-rashba* (ed. Vilna 1884), vol. 5, responsum 54, p. 9a.

[19] Rabbi Israel Goldstein in 1948, quoted in Wirth-Nesher, *Call It English*, p.

164.

[20] Tosafot to B. Berakhot 3a, s.v. *v'hayah l'kha l'hitpalleil t'fillah k'tzarah* . This translation is taken from Telsner, *Kaddish*, p. 36. The talmudic reference within the tosafist's comment is to B. Sotah 49a.

[21] *Sefer Ha-pardeis L'rashi z"l*, ed. H. L. Ehrenreich (Budapest: H.L. Ehrenreich, 1924), p. 326.

[22] See the teaching in the name of Rabbi Yoḥanan in B. Sotah 33a.

[23] This reading is from *Menorat Ha-ma·or* (ed. Amsterdam, 1721), §95, p. 85b.

[24] Zohar II 129b. This translation (with slight emendation in spelling) is by Daniel Matt, as published in *The Zohar: Pritzker Edition* (Stanford: Stanford University Press, 2009), vol.5, p. 209.

[25] This saying is from B. Sanhedrin 39b. The idea is that the handle of the axe is taken from the forest, which will then be cut down by the axe. This is a metaphor for the notion of an enemy within, that the causes of downfall can be inherent within one's own camp.

[26] *Likkutei Halakhot, Oraḥ Ḥayyim, Inyan Kaddish* §7 (Shomron: Bashan, 2014), vol. 1, p. 454. The translation is mine.

[27] Eugene B. Borowitz, "Musing on Mourning," *CCAR Journal* 53:3 (Summer 2006), p. 8.

Oseh Shalom: Giving Peace a Chance in Heaven and on Earth

Dan Ornstein

"All We Are Saying Is Give Peace A Chance"[1]

John Lennon's plaintive 1969 protest for world peace would later be drenched in blood-soaked irony when he became the murder victim of Mark David Chapman, a mentally ill man who shot him outside of his apartment building in New York City on December 8, 1980. In his later song "Imagine,"[2] Lennon, "the most famous Beatle," famously sang about contemplating an ideal world of peace free from strife and persecution—only to be felled by the very violence that he decried. What followed his tragic death was an international outpouring of grief and support for his family, as well as conspiracy theories that he was assassinated by right-wing government-backed operatives because of his outspoken political views. More than three decades later, his death reminds us of the dark truth that human violence will always be with us.

Jewish sources are emphatic about the stubborn propensity of human beings for violence and conflict—beginning with the early biblical story of Cain and Abel, the first homicide/fratricide, and continuing through today's writers who struggle to understand the religious, psychological, and ethical implications of the Holocaust and other genocides. Yet hard-boiled realism about what *is* is not the same as cynical despair about what *could be*. This essay explores *oseh shalom*, the poetic verse that ends the Full, Rabbinic, and Mourner's Kaddish and that has become an extremely popular song. It not only requests but demands that God bring about peace and harmony on earth. As with John Lennon's chant, we might sing its words gently. But I will show that these words are actually an explosive protest demanding that peace on earth must happen in our time, ending violent human reality. Because it is placed at the end of Kaddish, *oseh shalom* completes the eschatological ("end of history") themes of Kaddish by moving us, the worshippers, from hopes for God's universal sovereignty to demands for total peace, the result of that sovereignty.[3]

I will show the reader the provocative spiritual nature and power of *oseh shalom* by comparing it with a poem about peace that was written by the great American poet Emily Dickinson. Why employ such an unusual way to read and explain *t'fillot*, Jewish prayers? The philosopher Rabbi Abraham Heschel understands the connection between prayer and poetry in the following way:

> A word is a focus, a point at which meanings meet and from which meanings seem to proceed. In prayer, as in poetry, we turn to the words, not to use them as signs for things, but to see the things in the light of the words. In daily speech, it is usually we who speak the words, but the words are silent. In poetry, in prayer, the words speak.[4]

Rabbi Heschel calls our attention to the independent life and multiple meanings that words possess, apart from how we may use them to express ourselves in ordinary, everyday speech. Prayer and poetry are forms of verbal expression that are very different from an instruction manual, an email that I write to a friend, or even great prose. When I read a poem or chant a prayer, the words are supposed to have a profound emotional or spiritual effect upon me because of the beautiful artistic techniques used to express them, their many possible meanings, and the ways those meanings influence how I think about or see the world. I see "the things in light of the words" because the words speak to me, rather than serve exclusively as tools for me to say what I want to say. The comparison of poetry and prayer can deepen our appreciation for both and help us to hear their words meaningfully in our own lives. Such a comparison can awaken us to the poetic and spiritual richness of *oseh shalom*, as well as help us to direct our hearts more deeply to God and to our greatest hopes for peace.

Peace Is a Fiction of Our Faith

Emily Dickinson (1830–1886) gave voice to many important truths in her poetry, and her insights about human life and behavior far transcended the mostly reclusive and somewhat mysterious life that she led in Amherst, Massachusetts. As one of her biographers explained, Dickinson related to others in the same way that she wrote: by weaving a complex and often allusive web of metaphors, which she referred to as a kind of poetic algebra.[5] They allowed her to present her honest and penetrating struggles with love, faith, religion, despair, and death that would have challenged the orthodoxies of nineteenth-century New England culture and its declining Puritan religion. Her elusive style was less threatening to that society than a more direct approach would have been. Similarly, Dickinson often used the pattern of alternating four- and three-beat lines (eight syllables, then six syllables) in her poetry. This was a standard metrical pattern for New England church hymns, which would have been familiar to someone in her day and locale (and which was certainly familiar to her).[6] She may have done this to rebel against the accepted religious ideas and social mores of her time, from a position of safety, by couching her often unconventional insights in these conventional rhythms.[7]

In contrast to John Lennon, one of Dickinson's shortest poems—a four-line epigram—reflects sadly upon the naïve trust that we place in our ability to achieve peace:

> Peace is a fiction of our Faith—
> The Bells a Winter Night
> Bearing the Neighbor out of Sound
> That never did alight.[8]

Dickinson could be telling us that faith in peace—its presence or its achievement—is a lie. Faith of course can refer formally to organized religion, to personal religious faith, or to the general hope upon which we rely as individuals and communities for a sense of well-being. We do not know if Dickinson is referring to her personal inner turmoil and despair, to the well documented conflict that was ongoing in her extended family, to her ideas about death and life after death, or to the carnage of the American Civil War (which took place during her life).[9] The source of her despair is not of primary importance. One of the features of a great poem is its ability to suggest different powerful human emotions or ideas that resonate with numerous experiences using the smallest number possible of words, artfully arranged as evocative metaphors. I believe she has done exactly this in her poem.

Dickinson uses many idiosyncratic dashes in her poetry in place of punctuation and for poetic effect. (She also capitalizes many words mid-sentence.) The dash-line she adds after the word "Faith" appears to instruct us to pause, so that we contemplate the next three lines as her illustration of "Peace is a fiction of our Faith." She then tries to have us *feel this fiction*, by using a very simple yet haunting image. We hear the sleigh bells of a carriage that is carrying to us someone whom we have been expecting on a cold, lonely winter night: perhaps a loved one or a lover, a cherished friend, or someone else whom we have missed terribly. Dickinson hints at the person being anticipated, "the Neighbor"—though we want to be careful not to interpret this phrase too literally, since the word "neighbor" can allude to a friend, someone close to you, or someone who merely lives next door. I suggest that the neighbor here might also be a sad, even cynical allusion to all of humanity, echoing the biblical commandment to "Love your neighbor as yourself" (Leviticus 19:18). Dickinson may be using this word in a double sense: the elusiveness of real peace is like the carriage that passes with our neighbor in it; our neighbor is all people, with whom and among whom peace can never really be achieved, no matter how much we believe that it will be.[10] Ultimately, the carriage passes and we are left with an enduring sense of desolation. With this rich metaphor, the poet invites us to consider that faith in peace is colossal self-deception that, like our listening and hoping for that anticipated visit on a lonely winter night, brings us nothing but heartache and disillusionment. The person we longed to have stop in—perhaps all of humanity—is like the sound of those passing bells: increasingly, achingly distant, as is peace itself.

Rearranging and filling in Dickinson's words, we can read her evocative illustration as prose in the following way. Our false and misguided faith in peace is *(like) the bells of a carriage on a winter night, carrying out of the reach of sound the neighbor who never descends from that carriage.* The poet certainly could have simply said this in prose, but note how she instead uses rhyme and her distinctive rhythm in four compressed lines to give the reader the experience of having one's faith destroyed. Perhaps Dickinson uses here the alternating eight- and six-syllable lines that I mentioned above to intensify that feeling of descent for us. Longer lines suggest the effect of hopeful "longing," then they quickly sink into shorter lines that make us feel abruptly cut off when we read them. Like the longed-for neighbor at *night*, peace itself never *alights*; it never descends from the place toward which we direct our faith: heaven. As people and communities of faith, we can believe longingly that peace will finally drop by like a good neighbor, and that we should give it a chance; but our naïve hopes will be quickly dashed. Peace is that elusive, ringing bell we often hear (or wish to hear) in the desolate nighttimes of our lives, but whose passing sound moves quickly away, leaving us with nothing.

On Earth as It Is in Heaven

As I wrote above, *oseh shalom* ends of the recitation of every longer Kaddish. Though it likely originated as part of the Kaddish, it was added over time to the end of every silent Amidah (the silent, standing "prayer par excellence") and at the end of Birkat Ha-mazon (the traditional prayer of thanks after a meal). It is also a favored chant at Jewish-themed rallies, conferences, concerts, and youth gatherings. Though it might not formally be a poem, it has become an extremely popular song that has been set to music by many well-known Jewish composers. I believe this is because its Hebrew is simple and its rhythms are gentle, but its message is forceful and relentless. Below is my translation:

Oseh shalom bi-m'romav *hu ya·aseh shalom aleinu* *v'al kol yisrael.* *(V'imru amein.)*	May God, who imposes peace in God's heights, impose peace upon us and upon all of the people Israel. (And respond with: Amen.)

Even a casual glance at this passage reveals why people would be drawn to it. In ten brief Hebrew words, it emphasizes that genuine peace is imposed *by* God upon heaven (God's heights) and that we impose *upon* God to make that peace "alight," to descend directly upon us and upon the rest of the Jewish community. Realism about our violent present and faith in our tranquil future might struggle with each other, but despair about the eventual descent of peace is never allowed a voice here. *Oseh shalom* places the ultimate power to "impose" lasting peace upon us in God's hands, and the responsibility for "forcing" God to do this in our mouths. This verse encompasses literally the entire universe, in the sweep of its petition for peace. From the celestial heights of heaven down to each of us on earth, peace is something that we audaciously demand of God.

A deeper exploration of the language of *oseh shalom* shows how its author artistically conveys our demand that peace not be a mere fiction of our faith. The first part of the prayer borrows the Hebrew phrase *oseh shalom bi-m'romav* from the biblical Book of Job (25:2). Job is a thoroughly righteous man whose goodness is renowned. At the instigation of one of God's angels, God tests the purity of Job's motives for being so good by destroying his family, his property, and his health. God wants to see if he will maintain his faith and his goodness despite being hurt so badly. When Job lashes out bitterly at God for making him suffer, the three friends who have joined him, ostensibly to comfort him, set about to attack him for questioning God's justice and protesting his own innocence. In one response to Job, his friend Bildad exclaims:

> Dominion and dread are God's;
> God *imposes* peace in God's heights (*oseh shalom bi-m'romav*).[11]

Bildad then launches into a conventional defense of divine justice that relies upon denying the ability of human beings, even those as righteous as Job, to ever be vindicated morally before God. Many interpreters of the Bible assert that Bildad is referring to God's endless power to impose peace upon warring camps of angels and other celestial servants. His words are perhaps based upon an ancient Near Eastern myth about warring divine beings being subdued by the one God, or at least the most powerful god in the ancient pantheon. According to this view, Bildad asserts that God's power to coerce the heavenly hosts into harmony is, among other divine powers, so great that people can never expect to be justified before God.[12] Puny humankind steeped in its moral weakness and spiritual disabilities, including its incorrigible violence, is nothing before God, who singlehandedly reins in the violent chaos of the celestial beings—the very same beings that are far greater than humans. Where, then, did Job ever get the temerity to believe that he could call God to account for the violence being done to him and his family?

I suggest that the author of *oseh shalom* has consciously taken this fragment of Job 25:2 and turned it on its head.[13] In Bildad's eyes, no human being ever has the right to coerce or even request an accounting from God for anything that happens to him or her. God, after all, is the One who forcibly imposes peace upon the celestial powers. From the perspective of *oseh shalom*, every member of the community who chants it is attempting to "force" God, as it were, into imposing peace and harmony upon us. This is made clear by the parallelism between the first and second lines: we demand that God, who imposes peace on high, likewise impose it below upon us, those intoning these words, and upon the wider Jewish world as well. Our prayer expresses this presumptuous, seemingly unrealistic expectation of God in a highly deferential tone by retaining the third-person address to God that Bildad used to put Job in his place.[14] Yet tone and content are completely at odds here, as the translation above demonstrates.

A talmudic tradition beautifully emphasizes this very point while employing our passage in Job, perhaps as a reflection upon the meaning of *oseh shalom*:

[The sage] Bar Kappara said: Great is peace, for even the angels among whom there is no enmity, jealousy, hatred, strife, rivalry, or dissension [have need for] the blessed Holy One to make peace among them, as it is stated, "Dominion and [dread] are with God; God imposes peace in God's high places" (Job 25:2).

"Dominion" [is another name for the angel] Michael and "Dread" [is another name for the angel] Gabriel, one being of fire and the other of water, and yet they do not injure one another; how much more so then do mortal beings, among whom all these dispositions exist, [have need of peace].[15]

Note how this passage uses a rather formal, dry principle of logic employed by the ancient rabbis in legal arguments to make a very passionate claim. The principle, known as the "argument from minor to major" (*kal va-ḥomer*), emphasizes how simultaneously difficult, imperative, and possible is God's intervention in human affairs for the sake of imposing peace. The angels lack all propensity for violence, yet they still need divinely imposed peace and order because they are made of fire and water, mutually exclusive elements that could cancel each other out. If God prevents them from destroying each other, *how much more* does God need to prevent evil- and violence-prone humanity from doing so. Interestingly, this teaching retains the original meaning of Job 25:2 that we discussed above—namely, that God imposes peace and order upon the warring celestial parties— yet in a very different manner. On the one hand, the angels don't fight with each other, because only humans do that; yet God still exercises control over them, which makes God's coercive supervision of humanity even more important. On the other hand, the angels' "physical make-up"—sometimes fire and sometimes water—is inherently irreconcilable, yet God finds a way to keep the divine celestial entourage from mutual extinction. Humanity's violent tendencies are not an inherent part of our "physical make-up": we *choose* to be violent. Thus, how much easier should it be for God to stop us from behaving this way, given what God is able to achieve with the angels. We do not need to take any of this angel imagery literally to get the very serious point of this teaching and the point of *oseh shalom*, which is: we need God to help us give peace a real chance because we can't seem to figure this out for ourselves entirely. We know that with God's intervention in our efforts, there is no reason for peace to remain a fiction of our faith.

Just as I re-read and simplified Emily Dickinson's poem about peace as a fiction of our faith, let me also suggest a somewhat different, simplified reading of *oseh shalom*: *May the One who imposes coercive peace upon the warring parties in heaven…impose peace upon us and upon the whole of Israel!*[16]

Peace for the Jewish People and for All Humanity

Though the focus of this essay has mostly been on *oseh shalom* as a stand-alone prayer, we will now examine its literary context, the Kaddish—and especially the line of the Kaddish that precedes it. The line before *oseh shalom* reads, in Aramaic, as follows: *Y'hei sh'lama rabba min sh'maya, v'ḥayyim aleinu v'al kol yisrael (v'imru: Amein)*, "May great peace and life [descend] from [God in] heaven upon us and upon all of Israel (and say: *Amen*)." Is *oseh shalom* simply a free Hebrew translation of this last Aramaic language line of the Kaddish? Or does it consciously amplify and intensify that statement, by employing Job 25:2—and thus emphasizing the intense hope that peace be imposed upon us by God, here on earth? Whatever its original purpose for being placed where it is, what seems clear is that in the context of the Kaddish, *oseh shalom* moves our demand for God's peace from the distant future into the hopeful present, as we wait for it indignantly, edgily, impatiently.[17]

This volume about the Kaddish contains many essays that discuss the entire prayer in great detail. I will only mention here that it has very ancient roots in the Torah-study academies of Israel and Babylonia. It was recited to proclaim the name—the essential power—of God as eternally great and to console the listeners with messages of hope for that time at history's end when God would finally deliver the Jewish people and the world from lawlessness, evil, and violence. Professor Joseph Heinemann, the renowned scholar of liturgy, points out that the Kaddish and *oseh shalom* are part of a genre of prayers originating in the *beit midrash* (academy), prayers of praise for God and hopes for redemption with which teachers in the ancient academies used to end Torah study sessions. These prayers were later attached to the ends of other prayers, in order to reinforce the individual's and the community's demand that God bring us peace and release the Jewish people from persecution.[18] This appending of *oseh shalom* to the ends of other prayers is implied in the early rabbinic teaching that "Peace is so great, that all blessings and [Amidah] prayers end with words of peace."[19]

At first glance, *oseh shalom* seems to be a parochial prayer that focuses exclusively on the Jewish people. It prays for peace for one's local Jewish community as well as for the Jewish people as a whole, but not necessarily for the rest of humanity. I suggest that further examination of the sources and the context of *oseh shalom* will show that it should be read as a prayer of peace for the whole world. In the Book of Job, it is Bildad—a non-Jew[20]—who asserts that God imposes peace throughout the celestial heights. The use of *his* words possibly reflects the biblical author's subtle acknowledgment that the quest for peace in heaven and on earth belongs to everyone, not only Jews. Further, as I wrote above, we must look at how *oseh shalom* will show takes shape meaningfully when it is connected to the rest of the Kaddish. The first line of the Kaddish, *yitgaddal v'yitkaddash*, hopes for the day when God shall be magnified and sanctified victoriously as universal Ruler of the world that God has created. This first line echoes Ezekiel 38:23: *v'hitgaddilti v'hitkadishti, v'nodati l'einei goyim rabbim*, "Thus will I [that is, God] manifest My greatness and My holiness, and make Myself known in the sight of many nations." Ezekiel was a prophet who lived during the Jewish people's exile in Babylonia, likely several years before the Babylonians' destruction of the First Temple in Jerusalem in 586 B.C.E. His prophecies often comfort his fellow exiles with visions of redemption in the wake of the destruction of evildoers and those who hate the Jewish people. Ezekiel 38–39 is a long, violent prophecy that describes a great apocalyptic ("end-of-days") battle between God and the worldwide armies of evildoers (symbolized by the mythic kingdom of Gog), who are committed to the destruction of the Jewish people. God warns that Gog will be obliterated when God comes forth to redeem God's people, revealing that, on the day of punishment, "I will manifest My greatness and My holiness, and make Myself known in the sight of many nations. And they shall know that I am the Eternal" (38:23). The Kaddish draws directly from Ezekiel's vision of God finally vindicating the Jewish people in the sight of all humanity, and transforms that vision into a broader universal prayer for God's supreme rule over all humanity—something that we still await. Further, as we read in the talmudic tradition cited above, the Babylonian sage Bar Kappara early on drew an inference from Job 25:2 about the supreme importance of God imposing peace upon *all* human beings—not only the angels and not only the Jewish community. Thus, I detect a more universalistic undertone in *oseh shalom* than is usually acknowledged.

In our own time, many of us have become uncomfortable with the overtly parochial tone of *oseh shalom*. We must pray for peace for ourselves and our entire people, especially in light of attacks on the State of Israel and the persistence of anti-Semitism. Yet we must also pray for peace throughout the world—not only because peace is good for the Jewish people, but also because we fervently believe that God cares about all human beings and all living things. This is an authentically Jewish idea that is reflected in the famous Ashrei prayer.[21] Drawing upon the implicit universalism of *oseh shalom* that I discussed above, many people now add the Hebrew words *v'al kol yosh'vei teiveil*, "and upon all the earth's inhabitants," to the line after the words *v'al kol yisrael*, and this now appears in some printed editions of the prayerbook as well.

"Uncan'ting" the Can't

In Richard Powers' novel *The Time of Our Singing*, the father of one of the protagonists tells his African-American daughter that White America cannot hold her down and that she can do anything she wishes with her life. He exclaims, "What is history, except for 'uncan'ting' the can't?" His words later become ruthlessly ironic, as she and her white husband are repeatedly thwarted in their attempts to raise their children in the racist America of the 1950s, and she experiences horrible setbacks due to race that ultimately kill her. History is littered with tragic examples of when "can't" could not be undone, when limitless imagination and open-heartedness have been crushed mercilessly by the limits of dumb luck, closed minds, and hatred. How true this is with respect to the pursuit of genuine peace in the often ugly history of human behavior. About this much Emily Dickinson and the author of *oseh shalom* seem to agree: the existence of genuine peace *in real time* is nothing more than fiction, a matter that causes them—as it causes all people who love peace—the greatest anguish.

Whether or not Dickinson would have counseled us to abandon this fiction is largely irrelevant, for her words make clear what she believes: we cannot redeem ourselves from the hell that we, in our freedom, have created. By contrast, *oseh shalom* is a cry of protest from deep within the heart that demands—not requests—of God a thoroughgoing imposition of peace upon everything and everyone. The mirror image of this demand is an unrepentant Jewish hope for peace and justice that has its roots in the visions of our great prophets. The obstinate survival of that hope has carried us, and so many people of faith, forward through the long narrative of human evil with a counter-narrative, which insists that human life does not need to be all about brutality and violence. Those of us who believe it is God's prerogative to impose the terms of lasting peace upon the cosmos will hopefully continue to hold fast to this faith, which flies in the face of widespread cynicism and despair. Those of us who do not have faith in a dependable, all-powerful God who possesses such redemptive capacity will hopefully continue to reject despair nonetheless. For what can despair bring, other than the chronic sickness of more despair...especially despair that poses as a hard-knuckled realism that dismisses faith in peace as nothing more than silly fiction? If true peace never comes, at least not in our lifetimes, the plaintive words of *oseh shalom* can still goad good people to press forward, acting and living and teaching in ways that make us feel it is nearby. When we chant this little fragment of a prayer, all we are praying is "give peace a chance."

NOTES

[1] See https://en.wikipedia.org/wiki/Give_Peace_a_Chance for more information about the song's history.

[2] See https://en.wikipedia.org/wiki/Imagine_(John_Lennon_song) for more information about the song's history.

[3] *Oseh shalom* is also found at the end of the Amidah, the "prayer par excellence" of Jewish liturgy, and at the end of Birkat Ha-mazon, the Grace after Meals. As discussed above, an ancient rabbinic tradition explains that peace is so important that we have the practice of mentioning peace at the end of all blessings and prayers.

[4] Abraham Heschel, *Man's Quest For God: Studies In Prayer and Symbolism* (1954; rpt. New York: The Crossroad Publishing Company, 1987), p. 26.

[5] See Helen Vendler, *Dickinson: Selected Poems And Commentary* (Cambridge, MA: Harvard University Press, 2010), "Introduction," especially p. 9.

[6] Ibid, pp. 4–5.

[7] Richard Sewall, *The Life of Emily Dickinson* (Cambridge, MA: Harvard University Press, 1980), pp. 408 and 713–714. It should be noted, however, that only seven or eight of her poems were formally published in her lifetime. Dickinson carefully "published" many more poems in her many letters to friends and family, and the rest did not see the light of day until well after her death.

[8] #912 (untitled) in *The Complete Poems of Emily Dickinson*, ed. Thomas H. Johnson (Boston: Little, Brown, and Company, 1960), p. 430.

[9] This poem was likely written around 1864, four years into the bloody Civil War, during which more than 200,000 people died due to combat alone. Dickinson scholars increasingly acknowledge that some of her poetry, over half of which was written during the years of the war, reflects her anguish over the war's brutality and her protest against the popular religious idea that it was being fought to help God defeat Satanic forces and usher in a new era. See Shira Wolosky, "Emily Dickinson's War Poetry: The Problem Of Theodicy," in *Massachusetts Review* 25:1 (Spring 1984), pp. 22–41.

[10] Helen Vendler writes in her introduction (pp. 1 and 16) that Dickinson read the King James version of Hebrew Scriptures extensively, and one of the Dickinson Family Bibles translates Leviticus 19:18 in just this way. See *The Holy Bible, Containing the Old and New Testaments: Translated out of the Original Tongues* (Philadelphia: J. B. Lippincott & Co., 1843). The Dickinson Family Library copy is kept in the Emily Dickinson Room 8, Houghton Library, Harvard University, Cambridge, MA. The entire Dickinson Family Bible may be seen online at http://pds.lib.harvard.edu/pds/view/24025603. According to educators at the Dickinson House and Museum in Amherst, Massachusetts, the Dickinson family possessed nineteen copies of the King James Bible, of which the Harvard copy is one.

[11] NJPS translation, my emphasis. Note that God does not merely "create" peace in the usual sense of the Hebrew word *oseh*, usually translated as "make"; rather, God "imposes" peace in a much more forceful sense.

[12] *The Anchor Bible: Job,* ed. and trans. Marvin H. Pope (Garden City, NY: Doubleday, 1973), p. 181.

[13] This is a common literary technique in Jewish liturgy and Hebrew poetry known as intertextuality, wherein a writer uses the original words of a biblical or rabbinic source in a new, creative, or even radical way.

[14] This deferential third-person tone was actually quite common for prayers like this one, which were used to conclude public Torah study in ancient times. We will discuss this further below.

[15] M. Ginsberg, *"Perek Hashshalom*: Chapter on Peace," in *The Minor Tractates of the Talmud, Vol. II,* ed. and trans. Abraham Cohen (London: Soncino Press, 1965), p. 599, #8. I highly recommend this entire brief collection of Jewish sayings about peace to the reader, which can be found in Cohen, pp. 597–602. I have altered the translation of the verse from Job to match the one given above.

[16] Though I will not demonstrate it in detail in this essay, I suggest that the phrase *shalom aleinu v'al kol yisrael,* "peace upon us and upon all of the people Israel," is our poet's conscious echo of the prayer *shalom al yisrael,* ("peace be upon Israel"), which phrase is found twice in the biblical Book of Psalms (at 125:5 and 128:6). Psalm 125 seems a particularly apt source for our phrase in *oseh shalom,* since this psalm emphasizes God's assured and longed-for protection of good people, and of the entire people of Israel, in the face of evildoers who seek to destroy them—whom the psalmist assures us God will destroy. At the very end of this dual assurance and request for the vanquishing of evildoers, the psalmist exclaims, "Peace be upon Israel!" I imagine *oseh shalom* adapting this phrase as an echo of the psalmist's prayer: we ask God to bring us peace in the form of protection from evildoers, and we also know that God can make this happen.

[17] Ismar Elbogen, the nineteenth-century scholar of Jewish liturgy, writes: "We have no information as to when and where the same idea [found in the Aramaic line, *y'hei sh'lama rabba*] was later added again in Hebrew in the words *oseh shalom bi-m'romav...*" Elbogen assumes that the latter is an addition to the former, rather than a Hebrew-language expression of hope for redemption and God's peace that developed independently of (or even before) *y'hei sh'lama rabba*. There is consensus among traditional commentators that Kaddish was composed mostly in Aramaic because it was the language that most laypeople in Israel and Babylonia understood at that time. See Ismar Elbogen, *Jewish Liturgy: A Comprehensive History,* trans. Raymond P. Scheindlin (Philadelphia: Jewish Publication Society, 1993), pp. 80–84.

[18] Joseph Heinemann, *Prayer in The Talmud: Forms and Patterns,* trans. Richard Sarason (New York: Walter De Gruyter, 1977), chap. 10. One clue in *oseh shalom*

that it was originally such a prayer is the ending: *v'imru amein*, "Say *Amen!*" Likely a command by the teacher to the students to affirm his prayer of hope, it became such a popular part of *oseh shalom* that we recite it today as well—even though we normally would not command ourselves to respond *Amen* at the end of our own prayer.

[19] Cohen, *Minor Tractates*, p. 602, #19.

[20] Bildad is identified in Job 2:11 as a Shuḥite, from the family of Shuaḥ. Shuaḥ was one of Abraham's children through the latter's relationship with his concubine, Keturah, as we read in Genesis 25. According to that chapter, Abraham gave these children gifts but did not give them any of his estate as inheritance, before he sent them away eastward. This ensured that Isaac, Abraham's one son by his wife Sarah, would be the sole inheritor of his father's estate and the vehicle for God's promise to make Abraham's progeny into a great nation, the Jewish people. Bildad might be seen as hailing from a family of distant Abrahamic cousins to the Jewish people, who nonetheless were not included in the lineage of the Jews.

There are numerous Jewish traditions that Job is non-Jew. The general consensus of contemporary scholars is that Job and his friends are non-Jews and that the book was probably written by a Jew in the first millennium B.C.E., based on much earlier ancient Near Eastern folktales and poems. Though all four protagonists speak about God in exclusively monotheistic terms, their non-Jewish identities lend a distinctively universal tone to the book's concerns about God and human suffering. See Pope, *Job*, pp. xxiii–xlii. Also see Nahum N. Glatzer, *The Dimensions of Job: A Study and Selected Readings* (New York: Schocken, 1969), pp. 4, 16–17.

[21] Psalm 145:9, "The Eternal is good to all, and God's mercy is upon all God's works."

Translation
Grant peace everywhere goodness and blessing,
Grace, lovingkindness and mercy to us and unto all Israel

Transliteration
Sim shalom tovah u-v'rakhah
ḥein va-ḥesed v'raḥamim aleinu ve-al kol Yisrael amekha

שִׂים שָׁלוֹם*

שִׂים שָׁלוֹם טוֹבָה וּבְרָכָה
חֵן וָחֶסֶד וְרַחֲמִים עָלֵינוּ וְעַל כָּל יִשְׂרָאֵל עַמֶּךְ

* **Sim Shalom** (Hebrew: שִׂים שָׁלוֹם; "Grant Peace") is a blessing that is recited near the end of formal Jewish prayer services. The precise form of the blessing varies depending on the service and the precise denomination along the Jewish spectrum.

www.BlechTapes.com

a focused YouTube channel

Benjamin Blech Exegesis

on 10-theme Mesorah Matrix

sequence of 12 twenty-minute tapes:

intro + 10 themes + outro

www.UnifyingScienceSpirituality.com

About the Contributors

Adena K. Berkowitz is Scholar-in-Residence and co-founder of Kol HaNeshamah in New York, dedicated to re-energizing the spiritual life of both affiliated and not-yet-affiliated Jews. A graduate of the Benjamin N. Cardozo School of Law with a doctorate from the Jewish Theological Seminary, she is the co-author of *Shaarei Simcha: Gates of Joy* (KTAV, 2007), the mini-prayerbook that is the first liturgical work in the modern era written by Orthodox women. She is also a visiting lecturer at Yeshivat Chovevei Torah Rabbinical School.

Benjamin Blech served as co-editor of *Sanctification*, the first volume in this series. A Professor of Talmud at Yeshiva University since 1966, he is the author of fifteen highly acclaimed books—including his latest, *The Sistine Secrets* (HarperOne, 2009), now available in twenty-six countries and translated into sixteen languages—in addition to hundreds of articles in both scholarly and popular publications.

Herbert Bronstein has combined a successful vocation as a congregational rabbi with teaching and lecturing at various colleges and universities, publishing in scholarly journals, and serving as editor of Reform Judaism's *Passover Haggadah* (1974) and *Five Scrolls* (1984), both published by the CCAR Press. He served for many years as Chairman of the Joint Worship Commission of the Union of American Hebrew Congregations and as a member, and then Chairman, of the Liturgy Committee of the Central Conference of American Rabbis.

Reuven P. Bulka, C.M., has been the rabbi of Congregation Machzikei Hadas in Ottawa, Ontario, Canada, since 1967, and is presently its Rabbi Emeritus. He chairs the Trillium Gift of Life Network that is responsible for organ and tissue donation and transplantation in all of Ontario, and is President/CEO of Kind Canada Généreux. He and his wife Leah share many generations of children.

Geoffrey Claussen is the Lori and Eric Sklut Emerging Scholar in Jewish Studies, director of the Jewish Studies Program, and Assistant Professor of Religious Studies at Elon University. He is the current president of the Society of Jewish Ethics and is the author of *Sharing the Burden: Rabbi Simḥah Zissel Ziv and the Path of Musar* (SUNY Press, 2015).

Martin S. Cohen is the rabbi of the Shelter Rock Jewish Center in Roslyn, New York, and one of the senior editors of the Mesorah Matrix series. He is the author of *Our Haven and Our Strength: The Book of Psalms* (Aviv Press, 2004), *The Boy on the Door on the Ox* (Aviv Press, 2008), and four novels, and he served as senior editor of *The Observant Life*, published in 2012 by the Rabbinical Assembly. His translation and commentary on the Torah are forthcoming.

Noah Zvi Farkas serves as a rabbi at Valley Beth Shalom in Encino, California. He is the author of numerous articles on Jewish thought as well as the book *The Social Action Manual: Six Steps to Repairing the World* (Behrman House, 2010). He is an activist for social justice and a social entrepreneur.

Baruch Frydman-Kohl is Anne and Max Tanenbaum Senior Rabbi of Beth Tzedec Congregation, Toronto, and Senior Rabbinic Fellow of the Shalom Hartman Institute of Jerusalem.

Aubrey L. Glazer, Ph.D. (University of Toronto), is rabbi of Congregation Beth Sholom, San Francisco. As a graduate of the Institute for Jewish Spirituality, Aubrey continues studying and practicing Jewish meditation. Aubrey publishes reflections on contemporary spirituality, *Mystical Vertigo* (Academic Studies Press, 2013) and is completing a forthcoming book, called *Tangle of Matter & Ghost* on the intersection of Jewish mysticism and Rinzai Buddhism in the songbook of Leonard Cohen.

Mark B. Greenspan serves as rabbi of Beth Shalom Oceanside Jewish Center in New York. He has translated fifteen Hebrew commentaries on the Haggadah, most recently the *Minḥat Ani* by Rabbi Jacob Ettlinger.

David Greenstein serves as rabbi of Congregation Shomrei Emunah in Montclair, New Jersey and is also a painter who has exhibited his work in the US, France, and Israel. He has published essays in various journals, periodicals, and anthologies, and is the author of *Roads to Utopia: The Walking Stories of the Zohar* (Stanford University Press, 2014).

James Jacobson-Maisels is the founder of Or HaLev: A Center for Jewish Spirituality and Meditation (orhalev.org) and has been studying and teaching meditation and Jewish spirituality for over fifteen years. Rabbi Dr. Jacobson-Maisels teaches Jewish thought, mysticism, spiritual practices, and meditation at the Pardes Institute of Jewish Studies, Haifa University, Yeshivat Hadar, and in a variety of settings around the world. He strives to integrate his study and practice and to help teach and live Judaism as a spiritual discipline.

Elie Kaunfer is co-founder and executive director of Mechon Hadar (www.mechonhadar.org). A graduate of Harvard College, he completed his doctorate in liturgy at the Jewish Theological Seminary, where he was also ordained. A Wexner Graduate Fellow and Dorot Fellow, Rabbi Dr. Kaunfer is the author of *Empowered Judaism: What Independent Minyanim Can Teach Us About Building Vibrant Jewish Communities* (Jewish Lights, 2010).

Steven Kepnes is Professor of World Religion and Jewish Studies, and Director of Chapel House, at Colgate University, Hamilton, New York. He is the author of seven books, including *The Future of Jewish Theology* (Wiley Blackwell, 2013).

Peter S. Knobel is rabbi emeritus of Beth Emet-The Free Synagogue in Evanston, Illinois and teaches Jewish Studies at the Spertus Institute in Chicago. He chaired the editorial committee that produced *Mishkan T'filah,* the new *siddur* of the Reform Movement published in 2007, and recently re-edited the *Gates of the Season*, now entitled *Mishkan Moed - A Guide to the Jewish Year,* and *Gates of Mitzvah,* now called *Mishkhan Mitzvah - A Guide of the Jewish Life Cycle*, for the Central Conference of American Rabbis.

David A. Kunin is the spiritual leader of the Jewish Community of Japan. Interfaith relations having been an ongoing mark of his rabbinate, he served as board member and president of the Edmonton Interfaith Centre for Education and Action for many years and received the Alberta Centennial Medal in recognition of his community work. Rabbi Kunin is author of the recently published *Beyond the Golden Rule: A Jewish Perspective on Dialogue and Diversity* (Gaon Books, 2015).

Martin I. Lockshin is University Professor at York University in Toronto, where he has taught Jewish Studies for the last thirty-eight years. Rabbi Dr. Lockshin is the author of six books and many articles, mostly dealing with the history of Jewish Bible commentaries.

Michael Marmur is the Jack Joseph and Morton Mandel Provost of the Hebrew Union College-Jewish Institute of Religion. His *Abraham Joshua Heschel and the Sources of Wonder* was recently published by the University of Toronto Press. He lives in Jerusalem.

Dalia Marx, Ph.D., is Associate Professor of Liturgy and Midrash at the Jerusalem campus of Hebrew Union College-JIR, and teaches in various academic institutions in Israel and Europe. Rabbi Dr. Marx, a tenth-generation Jerusalemite, earned her doctorate at the Hebrew University and her rabbinic ordination at HUC-JIR in Jerusalem and Cincinnati, and is involved in various research projects as well as being active in promoting liberal Judaism in Israel. Marx writes for academic and popular journals and publications. Among her publications is *A Feminist Commentary of the Babylonian Talmud* (Mohr Siebeck, 2013).

Avi S. Olitzky is spiritual leader at Beth El Synagogue, St. Louis Park, Minnesota. Rabbi Olitzky recently co-authored *New Membership & Financial Alternatives for the American Synagogue: From Traditional Dues to Fair Share to Gifts from the Heart* (Jewish Lights Publishing, 2015).

Kerry M. Olitzky, D.H.L., is the executive director of Big Tent Judaism (formerly the Jewish Outreach Institute). Named one of the fifty leading rabbis in North America by *Newsweek*, Rabbi Olitzky formerly served on the faculty and administration of Hebrew Union College-Jewish Institute of Religion and is well known for his many inspiring books on Jewish spirituality, healing, and religious practice that bring the Jewish wisdom tradition into everyday life.

Dan Ornstein is rabbi at Congregation Ohav Shalom in Albany, New York. He blogs at the Times of Israel, writes essays for WAMC Northeast Public Radio, and has recently published poetry with the Jewish Literary Journal and the Pine Hills Review. He is also a rabbinic panelist for Jewish Values On Line.

Avram Israel Reisner, rabbi emeritus of Congregation Chevrei Tzedek in Baltimore, MD, is an Adjunct Professor at Towson University and St. Mary's Ecumenical Institute. Rabbi Dr. Reisner is a member of longstanding on the Conservative Movement's Committee of Jewish Law and Standards.

Jeremy Rosen is a graduate of Cambridge University and Mir Yeshivah in Jerusalem and has worked in the rabbinate, education, and academia in Britain and Europe. Now retired to New York, he writes and lectures and is the rabbi of a small congregation of Persian Jews.

Barbara Shulamit Thiede is a faculty member in the Department of Religious Studies at the University of North Carolina at Charlotte, where she teaches courses on the

Hebrew Bible, Jewish history, the history of anti-Semitism, and the legacy of the Holocaust. The spiritual leader of Temple Or Olam in Concord, North Carolina, Rabbi Dr. Thiede writes and publishes in both popular and academic settings and blogs at adrenalinedrash.com.

Orna Triguboff serves at Emanuel Synagogue in Sydney, Australia, having received her rabbinic and spiritual direction ordination from Aleph, the Jewish Renewal Movement. Rabbi Dr. Triguboff received her Ph.D. from the University of Sydney with a focus on Lurianic Kabbalah, and teaches Kabbalah and Jewish Meditation internationally.

Ruth Walfish is a senior lecturer in Bible and chair of the Bible Department at Efrata College of Education in Jerusalem, where she mentors student teachers in Bible pedagogy. Dr. Walfish's articles on Bible appear in the Hebrew-language journals *Megadim* and *Massekhet*, and in the *Jewish Bible Quarterly*.

Herbert A. Yoskowitz is a rabbi at Adat Shalom Synagogue in Farmington Hills, Michigan, a lecturer in Jewish Bioethics at Oakland University William Beaumont School of Medicine, and editor of *The Kaddish Minyan* (Eakin Press, 2001; second edition, 2003). His most recent articles have been featured in *Michigan Jewish History*.

special acknowledgement to

Nora Frydman

MESORAH MATRIX

10-BOOK SERIES
150+ Essayists

dimensions of

Spirituality & Kedushah

THE SPARK OF THE INFINITE DIVINE

Mesorah Matrix
Series

David Birnbaum

Editor-in-Chief

10-theme

10-volume

2015

2015

2016

2016

2017

2017

2018

2018

2019

2019

200+ original essays

jewish thought & spirituality

150+ global thought leaders

a decade-long unified endeavor

LIGHTS OF CREATION & TRANSCENDENCE
David Birnbaum / Mesorah Matrix Series

MESORAH MATRIX

10-BOOK SERIES
150+ Essayists

Sanctification

Tikkun Olam

Birkat Kohanim

The Kaddish

Modeh Ani

Havdalah

Search for Meaning

U-VACHARTA BA-CHAYIM

Ehyeh asher Ehyeh

V'Shamru

THE SPARK OF THE INFINITE DIVINE

Mesorah Matrix Series

Sanctification ("Kedushah")

Tikkun Olam ("Repair the World")

Birkat Kohanim (The Priestly Blessings: a contemporary take)

The Kaddish (specifically, The Mourner's Praise of God)

Modeh Ani (The solo daily morning prayer of Gratitude)

Havdalah (separating Holy from Secular: Sabbath > secular)

Search for Meaning (pegging-off of Viktor Frankl's classic)

U-VACHARTA BA-CHAYIM (The 613th precept-Choose Life)

Ehyeh asher Ehyeh ("I Will Be That Which I Will Be" – at the Burning Bush)

V'Shamru (The Sabbath)

21st CENTURY PUBLISHING

David.Birnbaum.NY@gmail.com

www.NewParadigmMatrix.com

MESORAH
MATRIX
VOLUME 1

David Birnbaum / Mesorah Matrix Series

LIGHTS OF CREATION & TRANSCENDENCE

Sanctification

Editors

David
Birnbaum & **Blech**
Benjamin

LEAD ESSAY: **Jonathan Sacks**

New Paradigm Matrix™

EXPLORING HIGHER DIMENSIONS

VOLUME—2

TIKKUN OLAM
JUDAISM, HUMANISM & TRANSCENDENCE

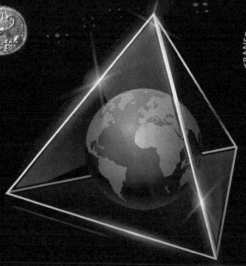

David Birnbaum / Mesorah Matrix Series
LIGHTS OF CREATION & TRANSCENDENCE

Editors
David
Birnbaum & Cohen
Martin S.

Associate Editor: **Saul J. Berman**

New Paradigm Matrix™

EXPLORING HIGHER DIMENSIONS

MESORAH MATRIX

VOLUME 3

BIRKAT KOHANIM

David Birnbaum | Mesorah Matrix Series

LIGHTS OF CREATION & TRANSCENDENCE

EXPLORING HIGHER DIMENSIONS

Editors

David
Birnbaum &
Martin S.
Cohen

Associate Editor: **Saul J. Berman**

New Paradigm Matrix

VOLUME 4

KADDISH

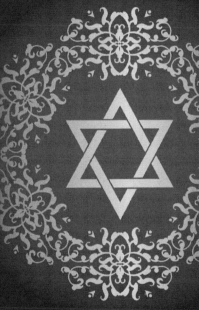

David Birnbaum / Mesorah Matrix Series

LIGHTS OF CREATION & TRANSCENDENCE

Editors

David
Birnbaum &

Martin S.
Cohen

Associate Editor: **Saul J. Berman**

New Paradigm Matrix™

EXPLORING HIGHER DIMENSIONS

VOLUME 5

Modeh Ani

THE TRANSCENDENT PRAYER OF GRATITUDE

Editors

David
Birnbaum & Cohen
Martin S.

Associate Editor: **Saul J. Berman**

New Paradigm Matrix™

LIGHTS OF CREATION & TRANSCENDENCE

David Birnbaum / Mesorah Matrix Series

EXPLORING HIGHER DIMENSIONS

MESORAH MATRIX
VOLUME 6

David Birnbaum

LIGHTS OF CREATION & TRANSCENDENCE

Mesorah Matrix Series

HAVDALAH

Editors

David
Birnbaum & Martin S.
Cohen

Associate Editor: **Saul J. Berman**

EXPLORING HIGHER DIMENSIONS

New Paradigm Matrix™

VOLUME 7

SEARCH FOR MEANING

Editors

David
Birnbaum & Martin S.
Cohen

Associate Editor: **Saul J. Berman**

New Paradigm Matrix™

LIGHTS OF CREATION & TRANSCENDENCE
David Birnbaum / Mesorah Matrix Series

EXPLORING HIGHER DIMENSIONS

MESORAH
MATRIX
VOLUME 8

LIGHTS OF CREATION & TRANSCENDENCE
David Birnbaum / Mesorah Matrix Series

U-VACHARTA
BA-CHAYIM

EXPLORING HIGHER DIMENSIONS

Editors

David
Birnbaum & Martin S.
Cohen

New Paradigm Matrix™

MESORAH MATRIX

VOLUME 9

LIGHTS OF CREATION & TRANSCENDENCE | Mesorah Matrix Series

David Birnbaum

Ehyeh asher Ehyeh

Editors

David
Birnbaum & Martin S.
Cohen

New Paradigm Matrix™

EXPLORING HIGHER DIMENSIONS

MESORAH MATRIX

VOLUME 10

David Birnbaum / Mesorah Matrix Series

LIGHTS OF CREATION & TRANSCENDENCE

V'shamru

Editors

David
Birnbaum &
Martin S.
Cohen

New Paradigm Matrix™

EXPLORING HIGHER DIMENSIONS

ESSAYISTS

Avivah Zornberg
Author

London, UK

David Ellenson
HUC-JIR

New York, NY

Saul Berman
Y.U. / Stern

New York, NY

Jonathan Sacks
United Hebrew
Congregations
London, UK

James Kugel
Bar Ilan University

Ramat Gan, Israel

Shalom Carmy
Yeshiva University,
Tradition Magazine
New York, NY

Rachel Barenblat
Bayit

Williamstown, MA

Rachel Friedman
Lamdeinu

New York, NY

W. Zeev Harvey
The Hebrew University of Jerusalem
Jerusalem

Rachel Adelman
Hebrew College

Newton Centre, MA

Shlomo Riskin
Ohr Torah Stone Colleges
Efrat, Israel

Mark Goldfeder
Emory University

Atlanta, GA

Hillel Goldberg
Intermountain Jewish News
Denver, CO

Lawrence Schiffman
NYU
New York, NY

Alan Cooper
Jewish Theological Seminary
New York, NY

Yonatan Feintuch
Bar Ilan University

Tel Aviv, Israel

Jacob Schacter
Yeshiva University

New York, NY

Aryeh Cohen
American Jewish
University
Los Angeles, CA

Avram Reisner
Chevrei Tzedek
Congregation
Baltimore, MD

Elliot Dorff
American Jewish
University
Los Angeles, CA

Michael Graetz
Congregation Eshel
Avraham
Omer, Israel

Steven Kepnes
Colgate University

Hamilton, NY

Reuven Bulka
Congregation
Machzikei Hadas
Ottawa, Canada

Adena Berkowitz
Kol Ha-neshamah

New York, NY

MESORAH
MATRIX

Alan Mittleman
Jewish Theological
Seminary
New York, NY

Tzvi Sinensky
Rosh Beit Midrash

Lower Merion, PA

Bradley Artson
American Jewish
University
Los Angeles, CA

Jill Jacobs
T'ruah: The Rabbinic
Call for Human Rights
New York, NY

Michael Broyde
Emory University

Atlanta, GA

Noam Zion
Hartman Institute

Jerusalem

Sid Schwarz
CLAL

New York, NY

Rahel Berkovits
Pardes Institute

Jerusalem

Howard Addison
Temple University

Philadelphia, PA

Robert Harris
Jewish Theological
Seminary
New York, NY

Samuel Lebens
Rutgers University

New Brunswick, NJ

Richard Hidary
Congregation
Shearith Israel
New York, NY

Jonathan Schorsch
Universität Potsdam
Potsdam
Germany

Eliezer Shore
Hebrew University
of Jerusalem
Jerusalem

Roberta Kwall
DePaul University
Law School
Chicago, IL

Alon Ferency
Heska Amuna
Synagogue
Knoxville, TN

Aubrey Glazer
Congregation Beth
Shalom
San Francisco, CA

Rebecca W. Sirbu
Rabbis Without
Borders, CLAL
New York, NY

Geoffrey Claussen
Elon University

Elon, NC

Jeremy Gordon
New London
Synagogue
London, U.K.

Shoshana Klein
Poupko
Ahavath Torah
Englewood, NJ

Michael
Wasserman
The New Shul
Scottsdale, AZ

Daniel Greyber
Beth El Synagogue

Durham, NC

Gail Labovitz
American Jewish
University
Los Angeles, CA

James Jacobson-Maisels
Or HaLev, Center for Jew-
ish Spirituality & Meditation
New York, NY

Yeshaya Dalsace
Dor Vador Com-
munaute Massorti
Paris, France

Kari Tuling
Congregation
Kol Haverim
Glastonbury, CT

Karyn Kedar
B'nai Jehoshua
Beth Elohim
Deerfield, IL

Nina Cardin
Rabbinical
Assembly
New York, NY

Aryeh Klapper
Center for Modern
Torah Leadership
Sharon, MA

Jonathan Wittenberg
New North London
Synagogue
London, UK

Michael Knopf
Temple Beth-El
Richmond, VA

Rivon Krygier
Congregation
Adath Shalom
Paris

Elie Spitz
Congregation
B'nai Israel
Tustin, CA

Ira Bedzow
Aspen Center for
Social Values
Aspen, CO

Yitzchak Blau
RCA

Jerusalem

Alfred Cohen
YU High School

New York, NY

Elliot Cosgrove
Park Avenue
Synagogue
New York, NY

Yehonatan
Chipman
Hitzei Yehonatan
Israel

David Flatto
Penn State Law

University Park, PA

MESORAH MATRIX

Shohama H. Wiener
Temple Beth-El

City Island, NY

David Evan Markus
Temple Beth-El

City Island, NY

Nathaniel Helfgot
Yeshivat Chovevei
Torah
New York, NY

Cass Fisher
University of South
Florida
Tampa, FL

Admiel Kosman
Postdam University

Germany

Simcha Krauss
Eretz Hatzvi

Jerusalem

Melanie Landau
Monash University

Australia

Vernon Kurtz
North Suburban
Synagogue Beth-El
Highland Park, IL

Rolando Matalon
B'nai Jeshurun

New York, NY

Shmuly Yanklowitz
Valley Beit Midrash
President & Dean
Scottsdale, AZ

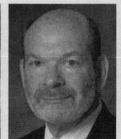

Peter Knobel
Beth Emet

Evanston, IL

Harvey Meirovich
Zacharias Frankel
College
Berlin, Germany

Aryeh Frimer
Bar-Ilan University

Ramat Gan

Martin Lockshin
York University

Ontario, Canada

Shai Cherry
Shaar Hamayim

Del Mar, CA

David Shatz
Yeshiva University

New York, NY

Jeremy Rosen
Persian Jewish
Center
New York, NY

David Greenstein
Congregation
Shomrei Emunah
Montclair, NJ

Avraham Walfish
Herzog College and
Michala Jerusalem
Tekoa, Israel

David Mescheloff
RCA

Israel

Barbara Thiede
UNC Charlotte

Concord, NC

Lawrence Troster
GreenFaith

Highland Park, NJ

Ruth Walfish
Herzog College and
Michala Jerusalem
Tekoa, Israel

Lenn Goodman
Vanderbilt
University
Nashville, TN

MESORAH
MATRIX

Dan Ornstein
Ohav Shalom

Albany, NY

Dena Freundlich
Ma'ayanot AMIT

Jerusalem

Elaine Goodfriend
California State
University
Northridge, CA

Berel Dov Lerner
Western Galilee
College, Herzl Inst
Northern Israel

Orna Triguboff
Neshama Life
Organisation
Sydney, Australia

Nehemia Polen
Hebrew College

Newton Centre, MA

Mark Greenspan
Oceanside Jewish
Center
Oceanside, NY

Richard Claman
Zeramim Journal

New York, NY

Avi Olitzky
Beth El Synagogue

St. Louis Park, MN

Michelle J. Levine
Stern College for Women
Yeshiva University
New York, NY

Yehuda Gellman
Ben-Gurion
University
Negev, Israel

Herbert Bronstein
Lake Forest
College,
Lake Forest, IL

Avraham Feder
Beit Knesset
Moreshet Yisrael
Jerusalem

Elyse Goldstein
City Shul

Ontario, Canada

Kerry M. Olitzky
Big Tent Judaism

New York, NY

Dalia Marx
Hebrew Union
College
Jerusalem

Jason Rubenstein
Mechon Hadar

New York, NY

Herbert Yoskowitz
Adat Shalom
Synagogue
Farmington Hills, MI

Mark Sameth
Pleasantville Com-
munity Synagogue
Westchester, NY

Catharine Clark
Congregation
Or Shalom
London, Ontario

Jacob Adler
Temple Shalom of
Northwest Arkansas
Fayetteville, AR

Jonathan Jacobs
John Jay College,
CUNY
New York, NY

David Kunin
Beth Shalom
Synagogue
Edmonton, AB

Michael Marmur
Hebrew Union
College
Jerusalem

MESORAH MATRIX

Mordechai Luria
Institute for Jewish
Ideas & Ideals
New York, NY

Noah Farkas
Valley Beth Shalom

Encino, CA

Alex Maged
Yeshiva University

New York, NY

Hayyim Angel
Yeshiva University

New York, NY

Elie Kaunfer
Mechon Hadar

New York, NY

Alex Sztuden
The Herzl Institute

Jerusalem

David Golinkin
Schechter Institute
of Jewish Studies
Jerusalem

Mark Washofsky
Hebrew Union
College
Cincinnati, OH

Edwin C. Goldberg
Temple Sholom of
Chicago
Chicago, IL

Baruch Frydman-Kohl
Beth Tzedec
Congregation
Toronto, Canada

Ora Horn Prouser
Academy for
Jewish Religion
Yonkers, NY

Howard Wettstein
University of
California
Riverside, CA

Zvi Grumet
Yeshivat Eretz
Hatzvi
Jerusalem

Erica Brown
The Jewish
Federation
Rockville, MD

Meesh Hammer-Kossoy
Pardes Institute
of Jewish Studies
Jerusalem

Michael J. Cook
Hebrew Union
College
Cincinnati, OH

James Diamond
University of
Waterloo
Ontario, Canada

Shira Weiss
Ben Gurion
University
Beer Sheba, Israel

Gidon Rothstein

Bronx, NY

Ariel Mayse
Stanford University
Stanford,
California

Dr. Elyssa Wortzman
Mindful art-based
spiritual education
San Francisco

Ellen LeVee
Spertus Institute

Chicago, IL

Kim Treiger-Bar-Am
Tel Aviv

Israel

David Maayan
Boston College

Newton, MA

Senior Editors

Benjamin Blech
Yeshiva University

New York, NY

Martin S. Cohen
Shelter Rock,
Jewish Center

Roslyn, NY

21st CENTURY PUBLISHING

David.Birnbaum.NY@gmail.com

www.NewParadigmMatrix.com

Sanctification

'Sanctification'
from Essay by Chief Rabbi Lord Jonathan Sacks

... And there is the priestly task of kedushah, sanctifying life by honouring the sacred ontology, the deep moral structure of the universe, through the life of the 613 commands, a life of discipline and self-restraint, honesty and integrity, respect and love, the code set out in the chapter of the Torah that opens with the momentous words, "Be holy for I, the Lord your God, am holy." Other cultures and faiths drew inspiration from its wisdom and prophetic traditions, but kedushah remained a specific Jewish imperative that made us different. Even so, it contains a message for the world, which Jews bear witness to whenever and wherever they remain faithful to it. Our vocation remains, to be mamlechet cohanim vegoi kadosh, "a kingdom of priests and a holy nation."

- The Ethic of Holiness, August 2012

to view series updated authors list,

see www.MesorahMatrix.com

Mesorah Matrix Series

Editors

David Birnbaum

Martin S. Cohen

Benjamin Blech
Editor

- born in Zurich in 1933, is an Orthodox rabbi who now lives in New York City.

Rabbi Blech has been a Professor of Talmud at Yeshiva University since 1966, and was the Rabbi of Young Israel of Oceanside for 37 years. In addition to his work in the rabbinate, Rabbi Blech has written many books on Judaism and the Jewish people and speaks on Jewish topics to communities around the world.

Benjamin Blech
Yeshiva University,
"Understanding
Judaism"

Education

Rabbi Blech received a Bachelor of Arts degree from Yeshiva University, a Master of Arts degree in psychology from Columbia University, and rabbinic ordination from the Rabbi Isaac Elchanan Theological Seminary.

Milestones

Rabbi Blech is the author of twelve highly acclaimed and best selling books, with combined sales of close to half a million copies, including three as part of the highly popular Idiot's Guide series. His book, *Understanding Judaism*: The Basics of Deed and Creed, was chosen by the Union of Orthodox Jewish Congregations as "the single best book on Judaism in our generation".

Martin S. Cohen

Martin S. Cohen

Martin S. Cohen has been a Senior Editor of the inter-denominational Mesorah Matrix series since 2012.

From 2000-2014, he served as Chairman of the Publications Committee of the quarterly journal *Conservative Judaism*, which was under the joint auspices of the JTS (Jewish Theological Seminary) and the RA (Rabbinical Assembly) during that span.

Rabbi Cohen also served as the senior editor of *The Observant Life*, a compendium of Jewish law, custom published by the Rabbinical Assembly in 2012.

Martin's weekly blog can be viewed at www.TheRuminativeRabbi. blogspot.com. He serves as rabbi of the Shelter Rock Jewish Center in Roslyn, New York.

Rabbi Cohen was educated at the City University of New York and at Jewish Theological Seminary of America, where he was ordained a rabbi and received his Ph.D. in Ancient Judaism. He is the recipient of fellowships at the Hebrew University (Jerusalem) in 1983 and Harvard University in 1993.

Martin Cohen has taught at Hunter College, the Jewish Theological Seminary of America, the Institute for Jewish Studies of the University of Heidelberg, as well as at the University of British Columbia and the Vancouver School of Theology.

His published works include *The Boy on the Door on the Ox* (2008) and *Our Haven and Our Strength: A Translation and Commentary on the Book of Psalms* (2004).

Rabbi Cohen is currently writing a translation and commentary on the Torah and the Five Megillot.

Saul Berman
Mesorah Editor

Saul Berman
Yeshiva University,
Stern College

Saul J. Berman is one of the world's leading Jewish intellects.

He is an American Jewish scholar and Modern Orthodox
rabbinic.

Rabbi Berman was ordained at Yeshiva University, from which
he also received his B.A. and his M.H.L. He completed a degree
in law, a J.D., at New York University, and an M.A. in Political
Sciesnce at the University of California, Berkeley, where he
studied with David Daube. He spent two years studying mishpat
ivri in Israel at Hebrew University of Jerusalem and at Tel Aviv
University. He did advanced studies in Jewish Law at Hebrew
University and Tel Aviv University Law Schools. Since 1971 Rabbi
Berman serves as Associate Professor of Jewish Studies at
Stern College for Women of Yeshiva University. Rabbi Berman
was Rabbi of Congregation Beth Israel of Berkeley CA (1963-
1969), Young Israel of Brookline, MA (1969-1971) and of Lincoln
Square Synagogue in Manhattan (1984-1990.) Since 1990
he has served as an Adjunct Professor at Columbia University
School of Law, where he teaches a seminar in Jewish Law. Aside
his academic appointments, from 1997 until 2006.

Rabbi Berman is a contributor to the *Encyclopedia Judaica* and
is the author of numerous articles which have been published in
journals such as *Tradition, Judaism, Journal of Jewish Studies,
Dinei Yisrael*, and others.

Rabbi Berman was the founder and director of the Edah
organization for the promotion of Modern Orthodoxy. Edah was
ultimately absorbed into Yeshivat Chovevei Torah.

He is married to Shellee Berman; they have four children and
seven grandchildren.

Wikipedia online, http://en.wikipedia.org/wiki/Saul_Berman (accessed February 15, 2013) +
The Tikvah Center for Law & Jewish Civilization online, http://www.nyutikvah.org/fellows/
saul_berman.html (accessed February 15, 2013)

Shalom Carmy
Contributing Editor

Shalom Carmy is an Orthodox rabbi teaching Jewish Studies and philosophy atYeshiva University, where he is Chair of Bible and Jewish Philosophy at Yeshiva College. He is an affiliated scholar at Cardozo Law School of Yeshiva University. He is also Editor of Tradition, an Orthodox theological journal.

Shalom Carmy
Yeshiva University,
Tradition Magazine

A Brooklyn native, he is a prominent Modern Orthodox theologian, historian, and philosopher. He received his B.A. in 1969 and M.S. from Yeshiva University, and received his rabbinic ordination from its affiliated Rabbi Isaac Elchanan Theological Seminary, studying under Rabbis Aharon Lichtenstein and Joseph Soloveitchik. He has edited some of R. Soloveitchik's work for publication. Carmy has written many articles on Biblical theology, Jewish thought, Orthodoxy in the 20th century, and the role of liberal arts in Torah education. He edited *Modern Scholarship in the Study of Torah*: Contributions and Limitations" (ISBN 1-56821-450-2), *"Jewish Perspectives on the Experience of Suffering"*, as well as several other works. He writes a regular personal column in *Tradition*, and contributes regularly on Jewish and general subjects to *First Things* and other journals. In addition to his exegetical and analytic work, Carmy's theological contribution is distinguished by preoccupation with the way religious doctrine and practice express themselves in the life of the individual.

http://en.wikipedia.org/wiki/Shalom_Carmy (accessed May 7, 2014)

LIGHTS OF CREATION & TRANSCENDENCE

David Birnbaum / Mesorah Matrix Series

Sanctification · VOLUME 1 · Birnbaum & Blech · New Paradigm Matrix · 2015

TIKKUN OLAM · VOLUME 2 · Birnbaum & Cohen · New Paradigm Matrix · 2015

BIRKAT KOHANIM · VOLUME 3 · Birnbaum & Cohen · New Paradigm Matrix · 2016

KADDISH · VOLUME 4 · Birnbaum & Cohen · New Paradigm Matrix · 2016

Modeh Ani · VOLUME 5 · Birnbaum & Cohen · New Paradigm Matrix · 2017

HAYYIM · VOLUME 6 · Birnbaum & Cohen · New Paradigm Matrix · 2017

SEARCH FOR MEANING · VOLUME 7 · Birnbaum & Cohen · New Paradigm Matrix · 2018

U-VACHARTA BA-CHAYIM · VOLUME 8 · Birnbaum & Cohen · New Paradigm Matrix · 2018

Ehyeh asher Ehyeh · VOLUME 9 · Birnbaum & Cohen · New Paradigm Matrix · 2019

U'shamru · VOLUME 10 · Birnbaum & Cohen · New Paradigm Matrix · 2019

March 2018

www.MesorahMatrix.com

www.NewParadigmMatrix.com

Frydman-Kohl

Berkowitz

Walfish

Marx

Olitzky

Claussen

Kunin

Blech

Yoskowitz

Thiede

Greenstein

Glazer

Marmur

Cohen

Jacobson-Maisels

Bronstein Triguboff

Bulka

Greenspan

Kaunfer

Ornstein Kepnes

Rosen Farkas

Reisner

Knobel

Lockshin

For the mountains shall erode

and the hills indeed collapse,

but My grace towards you shall never waver.

- Isaiah 54:10

כִּי הֶהָרִים יָמוּשׁוּ

וְהַגְּבָעוֹת תְּמוּטֶינָה

וְחַסְדִּי מֵאִתֵּךְ לֹא יָמוּשׁ

- יְשַׁעְיָהוּ 54:10

21st CENTURY PUBLISHING

David Birnbaum
Editor-in-Chief

New Paradigm Matrix
att: David Birnbaum
Tower 49
12 E 49th St.
11th Floor
New York, NY 10017

David.Birnbaum.NY@gmail.com

$16.00 / book

Kaddish

ISBN 978-0-9801710-6-8